D0782452

Inference, Explanation, and Other Frustrations

Pittsburgh Series in Philosophy and History of Science

Inference, Explanation, and Other Frustrations

Essays in the Philosophy of Science

EDITED BY
John Earman

UNIVERSITY OF CALIFORNIA PRESS
Berkeley Los Angeles Oxford

University of California Press
Berkeley and Los Angeles, California

University of California Press
Oxford, England

Library of Congress Cataloging-in-Publication Data

Inference, explanation, and other frustrations : essays
in the philosophy of science / edited by John Earman.
p. cm.—(Pittsburgh series in philosophy and history of
science; v. 14)
"Papers delivered in the annual lecture series (1986–1989)
sponsored by the University of Pittsburgh's Center for the
Philosophy of Science."—Intro.
Includes bibliographical references and index.
ISBN 0-520-07577-3 (alk. paper)
ISBN 0-520-08044-0 (pbk.: alk. paper)
1. Science—Philosophy. 2. Science—Methodology. 3. Inference.
4. Induction (Logic) I. Earman, John. II. Series.
Q175.3.I53 1992
501—dc20
91-40044
CIP

Printed in the United States of America
1 2 3 4 5 6 7 8 9

The paper used in this publication meets the minimum requirements
of American National Standard for Information Sciences—Permanence
of Paper for Printed Library Materials, ANSI Z39.48-1984 ∞

CONTENTS

INTRODUCTION

The present volume contains papers delivered in the twenty-seventh, twenty-eighth, and twenty-ninth annual Lecture Series (1986–1989) sponsored by the University of Pittsburgh's Center for the Philosophy of Science. The authors will be immediately recognized as among the leading lights in current philosophy of science. Thus, taken together, the papers provide a good sample of work being done at the frontiers of research in philosophy of science. They illustrate both the contemporary reassessment of our philosophical heritages and also the opening of new directions of investigation. The brief remarks that follow cannot hope to do justice to the rich and rewarding fare to be found herein but are supposed to serve only as a menu.

INFERENCE AND METHOD

Students in philosophy of science used to be taught to respect the distinction between "the context of discovery" and "the context of justification." The philosophy of science (so the story went) is concerned with the latter context but not the former. It seeks to provide principles for evaluating scientific hypotheses and theories once they are formulated, but it must remain modestly silent about the process of discovery since hypotheses and theories are free creations of the human mind and since the creative process is the stuff of psychology, not philosophy. The discovery/justification distinction is now under pressure from several directions, one of which stems from work in artificial intelligence and formal learning theory. Granted that scientists do in fact arrive at theories by a process of guesswork, intuition, or whatever, it remains to ask what true theories can be reliably discovered by what procedures. More specifically, for a specified kind of theory and a specified class of possible worlds, does there exist a procedure (recursive or otherwise) such that for every possible evidence sequence from any of the possible worlds the procedure eventually finds every true theory of the given type and eventually avoids every false theory of the given type? In their contribution, Clark Glymour and Kevin Kelly show how to make such questions precise, and for some precise versions they provide precise answers. But as they note, a host of such questions remain begging for further investigation.

Jaakko Hintikka's contribution draws out some of the implications for induction of his interrogative model of inquiry. This model conceptualizes scientific inquiry as a game played by a scientist against Nature. The scientist's goal is to derive a conclusion C from a starting premise P. To reach this goal, the scientist is allowed two kinds of moves: an interrogative move in which a question is put to Nature and an answer received, and a deductive move in which he draws logical consequences from P and the answers received to interrogative moves. A very striking feature of this model is the absence of any place for induction as it is traditionally conceived. Hintikka argues that Hume's classic problem of induction is an artifact of the mistaken assumption that the only answers Nature gives to queries are in the form of atomic (i.e., quantifier-free) sentences. Hintikka sides with the view, traceable to Newton and beyond Newton to Aristotle, that observation and experiment provide us with propositions that possess a significant generality. The residual, non-Humean problem of induction, as Hintikka conceives it, consists in extending the scopes of and unifying the general truths received from Nature.

According to the textbooks, modern science eschews Aristotelian natures in favor of laws of nature construed as codifications of regularities. In her provocative contribution Nancy Cartwright contends that this common wisdom is flawed, for in her view laws of nature are about natures. Thus, for Cartwright, Newton's law of gravitation doesn't say what forces bodies actually experience but rather what forces it is their nature, as massive objects, to experience. The exceptionless regularities required by the empiricist account are rarely found, she contends, and where they are found they result from arrangements that allow stable natures to be manifested. Cartwright supports her neo-Aristotelian conception of laws by arguing that it makes more sense of experimental methodology and inductive procedures than the more popular empiricist view.

If empiricism is the view that no matter of fact can be known a priori, then Hume was not an empiricist. For, as Barbara and Gerald Massey show in their contribution, Hume's account of animals attributes to them factual knowledge which is not learned from experience but which is imparted to them by "the original hand of Nature." Hume could be said to remain an empiricist insofar as he denies that human beings have specialized innate cognitive faculties or instincts as opposed to generalized instincts, such as the inductive propensity. But the distinction between specialized and generalized propensities is vague and, thus, the boundaries of empiricism are fuzzy. If Nelson Goodman is right, we are endowed with the propensity to project 'green' instead of 'grue.' And Noam Chomsky has championed the view that we are endowed with complex propensities to map linguistic evidence to linguistic knowledge. Do such propensities, which are at once special and general, lie inside or outside the boundaries of empiricism?

Logical positivism is a failed program. But its real shortcomings are quite different from those besetting the caricatures that dot the potted histories of philosophy. For example, the leading logical positivists (apart from Schlick) did not subscribe to the naive empiricism of a neutral observation language; indeed, as Michael Friedman notes in his contribution, the theory-ladenness of observation was explicitly emphasized by Carnap and others. Friedman argues that the ultimate shortcoming of positivism as embodied, say, in Carnap's *Logical Syntax of Language* lay in its failure to establish a neutral framework from which alternative languages or frameworks could be judged. Friedman traces this failure to Gödel's incompleteness theorems and argues that the demise of Carnap's program does not promote relativism—as expressed by a notion of truth relativized to a framework—but pulls the rug out from under this and other fashionable relativisms.

If asked to list the most important accomplishments of twentieth-century philosophy, the majority of the profession would surely give prominent place to Quine's slaying of one of two dogmas of empiricism—the existence of the analytic–synthetic distinction (that is, a principled distinction between truths of meaning and truths of fact). This accomplishment would not appear on Noam Chomsky's list. Indeed, in his paper for this volume, Chomsky argues that Quine's result is, ironically, an artifact of an overly behavioristic and a too narrowly positivistic conception of how the scientific investigation of language should and does proceed. In particular, he claims that the strictures imposed by Quine's paradigm of "radical translation" are not accepted in and would undermine the process of inquiry in the natural sciences.

THEORIES AND EXPLANATION

The theories of modern science tell stories of unobservable entities and processes. Scientific realists contend that these stories are not to be read as fairy tales and that observational and experimental evidence favorable to a theory is to be taken as evidence that the theory gives us a literally true picture of the world. Richard Boyd, one of the leading exponents of scientific realism, has in the past been concerned to combat the logical empiricists and their heirs who (with some notable exceptions such as Hans Reichenbach) contend that scientific theories are to be read instrumentally or else that we are never warranted in accepting a theory except as being adequate to saving the phenomena. Here Boyd is concerned with the more elusive and insidious opponent of realism who contends that the very notion of "the world" to which theories can succeed or fail in corresponding is a delusion since science is the social construction of reality. Some forms of constructivism have been successfully answered; for example, those that take their cue from Kuhnian incommensurability can be rejected on the basis of a causal theory of reference. Other more subtle forms of constructivism remain to be answered. Boyd's contribution is aimed at identifying the most interesting of these forms and showing that the "philosophical package" in which they come wrapped cannot be reconciled with the content and procedures of science.

Diderik Batens gives a resounding "No" to his query "Do We Need a Hierarchical Model of Science?" In place of both hierarchical and holistic models he proposes a contextualistic approach in which problems are always formulated and attacked with respect to a localized problem-solving situation rather than with respect to the full-knowledge situation. On Batens's account, methodological rules as well as empirical assertions are contextual. This has the interesting consequence that no a priori arguments can demonstrate the superiority of science to astrology; rather the superiority has to be shown on a case-by-case basis in a range of concrete problem-solving contexts.

What was once the "received view" of scientific theories, which emphasized the representation of scientific theories as a logically closed set of sentences (usually in a first-order language), has given way to a "semantic" or "structuralist" view, expounded in different versions by Patrick Suppes, Joseph Sneed, Fredrick Suppe, Bas van Fraassen, and others. But what exactly is the difference between these two ways of understanding theories? And what exactly was wrong with or lacking in the older view? In his contribution Richard Grandy argues that the proponents of the semantic view are offering not so much a new account of theories per se as a new account of the epistemology and application of theories. In his contribution Sneed responds to critics who charge that the semantic-structuralist reconstructions of theories are inadequate because they fail to provide syntactic representations of crucial items. By providing syntactic formulations of "lawlikeness," "theoretical concepts," and "constraints," Sneed paves the way for a reconciliation of the old and new views of theories, and at the same time he opens up a new avenue of research by connecting his structuralist account with previous work on data bases.

In his contribution Hilary Putnam explains why he has abandoned a view he helped to articulate and popularize—the computational or functional characterization of the mental. He continues to hold that mental states cannot be straightforwardly identified with physical states of the brain. But he now proposes to turn the tables on his former self by extending his own arguments, previously deployed to show that "software" is more important than "hardware," to show that mental states are not straightforwardly identical with computational states of the brain. What does Putnam propose as a replacement for functionalism? Some hints are to be found in the present paper and in his book *Representation and Reality* (Cambridge, Mass.: MIT Press, 1988), but for a complete answer the reader will have to stay tuned for further developments.

Hartry Field is more sanguine about another major "ism"—physicalism. He tries to chart a course between the Scylla of formulating the doctrine in such a strong form as to make it wholly implausible and the Charybdis of making it so weak as to have no methodological bite. The form of physicalism that Field takes to be worthy of respect is along the lines of reductionism, asserting (very roughly) that all good explanation must be reducible to physical explanation. He argues that weaker versions of physicalism, such as supervenience, that lack the explanatory requirement founder on the Charybdis. What remains to be specified to make physicalism a definite thesis is the reduction base: what are the considerations in virtue of which a science or a theory is properly classified as being part of physics?

John Earman
University of Pittsburgh

PART I

Inference and Method

ONE

Thoroughly Modern Meno

Clark Glymour and Kevin Kelly

1. INTRODUCTION

The *Meno* presents, and then rejects, an argument against the possibility of knowledge. The argument is given by Meno in response to Socrates' proposal to search for what it is that is virtue:

> Meno: How will you look for it, Socrates, when you do not know at all what it is? How will you aim to search for something you do not know at all? If you should meet with it, how will you know that this is the thing that you did not know?[1]

Many commentators, including Aristotle in the *Posterior Analytics*, take Meno's point to concern the *recognition of an object*, and if that is the point there is a direct response: one can recognize an object without knowing all about it. But the passage can also be understood straightforwardly as a request for a discernible *mark* of truth, and as a cryptic argument that without such a mark it is impossible to acquire knowledge from the instances that experience provides. We will try to show that the second reading is of particular interest.

If there is no mark of truth, nothing that can be generally discerned that true and only true propositions bear, Meno's remarks represent a cryptic argument that knowledge is impossible. We will give an interpretation that makes the argument valid; under that interpretation, Meno's argument demonstrates the impossibility of a certain kind of knowledge. In what follows we will consider Meno's argument in more detail, and we will try to show that similar arguments are available for many other conceptions of knowledge. The modern Meno arguments reveal a diverse and intricate structure in the theories of knowledge and of inquiry, a structure whose exploration has just begun. While we will attempt to show that our reading of the argument fits reasonably well with Plato's text, we do not aim to argue about Plato's intent. It is enough that the traditional text can be elaborated into a systematic and challenging subject of contemporary interest.[2]

2. THE MENO

In one passage in the *Meno*, to acquire knowledge is to acquire a truth that can be given a special *logical form*. To acquire knowledge of virtue is to come to know an appropriate truth that states a condition, or conjunction of conditions, necessary and sufficient for any instance of virtue. Plato's Socrates will not accept lists, or disjunctive characterizations.

> Socrates: I seem to be in great luck, Meno; while I am looking for one virtue, I have found you to have a whole swarm of them. But, Meno, to follow up the image of swarms, if I were asking you what is the nature of bees, and you said that they are many and of all kinds, what would you answer if I asked you: "Do you mean that they are many and varied and different from one another in so far as they are bees? Or are they no different in that regard, but in some other respect, in their beauty, for example, or their size or in some other such way?" Tell me, what would you answer if thus questioned?
>
> Meno: I would say that they do not differ from one another in being bees.
>
> Socrates: Suppose I went on to say: "Tell me, what is this very thing, Meno, in which they are all the same and do not differ from one another?" Would you be able to tell me?
>
> Meno: I would.
>
> Socrates: The same is true in the case of the virtues. Even if they are many and various, all of them have one and the same form which makes them virtues, and it is right to look to this when one is asked to make clear what virtue is. Or do you not understand what I mean?

There is something peculiarly modern about the *Meno*. The same rejection of disjunctive characterizations can be found in several contemporary accounts of explanation.[3] We might say that Socrates requires that Meno produce an appropriate and true universal biconditional sentence, in which a predicate signifying 'is virtuous' flanks one side of the biconditional, and a conjunction of appropriate predicates occurs on the other side of the biconditional. Let us so say. Nothing is lost by the anachronism and, as we shall see, much is gained.

Statements of evidence also have a logical form in the *Meno*. Whether the topic is bees, or virtue, or geometry, the evidence Socrates considers consists of instances and non-instances of virtue, of geometric properties, or whatever the topic may be. Evidence is stated in the singular.

The task of acquiring knowledge thus assumes the following form. One is presented with, or finds, in whatever way, a series of examples and non-examples of the feature about which one is inquiring, and from these examples a true, universal biconditional without disjunctions is to be produced. In the

Meno that is not enough for knowledge to have been acquired. To acquire knowledge it is insufficient to produce a truth of the required form; one must also *know* that one has produced a truth. What can this requirement mean?

Socrates and Meno agree in distinguishing knowledge from mere true opinion, and they agree that knowledge requires at least true opinion. Meno thinks the difference between knowledge and true opinion lies in the greater *reliability* of knowledge, but Socrates insists that true opinion could, by accident as it were, be as reliable as knowledge:

> Meno: ... But the man who has knowledge will always succeed, whereas he who has true opinion will only succeed at times.
>
> Socrates: How do you mean? Will he who has the right opinion not always succeed, as long as his opinion is right?
>
> Meno: That appears to be so of necessity, and it makes me wonder, Socrates, this being the case, why knowledge is prized far more highly than right opinion, and why they are different.

Socrates answers each question, after a fashion. The difference between knowledge and true opinion is in the special *tie*, the binding connection, between what the proposition is about and the fact of its belief. And opinions that are tied in this special way are not only reliable, they are liable to stay, and it is that which makes them especially prized:

> Socrates: To acquire an untied work of Daedalus is not worth much, like acquiring a runaway slave, for it does not remain, but it is worth much if tied down, for his works are very beautiful. What am I thinking of when I say this? True opinions. For true opinions, as long as they remain, are a fine thing and all they do is good, but they are not willing to remain long, and they escape from a man's mind, so that they are not worth much until one ties them down by an account of the reason why. And that, Meno my friend, is recollection, as we previously agree. After they are tied down, in the first place they become knowledge, and then they remain in place. That is why knowledge is prized higher than correct opinion, and knowledge differs from correct opinion in being tied down.

Plato is chiefly concerned with the difference between knowledge and true opinion, and our contemporaries have followed this interest. The recent focus of epistemology has been the special intentional and causal structure required for knowing. But Meno's argument does not depend on the details of this analysis; it depends, instead, on the capacity for true opinion that the capacity to acquire knowledge implies. That is the capacity to find the truth of a question, to recognize it when found, to stick with it after it is found, and to do so *whatever* the truth may be.

Suppose that Socrates could meet Meno's rhetorical challenge and recognize the truth when he met it: what is it he would then be able to do? Something like the following. In each of many different *imaginable* (we do not say *possible* save in a logical sense) circumstances, in which distinct claims about virtue (or whatever) are true, upon receiving enough evidence, and considering enough hypotheses, Socrates would hit upon the right hypothesis about virtue for that possible circumstance, and would then (and only then) announce that the correct hypothesis is indeed correct. Never mind just *how* Socrates would be able to do this, but agree that, if he is in the actual circumstance capable of coming to know, then that capacity implies the capacity just stated. Knowledge requires the ability to come to believe the truth, to recognize when one believes the truth (and so to be able to continue to believe the truth), and to do so whatever the true state of affairs may be.

So understood, Meno's argument is valid, or at least its premises can be plausibly extended to form a valid argument for the impossibility of knowledge. The language of possible worlds is convenient for stating the argument. Fix some list of predicates V, P1, . . . , Pn, and consider all possible worlds (with countable domains) that assign extensions to the predicates. In some of these worlds there will be true universal biconditional sentences with V on one side and conjunctions of some of the Pi or their negations on the other side. Take pieces of evidence available from any one of these structures to be increasing conjunctions atomic or negated atomic formulas simultaneously satisfiable in the structure. Let Socrates receive an unbounded sequence of singular sentences in this vocabulary, so that the sequence, if continued, will eventually include every atomic or negated atomic formula (in the vocabulary) that is satisfiable in the structure. Let ω range over worlds. With Meno, as we have read him, say that Socrates can come to know a sentence, S, of the appropriate form, true in world ω, only if

(i) for every possible sequence of presentation of evidence from world ω Socrates eventually announces that S is true, and

(ii) in every world, and for every sequence from that world, if there is a sentence of the appropriate form true in that world, then Socrates can eventually consider some true sentence of the appropriate form in that world, can announce that it is true in that world (while never making such an announcement of a sentence that is not true in that world), and

(iii) in every world, and for every sequence from that world, if no sentence of the appropriate form is true in the world, then Socrates refrains from announcing of any sentence of that form that it is true.

Meno's argument is now a piece of mathematics, and it is straightforward to prove that he is correct: no matter what powers we imagine Socrates to have, he cannot acquire knowledge, provided "knowledge" is understood to entail these requirements. No hypotheses about the causal conditions for knowledge defeat the argument unless they defeat the premises. Skepticism need not rest on empirical reflections about the weaknesses of the human mind. The impossibility of knowledge can be demonstrated a priori. Whatever sequence of evidence Socrates may receive that agrees with a hypothesis of the required form, there is some structure in which that evidence is true but the hypothesis is false; so that if at any point Socrates announces his conclusion, there is some imaginable circumstance in which he will be wrong.

We should note, however, that in those circumstances in which there is no truth of the required form, Socrates can eventually come to know that there is no such truth, provided he has an initial, finite list of all of the predicates that may occur in a definition. He can announce with perfect reliability the absence of any purely universal conjunctive characterizations of virtue if he has received a counterexample to every hypothesis—and if the number of predicates are finite, the number of hypotheses will be finite, and if no hypothesis of the required form is true, the counterexamples will eventually occur. If the relevant list of predicates or properties were not provided to Socrates initially, then he could not know that there is no knowledge of a subject to be had.

3. WEAKENING KNOWLEDGE

Skepticism has an ellipsis. The content of the doubt that knowledge is possible depends on the requisites for knowledge, and that is a matter over which philosophers dispute. Rather than supposing there is one true account of knowledge to be given, if only philosophers could find it, our disposition is to inquire about the possibilities. Our notion of knowing is surely vague in ways, and there is room for more than one interesting doxastic state.

About the conception of knowledge we have extracted from Meno there is no doubt as to the rightness of skepticism. No one can have *that* sort of knowledge. Perhaps there are other sorts that can be had. We could restrict the set of possibilities that must be considered, eliminating most of the possible worlds, and make requirements (i), (ii), and (iii) apply only to the reduced set of possibilities. We would then have a revised conception of knowledge that requires only a reduced *scope*, as we shall call the range of structures over which Socrates, or you or we, must succeed in order to be counted as a knower. This is a recourse to which we will have eventually to come, but let us put it aside for now, and consider instead what might otherwise be done about weakening conditions (i), (ii), and (iii).

Plato's Socrates emphasizes this difference between knowledge and mere true opinion: knowledge stays with the knower, but mere opinion, even true opinion, may flee and be replaced by falsehood or want of opinion. The evident thing to consider is the requirement that for Socrates to come to know the truth in a certain world, Socrates be able to find the truth in each possible world, and never abandon it, but not be obliged to announce that the truth has been found when it is found. Whatever the relations of cause and intention that knowledge requires, surely Meno requires too much. He requires, as we have reconstructed his argument, that we come to believe through a reliable procedure, a procedure or capacity that would, were the world different, lead to appropriately different conclusions in that circumstance. But Meno also requires that we know when the procedure has succeeded, and that seems much like demanding that we know that we know when we know. Knowing that we know is an attractive proposition, but it does not seem a prerequisite for knowledge, or if it is, then by the previous argument, knowledge is impossible. In either case, the properties of a weaker conception of knowledge deserve our study.

The idea is that Socrates comes eventually to embrace the truth and to stick with it in every case, although he does not know at what point he has succeeded: he is never sure that he will not, in the future, have to change his hypothesis. In this conception of knowledge, there is no mark of success. We must then think of Socrates as conjecturing the truth forever. Since Socrates did not live forever, nor shall we, it is better to think of Socrates as having a *procedure* that could be applied indefinitely, even without the living Socrates. The procedure has mathematical properties that Socrates does not.

For Socrates to know that S in world ω in which S is true now implies that Socrates' behavior accords with a procedure with the following properties:

(i*) for every possible sequence of evidence from world ω, after a finite segment is presented, the procedure conjectures S ever after, and

(ii*) for every possible sequence of evidence from any possible world, if a sentence of the appropriate form is true in that world, then after a finite segment of the evidence is presented the procedure conjectures a true sentence of the appropriate form ever after.

These conditions certainly are not sufficient for any doxastic state very close to our ordinary notion of knowledge, since Socrates' behavior may in the actual world accord with a procedure satisfying (i*) and (ii*) even while Socrates lacks the *disposition* to act in accord with the procedure in other circumstances. For knowledge, Socrates must have such a disposition. But he can only have such a disposition if there exists a procedure meeting conditions (i*) and (ii*). Is there? If the logical form of what is to be known is restricted to universal biconditionals of the sort Plato required, then there is indeed such a procedure. If Socrates is unable to acquire this sort of knowledge, then it is because of psychology or sociology or biology, not in virtue of mathematical impossibilities. Skepticism about this sort of knowledge cannot be a priori. There is no general argument of Meno's kind against the possibility of acquiring this sort of knowledge.

The weakening of knowledge may be un-Platonic, but it is not unphilosophical. Francis Bacon's *Novum Organum* describes a procedure that works for this case, and his conception of knowledge seems roughly to accord with it. John Stuart Mill's canons of method are, of course, simply pirated from Bacon's method. Hans Reichenbach used nearly the same conception of knowledge in his "pragmatic vindication" of induction, although he assumed a very different logical form for hypotheses, namely that they are conjectures about limits of relative frequencies of properties in infinite sequences.

So we have a conception of knowledge that, at least for some kinds of hypotheses, is not subject to Meno's paradox. But for which kinds of hypotheses is this so? We are not now captivated, if ever we were, by the notion that all knowledge is definitional in form. Perhaps even Plato himself was not, for the slave boy learns the theorem of Pythagoras, which has a more complicated logical form. We are interested in other forms of hypotheses: positive tests for diseases, and tests for their absence; collections of tests one of which will reveal a condition if it is present. Nor are our interests confined to single hypotheses considered individually. If the property of being a squamous cancer cell has some connections with other properties amenable to observation, we want to know *all about* those connections. We want to discover the whole theory about the subject matter, or as much as we can of it. What we may wish to determine, then, is what classes of *theories* can come to be known according to our weaker conception of knowledge. Here, as we use the notion of theory, it means the set of all true claims in some fragment of language. Wanting to know the truth about a particular question is then a special case, since the question can be formulated as a claim and its denial, and the pair form a fragment of language whose true claims are to be decided. What we wish to determine is whether all of what is true and can be stated in some fragment of language can be known.

Either the possibility of knowledge depends on the fragment of language considered or it does not. If it does, then many distinct fragments of language might be of the sort that permit knowledge of what can be said in them, and the classification of fragments that do, and that do not, permit such knowledge becomes an interesting task. For which fragments of language, if any, are there valid arguments of Meno's sort against the possibility of knowledge, and for which fragments are there not? These are straightforward mathematical questions, and their answers, or some of their answers, are as follows:

Consider any first-order language (without identity) in which all predicates are monadic, and there are no symbols taken to represent functions. Then any true theory in such a language can be learned, or at least there are no valid Menoan arguments against such knowledge.

If the language is monadic but with identity, or if the language contains a predicate that is not monadic, then neither the fragment that consists only of universally quantified formulas, nor the fragment that consists only of existentially quantified formulas, nor any part of the language containing either of these fragments, is such that every true theory in these fragments can be known.

In each of the latter cases an argument of Meno's kind can be constructed to show that knowledge is impossible.

4. TIMES FOR ALL THINGS

The weakened conception of knowledge is still very strong in at least one respect. It requires for the possibility of knowledge of an infinite wealth of claims that there be a time at which all of them are known—that is, a single time after which all and only the truths in a fragment of language are conjectured. We might instead usefully consider the following circumstance: When investigating hypotheses in a fragment of language, Socrates is able, for each truth, eventually to conjecture it and never subsequently to give it up; and Socrates is also able, for each falsehood, eventually *not* to conjecture it and never after to put it forward. Plato's Socrates illustrates that the slave boy can "recollect" the Pythagorean theorem from examples and appropriate questions, and presumably in Plato's view the slave boy could be made to recollect any other truth of geometry by a similar process. But neither the illustration nor the view requires that the slave boy, or anyone else, eventually be able to recollect the whole of geometry. There may be no time at which Socrates knows all of what is true and can be stated in a given fragment of language. Yet the disposition to follow a procedure that will eventually find every truth and eventually avoid every falsehood is surely of fundamental interest to the theory of knowledge. Call a procedure that has the capacity to converge to the whole truth at some moment, as in the discussion of the previous section, an EA learning procedure, and call an AE learner a procedure that for each truth has the capacity to converge to that truth by some moment, and for each falsehood avoids it ever after some moment. Every EA learner is an AE learner, but is the converse true? Or more to the point, are there fragments of language for which there are AE procedures but no EA procedures?

There are indeed. Consider the set of all universal sentences, with identity, and with any number of predicates of any arity and any number of function symbols of any arity. By the negative result stated previously, there is no EA procedure for that fragment of language, no procedure that, for every (countable) structure, and every way of presenting the singular facts in the structure, will eventually conjecture the theory (in the language fragment) true in that structure. But there is an AE procedure for this fragment. If, for knowledge about a matter, Socrates is required only to have a disposition to follow an AE procedure for the language of the topic, then no Menoan argument shows that Socrates cannot acquire knowledge, even if Socrates does not know the relevant predicates or properties beforehand.

The improvement does not last. If we consider the fragment of language that allows up to one alternation of quantifiers, whether from universal to existential or from existential to universal, it again becomes impossible to acquire knowledge; there are no AE procedures for this fragment that are immune from arguments of Meno's kind.

5. DISCOVERY AND SCOPE

Whether we consider EA discovery or AE discovery, we soon find that arguments of Meno's kind succeed. The same sort of results obtain if we further weaken the requirements for knowledge. We might, for example, abandon Plato's suggestion that when a truth is known it is not subsequently forgotten or rejected. We might then consider the requirement that Socrates be disposed to behave in accordance with a procedure that, as it considers more and more evidence about a question, is wrong in its conjectures only finitely often, is correct infinitely often, but may also suspend judgment infinitely often. Osherson and Weinstein have shown that even with this remarkably weak conception there are questions that cannot, in senses parallel to those above, be known. Or we might allow various sorts of approximate truth; for many of them, arguments parallel to Meno's are available.

The conceptions of knowledge we have discussed place great emphasis on *reliability*. They demand that we not come to our true beliefs by chance but in accordance with procedures that would find the truth no matter what it might be, so long as the procedures could be carried out. What the Meno arguments show is that in the various senses considered, for most of the issues that might invite discovery, procedures so reliable do not exist. The antiskeptical response ought to be principled retreat. In the face of valid arguments against the possibility of procedures so reliable, and hence against the possibility of corresponding sorts of knowledge, let us consider procedures that are not so reliable, and regard the doxastic state that is obtained by acting in accord with them as at least something better and more interesting than accidental true belief.

For each of the requirements on knowledge considered previously, and for others, we can ask the following kind of question: For each fragment of language, what are the classes of possible worlds for each of which there exists a procedure that will discover the truths of that fragment for any world in the class? The question may be too hard to parse. Let us define it in pieces. Let a discovery problem be any (recursive) fragment F of a formal language, together with a class K of countable relational structures for that fragment. One such class K is the class of all countable structures for the language fragment, but any subsets of this class may also be considered. A discovery procedure for the discovery problem is any procedure that, for every k in K and every presentation of evidence from k, "converges" to all of the sentences in F that are true in k. "Convergence" may be in the EA sense, the AE sense, or some other sense altogether (such as the weak convergence criterion considered two paragraphs previously).

What the results we have described tell us is that for many fragments F, if K is the set of all countable structures for F, then there are no discovery procedures for pairs $\langle F, K \rangle$. That does not imply that there are no discovery procedures for pairs $\langle F, K' \rangle$ where K′ is some proper subset of K. Must it be that for knowledge, true belief has been acquired in accordance with a procedure that would lead to the truth in *every* imaginable sequence?

Suppose we think of inquiry as posing discovery problems, a question or questions, and a class of possible worlds or circumstances that determine various answers to the question. Depending on which world or circumstance is ours, different answers will be true. Successful inquiry, which leads to some kind of knowledge, accords with a procedure that will converge to the truth of the matter, whatever it may be, in each of these possible circumstances. It is possible for procedures to have the capacity to find the truth in each of a class of circumstances without having the capacity to find the truth in every imaginable circumstance.

When attention is restricted to a discovery problem that contains a restricted class of possible worlds or circumstances, that restriction constitutes a kind of *background knowledge* brought to inquiry. The background knowledge says that the actual circumstance is one of a restricted class of circumstances or possible worlds. The theory of recollection, Plato's solution to Meno's paradox, claims that inquiry is conducted with a special sort of background knowledge, stamped in the soul before birth. Two different reconstructions of Plato's solution fit the story, and we offer them both without choosing between them.

In the first account, the correct *definitions* are stored in the soul and need only be brought to mind. The presentation of examples and the process of recollection eventually brings forth the truth, and provides knowledge, not because the process using that same background knowledge would succeed no matter how the world (or rather the forms) might imaginably be, but because there is a guarantee that the world (or, rather again, the forms) accords with knowledge the soul possesses. The background knowledge is so complete that no *inference* from examples is required; examples only ease access to knowledge we already have.

In the second account a complete list of *definientia*, each characterizing a distinct form, is stored in the soul. An inquiry into the nature of virtue must then match instances of the usage of "virtue" with the appropriate definiens in the list. In this case the process of recollections involves an inductive inference from particular examples to a universal biconditional connecting a definiens in the list with a term denoting the subject of inquiry. On the assumptions that no two forms are such that the same individuals participate in both, and that there are only finitely many forms, Socrates can eventually conjecture the form of virtue, know that his conjecture is correct, and can do so no matter which definiens in the list happens to represent the form of virtue.

On either reconstruction, Plato's reply to Meno's paradox has two aspects, and the slave boy's rediscovery of the theorem of Pythagoras illustrates each of them. First, knowledge may be had by means other than the means of inquiry. It may be inherited, innate, stamped on the soul, and not acquired by generalization from examples given in this life. Second, given such prior knowledge the task of discovery or the acquisition of knowledge is reconceived and becomes feasible, for the inquirer need not be able to fix upon the truth in every imaginable circumstance, but only in those circumstances consistent with prior knowledge.[4]

Plato has little to say in the *Meno* about what souls do that gives them the knowledge we recollect in successful inquiry. We (or our souls) have background knowledge through a causal process that is not itself inquiry. We could instead entertain the thought that we acquire background knowledge through inquiry conducted in our past lives. The second alternative raises a number of interesting questions.

When we inquire into a question, the discovery problem we address depends upon our knowledge. The class of alternative circumstances, and thus alternative answers, that need be considered is bounded by our prior knowledge. If we know nothing, it is the class of all imaginable circumstances; if we know a great deal, the class of alternative circumstances may be quite small. Suppose as we go through life (or through a sequence of lives) we form conjectures about the answers to various questions, and while we reserve the right to change these conjectures upon further evidence, in the meanwhile we use them as though they were background knowlege for still other questions. Should evidence later arrive that causes us to abandon our conjectures, we will also have to reconceive the discovery problems in which we had taken those conjectures as background knowledge.[5]

Since we are not only uncertain what discovery problems we shall face, but more profoundly, we may be wrong in our construal of the discovery problems we presently face, it would seem only prudent to rely on learning procedures that have the widest possible scope. We know from what has gone before that Meno's argument, and derivatives of it, show that there is no procedure adequate for all discovery problems, but some procedures may do better than others. We can characterize a dominance relation between discovery procedures: Procedure A dominates procedure B provided A solves (in whatever sense may be specified) every discovery problem B solves, but not vice versa. A procedure is then *maximal* if no procedure dominates it. We might then take prudence to require that our manner of inquiry accord with a maximal procedure. Some second thoughts are called for. In the well-studied case in which what is to be learned is not a theory but a language, it is known that every maximal procedure solves the discovery problem that consists of learning any finite language on a fixed vocabulary, but no procedure solves any larger problem, posed by any larger class of languages on that same vocabulary. There is no maximal procedure that identifies even one infinite language. For problems that concern the learning of theories, one should expect something analogous: the maximal procedures will be very sparse and will fail to solve discovery problems that are readily solved by other methods.

Since, in all likelihood, we cannot fix beforehand on maximal methods, prudence can only recommend something more modest. When we recognize that one discovery procedure dominates another then, *ceteris paribus*, it is prudent to use the dominant procedure rather than the dominated procedure. Whether that is a sensible or feasible recommendation depends on the dominance structure of discovery procedures. If, for example, there is a readily described infinite chain of procedures, later members of the sequence dominating all earlier members, then the recommendation would give us a task worthy of Sisyphus. We would ever be changing one procedure for another, without rest and without end. Sometimes, much as the existentialists say, the best thing to do is to stop preparing to make inquiries and make them.

6. HYPERMODERN MENO

Methodology amounts to recommendations restricting procedures of inquiry. Any such restriction can be thought of as determining a class of procedures, those that satisfy it. Besides methodology, psychology is another source of restrictions on procedures, and computation theory still another. For example, we might nowadays suppose that the discovery procedures available to us, even with the aid of machines, must be *computable* procedures, and invoking Church's thesis, restrict our attention to the class of Turing computable procedures for inquiry.

For any restriction on discovery procedures, the preceding discussion should suggest the following sort of question: What arguments of Meno's sort can be made against all procedures of this class? More exactly, for any restriction on discovery procedures, does the restriction also limit the class of discovery problems that can be solved? For both the EA and AE conceptions of successful inquiry, the requirement that procedures be computable limits the class of discovery problems that can be solved. There are discovery problems that can be solved by EA procedures but not by any computable EA procedures, and there are discovery problems that can be solved by AE procedures but not by any computable AE procedures. Methodological principles that are often regarded as benign also limit discovery when they are imposed in combination with the requirement of computability. A consistency principle applies to procedures that always conjecture theories consistent with the evidence; a conservative principle applies to procedures that never change a current conjecture until new evidence contradicts it. Either of these requirements, in combination with the requirement of computability, restricts the class of discovery problems that can be solved. It is easy to see that reverse is not true. That is, for every conservative, consistent, computable procedure, there is an inconsistent or unconservative (or both) procedure whose scope includes all discovery problems that can be solved by the first procedure.

When we investigate the restrictions on reliability that are implicit in methodological restrictions, we are entertaining recommendations to hop from one procedure to another. The picture of inquiry sketched in the previous section suggests the same thing for different reasons: as we reconceive the discovery problems with which we are faced, we may change our minds about which methods are appropriate. In that spirit, some philosophers have recommended methodological principles on empirical grounds: procedures that accord with the principles have worked in the past.[6]

The effect of hopping from one procedure to another can only be itself some procedure for discovery that mimics other procedures when given various pieces of evidence. From the inside, a hopping procedure may feel different from a procedure that does not hop, but behaviorally, the disposition to hop from procedure to procedure as evidence accumulates simply is a procedure, located somewhere in the vast ordering of possible discovery procedures. Recommendations about when and how to change procedures as evidence accumulates thus amount to restrictions on acceptable procedures, and form part (thus far an uninvestigated part) of methodology as we have just construed that subject. Despite these caveats, if we are familiar with only a small set of methods, as seems to be the case, hopping among them can constitute a better procedure.

Recommendations about preferences among procedures may also come from the study of the scope of procedures, but that study cannot be algorithmic. There is no computable function that will tell us, for all ordered pairs of indices of discovery procedures, whether the first member of the pair dominates the second. We are instead landed somewhere within the analytical hierarchy of recursion theory, and just where it is that we have landed is an open question.

The general notion of hopping among procedures suggests an apparent paradox: Can an effective procedure that hops among procedures hop from itself to some other procedure? Can it hop back to itself? In a sense it can. If we think of a hopping procedure as a program that simulates other programs, then (by the recursion theorem) it can at various stages pursue a simulation of itself, or cease to simulate itself, and thus accept or reject itself as a method. Of course, no procedure can *behave* differently than it does.

7. REAL LEARNING

Some people may think that results and questions such as those we have derived from the Meno paradox are remote from real concerns about the acquisition of knowledge. One might complain that these are all *formal* results, and because of that, for some reason mysterious to us, of no bearing on real science and its philosophical study. The study of the connection between logical form and the possibility of successful inquiry, in various senses, strikes us as both theoretically interesting and profoundly practical. For every question that has a logical form, or at least a tolerable variety of possible logical forms among which we may be undecided, these studies address the prospects for coming to know the answer.

Problems of a similar kind abound in the sciences, and questions (whose answers are in many cases unknown) about the existence of Menoan arguments against the acquisition of knowledge affect very practical issues about procedures of inquiry. We will give a few illustrations.

7.1. LANGUAGE LEARNING

Consider a child learning its first language. Somehow, within a few years, the child comes to be able to produce and to recognize grammatical sentences in the native language, and to distinguish such sentences from ungrammatical strings. Grammatical sentences of any possible language can be regarded as concatenations of symbols from some finite vocabulary. If we fix the finite vocabulary, then the number of distinct sets of strings built from that vocabulary is of course infinite, and in fact uncountably infinite. Suppose, however, we make the reasonable assumption that if a collection of strings is the collection of grammatical strings of some possible human language, then the collection is recursively enumerable. That is, for any set of strings of this kind there is a computable function such that, if a string is in the collection, the computable function will determine that it is. So, restricting attention to the languages that can be built on some particular vocabulary, the collection of possible natural languages is restricted to the recursively enumerable sets of strings made from that vocabulary. For each recursively enumerable set there is a program, actually an infinity of different programs, that when given an arbitrary string will compute "yes" if and only if the string is in the set (and will not return anything otherwise). The recursively enumerable sets can be effectively indexed in many different ways, so we can imagine each possible language to have a name that no other possible language has, and in fact we can imagine the name just to *be* a program of the kind just mentioned.

One way to think of the child's problem is this: on the basis of whatever evidence the environment provides, the child forms a sequence of programs that recognize a sequence of languages, until, eventually, the child settles on a program that recognizes the actual natural language in the child's environment. Psychological investigation suggests that children use *positive* evidence almost exclusively. That is, the evidence consists of strings from the language to be learned but does not include evidence as to which strings are not in the language.

With this setting, due essentially to E. Mark Gold,[7] an important aspect of human development is made formal enough to permit mathematical investigations to bear on issues such as the characterization of the collection of possible human languages. For a language to be possible for humans, humans must be capable of learning it. Assuming that any possible human language could have been learned by any one human, it follows that the collection of possible human languages must be identifiable, or learnable, in the sense that for every language in the collection a human child, if given appropriate positive evidence, can form a program that recognizes that language. There are surprising results as to which collections of languages are, and are not, learnable. Gold himself proved that any collection containing all finite languages and at least one infinite language cannot be identified. Imposing psychologically motivated constraints on the learner, Osherson and Weinstein have argued that any learnable collection of languages is finite. A wealth of technical results is now available about language learning.

7.2. STATISTICAL INFERENCE

One of the principal statistical tasks is to infer a feature of a population from features of samples drawn at random from that population. One can view an ideal statistician as drawing ever larger samples and using the statistical estimator to guess the value of the quantity of interest in the population. Some of the usual desiderata for statistical estimators are founded on this picture. For example, it is desired that an estimator be *consistent*, meaning that whatever value the quantity has in the population, for any positive epsilon the probability that the estimate of the quantity differs from the true value by more than epsilon approaches zero as the sample size increases without bound. This is clearly a convergence criterion; it implicitly considers a family of possible worlds, in each of which the quantity of interest has a distinct value. When the quantity is continuous, there will be a continuum of such possibilities. A consistent estimator must, given increasing samples from any one of these possible worlds, converge with probability one to a characterization of the value the quantity has in the world from which the data are obtained.

7.3. CURVE FITTING

Every quantitative empirical science is faced with tasks that require inferring a functional dependency from data points. Kepler's task was to determine from observations of planetary positions the function giving the orbits of planets. Boyle's task was to infer the functional dependency of pressure and volume from measures on gas samples. These sorts of challenges can usefully be viewed as discovery problems. Data are generated by a process that satisfies an unknown functional dependency, but the function is known (or assumed) to belong to some restricted class of functions. In principle, more data points can be obtained without bound or limit, although in practice we may lose interest after a while. In real cases, the data are subject to some error, but something may be known about the error—its bounds, for example, or its probability distribution. The scientist's task is to guess the function from finite samples of data points. The conjecture can be revised as more evidence accumulates.

Many procedures have been proposed for this sort of discovery problem. Harold Jeffreys,[8] for example, proposed a procedure that uses Bayesian techniques together with an enumeration of the polynomial functions. Nineteenth-century computational designs, such as Babbage's, used differencing techniques for computing polynomials, techniques that could (in the absence of error) be turned round into discovery procedures. More recently Langley et al.[9] have tried doing exactly that, and have described a number of other procedures for inferring functional dependencies from sample data.

For any of these procedures, and for others, the foremost questions concern reliability. For any procedure we can and should ask under what conditions the conjectures will converge to an appropriate function. We can ask such questions for many different senses of convergence, and for many different accounts of what makes a function (other than the correct one) appropriate, but we should certainly try to formulate the issues and answer them. Very little work of this kind has been done; neither Jeffreys nor Langley and his collaborators characterize exactly when their procedures will succeed, although in both cases it is easy enough to find many classes of functions (e.g., classes including logarithmic, exponential, and similar transcendental functions) for which the procedure will fail in the long run. A more systematic study has been done for a related class of problems in which the data are finite pieces of the graph of a recursive function, and the discovery task is to identify the function by guessing a program that computes it.[10]

7.4. GENERATING FUNCTIONS

One of the characteristic kinds of discovery tasks, at least in the physical sciences, is the discovery of generating functions. The idea is easiest to understand through an example. When monatomic gases are heated they emit light, but only light of certain definite frequencies. For example, when atomic hydrogen emits light, the spectrum contains a series of lines following a line whose wavelength is 6563 angstroms. In addition, the spectrum of hydrogen contains a number of other series of lines. The spectral likes of other elements, notably the alkaline earth and alkali metal elements, can also be arranged in various series. Here is a kind of discovery problem: given that one can obtain the spectrum of such a gas, and can identify lines as lines of a common series, what is the function that determines the frequencies (or wavelengths) of the lines in the series? For the principal hydrogen series, Balmer solved this problem in 1885. Balmer's formula is

$$1/\lambda = R(1/4 - 1/n^2)$$

where n is an integer greater than or equal to 3, λ is the wavelength, and R is a constant (the Rydberg constant). Balmer generalized his formula to give a parametric family

$$1/\lambda = R(1/m^2 - 1/n^2)$$

for which series for m = 1, 3, 4, and 5 have been found.

Balmer's formulas give a collection of discrete values for a continuous quantity, in this case the wave number, and they specify that collection by giving a (partial) function of the positive integers.

There are other famous discoveries in the natural sciences that seem to have an analogous structure. The central question in chemistry in the nineteenth century was the reliable determination of the relative weights of atoms. Alternative methods yielded conflicting results until in 1859 Cannizzaro noted that the relative vapor densities of compounds form series; for example, all compounds of hydrogen form a series, as do all compounds of oxygen, and so forth, for any element. Of the continuum of possible values for compounds of hydrogen, only a discrete set of values is founded, and Cannizzaro discovered that the vapor density of any hydrogen compound is divisible by half the vapor density of hydrogen gas. Analogous results held for compounds of other elements. Cannizzaro's discovery was of crucial importance in putting the atomic theory on a sound basis; Balmer's discovery formed the crucial evidence for the early quantum theory of matter.

We can imagine a scientist faced with the following kind of problem: an infinite but discrete series of values of a continuous quantity is given by some unknown function of a power of the integers, I^n, or of the positive integers, but the function may belong to a known class of functions of this kind. The scientist can observe more and more members of the series, without bound, and can form a series of conjectures about the unknown function as the evidence increases. The properties of discovery problems of this sort have not been investigated either in the scientific or in the philosophical literature; and aside from the obvious procedure of looking for common divisors of values of a quantity, we know of no discovery procedures that have been proposed.

7.5. THEORETICAL QUANTITIES AND FUNCTIONAL DECOMPOSITIONS

If you have only a number of resistance-free batteries, wires of varying but unknown resistances, and a device for measuring current through a circuit, you can discover Ohm's law, that voltage in a circuit equals the current in the circuit multiplied by the resistance in the circuit, even though you have no device to measure voltage or resistance, and even though at the beginning of the inquiry you have no belief that there are properties such as voltage and resistance. Pick a wire to serve as standard, and let the current through each circuit with each battery serve to measure a property of each battery. Pick a battery to serve as standard, and let the current through each circuit with each wire and that battery serve to measure a property of each wire. You will then find, by simple curve fitting, that the relations between these two properties and the current is described by Ohm's law. Langley et al. give a discovery procedure that solves this problem. But what is the general form of the problem?

Consider any real (or rational, or integer as the case may be) valued function of n-tuples of nominal variables. In the circuits considered previously, for example, current I is a function of each pair of values for the nominal pair (battery, wire). In general we have $F(X_1, \ldots, X_n)$, Let F be equal to some composition of functions on subsets of the nominal variables. For example, I(battery, wire) = V(battery)* R(wire), where * is multiplication. A discovery problem consists of a set of functions on subsets of tuples of nominal variables, and for each tuple and set of functions, a function that is a composition of (i.e., some function of) that set. The learner's task is to infer the decomposition from values of the composite function.

Evidently a lot of clever science consists in solving instances of problems of functional decomposition, and thus discovering important but initially unmeasured properties. The properties of discovery problems of this kind, and of algorithms for solving them, are almost completely unstudied.

7.6. "UNDERDETERMINATION," OR ANSWERABLE AND UNANSWERABLE QUESTIONS

A scientist often has in mind a particular question to which an answer is wanted. The aim is not to find the whole truth about the world, but to find the answer to one particular question. There is a tradition in philosophy, in physics, and even in statistics of considering contexts in which particular questions cannot be answered. Philosophers talk about "underdetermination" in such contexts, whereas physicists tend to talk about similar issues in terms of "physical meaningfulness" and statisticians in terms of "identifiability." The examination of such issues is in structure very much like Gold's consideration of classes of languages that cannot be identified. Arguments consider a collection of alternative structures of some kind, characterize the evidence generated from any structure, and establish that even "in the limit" some structures in the collection cannot be distinguished.

Consider a question about the shape of space: what is its global topology? In relativity, the evidence we can get at any time about that question is bounded by our past light cone; the discriminations we can make at any time are then determined by the data in that light cone and whatever general laws we possess. The general laws can be thought of as simply restricting the possible classes of space-time models. As time goes by, more and more of the actual universe is in the past of an imaginary, immortal observer. Are there collections of relativistic models for which such an observer can *never* determine the global topology of space? It turns out that there are, and some of them are not too difficult to picture. Imagine that space is a three-dimensional sphere, and that space-time is an infinite sequence of three-dimensional spheres. Suppose the radius of the sphere expands as time goes on. At any moment the past light cone of an observer may include, at each past moment, some but not all of the sphere of space at that past moment. If the radius of space expands fast enough, then at *no* moment will the past light cone include all of space. Now consider another space-time made mathematically from the first by identifying the antipodal points on the sphere of space at each moment. The shape of space will be different in the two space-times. The sphere is simply connected: any closed curve on the surface of a sphere, even a three-dimensional sphere, can be contracted smoothly to a point. The projective space obtained by identifying antipodal points on the sphere is not simply connected. The two spaces have different topologies. Now imagine that space expands with sufficient rapidity that the past light cone of any point never reveals whether one is in the spherical space of the projective space. Many other classes of indistinguishable space-times have been described.[11]

7.7. INDISTINGUISHABILITY BY A CLASS OF PROCEDURES

Issues of distinguishability also arise in settings that are remote from cosmology. In the social sciences, engineering, and parts of biology and epidemiology, we often rely on statistical models of causal relations. Often an initial statistical model is thought to be in error, and a variety of algorithmic or quasi-algorithmic techniques have been developed to find revisions. Factor analysis is one way; procedures that modify an initial model by means of "fitting statistics" are another; procedures that try to match the empirical constraints entailed by a model with those found in the data are still a third.

For each of these kinds of procedures the discovery framework poses a relevant question: For what classes of models can the procedure succeed in identifying in the limit? What are the collections of models such that, given data generated from any one model in the collection, as the size of the sample increases without bound the procedure will identify the model that actually generated the data?

Sometimes a variety of procedures share a feature; either they share a limit on the information they consider in forming a hypothesis, or they share a limit on the hypotheses they consider. In the latter case it is perfectly obvious that certain classes of models cannot be identified. In the former case, finding out what classes of models can and cannot be identified may take some work. The discovery paradigm emphasizes the importance of the work.

8. CONCLUSION

There is a lot of structure behind the words that translators have given to Plato's Meno and to Plato's Socrates. The structure is, we hope, plausibly attributed even though it is remarkably modern. That should be of no surprise to those who think philosophy really addresses enduring questions, and who think the questions of knowledge had the same force and urgency for the ancients as for ourselves.

NOTES

1. Plato, *Five Dialogues*, trans. G. Grube (Indianapolis: Hackett, 1981). All quotations are taken from this translation.

2. A view of inquiry related to ours has been championed by A. Goldman in his *Epistemology and Cognition* (Cambridge, Mass.: Harvard University Press, 1984). Recent commentaries on the Meno by historians of philosophy have varied in the importance they give to Meno's paradox, but none of them give it the reconstruction considered here. Compare T. Irwin, *Plato's Moral Theory* (Oxford, 1977); J. Maravcsik, "Learning as Recollection," in *Plato: A Collection of Critical Essays*, ed. G. Vlastos, vol. 1, *Metaphysics and Epistemology* (Garden City, N.Y.: Anchor Books, 1971); N. White, *Plato on Knowledge and Reality* (Indianapolis: Hackett, 1976). In what follows a variety of technical claims are asserted without proof. In all cases the claims are simple applications of results shown in D. Osherson, M. Stob, and S. Weinstein, *Systems That Learn* (Cambridge, Mass.: MIT Press, 1985); C. Glymour, "Inductive Inference in the Limit," *Erkenntnis* 21 (1984); D. Osherson and S. Weinstein, "Paradigms of Truth Detection," *Journal of Philosophical Logic*, 1989; K. Kelly and C. Glymour, "Convergence to the Truth and Nothing but the Truth," *Philosophy of Science*, 1990; K. Kelly and C. Glymour, "Theory Discovery from Quantified Data," *Journal of Philosophical Logic*, 1990.

3. For example, in H. Field, "Mental Representation," in *Philosophy of Psychology*, ed. N. Block (Cambridge, Mass.: Harvard University Press, 1980), and in R. Stalnaker, *Inquiry* (Cambridge, Mass.: MIT Press, 1984).

4. Chomsky gave a strictly parallel answer to questions about how children learn their native language. "Cartesian linguistics" ought perhaps to have been called "Platonic linguistics."

5. The result is a picture of inquiry something like that proposed by Isaac Levi. Compare his *The Enterprise of Knowledge* (Cambridge, Mass.: MIT Press, 1980).

6. Compare C. Glymour, *Theory and Evidence* (Princeton: Princeton University Press, 1980), and R. Boyd, "Realism, Underdetermination, and a Causal Theory of Evidence," *Nous* 7 (1973).

7. Aspects of the framework were developed independently and slightly earlier by Hilary Putnam.

8. See his *Scientific Inference* (Cambridge: Cambridge University Press, 1973).

9. See P. Langley, H. Simon, G. Bradshaw, and J. Zytkow, *Scientific Discovery* (Cambridge, Mass.: MIT Press, 1986).

10. See D. Angluin and C. Smith, *A Survey of Inductive Inference Methods*, Technical Report 250 (New Haven: Yale University Department of Computer Science, 1982).

11. See C. Glymour, "Indistinguishable Space-Times and the Fundamental Group," and D. Malament,"Indistinguishable Spacetimes," both in *Foundations of Space-Time Theories*, ed. J. Earman (Minneapolis: University of Minnesota Press, 1981).

TWO

The Concept of Induction in the Light of the Interrogative Approach to Inquiry

Jaakko Hintikka

1. THE INTERROGATIVE MODEL

This paper is a part of a larger enterprise. In the last few years I have developed an essentially new approach to inquiry, prominently including scientific inquiry.[1] This approach can be given the form of a model (or, more appropriately, a multidimensional spectrum of models) of inquiry, which I propose to call *the interrogative model of inquiry*. It can be used to understand a wide variety of phenomena and to solve a variety of problems. In this paper I will study one particular concept that can be put into an interesting systematic and historical perspective by means of the interrogative model, namely, the concept of *induction*.[2] In the study of this notion the interrogative model of inquiry turns out to be especially useful. Among other conclusions, we shall find interesting reasons for assigning induction in the accepted sense of the word a rather lowly place on the map of scientific methodology. At the same time, the interrogative model helps us to uncover a historically earlier sense of induction which in our days is virtually forgotten and to assign to it an important role in the scientific process.

I will assume familiarity with the main ideas of the interrogative model. There is in fact relatively little to be familiar with, as the main ideas on which this model is based are extremely simple. The model can be described in game-theoretical terms.[3] The model takes the form of a game which an idealized scientist, called the *Inquirer*, plays against *Nature* on a fixed model (universe of discourse). This model or "world" in practice is usually our actual world or some part of it. (Such parts as can serve as models of theories are often called in physics independent or isolated systems.) The game starts from a theoretical premise T. The Inquirer is trying to derive a preset conclusion C from T. At each stage, the Inquirer has a choice between a *deductive move*, in which a logical conclusion is drawn from what the Inquirer has reached already, and an *interrogative move*, in which the Inquirer puts a question to Nature and registers the answer, when forthcoming, as an additional premise. Speaking of such questions is what presupposes that a model of the combined language of T and C is given to which the questions pertain. Nature's answers are assumed to be true in this model. In the applications contemplated here, "questions put to Nature" are typically intended to be observations and experiments.

In different varieties of the model, different assumptions are made as to what kinds of questions Nature can answer. One important dimension is represented by different restrictions on the logical complexity of the available answers, as measured by the number of quantifier kind changes (i.e., changes from an evidential to a universal quantifier or vice versa) in the quantifier prefix of the answer. Quantifier-free answers are called $A^0 = E^0$ answers. A^{n+1}-answers have a prefix of the form $(\forall x_1)(\forall x_2) \ldots (\forall x_k)$ + an E^n-prefix, and E^{n+1}-answers have a prefix of the form $(\exists x_1)(\exists x_2) \ldots (\exists x_k)$ + an A^n-prefix. A^2-prefixes will also be called AE-prefixes.

Restricting Nature's answers to the $A^0 = E^0$ case is tantamount to restricting answerable questions to yes-or-no questions concerning the truth or falsity of atomic propositions in M. The restriction that limits Nature's answers to this case I have called the *Atomistic Postulate*. At first sight, it seems to characterize the logic of empirical sciences. For Nature will not tell us in one fell swoop what happens always and everywhere. All that she will directly inform the Inquirer of is what happens in particular cases—in particular observations or measurements. And this restriction is precisely what the Atomistic Postulate is calculated to capture.

It can in fact be argued that practically all recent philosophy of science has been based on the Atomistic Postulate, tacitly if not explicitly.[4] Yet this postulate is unacceptable, for when a controlled experiment is construed as Nature's answer to the Inquirer's question, the logical complexity of the answers is at least of the AE variety. Hence the logic of experimental sciences (as distinguished from purely observational sciences) is an AE logic rather than one characterized by the Atomistic Postulate.[5] This result prompts a major reevaluation of contemporary philosophy of science. The present paper is a part of that reevaluation.

2. CONVENTIONAL INDUCTION PLAYS NO ROLE IN THE INTERROGATIVE MODEL

The first observation that can be made here is that induction in our accustomed twentieth-century sense play absolutely no role in the original interrogative model. In this sense, induction means, in the first place, inference from particular cases to general truths and, secondarily, inference from particular cases to other particular cases. I shall here disregard the latter aspect, for the following reason: If inferences from particulars to particulars satisfy certain conditions, the principles according to which they are made are logically equivalent to principles governing inferences from particulars to generalizations.[6] Hence it suffices for most purposes to consider only inferences from particular instances to general laws.

As the reader can ascertain, there is in the original interrogative model absolutely no slot for the kind of inference that induction is supposed to be. The only inferences that take place in an interrogative inquiry are deductive. The other moves (other than deductive ones) include in the first place interrogative ones. In them, no inferences are drawn. Instead, a question is addressed by the Inquirer to Nature and (depending on conditions that are defined when the interrogative model is further specified) answered by Nature. In some varieties of the model, the Inquirer can, instead of an interrogative or a deductive move, perform a definitory move (introduce a new concept by an explicit definition) or strengthen the conclusion to be proved (assertoric move). But in none of these extensions of the interrogative model is anything like an inductive move possible.

The original unreconstructed interrogative model of inquiry hence already leads to a remarkable result. It shows that it is possible to develop a rich and realistic model of at least some central aspects of the scientific enterprise without as much as mentioning induction. *A fortiori*, if the interrogative model should turn out to be, not only the truth and nothing but the truth, but the whole truth, Hume's problem would play no role whatsoever in a serious theory of the scientific method and of the scientific process.

What is especially interesting here is that the most important extensions of the original interrogative model also fail to vindicate the received concept of induction. I cannot examine these extensions in detail here. The main idea is nevertheless easy to appreciate.[7] Instead of assuming that the answers given by Nature are always true, it can be assumed that each such answer is true only with a certain probability. This does not yet specify a unique model, for it does not tell us how the probabilities of a true answer on different occasions depend on (or are independent of) one another. By choosing these probabilities in different ways we can adapt the interrogative model to different evidential situations. For instance, if Nature's answers to repetitions of one and the same question are independent of one another, the best way for the Inquirer to ascertain that Nature's answer is veridical may be to repeat the same question and hope for the same answer. This corresponds to a scientific situation in which an experiment or observation does not involve a systematic bias or other systematic mistakes.

It may happen, however, that an answer by Nature to a given question makes it likely that Nature should give the same answer to its repetitions. Then the best strategy for ascertaining Nature's veracity may very well be to try to derive the same conclusion by an altogether different line of reasoning. In this way, the famous old idea of the consilience of scientific inference can be explained and vindicated.[8]

In all these different situations, however, we are still dealing with deductive rather than inductive reasoning. More accurately, we are dealing with strict inferences from merely probable premises. The is diametrically opposite to typical cases of inductive inference, which are nonbinding inferences from (typically indubitable) premises. It is seen, not only that inductive inferences are not incorporated in the extended interrogative model, but that there is no place for them in the interrogative model or in any of its most natural extensions.

3. THE PROBLEM OF INDUCTION AND THE ATOMISTIC POSTULATE

One can say much more here, however. Indeed, one can put the entire concept of induction in a sharper historical relief.

The concept of induction goes back to Aristotle's idea of *epagoge*.[9] Indeed, the Latin term *inductio* was first introduced as a translation of *epagoge*. It is far from clear, however, that *epagoge* really is the same idea as our received concept of induction, and it will be argued below that it is not. In any case, the "problem of induction," by which everybody means the problem of *justifying* induction, was only thrust to the forefront of philosophical discussion almost two thousand years after Aristotle by David Hume.[10] Why the time lag? Were pre-Humean philosophers too confused or too naive to appreciate the importance of the problem of induction? I don't think that they were. It can be shown, if I am right, that the ascendancy of "Hume's Problem" of induction is part and parcel of the same problem situation as contemporary philosophers' virtually unanimous assumption of the Atomistic Postulate. In fact, this is a natural occasion to put the entire concept of induction into an overall historical perspective.

First, it can be seen where the idea of inductive inference as an essential ingredient of the scientific process comes from. It is one possible reaction to the problem situation created by the assumption of the Atomistic Postulate. If this postulate is adopted, then a scientific theory (e.g., the initial theoretical premise T) cannot itself be derived by means of the interrogative procedure without an equally strong or stronger theoretical premise. For no nontrivial general laws can be deduced from particular propositions, for instance, from Nature's answers to questions concerning particular cases or particular situations. Hence, the suggestion goes, the two kinds of steps of the interrogative procedure, questions and deductive inferences, have to be supplemented by a third kind of step. This step is calculated to lead us from Nature's particular answers to general truths. And it is this role of generalizing steps that inductive inferences are supposed to play.

At the moment I am not discussing the intrinsic merits or demerits of this idea. What is relevant here is a simple historical prediction (or retrodiction) that can be based on my diagnosis of the rationale of the general idea of inductive inference. What follows from my analysis is that, for those philosophers and scientists who did not adopt that Atomistic Postulate, our received idea of induction was not likely to play the same role as it does for us. It was not needed as a supplement to deductive inference. There did not exist for such philosophers any Humean problem of justifying induction, for induction in our sense could largely be dispensed with. If such thinkers used the idea of induction, it was in some different kind of role altogether.

In particular, it can be expected that philosophers and methodologists who do not believe in the Atomistic Postulate will not abide by the current idea of induction as an inference from particular cases to a generalization. For, in the face of the Atomistic Postulate, it was precisely this kind of generalization that induction was supposed to mediate. If you don't accept the postulate, you don't need induction for this purpose.

Likewise, it is clear that the central role of "the problem of induction" is due to philosophers' adoption of the Atomistic Postulate.[11] Hence this problem of "justifying induction" can be expected to occupy only those philosophers who have tacitly accepted the postulate. This observation helps in fact to explain why "Hume's Problem" became a central problem in philosophy when it did—and also how, as I will show below.

Now, as a matter of historical fact, the Atomistic Postulate was not adopted in the earlier tradition of philosophy and science from Aristotle to Newton (inclusive), though for different reasons in the case of different historical figures. In the Aristotelian tradition, even perception can give us forms, which are already by themselves general concepts. Moreover, their presence in the soul *ipso facto* implied according to Aristotle awareness of certain general laws, namely, those laws that specify what forms necessarily accompany the given ones.[12] (Thinking of a certain form is for Aristotle to have it realized in one's soul. Hence what necessarily accompanies this form is also automatically present in the soul, that is, is also necessarily thought of.)

This rejection of the Atomistic Postulate by Aristotle is seen in other ways, too. Another indication is the fact, brought out by G. E. L. Owen and others, that the *phainomena* and *endoxa* which a theory was supposed to account for according to Aristotle, were not all particular facts but could include general laws.[13]

In Newton, his reason for dispensing with the Atomistic Postulate is different. It is Newton's firm belief in the experimental method as being able to give the Inquirer general laws as answers to experimental "questions put to nature."[14] Hence induction in our contemporary sense was not needed by Newton.

In either type of case, induction can therefore be expected to amount to something essentially different from our post-Humean conception. A widespread failure to appreciate this historical fact has in my judgment seriously impaired philosophers' understanding of the early history of the concept of induction. I don't think that most philosophers or historians really have a realistic idea of what Aristotle or Newton meant by induction.

4. EXPERIMENTAL QUESTIONS AND THEIR PRESUPPOSITIONS

In spite of all this, the interrogative model nevertheless assigns to a somewhat different (but historically authentic) concept of induction an extremely interesting role. In order to see this, a starting point is offered by the logical situation outlined in my paper, "What Is the Logic of Experimental Inquiry?"[15] When carried further, this analysis naturally, not to say inevitably, leads to further insights. In the earlier discussion, the reader was probably bothered by the question as to how much new force answers to AE questions (and to more complicated questions) really give us—and what kind of information they do yield. For from the perspective used there it may legitimately look as if the presuppositions of the questions in question are so strong that they are unlikely even to have been established in a realistic situation of inquiry and so strong that answers to them will yield relatively little new information anyway. Witness, for example, the question whose presupposition is:

$$\begin{matrix} (\forall x)\,(\exists y) \\ (\forall z)\,(\exists u) \end{matrix} > S[x, y, z, u] \qquad (1)$$

The logic of such sentences alone is almost tantamount to the entire second-order logic.[16] Hence the step from the presupposition (1) of a question put to Nature to its answer

$$K(\forall x)\,(\forall z)\,S[x, f(x), z, g(z)] \qquad (2)$$

or even to the desideratum

$$(\exists f)\,(\exists g)\,K(\forall x)\,(\forall z)\,S[x, f(x), z, g(z)] \qquad (3)$$

appears not to add terribly much new force to what the Inquirer already has.

Moreover, it is clear that the force of the presupposition (1) is largely due to the fact that it codifies certain independencies between different experimental variables. Now we normally think that such independencies can only be established experimentally. This expectation seems to me justified. But how can any experiment establish such independencies if they must have been found and incorporated into the presupposition of a question before the experimental question is put to Nature and answered by her?

These are genuine problems, and they force us to have another look at the most basic ideas on which the interrogative model is based. More specifically, we must have some second thoughts about the role of presuppositions. Right from the beginning, I could have built the model in a slightly different way. I could have eliminated the role of the presupposition of a question altogether as a prerequisite to asking the questions. Of course, I must then allow the answerer to respond, even when the question does otherwise qualify as an answerable one, by rejecting its presupposition rather than by providing the Inquirer with an answer to it.[17]

This rule change seems to result in a better model of scientific inquiry than the previous one, at least in many applications. It goes some distance toward solving the problems just pointed out. However, a little bit more has to be said of the failures of the presupposition of a question in different cases. For a propositional question,

$$(S_1 \text{ or } S_2 \text{ or} \ldots \text{or } S_k)? \tag{4}$$

the failure of the presupposition

$$(S_1 \vee S_2 \vee \ldots \vee S_k) \tag{5}$$

makes the question completely otiose, and likewise for simple wh-questions. But consider a question whose presupposition is:

$$(\forall x)\,(\exists y)\,S[x, y] \tag{6}$$

Such a presupposition fails if for *some* values of x *no* y satisfies S[x, y]. Then the Inquirer ought not to ask which y does the job for those fruitless values of x. But there is no harm in asking the question for other values of x. And even more so if the presupposition (6) is true but has not been shown to be true for some values of x. This should not bar the Inquirer from raising the question.

In such cases, Nature's response to a question whose presupposition used to be (6) is naturally taken to be of the same form

$$(\forall x)\,S[x, f(x)] \tag{7}$$

as before, with f such as to sustain the existential generalization from

$$K\,(\forall x)\,S[x, f(x)] \tag{8}$$

to

$$(\exists g)\,K\,(\forall x)\,S[x, g(x)], \tag{9}$$

except that f can now be a partial function, that is, defined only for some values of x. This can be expressed in the usual notation by turning the reply (8) (minus "K") into a conditional one:

$$(\forall x)\,((x_1 < x < x_2) \supset S[x, f(x)] \tag{10}$$

Instead of just one interval, we can of course in principle have in (10) several different nonoverlapping intervals. This, then, is what is natural to think of as Nature's answer to an AE-type question. I shall assume in the following that this is what Nature's answers are like. Nature's reply may also include a rejection of the presupposition for certain values of x:

$$(\forall x)((x' < x < x'') \supset \sim(\exists y)S[x, y]) \tag{11}$$

I shall ignore this possible component of Nature's response in what follows, however. It is the less important and less interesting part of the reply.

Thus it is seen that the natural way of defining the interrogative model is to allow the Inquirer to put AE questions to Nature even when the presupposition is not established. Nature's reply is not the negative of the (former) presupposition, even when it is false. Rather, it is a restricted functional dependence like (10).

5. INDUCTION AS THE TASK OF EXTENDING LIMITED GENERALIZATIONS

From what has been said, it is seen that there is an important dimension of the progress of scientific inquiry which we have not yet considered and which has not been considered very often in recent philosophy of science. It is not, strictly speaking, any longer an application of the interrogative model. However, its importance is in effect predicted by the interrogative model in the light of the remarks just made.

This dimension concerns the extension of a generalization like (10) to further values of x, that is, a step from (10) to

$$(\forall x)((x_1' < x < x_2') \supset S[x, f(x)]) \tag{12}$$

where $x_1' < x_1, x_2 < x_2'$.

More generally, the Inquirer has a number of partial generalizations

$$(\forall x)((x_{i1} < x < x_{i2}) \supset S[x, f_i(x)]) \tag{13}$$

($i = 1, 2, \ldots, k$), where the intervals $x_{i1} < x < x_{i2}$ are assumed not to overlap. These may have been established in part as (partial) answers to the same question, and in part as (partial) answers to different questions.

The dimension I have in mind is now twofold: (i) the Inquirer is trying to extend a generalization like (10) or (13) to longer intervals, perhaps to an unrestricted generalization; and (ii) the Inquirer is trying to unify the different partial dependences (laws, functions) $f_i(x)$ into one law, for example, into one and the same mathematical law.

This dual dimension is the focus of this paper. I have shown why it is important from the systematic viewpoint offered to us by the interrogative model. I will return to this systematic significance later in this paper. The main historical thesis I am proposing also concerns the same dimension. What this thesis says is that the generalization and reconciliation task this dimension deals with is what was earlier meant by induction.

6. NEWTONIAN INDUCTION

This historical thesis deserves a few comments and explanations. Indeed, Newton's idea of induction is seen from his famous methodological statement in the *Opticks*:

> As in mathematics, so in natural philosophy, the investigation of difficult things by the method of analysis ought ever to precede the method of composition. This analysis consists in making experiments and observations, and in drawing general conclusions from them by induction, and admitting no objections against the conclusions but such as are taken from experiment, or other certain truths. For hypotheses are not to be regarded in experimental philosophy. And although the arguing from experiments and observations by induction be no demonstration of general conclusions, yet it is the best way of arguing which the nature of things admits of, and may be looked upon as so much the stronger by how much the induction is more general. And if no exception occur from phenomena, the conclusion may be pronounced generally. But if at any time afterward any exception shall occur from experiments, it may then begin to be pronounced with such exceptions as occur. By this way of analysis we may proceed from compounds to ingredients and from motions to the forces producing them, and in general from effects to their causes and from particular causes to more general ones, till the argument end in the most general. This is the method of analysis; and the synthesis consists in assuming the causes discovered and established as principles, and by them explaining the phenomena proceeding from them and proving the explanations.[18]

Here we can see the kind of concept of induction I propose to call the Newtonian one at work. Induction in this sense of the word occupies a niche in the scientific procedure indicated by the analysis carried out earlier in this paper. Induction is, in the simplest case, the step from a limited generalization of the form (10) to a less restricted generalization (12). In the extreme (ideal) case, the entire restriction (antecedent) in (10) is eliminated. This optimal case is what Newton describes as saying: "And if no exception occur from phenomena, the conclusion may be pronounced generally." What distinguishes a Newtonian inductive step from inductive inference in the twentieth-century sense is that its starting point is not a number of particular propositions but propositions which, logically speaking, normally possess already limited generality. For, as I have argued elsewhere, experiments could according to Newton yield as their result a general law.[19] (This is among other things seen from Newton's practice of resorting to results of experiments in proving general theorems and solving general problems in his *Opticks*.) Induction thus increases the generality of the propositions the Inquirer has established, but in an entirely different sense from the twentieth-century idea of induction as an inference from the particular to the general. For in Newtonian induction, the increase in generality is one of degree, not of kind. Newton is in fact quite consistent in speaking of induction as a way of arguing from "observations and experiments." Given his conception of experiment, this means that the starting point of an inductive step can already possess (limited) generality.

It is not clear in what sense a Newtonian induction is an inference, either. In principle, the extension of the scope of a generalization can take place experimentally. This is not what Newton means, however. For he says that "although the arguing from experiments and observations by induction be no demonstration of general conclusions, yet it is the best way of arguing which the nature of things admits of." What Newton has in mind is a fact of scientific life familiar to all experimentalists. Even though a controlled experiment (or equivalent) can establish a generalization, the actual range over which the controlled variable can be varied is typically very narrow, indeed so narrow that the resulting restricted generalization is useless in studying other phenomena unless it can be further generalized by widening its scope (as is the step from (10) to (12) above), even before other experiments and observations have been made to help us extend it. This implies that induction in the sense of widening the scope of a generalization is a corrigible step of argument in a sense which, for example, Nature's limited-scope answer to an experimental question is not. I will return to this point later.

At the same time, the quotations from Newton show how tempting it might easily seem to be to assimilate Newtonian induction to our latter-day namesake conception. It is indeed possible that Newtonian induction was intended to comprise as a degenerate special case steps from particular measurement results to a generalization. But this temptation is nevertheless misleading. It has in some cases even misled translators. For instance, this is illustrated by the Motte-Cajori translation of *Principia* where one of the crucial sentences is made to disagree with our interpretation:

> In this [experimental] philosophy particular propositions are inferred from the phenomena, and afterwards rendered general by induction.[20]

But there is no "particular" in the original, and the netural term "inferred" is a bad substitute for Newton's explicit word for deduction:

> In hac philosophia propositiones deducuntur ex phaenomenis, & redduntur generales per inductionem.[21]

The correct translation thus goes somewhat as follows:

> In this philosophy, propositions are deduced from phenomena and rendered general by induction.

If anything, Newton's terminology supports my interpretation, for a "proposition" normally meant in an axiomatic context of his day a *general* proposition.

Earlier in this paper, we saw that for Aristotle, phenomena could be the source of general truths (or general beliefs) and not just particular ones. The same is now seen to be true of Newton. For instance, in speaking of his laws of motion (which of course are supposed to be general truths *par exellence*) Newton, on one occasion writes:

> These Principles are *deduced from Phaenomena* and made general by Induction.[22] [emphasis added]

Since Newton uses "deduce" in a fairly strict sense, this makes sense only if Newton's "Phaenomena" are already general. Similar evidence is easily found elsewhere. (Cf. also what was established above.)

Thus those few hardy souls who have maintained that Newton's methodology was an "inductivist" one may after all have something going for them. But, of course, Newton was speaking of "induction" in a sense different from theirs.

7. NEWTON AND MATHEMATICAL MODELING

There is yet another similarity between Newton and Aristotle which has not been utilized in the literature on Newton. It is the role of induction in establishing the first principles of science in Aristotle. The way this oversight has pointed historians' and philosophers' attention in a wrong direction is seen in the views of those commentators who construe Newton's method as a construction of mathematical models.[23] This idea has been encouraged by Newton's relatively sparse mention of experiments and observations in the early books of the *Principia*. This seems to differentiate his procedure from that prescribed by the interrogative model, which apparently squares better with what Newton does in the *Opticks*.

The answer is that Newton assumes that most of the pertinent questions had been put to Nature before the definition and axioms (laws of motions) are formulated. We have in fact seen that Newton claimed in so many words that those laws (principles) were "deduced from Phaenomena & made general by Induction."[24] Hence the principles of the *Principia* do not just define a mathematical model. They are themselves not only somehow inspired by experience, as in any old mathematical model, but in fact derived from phenomena, Newton claims. This distinguishes Newton's procedure from typical hypothetico-deductive model construction, and it is well in keeping with the Aristotelian conception of a particular empirical science.

That Newton himself looked upon the *Principia* in this way is amply demonstrated by evidence. The following is a part of Newton's self-description of what he did in the *Principia*:

> The Propositions in the following book were invented by Analysis. But considering that the Ancients (so far as I can find) admitted nothing into Geometry before it was demonstrated by Composition I composed what I invented by Analysis to make it Geometrically authentic & fit for the publick. And this is the reason why this Book was written in words at length after the manner of the Ancients without Analytical calculations. But if any man who understands Analysis will reduce the Demonstrations of the Propositions from their composition back into Analysis (which is very easy to be done,) he will see by [what] method of Analysis they were invented. [And] by this means the Marquess de l'Hospital was able to affirm that this this [sic] Book was [presque tout de ce Calcul.] almost wholly of the infinitesimal Analysis.[25]

And here is another Newtonian self-description, this time anonymous:

> By the help of the new Analysis Mr. Newton found out most of the Propositions in his *Principia Philosophiae*: but because the Ancients for making things certain admitted nothing into Geometry before it was demonstrated synthetically, he demonstrated the Propositions synthetically, that the Systeme of the Heavens might be founded upon good Geometry. And this makes it now difficult for unskillful Men to see the *Analysis* by which those Propositions were found out.[26]

8. INDUCTION AND CONCEPT FORMATION

Already at the stage of analysis we have reached, a suggestive resemblance between Newtonian and Aristotelian induction is beginning to emerge. For Aristotle, the problem of induction was not first and foremost a problem of inference from particulars to a generalization. It was a problem of concept formation.[27] Particular cases were stepping-stones to the concepts or forms "induced" to be realized in the soul. Once they are formed, the laws governing them are obvious. (This is very closely related to Aristotle's rejection of the Atomistic Postulate.) Hence there is no such problem as the justification of induction for Aristotle. For Newton, too, the crucial step was the formation of the mathematical law on the basis of an experiment. The extension of this law to other cases is a lesser problem, and a problem that is at least partly mathematical (and hence conceptual) in nature, as we shall see later.

This similarity is not accidental, and it can be deepened by noting other points of contact between Newton and Aristotle.

9. HUME MISINTERPRETED NEWTON

Some light on the history of the problem of induction in thrown by its origin. It was made a centerpiece of epistemology and philosophy of science by Hume. Now Hume's approach to methodological matters is characterized concisely as a misinterpretation of Newton's methodology. Hume wanted to introduce what he called the experimental method into philosophy.[28] For Hume, however, the term 'experimental' was merely a near-synonym of 'empirical', as one can easily show.[29] In general, the good David did not have any idea of a genuine controlled experiment. In particular, Hume totally failed to understand Newton's idea that an experiment can yield general laws (dependencies). Instead, he firmly assumed the Atomistic Postulate. Hence the logico-methodological reasons which I showed to underlie the modern (post-Humean) preoccupation of philosphers with "Hume's Problem" are exemplified in an actual historical setting by the originator of this alleged problem himself.

I will return later to the relation of Hume's problem to Newton's explicitly acknowledged admission of the corrigibility of induction.

10. RECONCILING DIFFERENT PARTIAL GENERALIZATIONS

All this nevertheless amounts to treating only the simplest kind of inductive task, namely, the task of extending a generalization established for one interval of values of the controlled variable. (Cf. (1) above.) In the general case, the Inquirer faces the task of not only extending one interval but combining different kinds of functional dependence found to obtain over different (nonoverlapping) intervals. In this case, the problem is not simply extending a generalization but also reconciling with other partial generalizations. I will refer to this second aspect as the reconciliation problem.

This kind of reconciliation problem is not atypical in the history of science. A reader may in fact have here a déjà vu experience. For consider the problem situation which Planck faced and which I used as an example in the paper, "What Is the Logic of Experimental Inquiry?"[30] This problem situation is precisely one of reconciling partial generalizations with one another. Another important case in point is perhaps Einstein's discovery of the special theory of relativity, which may be considered a grand reconciliation of Newtonian mechanics and Maxwell's theory of electromagnetism. Other examples are easily found in the actual history of science.[31]

In Newton's own case, the combination and reconciliation problem is perhaps instantiated by his discovery of the law of gravitation. Newton had several ranges of two-body systems to generalize from, including those formed by falling terrestrial bodies and the earth; by the earth and the moon; and by the sun plus a planet obeying Kepler's laws. In this case, the reconciliation consisted mainly in ascertaining that the same gravitational constant was obtained in all the cases, for the laws themselves were of the same inverse-square form.

This kind of reconciliation task is an important variety of induction in the Newtonian sense of the word. It represents a problem situation which has played a major role in the development of science and which is therefore worth a study in its own right.

11. THE RECONCILIATION PROBLEM AND ARISTOTELIAN INDUCTION

Before studying the structure of the reconciliation problem, it is in order to point out a remarkable similarity between an inductive reconciliation of different restricted mathematical laws and Aristotelian induction. I have analyzed in detail Aristotle's conception of *epagoge* in an earlier paper.[32] Since induction was calculated to establish at least some of the first premises of a science according to Aristotle, and since those first premises were identified by Aristotle with definitions, the process of induction in Aristotle must be the same as a search for a definition. Now Aristotle gives a vivid example of the search for a definition in *Posterior Analytics* B 13. The notion to be defined there is *megalopsychia*, an interesting notion that is likely to intrigue any student of Greek moral philosophy in its own right. Now how is it that Aristotle proposes to look for a definition of *megalopsychia*? Here is his description:

> I mean, e.g. if we were to seek what *megalopsychia* is we should inquire, in the case of some *megalopsychia* we know, what one thing they all have as such. For instance, if Alcibiades is *megalopsychos*, or Achilles and Ajax are *megalopsychoi*, what one thing do they all have? Intolerance of insults; for one made war, one waxed wroth, and the other killed himself [because of this intolerance]. Again in the case of others, e.g. Lysander and Socrates. Well, if here it [sc. the common characteristic that makes them *megalopsychoi*] is being indifferent to good and bad fortune, I take these two things and inquire what both indifference to fortune and not brooking dishonour have that is the same. . . . then we must again inquire if what we have now got have anything that is the same (with still other cases)—until we come to a single account; for this will be the definition of the object.[33]

The analogy with the reconciliation problem is striking. What Aristotle is in effect saying is that one first has to establish a number of restricted generalizations, each specifying the defining characteristic of *megalopsychia* in one type of case. The task of finding the definition of *megalopsychia* then consists in reconciling these partial generalizations, that is, in finding what (if anything) the different partial definitions have in common. In my paper "Aristotelian Induction" I showed that the structure of this kind of definition seeking is precisely the same as the so-called syllogistic induction Aristotle describes in *Prior Analytics* B 23.[34]

The differences between a typical Aristotelian induction and the inductive reconciliation problem are also clear. First, for Aristotle the partial generalizations to be integrated with one another are not established experimentally, but by examining our own reasons for calling a class of people *megalopsychoi*. Second, the partial generalizations in question are typically qualitative and not quantitative. However, neither of these differences affects essentially the similarity of the two reconciliation problems.

Here we have an interesting glimpse of what the cash value of the term 'induction' (or *epagoge*) really was in pre-Humean philosophy of science.

It is especially interesting historically to see that the Aristotelians of the early modern period explicitly connected Aristotle's *epagoge* with his description of the search of a definition in *Posterior Analytics* B 13 and otherwise interpreted *epagoge* along the same lines I have done. It is also known that the young Newton read the *Organon* as well as the Aristotelian methodologists of his day. What historical insights a study of his notebooks might yield remains to be seen.

12. THE STRUCTURE OF A RECONCILIATION PROBLEM

It is now in order to discuss the reconciliation problem in its own right. What is the structure of induction in the sense of reconciliation of different partial generalizations? If a simple answer were forthcoming, we would understand the nature of scientific discovery much better than we actually do. Certain things can nevertheless be said. The task is to transform the different mathematical laws to a form where they can be seen to be special cases of a more general regularity. For instance, what Planck did was to argue that the Rayleigh-Jeans law amounts essentially to

$$\frac{\partial^2 S}{\partial U^2} = \frac{\text{Constant}}{U^2} \tag{14}$$

where S is the entropy of an oscillator and U the energy.[35] In contrast, Wien's law goes together with the different law, namely:

$$\frac{\partial^2 S}{\partial U^2} = \frac{\text{Constant}}{U} \tag{15}$$

Planck reconciled the laws (14) and (15) by regarding them as special cases of:

$$\frac{\partial^2 S}{\partial U^2} = \frac{a}{U(U + b)} \tag{16}$$

For small values of U this reduces to Wien's law and for large values of U essentially to the Rayleigh-Jeans law, which had been experimentally established by Rubens and Kurlbaum.

Once again, the final reconciliatory step appears both trivial and arbitrary. Jammer says that this step, "though mathematically a mere trifle, was one of the most significant and momentous contributions ever made in the history of physics."[36] The significance is of course not due to this one step but is in the line of thought that led Planck to a point where the competing partial generalizations are directly comparable—or, rather, directly reconcilable. Such a line of thought normally takes the form of a mathematical manipulation of the laws in question. But such a manipulation of mathematical formulas must be guided by an insight into the actual physical situation. For instance, we can ask: How did Planck get from the original experimentally established radiation laws to the simple equations (14) and (15), which are not directly verifiable? In order to reach these equations, Planck has among other things to introduce a new concept, the concept of entropy, which he shunned earlier but which he now found himself forced to use. And this reliance on the concept of entropy is not just a facet of clever manipulation of mathematical expressions. It reflects Planck's newfound respect for statistical concepts in the analysis of physical situations. Unmistakably, such a combination of mathematical and physical considerations has something of the character of conceptual analysis. Small wonder, therefore, that Planck's line of thought led to a momentous new concept, namely, that of a quantum of energy.

Perhaps it is not too far-fetched to say that a physicist has to have some grasp of why each of the limited generalizations to be reconciled holds in its range, just as Aristotle assumed that in our search for a definition of *megalopsychia* we have to know, for each of the restricted ranges of cases we regard as stepping-stones toward a definition, why members of that class are called *megalopsychoi*: Socrates and Lysander because of their indifference to good and bad fortune, Alcibiades and Ajax and their ilk because of their intolerance to insult, and so on.

These observations also put in an interesting perspective the use of mathematics in an experimental science like physics. They show that the role of mathematics is far subtler than is usually spelled out. Mathematics is not just an aid in registering the outcomes of experiments. It is a tool, albeit not a mechanically applicable tool, that can be used to *analyze* a physical phenomenon. Mastering the mathematics used in a physical theory is very closely related to mastering the basic physical concepts of this theory. (Just think of what a crucial breakthrough von Neumann's work on the mathematical principles of quantum theory was for the actual development of this branch of physics.) In particular, the experimentation with mathematical equations which is calculated to bring the different mathematical laws (empirical generalizations) under the same roof inevitably takes on something of the character of conceptual analysis of the relevant physical situation.

The subtlety of the reconciliation problem shows how far a cry actual scientific argumentation is from the inductivist paradigm of making generalizations from particular cases. By the same token, it shows how much interesting argumentation is left untreated by the hypothetico-deductive conception of science.

Admittedly, there is a certain similarity between a reconciliation problem and the problem of establishing an inductive generalization in the twentieth-century sense of the term. In both uses, an inquirer moves from special cases to a more general proposition. There nevertheless are important differences between the typical forms of modern induction and of the task of fitting several restricted laws under a more general one (in the sense of a law defined for a larger range of argument values). For one important thing, the restricted laws have to be reinterpreted in the reconciliation process. They cannot simply be considered instances of a generalization. For this reason, the reconciliation problem cannot, for example, be dealt with by means of existing inductive logics.

13. THE UNCERTAINTIES OF INDUCTION

Newton acknowledges that induction in his sense is not an incorrigible step:

> And although the arguing from experiments and observations by induction be no demonstration, yet it is the best way of arguing which the nature of things admits of.[37]

It is of interest to ask, however, what in practice is the source of the uncertainty of a Newtonian (step of) induction. Does the source of trouble perhaps lie in unexpected discontinuities of nature? An experiment can establish a precise mathematical function. If this function is analytic, it has a Taylor expansion. That means that its behavior for the entire range of values for which it is defined by the same Taylor series is determined by its behavior in an arbitrarily small neighborhood of any point for which it is defined. Hence the kind of extension that is involved in "extrapolating" an analytic function seems to be a purely mathematical operation, and not conjectural at all. The only possible source of trouble seems to be hidden discontinuities of the function or of its derivatives outside the range of cases in which it has experimentally been found to hold.

It turns out, however, that this is not the only or even the main source of the uncertainty of Newtonian induction. Consider, for instance, Planck's problem situation. The two radiation laws he was trying to reconcile of course could not be considered precise special cases of a more general law. Rather, they were good approximations to the general law for different ranges of values, so good, indeed, that approximation fell within the range of observational error.

Hence the logic of Newtonian induction appears to be inextricably intertwined with the notions of approximation and of the margin of experimental or observational error. This is not the case logically speaking, however. Logically, the problem of inductive reconciliation of partial laws can arise and have the same logical properties also when the approximative character of the partial laws plays no role. For instance, Newton knew that Kepler's laws could not be completely accurate, because of the gravitational influence of different planets on one another's movements. Likewise, the orbit of the moon around the earth was known by him to be subject of the sun's perturbatory influence. But the logical problem of reconciliation would have been the same even if he had in both cases been able to observe pure two-body systems.

In Planck's case, the two radiation laws are likewise approximations only. However, they would be precise laws if we could push the value of one of the variables to its limiting values (zero and infinity, respectively).

Hence what the crucial judgment-call typically is in a Newtonian induction is an independence or near-independence assumption. It has to be assumed either that the functional dependence that has been established is independent of further "hidden variables" or else that it is so nearly free from further factors that it can be considered the precise law for a suitable special case or range of values. Once again, the source of logical strength in scientific inference turns out to lie in establishing or assuming functional independence. This is in keeping with what was found in my paper "What Is the Logic of Experimental Inquiry?"[38]

Hence the logic of Newtonian induction is not essentially dependent on the quantitative character of the partial laws that have been established or on their character as approximations. In principle, a similar problem situation can arise in a theory expressible in a first-order language.

Notice also that this kind of uncertainty of Newtonian induction is rather different from the general uncertainty to which Hume called philosophers' attention.

Among other observations, we can now see that Popper's criticism of Newton's claim for having derived his law of gravitation from phenomena is without any force whatsoever.[39] Popper bases his criticism on the fact that Kepler's laws, which were the starting point of Newton's line of thought, cannot be strictly true if Newton's law of gravitation holds, for they do not allow for the gravitational interaction between different planets. How could Newton possibly have derived the true law of gravitation from false empirical generalizations, Popper asks? Yet we have seen that the merely approximate character of Kepler's laws is completely beside the point in evaluating the kind of "inductive" reasoning Newton used. It was perfectly possible for him to think of Kepler's laws as holding strictly for certain two-body systems. For those systems, the law of gravitation was, strictly speaking, implied by the laws of motion of a planet. The inductive step was then to note that the resulting law, established so far only for a certain range of two-body systems, agrees with other partial generalizations established for other ranges of cases. Popper's criticisms show merely that he has not begun to understand Newton's actual conception of scientific inference in general and of the role of induction in science in particular.

NOTES

1. See the following papers of mine: "Knowledge Representation and the Interrogative Approach to Inquiry," forthcoming in a survey volume edited by Keith Lehrer

and Marjorie A. Clay; "What Is the Logic of Experimental Inquiry?" *Synthese* 74 (1988): 133–190; "The Interrogative Approach to Inquiry and Probabilistic Inference," *Erkenntnis* 26 (1987): 429–442; "The Logic of Science as Model-oriented Logic," in *PSA 1984*, ed. P. Asquith and P. Kitcher (East Lansing, Mich.: Philosophy of Science of Association, 1984), 1: 177–185; "A Spectrum of Logics of Questioning," *Philosophica* 35 (1985): 135–150; "Questioning as a Philosophical Method," in *Principles of Philosophical Reasoning*, ed. James Fetzer (Totowa N.J.: Rowman and Allanheld, 1984), 25–43; "Rules, Strategies and Utilities in Interrogative Games," in *Cognitive Constraints on Communication*, ed. Lucia Vaina and Jaakko Hintikka (Dordrecht: D. Reidel, 1984), 277–294; (with Merill B. Hintikka), "Sherlock Holmes Confronts Modern Logic," in *Argumentation: Approaches to Theory Formation*, ed. E. M. Barth and J. L. Martens (Amsterdam: Benjamins, 1982), 55–76.

2. For a lucid and informative survey of the problem of induction in its twentieth-century sense see G. H. von Wright, *The Logical Problem of Induction*, 2d ed. (New York: Macmillan, 1957).

3. The point in using game-theoretical concepts and conceptualizations is of course not to be able to use the mathematical results of game theory, but to do justice to the importance of research strategies in science, modeled in the interrogative model by different questioning strageties.

4. Later (see sec. 9 below) it will be indicated how the Atomistic Postulate can serve to motivate an inductivist approach to the progress of science. By almost the same token, if a philosopher of science rejects the idea of inductive inference, virtually the only remaining alternative is to consider general scientific theories as hypothetical constructs in the sense that they are not derived from experience by any rule-governed procedure. Theories can only be tested against evidence via their observable consequences, but not derived from them. This is, roughly speaking, the hypothetico-deductive conception of science, which, like the inductivist one, has to be radically reconsidered if the Atomistic Postulate in given up.

Other views, including certain Kuhnian ones, are also arguably inspired in part by a tacit belief in the Atomistic Postulate.

5. This is argued in "What Is the Logic of Experimental Inquiry?" (n. 1 above).

6. In Carnap's terms, the characteristic function of an inductive method can be such that it assigns definite prior probabilities (between zero and one) to generalizations. Conversely, the prior probabilities of generalizations determine partly the characteristic functions (right betting ratios of the next randomly observed individual). Cf. here, e.g., Jaakko Hintikka and Ilkka Niiniluoto, "An Axiomatic Foundation for the Logic of Inductive Generalization," in *Studies in Inductive Logic and Probability*, ed. Richard Jeffrey (Berkeley, Los Angeles, London: University of California Press, 1980), 157–181.

7. Cf. here "The Interrogative Approach to Inquiry and Probabilistic Inference" (n. 1 above).

8. Ibid., especially pp. 432–435.

9. See here Jaakko Hintikka, "Aristotelian Induction," *Revue Internationale de Philosophie* 34 (1980): 422–439; K. von Fritz, *Epagoge bei Aristoteles*, Sitzungsberichte der Bayerischen Akademie der Wissenschaften, Phil.-hist. Klasse, Heft 3 (Munich: C. H. Beck, 1964); D. W. Hamlyn, "Aristotelian Epagoge," *Phronesis* 21 (1976): 167–184; Gerd Buchdahl, *Induction and Necessity in the Philosophy of Aristotle*, Aquinas Paper no. 40 (London: Aquin Press, 1963).

10. Cf. Jaakko Hintikka, "Concepts of Scientific Method from Aristotle to Newton," *Knowledge and the Sciences in Medieval Philosophy* (Proceedings of the Eighth International Congress of Medieval Philosophy, ed. Monika Asztalos et al.), *Acta Philosophica Fennica* 48 (1990): 72–84.

11. Notice, however, that the restrictive consequences of the Atomistic Postulate can be counteracted to some extent by strengthening the initial theoretical premise or premises T from which an interrogative inquiry starts. Hence induction became a problem for philosophers only after they accepted the Atomistic Postulate and rejected such sources of general truths as innate ideas. This is the underlying reason why the problem of induction became Hume's problem and, not, say, Duns Scotus's problem.

12. Cf. here Jaakko Hintikka, "Aristotle's Incontinent Logician," *Ajatus* 37 (1978): 48–65.

13. See G. E. L. Owen, "Tithenai ta phainomena," in *Aristotle et les problèmes de méthode*, ed. S. Mansion (Louvain: Publications universitaires, 1961), 83–103.

14. See here Jaakko Hintikka and James Garrison, "Newton's Methodology and the Interrogative Logic of Experimental Inquiry," forthcoming in the proceedings of the 1987 workshop in Israel on "Three Hundred Years of the *Principia*-Realism Then and Now."

15. See n. 1 above.

16. The two are equivalent in the sense that their decision problems have the same degree of difficulty. See Jaakko Hintikka, "Quantifiers vs. Quantification Theory," *Linguistic Inquiry* 5 (1974): 153–177.

17. Another way of handling the situation would be by means of the idea of partial answer.

18. I quote from the Dover Books edition (New York, 1952), 404.

19. Cf. here "Newton's Methodology and the Interrogative Logic of Experimental Inquiry" (n. 14 above).

20. (Berkeley and Los Angeles: University of California Press, 1934), 2: 547.

21. See the critical edition by Alexandre Koyre and I. Bernard Cohen (Cambridge, Mass.: Harvard University Press, 1972).

22. See I. Bernard Cohen, *Introduction to Newton's "Principia"* (Cambridge, Mass.: Harvard University Press, 1978), 241.

23. Cf., e.g., I. Bernard Cohen, *The Newtonian Revolution* (Cambridge: Cambridge University Press, 1980).

24. Cohen, *Introduction*, 241.

25. Quoted in Cohen, *Introduction*, 294.

26. Cohen, *Introduction*, 295.

27. For Aristotle, whatever necessarily accompanies a form in general accompanies it when it is realized in the human soul (cf. "Aristotle's Incontinent Logician" [n. 12 above]). Hence there is no difficulty according to Aristotle in seeing what is implied by a certain concept once this concept is fully formed in one's mind. Hence the primary premises of a science are for him definitions. (Cf., e.g., *Posterior Analytics* B 3, 90b24.) Hence also our problem of induction is replaced in Aristotle's thought by problems of definition seeking and concept formation.

28. See the subtitle to the *Treatise* (1739): *An attempt to introduce the experimental Method of Reasoning into Moral Subjects.*

29. Hume occasionally speaks of "millions of experiments" (see *Treatise*, Selby-

Bigge ed., 105) that are supposed to have confirmed his views. But they cannot conceivably be controlled experiments of the kind Newton habitually was referring to by the term 'experiment', and they could scarcely even all involve purposive interference with the normal course of events.

30. See n. 1 above.

31. Another example is the way in which van der Waals's gas law unifies Boyle's law with what is known experimentally of the behavior of gases at low temperatures (i.e., near their liquefaction point) and with the known behavior of liquids. This example is also instructive in that van der Waals's law is based on an analysis of the forces governing the interaction of molecules.

32. See n. 9 above.

33. I am using, with some modifications, Jonathan Barnes's translation: see *Aristotle's Posterior Analytics*, ed. Jonathan Barnes, Clarendon Aristotle series (Oxford: Clarendon Press, 1975), 74.

34. See n. 9 above.

35. For Planck's reconciliation of the two laws, cf. Thomas S. Kuhn, *Black-Body Theory and the Quantum Discontinuity 1894-1912* (Oxford: Clarendon Press, 1978); Max Jammer, *The Conceptual Development of Quantum Mechanics* (New York: McGraw-Hill, 1966); and Armin Hermann, *The Genesis of Quantum Theory (1899–1913)* (Cambridge, Mass.: MIT Press, 1971).

36. Jammer, *Conceptual Development*, 18.

37. Newton, *Opticks* (see n. 18 above).

38. See n. 1 above.

39. See Karl R. Popper, "The Aim of Science," *Ratio* 1 (1957): 24–35; reprinted in Popper's *Objective Knowledge* (Oxford: Clarendon Press, 1972), 191–205.

THREE

Aristotelian Natures and the Modern Experimental Method

Nancy Cartwright

1. HISTORICAL BACKGROUND

One of the great achievements of the scientific revolution, according to its adherents, was the banishment from modern science of the Aristotelian schemes of explanation which had dominated Scholastic studies. Aristotle was derided as a cuttlefish, a squid: the ink he discharged cast everything into obscurity. Consider one typical case, Pierre Gassendi in his *Exercises against the Aristotelians* (1624). Gassendi complains that Aristotelian explanations fail to explain. About the definition of motion as "the act of being in potentiality insofar as it is in potentiality," he remarks: "Great God! Is there any stomach strong enough to digest that? The explanation of a rather familiar thing was requested, but this is so complicated that nothing is clear anymore. . . . The need for definitions of the words in the definitions will go on *ad infinitum*" (book 2, exercise 4, article 4).

The scientific revolutionaries favored the certainty of mathematics to the ambiguity of Scholastic accounts. Mathematics was "built on clear and settled signification of names, which admit of no ambiguity." This remark comes from Joseph Glanvill, whose defense of modern thought in *Scepsis Scientifica* earned him a place in the Royal Society in 1664. On Glanvill's account, Aristotle was exactly the opposite: "Peripatetic philosophy is litigious"; its accounts are "circular"; and its terms are "empty," "ambiguous," and lacking "settled, constant signification." The science of the Scholastics was involved in endless quarrels about words and very little actual investigation, in large part because it tried to explain the behavior of things by reference to their natures. But knowledge of natures, according to the new empiricists of the scientific revolution, is forever beyond our grasp; it is divine, not human. As Gassendi argues, it is not possible for mere humans to know "that something is by nature and in itself, and as a result of basic, necessary infallible causes, constituted in a certain way" (book 6, article 1). Rather, "it can only be known how a thing appears to one or another" (book 6, article 6).

It is on account of this twofold fact that the Aristotelians got into useless debates over meanings: on the one hand, natures stood at the core of explanation for them; on the other, these natures were intrinsically unknowable. According to the empiricists, then, the Aristotelians inevitably resolved things into qualities that were occult; they could never be genuinely understood but only grasped by definition. Invariably this leads to a total circularity of explanation. The favored example is that of gravity. Glanvill tells us:

> That heavy bodies descend by gravity is no better account than we would expect from a rustic; that gravity is a quality whereby a heavy body descends, is an impertinent circle, and teaches nothing. (*Scepsis Scientifica*, chap. 20)

For the empiricists, we must throw over this attempt to found science on occult natures and instead base everything on the kinds of qualities that appear to us in experience. Even here there is a danger that we may become too ambitious, and Glanvill warns: "If we follow manifest qualities beyond the empty signification of their names, we shall find them as occult as those which are professedly so" (*Scepsis Scientifica*, chap. 20).

Most modern accounts in the philosophy of science take it that the attempts of the scientific revolution to banish natures from science were successful. The idea of natures operating in things to determine their behaviors was replaced by the concept of a law of nature. Here is a short history, told by a modern-day empiricist, to illustrate:

> Aquinas was at pains to contest a preceding scholastic view that everything which happens, does so because it is directly and individually willed by God. This would seem to make science a pointless enterprise; according to Aquinas it also denigrates creation. Yet theology points to God as ultimate cause. The reconciliation Aquinas offered was this: to explain why phenomena happen as they do, requires showing why they must; this necessity however derives from the natures of the individual substances involved—which themselves are as they are because of God's original design. Thus the necessity does derive *ultimately* from God's decrees for the world as a whole, made at the point of creation—but derives *proximately* from the local conditions and characters in the Aristotelian pattern. . . .
>
> . . . if we look more closely at the seventeenth century we see an insistence, even more adamant than Aquinas', upon the autonomy of physics from theology. Descartes insists on it most stringently. . . .
>
> The *Drang nach Autonomie* of physics, even as developed by such theological thinkers as Descartes, Newton, and Leibniz, needed an intermediate link between God's decree and nature. Aquinas had needed such a link to explain proximate causation, and found it in the Aristotelian substantial forms (individ-

> ual natures). For the seventeenth century another kind was needed, one that could impose a global constraint on the world process. In general terms, this link was provided by the idea that nature has its inner necessities, which are not mere facts, but constrain all mere facts into a unified whole. The theological analogy and dying metaphor of law provided the language in which the idea could be couched. (Bas van Fraassen, *Laws and Symmetry* [Oxford: Clarendon Press, 1989], 4–6)

My thesis here is that this story is distorted (at least as it applies to modern experimental science). We have not replaced *natures* by *laws of nature.* For laws of nature are typically about natures, and what they produce. Rather, what we have done is to replace occult powers by powers that are visible, though it may take a very fancy experiment to see them. This is already apparent in Francis Bacon. Bacon still employs the Aristotelian idea of natures or essences, but for him these are not hidden. Bacon looks for the explanatory essences, but he looks for them among qualities that are observable. Consider his hunt for the essence of heat. He makes large tables of situations in which heat occurs, in which it is absent, and in which it varies by degrees. "Instances agreeing in the Form of Heat" (*Novum Organum*, 1620) include, for instance, rays of the sun; damp, hot weather; flames; horse dung; strong vinegar; and so forth. Then he looks to see what other quality is always present when heat is present, and always absent when heat is lacking. In this way, he finds the true, simple nature that consitutes heat: motion. The point is that Bacon still hopes to find the nature of heat, but among visible, not occult, qualities.

Modern explanation similarly relies on natures, I will argue; the modern natures are like Bacon's and unlike those of the Scholastics, in that they are attributed to observable structures and qualities. Generally they differ from Bacon's in that they do not lie on the surface and are not to be observed with the naked eye. Rather, we often need very subtle and elaborate experiments in order to see them. Modern science insists that we found explanation on experimentally identifiable and verifiable structures and qualities. But, I maintain, what we learn about these structures and qualities is what it is in their natures to do.

What we have done in modern science, as I see it, is to break the connection between what the explanatory nature is—what it is, in and of itself—and what it does. An atom in its excited state, when agitated, emits photons and produces light. It is, I say, in the nature of an excited atom to produce light. Here the explanatory feature—an atom's being in the excited state—is a structural feature of the atom, which is defined and experimentally identified independently of the particular nature that is attributed to it in this case.[1] It is in the nature of the excited atom to emit light, but that is not what it is to *be* an atom in an excited state. For modern science, what something really is—how it is defined and identified—and what it is in its nature to do are quite separate things. So even a perfect and complete modern theory would never have the closed, deductive structure that the Aristotelians envisaged. Still, I maintain, the use of Aristotelian-style natures is central to the modern explanatory program. We, like Aristotle, are looking for "a cause and principle of change and stasis in the thing in which it primarily subsists" (*Physics* 2.1.192b22), and we, too, assume that this principle will be "in this thing of itself and not *per accidens*."

Yet, even at this very cursory level of description, we differ from Aristotle in three important ways. First, as in my example of an atom in an excited state, we assign natures not to substances but rather to collections or configurations of properties, or to structures. Second, like the early empiricists and the mechanical philosophers of the scientific revolution, modern physics supposes that the "springs of motion" are hidden behind the phenomena and that what appears on the surface is a result of the complex interaction of natures. We no longer expect that the natures that are fundamental for physics will exhibit themselves directly in the regular or typical behavior of observable phenomena. It takes the highly controlled environment of an experiment to reveal them. Third, having made the empiricist turn, we no longer identify natures with essences. As I have described in this section, in modern science we separate our definition of a property from our characterization of what kind of change it naturally produces. Still, when we associate a particular principle of change with a given structure or characteristic, we expect that association to be permanent, to last so long as the structure is what it is. Indeed, it is this permanence of association that I will underline by claiming that modern science still studies Aristotelian-style natures. Of course, these are not really Aristotelian natures. For one thing, we seem to share none of the concerns about substance and individuation in which Aristotle's concept was embedded. There are a number of other differences as well. Nevertheless, I call them "Aristotelian" because of the inheritance through the Scholastics to the "New Philosophy" of Galileo, Bacon, and Descartes.

What I will do in the remainder of this paper is: first, explain in more detail what this claim amounts to by contrasting it with a more standard empiricist account of laws of nature; and second, provide one argument in favor of the thesis—an argument that says that one cannot make sense of modern experimental method unless one assumes that laws are basically about natures. The basic point of view I urge here is similar to that which I have written about at length in *Nature's Capacities and Their Measurement* (Oxford: Oxford University Press, 1989), but the fundamental argument is new.

2. NATURES AND THE ANALYTIC METHOD

In defending natures, I take my principal antagonist to be the modern empiricist account of laws which rests on a distinction crucial to the thought of Locke, Berkeley, and Hume: the distinction between powers and sensible qualities. According to Hume, powers are not accessible to us through our senses, and hence must be excluded from science. Nowadays, the distinction takes a slightly different form, between the power things have to behave in certain ways, on the one hand, and the actually exhibited behaviors, on the other. But modern empiricists in the Hume tradition remain just as eager as Hume himself to reject powers. Laws of nature, they insist, are about *what things do.* I want to maintain, by contrast, that fundamental laws are generally not about what things do but what it is in their nature to do. Consider Coulomb's law of electrostatic attraction and repulsion. Coulomb's law says that the force between two objects of charge q_1 and q_2 is equal to $q_1 q_2/r^2$. Yet, this is not the force the bodies experience; they are also subject to the law of gravity. We say that Coulomb's law gives the force *due to* their charge. But this is no concept for an empiricist: Coulomb's is not the force that actually occurs; rather, it is a hypothetical power hidden away in the actual force.

I think the best account we can give is in terms of natures. Coulomb's law tells not what force charged particles experience but rather what it is in their nature, qua charged, to experience. Natures are something like powers. To say it is in their nature to experience a force of $q_1 q_2/r^2$ is to say at least that they *can* experience this force if only the right conditions occur for the power to exercise itself; for instance, if they have very small masses so that gravitational effects are negligible. It is also to say that their tendency to experience it persists, even when the conditions are not right; for instance, when gravity becomes important. Qua charged, they tend to experience a mutual force $q_1 q_2/r^2$; qua massive, they tend to experience a different force ($Gm_1 m_2/r^2$). What particles that are both massive and charged actually experience will be a function of what they experience qua charged and what they experience qua massive.

It is to mark this fact, the fact that charge always "contributes" the same force, that I use the Aristotelian notion of nature. But, as I remarked in referring to Bacon, these modern natures differ from Aristotle's in one very central respect. Although it is in the nature of charge to be subject to a force of $q_1 q_2/r^2$, in the sense that this is what particles experience qua charged, this nature does not in any proper Aristotelian way reveal the essence of charge. What charge is depends on a lot of factors independent of Coulomb's law. As Gerd Buchdahl puts it, there is a mere "brute-fact connection" between what charge is and how charged particles behave qua charged (*Metaphysics and the Philosophy of Science* [Oxford: Blackwell, 1969]).

One customary response that Humeans make to the kinds of problems I am raising is to resort to counterfactuals. They talk not in terms of actually exhibited qualities and behavior but in terms of possible qualities and behaviors. Coulomb's law gives the force two bodies *would* experience if their masses were equal to zero. From an empiricist point of view this is a peculiar kind of counterfactual to find at the foundation of our study of motion, for it is one whose antecedent can never be instantiated. But that is not my principal concern.

Instead, I want to point out two other nonempiricist elements that are concealed in this account. The first comes to light when we ask, "Why do we want the masses to go to zero?" The answer: "Because we want to find out what the total force would be, were there no other forces at work." It is the "at work" that one should notice. Put in this blunt fashion, it suggests that the counterfactual account itself is grounded in ideas about powers and their operation, as no good Humean would allow. So the counterfactual antecedent "were the masses equal to zero" is used instead.

My second concern becomes apparent when one asks the obvious next question, "Why do we want to know what the force between charged bodies would be were no other forces at work?" This case is just one particular case among all conceivable ones, and a peculiarly inconvenient one at that. Why, then, are these circumstances so special? They are special because these are the circumstances in which all the hindrances are stripped away so that we can find out what charged particles do "on their own"—that is, what they do by virtue of being charged. This is how they would attract or repel one another were "only" charge at work; and it is how they try to behave even when other factors impede them.

We discover the nature of electrostatic interaction between charges by looking in some very special circumstances. But the charge interaction carries that nature with it, from one circumstance to another. That is why what we call *the analytic method* in physics works: to understand what happens in the world, we take things apart into their fundamental pieces; to control a situation we reassemble the pieces, we reorder them so they will work together to make things happen as we will. You carry the pieces from place to place, assembling them together in new ways and new contexts. But you always assume that they will try to behave in new arrangements as they have tried to behave in others. They will, in each case, act in accordance with their nature.[2]

The talk of pieces and assembly is a metaphor. How do the behaviors dictated by different natures combine when they are constrained to operate together? There is no general receipt; the answer is, at best, subject-specific. In mechanics, a total force is constructed by vectoral addition from the forces that each component tries separately to create. In the simultaneous-equation models of econometrics, the natural behavior of each independent mechanism is represented in a different equation; when a number of mechanisms work together, all the equations must be satisfied at once. The way in which literal mechanical pieces function together is different again. We employ the method of analysis and synthesis to make predictions and to shape behavior to our own wishes. In each case, we exploit the fact that the pieces when assembled together each continue to "contribute" in accord with their natures. What actually results in a specific case is fixed not only by the natures of the parts but also by the rules that dictate what happens in that domain when natures act together.

The analytic method is closely associated with what we often call Galilean idealization. Together idealization and abstraction form a familiar two-tiered process that lies at the heart of modern scientific inquiry. First, we try to find out by a combination of experimentation, calculation, and inference how the feature under study behaves, or would behave, in a particular, highly specific situation. By controlling for, or calculating away, the gravitational effects, we try to find out how two charged bodies would interact if their masses were zero. But this is just a stage; in itself this information is quite uninteresting. The ultimate aim is to find out how the charged bodies interact not when their masses are zero, nor under any other *specific* set of circumstances, but rather how they interact qua charged. That is the second stage of the inquiry: we abstract the nature of the charge interaction from how charges behave in these specially selected "ideal" circumstances.

The key here is the concept "ideal." On the one hand, we use this term to mark the fact that the circumstances in question are not real or, at least, that they seldom obtain naturally but require a great deal of contrivance even to approximate. On the other, the "ideal" circumstances are the "right" ones—right for inferring what the nature of the behavior is, in itself. Focusing on the first aspect by itself downplays our problems. We tend to think that the chief difficulties come from the small departures from the ideal that will always be involved in any real experiment: however small we choose the masses in tests of Coulomb's law, we never totally eliminate the gravitational interaction between them; in Galilean experiments on inertia, the plane is never perfectly smooth nor the air resistance equal to zero; we may send our experiments deep into space, but the effect of the large massive bodies in the universe can never be entirely eliminated; and we can perform them at cryogenic temperatures, but the conditions will never, in fact, reach the ideal.

The problem I am concerned with is not whether we can get the system into circumstances where it can operate on its own but rather: what does it mean when we say that the circumstances are ideal, or that the system is operating "on its own"? What is it that dictates which other effects are to be minimized, set equal to zero, or calculated away? This is the question, I maintain, that cannot be answered given the conventional empiricist account of laws. No doubt, in any particular experiment, the equipment we move about, the circumstances we contrive, and the properties we calculate away, are ones that can be described without mentioning natures. But in each case, what makes that arrangement of equipment in those particular circumstances "ideal" is the fact that these are the circumstances where the feature under study operates, as Galileo taught, without hindrance or impediment, so that its nature is revealed in its behavior. Until we are prepared to talk in this way about natures and their operations, to fix some circumstances as felicitous for a nature to express itself, and others as impediments, we will have no way of determining which principle is tested by which experiment. It is this argument that I want to develop in the rest of this paper.

3. HOW DO WE KNOW WHAT WE ARE TESTING?

For anyone who believes that induction provides the primary building tool for empirical knowledge, the methods of modern experimental physics must seem unfathomable. Usually the inductive base for the principles under test is slim indeed, and in the best experimental designs, where we have sufficient control of the materials and our knowledge of the requisite background assumptions is secure, one single instance can be enough. The inference, of course, is never certain, nor irrevocable. Still, we proceed with a high degree of confidence, and indeed, a degree of confidence that is unmatched in large-scale studies in the social sciences, where we do set out from information about a very great number of instances. Clearly, in these physics experiments we are prepared to assume that the situation before us is of a very special kind: it is a situation in which the behavior that occurs is repeatable. Whatever happens in this situation can be generalized.

This peculiar kind of repeatability that we assume for physics experiments requires a kind of permanence of behavior across varying external conditions that is comparable to that of an essence, although not as strong. For example, we measure, successfully we think, the charge or mass of an electron in a given experiment. Now we think we know the charge or mass of all electrons; we need not go on, measuring hundreds of thousands. In so doing, we are making what looks to be a kind of essentialist assumption: the charge or mass of a fundamental particle is not a variable quantity but is characteristic of the particle so long as it continues to be the particle it is.

In most experiments we do not investigate just the basic properties of systems such as charge, but rather more complicated trains of behavior. Diagrammatically, we may think of Galileo's attempts to study the motions of balls rolling down inclined planes; or, entirely at the opposite end of the historical spectrum, the attempts in Stanford's Gravity-Probe-B experiment to trace the precession of four gyroscopes in space, to see how they are affected by the space-time curvature relativistically induced by the earth. Here, too, some very strong assumptions must back our willingness to draw a general conclusion from a very special case. On the surface, it may seem that the license to generalize in these cases can be put in very local terms that need no reference to natures. We require only the assumption that all systems so situated as the one in hand will behave identically. But I think on closer inspection we can see that this is not enough.

We may begin to see why by considering Hume himself. Hume maintained the principle "same cause, same effect." For him, every occurrence is an exemplar of a general principle. It is simply a general fact about the world, albeit one we can have no sure warrant for, that identically situated systems behave identically. Hence for Hume, the license to generalize was universal. But not for us. We cannot so easily subscribe to the idea that the same cause will always be succeeded by the same effect. Hume assumed the principle to be true, though not provable. He worried that principles like this one could only be circularly founded, because they could have no evidence that is not inductive. But nowadays we question not just whether our belief in them can be well-founded but whether they are true. Even if we were content with merely inductive warrant, in what direction does our evidence point? The planetary motions seem regular, as do the successions of the seasons, but in general, Nature in the mundane world seems obstinately chaotic. Outside the supervision of a laboratory or the closed casement of a factory-made module, what happens in one instance is rarely a guide to what will happen in others. Situations that lend themselves to generalization are very special, and it is these special kinds of situations that we aim to create, both in our experiments and in our technology. My central thesis here is that what makes these situations special is that they are situations that permit a stable display of the nature of the process under study, or the stable display of the interaction of several different natures.

The case is especially strong when we turn from fictional considerations of ideal reasoning to considerations of actual methodology. Here questions of true identity of circumstance drop away. We never treat complete descriptions; rather we deal with *salient characteristics* and *relevant similarities*. This is a familiar point. You do not have to specify everything. If the right combination of factors is fixed, you are in a position to generalize. Yet what makes a specific combination a right one? What is the criterion that makes one similarity relevant and another irrelevant? Case by case, after the fact, it seems we can avoid an answer. We need only say, "In this case, we have picked thus-and-so set of factors; and we assume that so long as this particular set of factors is fixed, the behavior that obtains will be general."

This is the position we arrived at a few paragraphs ago. It provides a defense, of kinds, one by one, of each generalization that we are willing to make on the basis of an experimental study. But it provides no account of what we do. Experiments are designed with intense care and precision. They take hard work, and hard thought, and enormous creative imagination. The Gravity-Probe experiment which I mentioned above is an exaggerated example. It will only be set running twenty years—twenty years of fairly continuous effort—after it was initiated, and it will have involved teams from thirty or forty different locations, each solving some separate problem of design and implementation.

What can account for our effort to make the experimental apparatus *just so* and no other way? Take the Gravity Probe as a case in point. Each effort is directed to solve a specific problem. One of the very first in the Gravity Probe involved choosing the material for the gyroscopes. In the end, they are to be made of fused quartz, since fused quartz can be manufactured to be homogeneous to more than one part in 10^6. The homogeneity is crucial. Any differences in density will introduce additional precessions, which can be neither precisely controlled nor reliably calculated, and these would obscure the nature of the general-relativistic precession that the experiment aims to learn about.

In this case, we can imagine that the physicists designing the experiment worked from the dictum, which can be formulated without explicit reference to natures, "If you want to see the relativistic precession, you had better make the gyroscope as homogeneous as possible," and they wanted to do that because they wanted to eliminate other sources of precession. But more than that is necessary. The total design of the experiment must take account not only of what else might cause precession but also of what kinds of features would interfere with the relativistic precession, what kinds of factors could inhibit it, and what is necessary to ensure that it will, in the end, exhibit itself in some systematic way. When all these factors are properly treated, we should have an experiment that shows what the nature of relativistic precession is. That is the form, I maintain, that the ultimate conclusion will take.

But that is not the immediate point I want to make. What I want to urge is that, by designing the experiment to ensure that the nature of relativistic precession can manifest itself in some clear sign, by blocking any interference and by opening a clear route for the relativistic coupling to operate unimpeded—according to its own nature—by doing just this, the Gravity-Probe team will create an experiment from which it is possible to infer a general law. At the moment, the form of this law is not my chief concern. Rather, what is at stake is the question, "What must be true of the experiment if a general law of any form is to be inferred from it?" I claim that the experiment must succeed at revealing the nature of the process (or some stable consequence of the interaction of natures) and that the design of the experiment requires a robust sense of what will impede and what will facilitate this. The facts about an experiment that make that experiment generalizable are not facts that exist in a purely Humean world.

It is, of course, not really true that my thesis about the correct form of natural laws is irrelevant to my argument. Put in the most simple-minded terms, what I point out is the apparent fact that we can generalize from a single observation in an experimental context just because that context is one in which all the relevant sources of variation have been taken into account. Then, after all, what I claim is that it is laws in the form I commend—that is, laws about natures—that determine what is and what is not relevant. This sets the obvious strategy for the Humean reply: laws, in the sense of universal or probabilistic generalizations, determine the relevant factors an experiment must control to ensure that it is repeatable. I will discuss this strategy briefly in the next section. Before turning to it, though, I want to make some clarifications about the concept of generalizability.

I have been using the term 'generalizable' and the term 'repeatable'. Both can be taken in two senses in this discussion. I claim that the Gravity Probe aims to establish a general law about the nature of the coupling of a spinning gyroscope to curved space-time and thereby to learn something about the truth of the general theory of relativity. But along the way, as a by-product, the experiment will reveal, or instantiate, another considerably less abstract law, a law that can far more readily be cast into the conventional form of a universal generalization. This is a law to the effect that any fused-quartz gyroscope of just this kind—electromagnetically suspended, coated uniformly with a very, very thin layer of superfluid, read by a SQUID detector, housed in a cryogenic dewar, constructed just so ... and spinning deep in space—will precess at the rate predicted. We expect a law like this to obtain because we expect the experiment to establish a stable environment in which whatever happens would happen regularly; that is, we expect the experimental results to be repeatable.

This is a sense of repeatability internal to the experiment itself: given that the experiment is a good one, if it were to be rerun in the same way with the same apparatus, it should teach the same lesson. We need not demand that the regularity instantiated be expressible in some particular language—or in any language, for that matter; nor, as Harry Collins stresses (*Changing Order* [London: Sage Publications, 1985]), need we insist that the knowledge of how to build the apparatus be explicit knowledge that could be read from the experimenter's notebooks or that could be written in a "how-to-build-it" manual.[3] Yet, if the experiment is to bear on the more general conclusion which we, in the end, want to establish, we do want to insist on the regularity. For part of what is meant by the hypothesis that the coupling between the gyroscope and the curvature has a special nature that bears on the truth of general relativity is that there is a proper, predictable way in which it will behave on its own, if only the circumstances are propitious. To the degree that we doubt that the experiment is repeatable, to that degree at least must we doubt that the behavior we see is a sign of the nature we want to discover.

Although the general (albeit low-level) law that expresses this first kind of repeatability is, it seems, a universal generalization of the conventional form, still the argument I want to make for the necessity of some nonstandard forms in the background bears on it just as forcefully as on the more abstract law that seems directly to describe natures. As with the higher-level law, so too, with the lower-level: if we want to understand why we are entitled to accept this law on such a thin inductive base as the Gravity Probe's four gyroscopes, and if we want to understand the painstaking details of design the experimenters labor over to produce the conditions of the law, we will have to use the idea of a nature, or some related non-Humean notion.

Indeed, I want to make a fairly strong claim here. In the order of generality, the low-level generalization about what happens in just this kind of experimental setup comes first, and the more abstract claim about the general nature of the coupling comes second. We tend to think that the order of warrant is parallel: the low-level generalization comes first and is most secure; the more abstract law derives what warrant it gets from the acceptance of the generalization. I want to urge that there is an aspect of warranting for which this picture is upside down. It is just to the extent that we acknowledge that the experiment is well designed to find out the natures of the interaction, described in the higher-level law, that we are entitled to accept the low-level generalization on the basis of the experimental results.[4]

This is the central argument with which this section began. But it bears repeating now that the distinction between low-level laws, in the form of generalizations, and high-level abstractions has been drawn. Most situations do not give rise to regular behavior. But we can make ones that do. To do so, we deploy facts about the stable natures of the processes we manipulate, and the circumstances that will allow these natures either to act unimpeded or to suffer only impediments that can have a stable and predictable effect. When we have such a situation, we are entitled to generalize from even a single case.[5]

The philosophical underpinning that supports these claims is a more radical shift from the picture in which the conventional view of laws is embedded than I have admitted so far. The conventional view sees laws as universal generalizations and thus takes regularities as given in Nature, as the things that Nature sets, by law. I want to urge that not only must we admit natures into our scientific world picture, contrary to Humean predilections, but in a sense we must eliminate regularities. These are, after all, very rare—at least when we focus on quantitatively exact behavior of the kind we study in physics[6]—and when they occur, either naturally or as a result of human contrivance, they can very plausibly be seen as the consequence of particularly fortunate arrangements that allow the processes involved to play out their stable natures in their occurrent behavior.

Return now to the two senses of repeatability. The first sense is internal to the specific experiment and bears on the low-level generalization that is instanced there. The second sense crosses experiments and bears on the high-level, abstract principle that is established: the results of an experiment should be repeatable in the sense that the high-level principles inferred from a particular experiment should be borne out in different experiments of different kinds. In *Nature's Capacities and Their Measurement*, this kind of repeatability played a central role in arguing for the abstract character of our high-level laws in physics and for the claim that these abstract laws describe what I here call "natures."[7] Low-level generalization is not enough. It is too tied to the specific details of the particular experiment; a generalization about what occurs there simply does not cover what occurs elsewhere.

We might think that the problem arises merely from the fact that the language of these low-level laws is not abstract enough: we should not be talking about what happens to a spherically homogeneous ball of fused quartz, coated with a superconductor and spinning, electromagnetically suspended, in midair. Rather, we should talk about a gyroscope, and how it precesses. Still the move to more abstract language will not permit us to retain the simple, unproblematic form of a universal generalization. For we do not want to record what all gyroscopes facing a significant space-time curvature *do*. Rather, we want to record what part the curvature-coupling contributes to how a gyroscope precesses, no matter what, in the end, various and differently situated gyroscopes do. As I described in section 2, that is the core of the analytic method. The point is that we want to learn something from an experiment that is transportable to entirely new situations where quite different circumstances obtain. We do that not by constructing super-abstract generalizations but rather by learning the nature of the pieces from which the new situations are built.

I will not dwell on this argument. More about it can be found in *Nature's Capacities*. The argument I have wanted to make here is different. In *Nature's Capacities*, I argue that we need something like natures if we are to generalize in the second sense—to infer from the results of one experiment some kind of law that can cover other situations as well. Here, I want to urge that we need the notion of natures to generalize in the first sense as well—to infer from the results of the experiment some general law that describes what happens, just in this experimental situation, whenever the experiment is run again. Returning to the remarks at the beginning of this section, I may put the point another way. How do we know which generalization, in this low-level sense, the experiment is testing? Not every feature of it is necessary to ensure its repeatability. The answer requires the notion of natures: the features that are necessary are exactly those which, in this very specific concrete situation, allow the nature of the process under study to express itself in some readable way. No weaker account will do. Without the concept of natures we have no way of knowing what it is that we are testing.

4. TWO OBJECTIONS

I have been arguing that in order to understand what makes experiments special, what ensures that we can generalize from them, we must employ concepts repugnant to a Humean, such as nature, power, impediment, operation. The most obvious responses for a Humean to make would be either that the job can be equally well done by referring only to "occurrent properties" and their regular associations or else that this is a job that does not need to be done.

a. Consider the first objection. We want to figure out what factors are relevant—what factors need to be controlled in a given experiment if that experiment is to be replicable. Imagine, for the sake of argument, that we have available an entire register of all lawlike regularities and that we are not going to quibble about the fact that most of these are as foreign to our world as unicorns. How are we to deploy them? What do we do to determine from this register whether a given factor in our experiment is relevant or not, and needs to be controlled? I suppose the procedure envisaged by the Humean is, very roughly, this: take all those laws whose consequents describe the same kind of behavior (for example, precessing in a gyroscope) as that of the law we wish to infer from our experiment; any factor that appears in the antecedents of one of these laws is a relevant factor—that is, a factor that must be controlled in any experiment to test the law at hand. But at which level of law are we to conduct our search?

At the lower level, there are a very great number of laws indeed. Gyroscopes of all shapes and materials and forms can precess, or fail to precess, in an inconceivable number of different determinate ways in a plentitude of different circumstances. The conditions are too numerous. They give us too many factors to control. Our experiments would be undoable, and the laws they entitle would be narrowed in scope beyond all recognition. But there is a deeper problem: how are these laws to be read? For the Humean, they must be the source of information about not only what factors are to be controlled but in exactly what way. Yet they cannot tell us that, for how a factor operates, at this very concrete level, is far too context-dependent. I give some examples of this kind of context dependence elsewhere.[8]

But I think the point is easy to see. To know exactly what to do with the superconducting coating in the Gravity Probe, one needs to know about the detailed construction of that particular experiment; and the laws one wants to look at are not more laws about precessions but rather laws about superconductors. The point is not whether these further laws are Humean in form or not but rather, how is the Humean to know to look at them? What is the prescription that sorts from among all the factors that appear in all the universal generalizations true in the world, which ones are to be fixed, and how, in this particular experiment?

Perhaps the answer comes one level up. Here I think is where we get the idea that there might be a relatively small number of fixed, probably articulable, factors that are relevant. We may think in terms of forces, how few in kind they are; or of long lists of causes and preventives. What is crucial is that at the abstract level, context seems irrelevant. Either it is or it is not the case that magnetic fields deflect charged particles; or that, as quantum mechanics teaches, an inversion in a population of molecules can cause lasing. Perhaps we can even find a sufficiently abstract law so that the problem seems to evaporate. For example, if we are thinking of an experiment where the effect we look for involves particle motions, we turn to the law $F = ma$, and that tells us that we must control all sources of force. In the gyroscope experiment, the law of choice in this case would be

Procession: $\dot{n}_s^r = \Gamma^r \times n_s / I\omega_s$

which gives the drift rate ($\dot{n}_s^r$) of a gyrospin vector as a function of the total torque (Γ^r) exerted on the gyro along with its moment of inertia (I), and its spin angular velocity (ω_s). From this we learn: control all sources of torque except that due to the relativistic coupling, as well as any sources of deviation in the angular velocity and in the moment of inertia.

The difficulty with this advice is that it does not justify the replicability we expect unless we join to it a commitment to stable powers of the kind I have been calling natures, or something very much like them. To see why, imagine a single successful run of the experiment, successful in the sense that first, we have indeed managed to set the total net torque, barring that due to relativistic coupling, equal to zero—or, as the Gravity Probe hopes to do, at least to an order of magnitude lower than that predicted for the relativistic effect; and second, it turns out that the observed precession is just that predicted. We seem to have succeeded in giving a purely Humean receipt for when to generalize, and this case fits. Roughly, we can generalize the quantitative relation we see between a designated input (here the relativistic coupling) and the precession actually observed in a given situation if that situation sets the remaining net torque equal to zero (or, more realistically, calculates it away), where the rationale for picking *net torque = 0* as the relevant feature comes from the "Humean association" recorded in the functional law that describes the size of precessions.

The problem is that this does not get us the detailed generalization we expect (at the first, lower level). The Gravity-Probe team has worked hard to set the total net torque extremely low, by a large number of specific hard-won designs; and they are entitled to think that the results are replicable in *that* experimental design. What the Humean prescription entitles them to is weaker. It gives them the right to expect only that on any occasion when the net nonrelativistic torque is zero, the precession will be the value predicted from the general theory of relativity. But we expect the more concrete general claim to hold as well.

Consider the table of design requirements for the gyroscope experiment (diagram 1). The table tells how controlled each foreseeable source of torque must be in order for the total extraneous precession to be an order of magnitude smaller than that predicted from the relativistic coupling. Each such source—rotor homogeneity, rotor sphericity, housing sphericity, optimum preload, and so on—presents a special design problem; and for each, the experiment has a special solution. Using fused quartz to get maximum rotor homogeneity is, for example, the starting point for the solution of the first problem. What all this careful planning, honing, and calculation entitles us to is a far more concrete generalization than the one above about (near) zero

			Requirement	Explanation
Gyroscope	Mechanical parts	Rotor homogeneity	$\frac{\Delta\rho}{\rho} \sim 3 \times 10^{-7}$	Mass unbalance and gravity gradient torques
		Rotor sphericity at rest	$\frac{\Delta r'}{r} \sim 5 \times 10^{-7}$ $\Delta r' \sim 0.4\mu in$	Suspension torques
		Housing sphericity	$\frac{\Delta r''}{r} \sim 2 \times 10^{-5}$ $\Delta r'' \sim 15.\mu in$	Second-order suspension torques and torques due to static charge on rotor
	Suspension systems	Optimum preload	$h \sim 10^{-7}$ g voltage = 0.2V	Suspension torques and cyclic acceleration on rotor
		Preload symmetry	$\zeta \sim 1\%$	Suspension torques
		Centering accuracy	$t/d \sim 1\%$ $t = 15\mu in$	Suspension torques plus readout errors
	Other	Optimum spin speed	$\omega_s \sim 170$ Hz	Centrifugal distortion of rotor
		Torque switching ratio for spin up system	$\Gamma_r/\Gamma_s \sim 2 \times 10^{-13}$	See Section C(2)
		Distance from drag-free proof mass	$\ell < 20$ cm	To minimize cyclic accelerations on rotors

		Requirement	Explanation
Environment	Drag-free acceleration level	$< 10^{-10}$ g	Suspension and mass unbalance torques
	Orbit eccentricity	< 0.1	Suspension and mass unbalance torques
	Magnetic fields	$< 10^{-7}$ g	Readout linearity (see Section C(3) (j) plus magnetic torques
	Electric charge on ball	10^9 electrons 0.3V	Torques plus preload requirement
	Gas pressure	Magnitude $< 10^{-9}$ torr Gradients $\sim 6\%$ variations allowed	Gas torques

Diagram 3.1. Design Requirements for a Relativity Gyroscope with Limiting Accuracy of 0.5×10^{-16} rad/sec (0.3 milliarc-sec/year) (From C. W. F. Everitt, coordinator, *Report an a Program to Develop a Gyro Test of General Relativity* [Stanford, Calif.: W. W. Hansen Laboratories, Stanford University, 1980].)

external torque. We are entitled to infer from a successful run that in any experiment of this very *specific* design, the observed precession should be that predicted by the general theory of relativity.[9]

The table of requirements highlights the analytic nature of this kind of experiment, which I discussed in section 2. What happens if something goes wrong with the rotor housing as it was originally planned, and the fault cannot be repaired? With a lot of effort, the Probe team will make a new design and slot it into the old general scheme, making appropriate changes. Because we are working in a domain where we trust analytic methods, a peculiar kind of sideways induction is warranted: from the successful run with the original design plus our confidence in the new rotor housing and its placement, we are entitled to infer a second, highly specific "low-level" generalization to the effect that the precession in situations meeting the new design will be that predicted for relativistic coupling as well. Again, the new situation will indeed be one that falls under the "Humean" generalization involving zero torques. What is missing is the connection. The new situation is one of very small extraneous torque; but the expectation that it should be cannot be read from the regularities of nature.

The regularity theorist is thus faced with a dilemma. In low-level, highly concrete generalizations, the factors are too intertwined to teach us what will and what will not be relevant in a new design. That job is properly done in physics using far more abstract characterizations. The trouble is that once we have climbed up into this abstract level of law, we have no device within a pure regularity account to climb back down again.

b. The second argument is a more transcendental one. It does not attempt to show how it is possible to fix relevance in a world without natures but rather that it must be possible to do so. I borrow the form from arguments made by Bas van Fraassen and by Arthur Fine in debating more general questions of scientific realism. The argument presupposes that we can make available a pure data base, cleansed of natures and their non-Humean relatives. The objection goes like this: "You, Cartwright, will defend the design of a given experiment by talking about what impedes and what facilitates the expression of the nature in question. I take it this is not idle faith but that in each case you will have reasons for that judgment. These reasons must ultimately be based not in facts about natures, which you cannot observe, but in facts about actual behavior, which you can. Once you have told me these reasons, I should be able to avoid the digression through natures and move directly to the appropriate conclusions about relevance. Talk of natures may provide a convenient way to encode information about behaviors, but so long as we insist that scientific claims be grounded in what can be observed, this talk cannot contribute any new information."

But what about this decontaminated data base? Where is it in our experience? It is a philosophical construction, a piece of metaphysics, a way to interpret the world. Of course, we cannot do without interpretation. But this construction is far more removed from our everyday experience of the world as we interact with it and describe it to others than are homely truths about triggering mechanisms, precipitating factors, impediments, and the like which mark out the domain of natures. Consider an adaptation of van Fraassen's objection to causes, which is a version of essentially the same argument. The objection proceeds from the assumption that there is some defensible notion of a sensible property which is conceptually and logically distinct from any ideas connected with natures. We are then confronted with a challenge to explain what difference natures make: "Imagine a world identical with our own in all occurrences of its sensible qualities throughout its history. How would that world differ from our world?"

On one reading, this argument may be about sequences not of properties in the world but of our experiences of the world. These sequences are to remain the same, but we are to imagine that they are not caused in the usual way by what is going on in the world around us. This reading cannot be the one intended, though, since it does not cut in the right way, revealing special virtues for descriptions like 'is red' or 'is a jet-stream trail' in contrast with ones like 'has the power to relieve headaches' or 'attracts others, qua charged'.

I might further be invited to inspect my experiences and to notice that they are "really" experiences of successions of color patches, say, with powers nowhere to be found. The philosophical dialogue along this line is well rehearsed; I merely point in the familiar directions. My experiences are of people and houses and pinchings and aspirins, all things which I understand, in large part, in terms of their natures. I do not have any raw experience of a house as a patchwork of colors. Even with respect to colors, my experience is of properties like red, whose nature it is to look specific ways in specific circumstances. Sense data, or *the given*, are metaphysical constructs which, unlike natures, play no role in testable scientific claims. Once there was a hope to mark out among experience some raw pieces by using an epistemological yardstick: the "real" experiences were the infallible ones. After a great deal of debate it is not clear whether this criterion even lets in claims about felt pains; but it surely does not distinguish claims like 'The stripes are red' from 'Your pinching makes my arm hurt'.

The contemporary version of this argument tends, for these reasons, not to be in terms of sense experiences but in terms of sensible properties. But here there is a very simple reply. A world with all the same sensible properties as ours would already be a world with natures. As I remarked above, redness is the property whose nature, among other things, is to look just *this* way in normal circumstances, and to look systematically different when the circumstances are systematically varied.

Perhaps we are misled here by carrying over the conclusions of an earlier metaphysics, conclusions for which the premises have been discarded. These premises involve the doctrine of impressions and ideas. In the immediately post-Cartesian philosophy of the British empiricists, sensible properties could be picked out because they looked like their impressions. Gaze at the first stripe on the American flag: redness is the property that looks like *that*. We do not have this copy theory; so we do not have properties that are identified like that. Correlatively, we can no longer make the same distinction separating powers and their properties as did these seventeenth-century empiricists. On their doctrine, the way things looked could get copied in the perceiver's impressions of them; but the various powers of a property could not. Since their ideas were copies of their impressions, necessarily their world, as imaged, had only inert properties. But we do not have the copy theory of impressions, nor do we adopt this simple theory of concept formation. For us, there are properties, and all properties have powers. (Perhaps, following Sydney Shoemaker, they are all just conglomerates of powers: cf. *Identity, Cause, and Mind* [Cambridge: Cambridge University Press, 1984], chap. 10.) What they are is given not by how they look but by what they do. When we use a particular power word to describe a property, we focus on one specific aspect of what it can accomplish. When we use an "occurrent" or "sensible" predicate, we refer to the property without highlighting any one thing it does, or any one particular way of identifying it. That is only a very rough characterization of the rules of use. But it points to the fact I want to stress: the distinction is one in language and in what we want to accomplish on specific occasions by using that language. Predicates can be roughly divided into types; but properties and powers are not separable in that way. The question of "How does the Hume world differ from ours?" may have made sense for Locke, Berkeley, and Hume; but without the copy theory of impressions and the related associationist theory of concept formation, nowadays it has an entirely trivial answer.

5. A HISTORICAL ILLUSTRATION

So far, I have couched the discussion in terms of making inductions from paltry samples, and that is because induction is the method that Humeans should favor for confirming laws. I think, though, that the process is far better understood as one of deduction; we accept laws on apparently slim experimental bases exactly when we can take for granted such strong background assumptions that (given these assumptions) the data plus the description of the experimental setup deductively imply the law to be established. Probably the most prominent advocate of a deductive method in reasoning from experiment to law is Isaac Newton. I think it will be helpful to look briefly at Newton's use of the "crucial experiment" in his theory of light and colors, and more particularly at Goethe's criticisms of it.

Newton's *experimentum crucis* is described in his first letter in 1671 to the

Royal Society in which he introduces his theory that white light consists of diverse rays of different refrangibility (that is, they are bent by different amounts when the light passes through a prism) and that color is a property of the ray which depends on its refrangibility. The work reported in the letter is generally taken as a model of scientific reasoning. Thomas Kuhn, for instance, claims that "Newton's experimental documentation of his theory is a classic in its simplicity." According to Kuhn, the opposition view might eventually have accounted for some of the data that appeared to refute it, "but how could they have evaded the implications of the *experimentum crucis*? An innovator in the sciences has never stood on surer ground" ("Newton's Optical Papers," in *Isaac Newton's Papers and Letters*, ed. I. B. Cohen [Cambridge, Mass.: Harvard University Press, 1958], 36).

It is important to keep in mind that Newton believed that his claims were *proved* by his experiments. He claims "the Theory, which I propounded, was evinced by me, not inferring tis thus because not otherwise, that is, not by deducing it only from a confutation of contrary suppositions but by deriving it from experiments concluding positively and directly." Or, "If the Experiments, which I urge, be defective, it cannot be difficult to show the defects; but if valid, then by proving the theory they must render all objections invalid." One last remark to illustrate the steadfastness of Newton's views on the role of the *experimentum crucis* in proving this claim appears in Newton's letter of 1676, four years after his initial report to the Royal Society. This letter concerned the difficulties Anthony Lucas had reported in trying to duplicate Newton's experiments and also some of Lucas's own results that contradicted Newton's claims. Newton replies, "Yet it will conduce to his more speedy and full satisfaction if he a little change the method he has propounded, and instead of a multitude of things try only the *Experimentum Crucis*. For it is not number of experiments, but weight to be regarded; and where one will do, what need many?"

Goethe's point of view is entirely opposite to Newton's: "As worthwhile as each individual experiment may be, it receives its real value only when united or combined with other experiments. . . . I would venture to say that we cannot prove anything by one experiment or even several experiments together" ("The Experiment as Mediator between Object and Subject," in Johann Wolfgang von Goethe, *Scientific Studies*, ed. and tr. Douglas Miller [New York: Suhrkamp, 1988]). For Goethe, all phenomena are connected together, and it is essential to follow through from each experiment to another that "lies next to it or derives directly from it." According to Goethe, "To follow every single experiment through its variations is the real task of the scientific researcher." This is illustrated in his own work in optics where he produces long series of "contiguous" experiments, each of which is suggested by the one before it. The point is not to find some single set of circumstances that are special but rather to lay out all the variations in the phenomena as the circumstances change in a systematic way. Then one must come to see all the interrelated experiments together and understand them as a whole, "a single piece of experimental evidence explored in its manifold variations."

Goethe is sharp in his criticisms of Newton. Two different kinds of criticism are most relevant here. The first is that Newton's theory fails to account for all the phenomena it should, and that that is no surprise since Newton failed to look at the phenomena under a sufficient range of variation of circumstance. Second, Newton's inferences from the experiments he did make were not valid; the *experimentum crucis* is a case in point. The chief fault which Goethe finds with Newton's inferences is one that could not arise in Goethe's method. Newton selects a single revealing experiment to theorize from; since he does not see how the phenomena change through Goethe's long sequence of experiments, he does not recognize how variation in circumstance affects the outcome: "[Newton's] chief error consisted in too quickly and hastily setting aside and denying those questions that chiefly relate to whether external conditions cooperate in the appearance of color, without looking more exactly into the proximate circumstances" (Dennis L. Sepper, *Goethe contra Newton* [Cambridge: Cambridge University Press, 1988], 144).

The crucial experiment involves refracting a beam of light through a prism, which elongates the initial narrow beam and "breaks" it into a colored band—violet at the top, red at the bottom. Then differently colored portions of the elongated beam are refracted through a second prism. Consider diagram 2, which is taken from Dennis L. Sepper's study, *Goethe contra Newton.* In all cases, the color is preserved, but at one end of the elongated beam the second refracted beam is elongated more than it is at the other. In each case, there is no difference in the way in which the light falls on the prism for the second refraction. Newton immediately concludes, "And so the true cause of the length of the image was detected to be no other than that *light* consists of *rays differently refrangible*" (Newton's first letter to the Royal Society, 1671).

We should think about this inference in the context of my earlier cursory description of the modern version of the deductive method, called bootstrapping by Clark Glymour, who has been its champion in recent debates. In the bootstrapping account, we infer from an experimental outcome to a scientific law, as Newton does, but only against a backdrop of rather strong assumptions. Some of these assumptions will be factual ones about the specific arrangements made—for example, that the angle of the prism was 63°; some will be more general claims about how the experimental apparatus works—the theory of condensation in a cloud chamber, for instance; some will be more general claims still—for example, all motions are produced by forces; and some will be metaphysical, such as the "same cause, same effect" principle mentioned in section 3. The same is true of Newton's inference. It may be a perfectly valid inference, but there are repressed premises. It is the repressed premises that Goethe does not like. On Goethe's view of nature, they are not

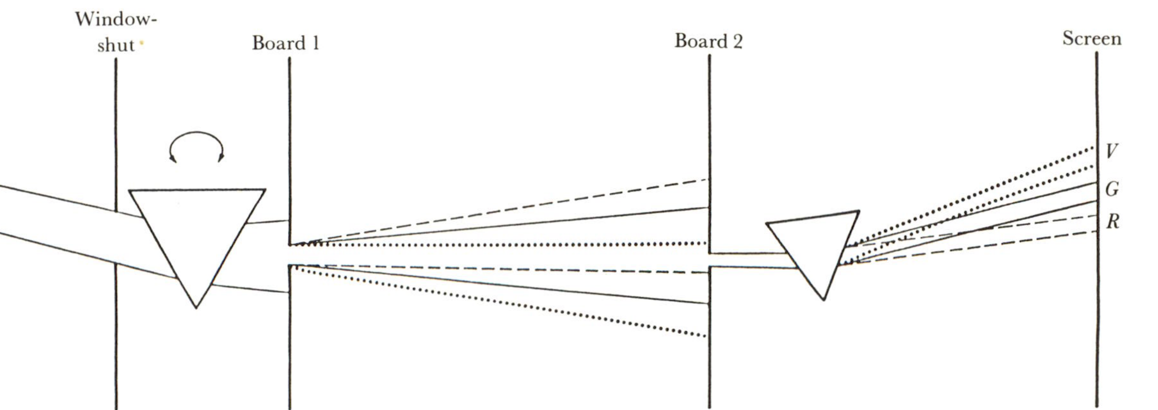

Newton's experimentum crucis. *Rotating the first prism (on the left) while keeping the other prism and the two boards with apertures stationary makes the complete spectrum cast on the second board move up and down, so that different colors fall on the aperture and pass through. The violet portion is refracted most (to* V*), the red the least (to* R*), green and other colors intermediately. (This figures is not drawn to scale.)*

Diagram 3.2 (From Dennis L. Sepper *Goethe contra Newton* [(Cambridge: Cambridge University Press, 1988].)

only badly supported by the evidence; they are false. Colors, like all else in Goethe's world,[10] are a consequence of the action of opposites, in this case light and darkness:

> We see on the one side light, the bright; on the other darkness, the dark; we bring what is turbid between the two [such as a prism or a semitransparent sheet of paper], and out of these opposites, with the help of this mediation, there develop, likewise in an opposition, colors. (*Theory of Colors*, didactic part, paragraph 175)

Newton's argument requires, by contrast, the assumption that the tendency to produce colors is entirely in the nature of the light, and that is why this dispute is of relevance to my point here. As Sepper says, for Newton "the cause is to be sought only in the light itself."

Let us turn to Newton's reasoning. The argument is plausible, so long as one is not looking for deductive certainty. From Newton's point of view (though not from that of Goethe, who imagines a far richer set of possibilities), the two hypotheses to be decided between are: (a) something that happens involving white light in the prism produces colored light; or (b) colored light is already entering the prism in the first place. We can see the force of the argument by thinking in terms of inputs and outputs. Look at what happens to, say, the violet light in the second prism (diagram 3):

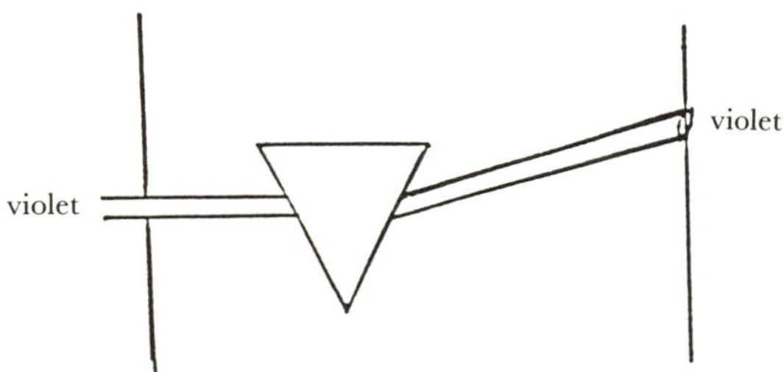

Diagram 3.3.

Compare this with the production of violet light in the first prism (diagram 4):

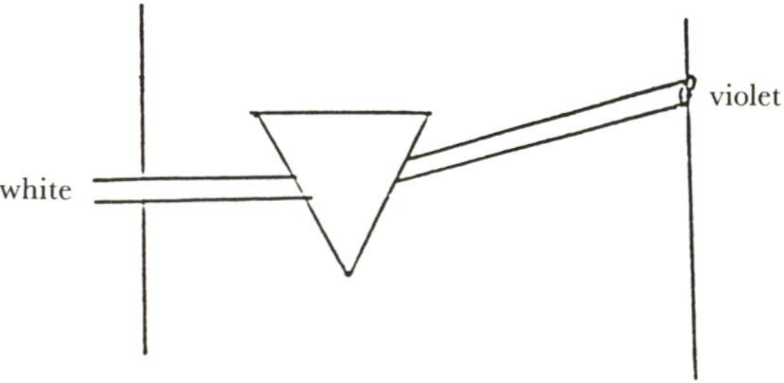

Diagram 3.4.

In both cases, the outputs are the same. The simplest account seems to be that the prism functions in the same way in both cases: it just transports the colored light through, bending it in accord with its fixed degree of refrangibility.

Consider an analogous case. You observe a large, low building. Colored cars drive through. Cars of different colors have different fixed turning radii. You observe for each color that there is a fixed and color-dependent angle between the trajectory on which the car enters the building, and the trajectory on which it exits; moreover, this is just the angle to be expected if the cars were driven through the building with steering wheels locked to the far left. Besides cars, other vehicles enter the building, covered; and each time a covered vehicle enters, a colored car exits shortly afterward. It exits at just that angle that would be appropriate had the original incoming vehicle been a car of the same color driven through with its steering wheel locked. Two hypotheses are offered about what goes on inside the building. Both hypotheses treat the incoming colored cars in the same way: on entering the building, their steering wheels get locked and then they are driven through. The two hypotheses differ, however, about the covered vehicles. The first hypothesis assumes that these, too, are colored cars. Inside the building they get unwrapped, and then they are treated just like all the other colored cars. The second hypothesis is more ambitious. It envisages that the low building contains an entire car factory. The covered vehicles contain raw material, and inside the building there are not only people who lock steering wheels, but a whole crew of Fiat workers and machinery turning raw materials into cars.

Obviously, the first hypothesis is simpler, but it has more in its favor than that. For so far, the second hypothesis has not explained why the manufactured cars exit at the angle they do, relative to their incoming raw materials; and there seems to be no immediate natural account to give on the second story. True, the cars are manufactured with fixed turning radii, but why should they leave the factory at just the same angle relative to the cart that carries in their raw materials as a drive-through does relative to its line of entry? After all, the manufactured car has come to exist only somewhere within the factory, and even if its steering wheel is locked, it seems a peculiar coincidence should that result in just the right exit point to yield the required angle vis-à-vis the raw materials. In this case, barring other information, the first, Newtonian, hypothesis seems the superior. The caveat, "barring other information," is central, of course, to Goethe's attack. For, as I have already remarked, Goethe was appalled at the small amount of information that Newton collected, and he argued that Newton's claim was in no way adequate to cover the totality of the phenomena. What looks to be the best hypothesis in a single case can certainly look very different when a whole array of different cases have to be considered.

The principal point to notice, for my purpose, is that the argument is not at all deductive. It can only become so if we already presuppose that we are looking for some fixed feature in light itself that will account for what comes out of the prism—something, as I would say, in the nature of light. Any assumption like this is deeply contrary to Goethe's point of view. The first few paragraphs of Newton's letter, before the introduction of the crucial experiment, give some grounds for such an assumption on his part; Goethe makes fun of them:

> It is a fact that under *those circumstances* that Newton exactly specifies, the image of the sun is five times as long as it is wide, and that this elongated image appears entirely in colors. Every observer can repeatedly witness this phenomenon without any great effort.
>
> Newton himself tells us how he went to work in order to convince himself that no *external cause* can bring this elongation and coloration of the image. This treatment of his will, as already was mentioned above, be subjected to criticism for we can raise many questions and investigate with exactness, whether he went to work properly and to what extent his proof is in every sense complete.
>
> If one analyzes his reasons, they have the following form:
>
> When the ray is refracted the image is longer than it should be according to the laws of refraction.
>
> Now I have tried everything and thereby convinced myself that no external cause is responsible for this elongation.
>
> Therefore it is an inner cause, and this we find in the divisibility of light. For since it takes up a larger space than before, it must divided, thrown asunder; and since we see the sundered light in colors, the different parts of it must be colored.
>
> How much there is to object to immediately in this rationale! [Goethe, 1793; quoted from Sepper, p. 101]

The contrast that I want to highlight is between Newton's postulation of an inner cause in light versus Goethe's long and many-faceted row of experiments. Goethe often remarks that he and Newton both claim to be concerned with *colors*; Newton after all labels his account in the 1671 letter his "new theory of light and colors." But, in actuality, Goethe points out, Newton's work is almost entirely about the behavior of rays—that is, about the inner nature of light. Goethe's experiments often involve light, but it is not light that he studies. The experiments describe entire interacting complexes, such as evening light entering a room through a hole in a white blind on which a candle throws light ("snow seen through the opening will then appear perfectly blue, because the paper is tinged with warm yellow by the candlelight" [*Theory of Colors*, didactic part, paragraph 79]), or sunlight shining into a diving bell (in this case "everything is seen in a red light ... while the shadows appear green" [*Theory of Colors*, didactic part, paragraph 78]), or a particularly exemplary case for the existence of colored shadows, a pencil placed on a sheet of white paper between a short, lighted candle and a window so that the twilight from the window illuminates the pencil's shadow from the candle ("the shadow will appear of the most beautiful blue" [*Theory of Colors*, didactic part, paragraph 65]). Even when described from the point of view of Goethe's final account of color formation, in the prism experiments Goethe is not looking at light but rather at light (or darkness)-in-interaction-with-a-turbid-medium.

Newton focuses on his one special experiment and maintains that the account of the phenomena in that experiment will pinpoint an explanation that is generalizable. The feature that explains the phenomena in that situation will explain phenomena in other situations; hence he looks to a feature that is part of the inner constitution of light itself. To place it in the *inner* constitution is to cast it not as an observable property characteristic of light but rather as a power that reveals itself, if at all, in appropriately structured circumstances. To describe it as part of light's *constitution* is to ascribe a kind of permanence to the association: light retains this power across a wide variation in circumstance—indeed, probably so long as it remains light. That is, I maintain, to treat it as an Aristotelian-style nature. This is why Newton, unlike Goethe, can downplay the experimental context. The context is there to elicit the nature of light; it is not an essential ingredient in the ultimate structure of the phenomenon.

6. CONCLUSION

My argument in this paper hinges on a not surprising connection between methodology and ontology. If you want to find out how a scientific discipline pictures the world, you can study its laws, its theories, its models, and its claims—you can listen to what it says about the world. But you can also consider not just what is said but what is done. How we choose to look at the world is just as sure a clue to what we think the world is like as what we say about it. Modern experimental physics looks at the world under precisely controlled or highly contrived circumstances; and in the best of cases, one look is enough. That, I claim, is just how one looks for natures, and not how one looks for information about what things do.

Goethe criticizes Newton for this same kind of procedure that we use nowadays, and the dispute between them illustrates my point. Newton's conclusions in his letter of 1671, as well as throughout his later work in optics, are about the inner constitution of light. I claim that this study of the inner constitution is a study of an Aristotelian-style nature and that Newton's use of experiment is suited to just that kind of enterprise, where the *experimentum crucis* is an especially striking case. The colored rays, with their different degrees of refrangibility, cannot be immediately seen in white light. But through the experiment with the two prisms, the underlying nature expresses itself in a clearly visible behavior: the colors are there to be seen, and the purely dispositional property, *degree-of-refrangibility*, is manifested in the actual angle through which the light is bent. The experiment is brilliantly constructed: the connection between the natures and the behavior that is supposed to reveal them is so tight that Newton takes it to be deductive.

Goethe derides Newton for surveying so little evidence, and his worries are not merely questions of experimental design: perhaps Newton miscalculated, or mistakenly assumed that the second prism was identical in structure with the first, or Newton takes as simple what is not . . . Goethe's disagreement with Newton is not a matter of mere epistemological uncertainty. It is rather a reflection of deep ontological differences. For Goethe, all phenomena are the consequence of interaction between polar opposites. There is nothing in light to be isolated, no inner nature to be revealed. No experiment can show in a single behavior what light does qua light, for by itself there is nothing, no special single thing that it is in the nature of light to do. The empiricists of the scientific revolution wanted to oust Aristotle entirely from the new learning. I have argued that they did no such thing. Goethe, by contrast, did dispense with natures; there are none in his world picture. But there are, I maintain, in ours.

NOTES

I owe special thanks to Hasok Chang, as well as to the members of the Philosophy of Language and Science Seminar, and the Romanticism and Science Seminar at Stanford University, fall and winter terms, 1989–90. This essay is dedicated to Eckart Förster.

1. Though in each case the independent methods of identification will themselves depend on some different aspect of the nature of the property in question; otherwise the methods of identification could not be expected to indicate the presence of the property reliably and repeatably. For a brief discussion of the connection among these different natures all of the same property, see sec. 4.b below.

2. Not all physics is based on the analytic method. Space-time theories that purport to study the whole manifold all at once are a case in point. What I claim to be characteristic of laws in classical mechanics, quantum mechanics, thermodynamics, and electromagnetic theory will not be so readily applicable in these nonanalytic domains.

3. Still, the knowledge cannot be too implicit. Trivially, where the experiment is to serve as a test, we must know enough to be assured that the behavior we see is a manifestation of the nature of the phenomenon we want to study and not a manifestation of some other side aspect of the arrangement.

4. I do not mean to suggest that there can be no other basis for this generalization. Sheer repetition will serve as well, and that is an important aspect of claims like those of Ian Hacking (*Representing and Intervening* [Cambridge: Cambridge University Press, 1984]), that the stable phenomena that are created in the experimental setting have a life of their own and continue to persist across great shifts in their abstract interpretation.

5. Our degree of confidence in the generalization will be limited, of course, by how certain we are that our assessment of the situation is correct.

6. The world, of course, is full of relatively reliable, rough regularities. Not only are all men mortal; in general, organisms exhibit regular developmental sequences peculiar

to their species. I do not discuss these, not only from a lack of expertise but also to avoid old issues of vitalism and mysticism. Part of the reason for looking at physics is that physics provides our paradigm for precisely testable claims. If physics treats of natures, or some similar concept suitable for making sense of the analytic method, then natures need not automatically commit us to mystical processes that lie fundamentally beyond our sure understanding.

7. In *Nature's Capacities and Their Measurement*, I call them "capacities" since my concern there is primarily with *causal* laws.

8. Cf. *Nature's Capacities*; also "Capacities and Abstractions," in *Scientific Explanation*, ed. Philip Kitcher and Wesley Salmon (Minneapolis: University of Minnesota Press, 1988).

9. The inference is *ceteris paribus*, of course—"so long as nothing goes wrong." The "zero torque" generalization apparently has the advantage that it needs no such *ceteris paribus* clause. But that is a mixed blessing since the advantage is bought at the cost of making "zero torque" a concept that is not identifiable independently of its effect. As soon as we begin to fill in what *makes for* zero torque, anything we say will inevitably have to contain a *ceteris paribus* proviso.

10. See, for example, paragraph 739 of the didactic part of his *Theory of Colors* (1810): "True observers of nature, however they may differ in opinion in other respects, will agree that all which presents itself as appearance, all that we meet with as phenomenon, must either indicate an original division which is capable of union, or an original unity which admits of division, and that the phenomenon will present itself accordingly. To divide the united, to unite the divided, is the life of nature; this is the eternal systole and diastole, the eternal collapsion and expansion, the inspiration and expiration of the world in which we live and move."

FOUR

Genetic Inference

A Reconsideration of David Hume's Empiricism

Barbara D. Massey and Gerald J. Massey

1. HUME'S FORK

What could be more banal than Hume's fork, the bifurcation of objects of inquiry (true propositions) into *relations of ideas* and *matters of fact*? Surely historians have so thoroughly scrutinized this celebrated dichotomy that we can be confident of their deliverances on this topic. Let us review, then, the received view of Hume's fork.

True propositions like '3 times 5 equals one-half of 30' and the Pythagorean theorem express relations of ideas, while ones like 'Fire burns' and 'The sun will rise tomorrow' record matters of fact or real existence. What is distinctive about a relation of ideas is that its negation entails a contradiction. The negation of every matter-of-factual truth, in contrast, is conceivable and so does not entail a contradiction because whatever is conceivable is possible. Hume's taxonomy of true propositions (objects of inquiry) is clearly disjoint and exhaustive: each true proposition falls into one and only one of his two compartments. And that the classification is dichotomous, that is, *necessarily* disjoint and exhaustive, can be grasped a priori because it is based on the presence or absence of a single property, namely, conceivability of the proposition's negation.[1]

Against the received view we note that Hume regularly uses his fork as if it speared all propositions, the false ones no less than the true. For example, he often makes the prior assessment that a given proposition is matter-of-factual or a relation of ideas an important part of his determination of its truth value, as in this passage from the first *Enquiry*:

> It is a question of fact, whether the perceptions of the senses be produced by external objects resembling them. How shall this question be determined? By experience surely, as all other questions of a like nature. But here experience is,

> and must be entirely silent. The mind has never any thing present to it but the perceptions, and cannot possibly reach any experience of their connexion with objects. The supposition of such a connection is, therefore, without any foundation in reasoning.[2]

But this is to argue in a circle and bears witness to a fundamental incoherence in Hume's system of philosophy.

Nor is it clear that the classification is dichotomous even when limited to true propositions. Perhaps Hume did intend initially to make a true proposition's classification depend solely on the conceivability of its negation. If so, he soon forgot his resolve. For whether a proposition is matter-of-factual or a relation of ideas becomes for Hume as much a matter of how it can be known (via intuition and demonstration or via observation and causal inference) as a matter of how its negation can be conceived. For the most part this ambivalence causes Hume little discomfort, for the two ways of understanding the classificatory basis match up pretty well. But when they fail to line up, watch out! And, unluckily for Hume, they do indeed sometimes fail to line up—for example, in such important cases as the allegedly factual thesis of the double existence of objects and perceptions. Quine's doctrine that definitional status is a passing trait of the truths of science surely took its inspiration from verbal behavior like Hume's![3]

We are told that Hume's fork answers tolerably well to our necessary/contingent distinction and even to our a priori/a posteriori distinction. Furthermore, the story goes, Kant pretty much took over Hume's dichotomy while embellishing it in two significant ways. First, he promoted strict universality and necessity as the marks of the a priori, that is, of relations of ideas. Second, he subdivided the a priori itself into analytic and synthetic, thereby setting the stage for his famous interrogative "How are synthetic judgments a priori possible?"

But, as we shall shortly see, Kant fundamentally misunderstood Hume. Kant failed to see that Hume, the champion of modern empiricism, himself posited faculties of synthetic a priori cognition beyond anything that he, Kant, ever dreamed of. Kant should perhaps not be much faulted for this latter oversight, however. For, *mirabile dictu*, Hume himself failed to take much notice of the faculties of synthetic a priori cognition with which he liberally sprinkled his system of philosophy. So, anyway, we will argue.

2. HUME'S VIEW OF ANIMALS

Let's begin our rethinking of Hume's fork by remarking upon a trait of David Hume that sets him apart from virtually all his contemporaries and predecessors and that has endeared him to animal lovers everywhere, namely, his resolute solidarity with "beasts." Never the species chauvinist, Hume saw human beings as animals among animals, distinguished in certain ways from beasts but only *extrinsically* marked off from them by the greater power and subtlety of shared cognitive powers:

> Next to the ridicule of denying an evident truth, is that of taking much pains to defend it; and no truth appears to me more evident, than that beasts are endow'd with thought and reason as well as men. The arguments are in this case so obvious, that they never escape the most stupid and ignorant.
>
> We are conscious, that we ourselves, in adapting means to ends, are guided by reason and design, and that 'tis not ignorantly or casually we perform those actions, which tend to self-preservation, to the obtaining pleasure, and avoiding pain. When therefore we see other creatures, in millions of instances, perform like actions, and direct them to like ends, all of our principles of reason and probability carry us with an invincible force to believe the existence of a like cause.[4]

Further, Hume notes that the three primitive relations of his associationist psychology operate in animals no differently than in humans:

> . . . there is evidently the same *relation* of ideas, and deriv'd from the same causes, in the minds of animals as in those of men. A dog, that has hid a bone, often forgets the place; but when brought to it, his thought passes easily to what he formerly conceal'd, by means of the contiguity, which produces a relation among his ideas. In like manner, when he has been heartily beat in any place, he will tremble on his approach to it, even tho' he discover no signs of any present danger. The effects of resemblance are not so remarkable; but as that relation makes a considerable ingredient in causation, of which all animals shew so evident a judgement, we may conclude that the three relations of resemblance, contiguity and causation operate in the same manner upon beasts as upon human creatures.[5]

The fact that human and animal behavior closely resemble each other, and hence that the animal mind is like the human mind,

> furnishes us with a kind of touchstone, by which we may try every system in this species of philosophy. 'Tis from the resemblance of the external actions of animals to those we ourselves perform, that we judge their internal likewise to resemble ours. . . . When any hypothesis, therefore, is advanc'd to explain a mental operation, which is common to men and beasts, we must apply the same hypothesis to both; and as every true hypothesis will abide this trial, so I may venture to affirm, that no false one will ever be able to endure it.[6]

Here, then, is a philosopher who knows animals and takes them seriously. He prides himself on the alleged fact that his own philosophical system deals evenhandedly with humans and animals. He justifies this pride by a theory of evidence that characterizes as better supported those systems that are evenhanded in the aforementioned respect. It may come as a shock, therefore, when we demonstrate shortly that Hume's treatment of the cognitive powers of humans and animals is decidedly asymmetrical. Even more surprisingly, we will show that the imbalance favors beasts. More surprising still will be the consequences of this psychological asymmetry for Hume's system, and for Kant's as well.[7]

Hume observes in the Section "Of the reason of animals" in Book I of the *Treatise* that:

> men are not astonish'd at the operations of their own reason, at the same time, that they admire the *instinct* of animals, and find a difficulty in explaining it, merely because it cannot be reduc'd to the very same principles. To consider the matter aright, reason is nothing but a wonderful and unintelligible instinct in our souls, which carries us along a certain train of ideas. . . . This instinct, 'tis true, arises from past observation and experience; but can any one give the ultimate reason, why past experience and observation produces such an effect, any more than why nature alone shou'd produce it? Nature may certainly produce whatever can arise from habit: Nay, habit is nothing but one of the principles of nature, and derives all its force from that origin.[8]

Hume's writings are replete with talk of cognitive *instincts*, cognitive *propensities*, cognitive *inclinations*, and the like. These instincts or propensities seem to come in two quite different varieties which we will call *generalized* and *specialized*. A good illustration of a generalized cognitive instinct is the inductive propensity, the cognitive instinct that Hume has in mind in the passage just cited. The inductive instinct determines us to pass to the idea of B when presented with the idea of A, and to transfer vivacity from the idea of A to that of B, when we have experienced a number of cases where an A is followed by a B and no cases where a B has failed to follow an A. It is a propensity shared by humans and animals alike. Other generalized cognitive instincts will be enumerated presently and will be found also to be common to humans and animals.

By *specialized cognitive instincts* we mean what people commonly refer to as *instincts*, that is, those cognitive endowments responsible for complex behavior that is adaptive but unlearned. Hume describes the affinity of "experimental reasoning," notably the inductive propensity, to the specialized cognitive instincts with an eloquence unsurpassed anywhere in his writings:

> But though animals learn many parts of their knowledge from observation, there are also many parts of it, which they derive from the original hand of nature; which much exceed the share of capacity they possess on ordinary occasions; and in which they improve, little or nothing, by the longest practice and experience. These we denominate INSTINCTS, and are so apt to admire, as something very extraordinary, and inexplicable by all the disquisitions of human understanding. But our wonder will, perhaps, cease or diminish; when we consider, that the experimental reasoning itself, which we possess in common with beasts, and on which the whole conduct of life depends, is nothing but a species of instinct or mechanical power, that acts in us unknown to ourselves; and in its chief operations, is not directed by any such relations or comparisons of ideas, as are the

> proper objects of our intellectual faculties. Though the instinct be different, yet still it is an instinct, which teaches a man to avoid the fire; as much as that, which teaches a bird, with such exactness, the art of incubation, and the whole economy and order of its nursery.[9]

For Hume, much and perhaps even most animal *knowledge* is instinctive. Such knowledge is not learned or acquired through experience. On the contrary, it is directly implanted in the animal by a providential Nature independently of experience. Modern ethology and contemporary cognitive science support Hume's contention. The newborn wildebeest (gnu) does not have to learn that the lioness bearing down on it is dangerous, or that this circumstance calls for rapid locomotion in an opposite direction; it comes into the world ready-equipped with such vital information. Even more to our point, the neonatal wildebeest, unlike the human infant, is not condemned to acquire knowledge of its visual space experimentally; it derives from the original hand of Nature the spatial knowledge that the human baby must learn slowly and painfully. That is to say, much that in humans is or would have to be learned experimentally by means of the inductive instinct is possessed innately by beasts. A generous Mother Nature lavishes true matter-of-factual beliefs on animals, but she only begrudgingly grants humans a generalized cognitive endowment by means of which they can wrest from her those facts of life they must know to survive. In short, Hume's Nature functions not as a solicitous Mother to the human species but as a cold Stepmother who sends her charges into the world impoverished and uninstructed to survive on their wits alone.

These decidedly Humean doctrines explode the myth of evenhandedness in Hume's psychological treatment of animals and humans. True, both humans and animals possess generalized cognitive endowments like the inductive propensity, but only animals possess specialized cognitive endowments that afford them a priori knowledge of countless matters of fact or real existence.

3. A SECOND LOOK AT HUME'S FORK

According to the received view, Hume championed *empiricism* by demonstrating that no matter of fact or real existence can be known a priori; experience alone makes such knowledge possible. Certainly, Hume himself claims to have done just this. But we have seen that Hume attributes to animals a priori knowledge of matters of fact with a liberality that would astonish even the most rabid rationalist. Had Kant rightly understood Hume, he would have rephrased his famous query thus: "How is a priori knowledge of matters of fact possible *for animals* when it is not possible for *human beings*?"

To ask this question is almost to answer it. For we cannot then help but notice that it is clearly an empirical matter whether human beings or any other organisms possess a priori knowledge of matters of fact. No one should have appreciated this circumstance better than Hume. In the already cited passage from the *Treatise* about reason's status as instinct, Hume expressly remarks that "Nature may certainly produce whatever can arise from habit: Nay, habit is nothing but one of the principles of nature, and derives all its force from that origin." He surely intends that any matter-of-factual belief acquired by an organism by means of its inductive instinct could have been planted directly in the organism by Nature; that is, it could have been part of the organism's native endowment.

What, then, of Hume's celebrated demonstration that knowledge of matters of fact or real existence is impossible a priori, that all such knowledge is and must be predicated on experience? Hume's argument turns crucially on the conceivability of alternatives to every matter of fact. Even to Adam's reason in the fullness of its paradisiacal powers, the proposition that fire burns would have recommended itself no more and no less than the proposition that fire freezes; only repeated experience of fire enabled poor Adam, no doubt suffering acutely from second-degree burns, to infer that fire does indeed consume:

> And as the power, by which one object produces another, is never discoverable merely from their idea, 'tis evident *cause* and *effect* are relations, of which we receive information from experience, and not from any abstract reasoning or reflexion. There is no single phaenomenon, even the most simple, which can be accounted for from the qualities of the objects, as they appear to us; or which we cou'd foresee without the help of our memory and experience.[10]

If you understand "reason" narrowly enough, you will find that Hume's argument is *sound but irrelevant* to the issue whether matters of fact can be known a priori. But if you take "reason" broadly enough to make the argument *relevant*, you will discover it to be *unsound*. Here's why.

Let *narrow reason* be a faculty limited to concepts, that is, a faculty of forming concepts and of analyzing and comparing them. Hume's argument does indeed show that narrow reason cannot discriminate among matter-of-factual propositions in a nonarbitrary way. But of course there is much more to *mind* than narrow reason. In particular, mind may encompass other cognitive faculties that exhibit partiality to certain matter-of-factual propositions, perhaps even to many of the true propositions belief in which is requisite to survival and well-being. This is no mere speculative hypothesis. We know from our experience of animals that their minds must include some such faculties of a priori factual cognition.

Let *broad reason* be a faculty coextensive with mind. To show that all factual propositions fare alike at the tribunal of broad reason would indeed be to show that "our reason, unassisted by experience, [can never] draw any inference concerning real existence and matter of fact."[11] But Hume's appeal to the conceivability of the negation of every matter-of-factual proposition reveals nothing about the capacity of broad reason innately to seize upon certain factual propositions while rejecting others.

We did not ourselves conjure up the distinction between narrow reason and broad reason, handy though it is for making our point. The honor of authorship is dubiously Hume's. You will find an ambiguity corresponding to the distinction traded on in all his arguments against the a priori knowability of causal connections. It is unfortunate that this ambiguity blinded him and a legion of later philosophers to the fallaciousness of his favorite demonstration.

Let us look again at the two bases for classifying propositions as relations of ideas or matters of fact, namely, whether their negations are conceivable and whether they are knowable through mental activity independently of experience. Whether or not a proposition like 'Fire burns' or 'The sun will rise tomorrow' is matter-of-factual will itself be an empirical matter, a matter of fact, if we adopt the second basis, that is, if we make the proposition's status a matter of the manner in which it can be known. When we give Hume's fork this basis, we discover that *his celebrated empiricist thesis*—no factual proposition can be known a priori—*becomes itself empirical*, a genuinely Humean line but perhaps not genuinely Hume's. By contrast, to choose the first basis for Hume's fork saves more of the letter of Hume's philosophy but only by cutting against its grain.

Hume was a supremely sharp and meticulous thinker. How, then, could he have been blind to the glaring defects in his empiricist doctrines that we have pointed out? We hinted at an answer earlier. So long as he ignored the a priori cognition of animals while denying to humans any specialized cognitive instincts or endowments, the two bases for his fork matched up pretty well, close enough anyway for philosophical work!

Can we defend Hume against the charge of invidious anomaly which we have leveled at his philosophical psychology, namely, that it credits animals with both generalized and specialized cognitive instincts but credits humans only with generalized ones? One tack might be to argue that specialized cognitive instincts like those found in animals are incompatible with highly developed generalized cognitive instincts of the sort found in humans, that is, that the highly developed generalized cognitive instincts would cancel or so completely dominate the specialized ones that the latter would have no cognitive role to play.

But this is not a tack on which Hume can easily sail. He delights in asserting that nature so ruthlessly dominates reason that competition between them is no contest at all. At best, reason will enjoy the upper hand only briefly, because

> there is a great difference betwixt such opinions as we form after a calm and profound reflection, and such as we embrace by a kind of instinct or natural impulse, on account of their suitableness and conformity to the mind. If these opinions become contrary, 'tis not difficult to foresee which of them will have the advantage. As long as our attention is bent upon the subject, the philosophical and study'd principle may prevail; but the moment we relax our thoughts, nature will display herself, and draw us back to our former opinion. Nay she has

> sometimes such an influence, that she can stop our progress, even in the midst of our most profound reflections, and keep us from running on with all the consequences of any philosophical opinion.[12]

For Hume, therefore, if either is to annihilate the other, the specialized cognitive instincts will cancel the generalized ones.

Here is a more promising tack. Perhaps the "anomaly," as we call it, is no embarrassment to Hume at all. Perhaps it registers a plain matter of fact recognized by Hume and taken account of in his philosophical psychology. After all, contemporary scientists and philosophers agree that human beings innately possess various generalized cognitive endowments, but they heatedly debate whether humans innately possess specialized cognitive endowments. Consider, for example, the Skinner-Chomsky-Quine controversy over innate linguistic endowments. Chomsky pleads that specialized cognitive endowments are needed to explain certain features of linguistic behavior; Quine and Skinner insist that we can explain all aspects of verbal behavior by means of the experience and generalized cognitive endowments of language-users; anything more is unneeded and undesirable.[13]

4. HUME: EMPIRICIST OR RATIONALIST?

Hume is liberal, almost profligate, in endowing human beings with cognitive instincts. For example, in addition to the inductive instinct already encountered, there is what we will call the *externalizing propensity*, the instinct that determines rustics to attribute unbroken duration to certain of their intermittent perceptions and that determines the learned to posit a universe of enduring, mind-independent objects. It is not peculiar to humans; animals too possess the externalizing propensity. Then there is the *egoizing propensity*, the instinct that determines human beings to take themselves to be substantial selves, that is, to personify certain bundles of perceptions. Animals, too, seem to possess the egoizing propensity. There may also be a *causal propensity* that determines both humans and animals to expect a cause of every event they meet with, but this conjecture is more controversial and we will not insist upon it. One stumbles upon many other cognitive propensities or instincts in Hume's philosophy, but this is not the place to enumerate them.[14]

Notice that all these cognitive instincts are generalized endowments. The beliefs that the externalizing propensity and the egoizing propensity occasion, Hume's so-called *natural beliefs*, are themselves quite general: belief in bodies, belief in external objects, belief in personal selves. Experience is required to trigger them, but no particular experiences. Whatever be the experience of a human or animal, it will come to have these natural beliefs, at least so long as its experience or train of impressions exhibits a modicum of coherency. Inductive beliefs, that is, the beliefs produced by the inductive propensity, are different. They are particular beliefs such as 'Fire burns' or 'The sun will rise tomorrow'. Not any old experiences trigger them. Unless Adam consorts frequently enough with fire, he will never acquire the belief that it burns. (At least he will not acquire this belief directly through the inductive propensity. He may come to hold this belief because of something Eve told him, thereby acquiring it indirectly through the inductive propensity, or madness or disease contracted after their expulsion from Paradise might perhaps produce it in him.)

We have already seen that Hume took Nature to implant many particular beliefs of the 'Fire burns' variety directly into animals, beliefs determined by specialized cognitive endowments or instincts. What experiences trigger these beliefs, if indeed they are triggered by experience? It would seem that no special experiences are required to trigger them; if they are triggered at all, they are triggered by any experiences whatsoever. But this cannot be the whole story. Surely the neonatal wildebeest contentedly sucking its mother's teat is not thinking about lions until sight of the charging lioness triggers its belief that lions are dangerous. Shall we say that the terrified wildebeest had the dispositional belief that lions are dangerous all along but that the awesome spectacle presented by the charging lioness triggered its occurrent belief that lions are dangerous? That is, shall we say that the beliefs produced by specialized cognitive instincts are dispositional, that they are present in the animal apart from and prior to any experience, and that relevantly appropriate particular experiences are requisite only to trigger the corresponding occurrent beliefs?

We might as well say so, for Hume's writings offer no help. You will search them in vain for the distinction between dispositional and occurrent belief, partly because eighteenth-century philosophers did not make much of it and partly because the distinction ill comports with his theory of belief as a certain feeling connected to a proposition.

Let us take stock of where we have arrived in our attempt to defend Hume. We have seen that Hume posited a number of generalized cognitive instincts common to humans and animals, that some of these generalized instincts engender very general beliefs (the so-called *natural beliefs*) in both humans and animals, that these generalized instincts generate these general beliefs independently of particular experiences, that the inductive instinct (itself a generalized instinct) gives rise to particular beliefs in both humans and animals but only when triggered by particular experiences of a relevant kind, and that animals are innately endowed with specialized cognitive instincts that engender many particular dispositional beliefs independently of experience although appropriate experiences are needed to trigger the corresponding occurrent beliefs. To save Hume, we need add only one more item to this litany, namely, that our experience of human beings gives us no reason to suppose that they are innately endowed with any specialized cognitive instincts, the ones that generate particular beliefs independently of particular experiences.

There still remains an anomaly in Hume's philosophical psychology, that is, a respect in which humans and animals do not fare alike, but it is an anomaly that does Hume's reputation more credit than injury. According to Hume, only animals possess specialized cognitive instincts, not because some unbridgeable spiritual divide separates humans from animals, nor because of any philosophical preconceptions or biases about the human or the animal mind, but because of *the brute fact that only brutes have instincts keyed to brute facts.* It might well have been different. If newborn humans behaved more like neonatal wildebeests, then we would credit ourselves, too, with specialized cognitive instincts, with a generous portion of instinctive knowledge of matters of fact served up by a benevolent Mother Nature.

So, if we understand by *empiricism* the doctrine that *no organism* can have a priori knowledge of particular matters of fact, Hume turns out to be an anti-empiricist, indeed an unbridled rationalist. But if we take empiricism to be the thesis that *human beings* do not have a priori knowledge of particular matters of fact but must acquire such knowledge on the basis of appropriate particular experiences, Hume was an empiricist for pretty convincing empirical reasons. And, for an empiricist, could there be a better kind of reason for being an empiricist?

Does Hume then deserve to be canonized as the patron saint of modern empiricism? It all depends on whom you survey. What one might call *dogmatic empiricism* refuses a priori knowledge of any fact, general as well as particular, to every organism. Dogmatic empiricists will find Hume's attribution to both animals and humans of generalized cognitive instincts, cognitive endowments productive of such general knowledge as the natural beliefs in an external world and a substantial self, altogether as noxious as the specialized cognitive instincts which he attributed to beasts alone. These dogmatists might well upbraid Hume for failing to recognize that his fork has no tine for the natural beliefs. (The negations of these propositions are conceivable and so they are factual, yet they can be known more or less independently of experience.) So, even if he had not professed to find specialized cognitive endowments in animals, Hume's treatment of the natural beliefs itself and alone constitutes a betrayal of empiricism in the eyes of these zealots. Hence, dogmatic empiricists will not hesitate to deliver their verdict loud and clear: David Hume sold out to rationalism.

But neither in philosophy nor in ordinary life should we permit fanatics to decide what is virtuous. In its widest signification, *empiricism* denominates those varieties of philosophy that take observation and experience seriously, especially scientific observation and scientific experimentation. Nothing we have said about Hume detracts from his reputation in this regard. True, his system of philosophy recognizes a great deal of a priori knowledge of matters of fact, both general and particular. But from an empiricist point of view, the saving grace is that this recognition is itself based on observation and experience of a fairly compelling sort. By grounding his innatist views about cognitive endowments thoroughly in observation and experience, that is, by making a priori knowledge an a posteriori matter, Hume earned forever the respect and admiration of nondogmatic empiricists.

A close examination of Hume's philosophy shows that the choice between empiricism and rationalism, as philosophical doctrines rather than philosophical attitudes or approaches, is not the binary a priori matter that many philosophers seem to take it to be. Hardheaded empiricists may countenance numerous faculties of a priori factual cognition without forfeiting membership in Hume's Club. Other empiricists may be more restrained in their postulation of such faculties. Still others may eschew them altogether. Nevertheless, their respective memberships in Hume's Club are secure so long as observation and experience furnish the reasons why they hold these views. However, some philosophers might, for essentially a priori reasons, repudiate all faculties of a priori factual cognition and yet suffer the humiliation of having their membership applications rejected by Hume's legatees. For it is not one's *views* about a priori factual cognition but one's *reasons* for them that make an empiricist or a rationalist out of a philosopher!

NOTES

A somewhat expanded version of this joint paper was first presented by Gerald Massey in December 1985 in the Lecture Series in the Philosophy of Science sponsored by the Center for Philosophy of Science at the University of Pittsburgh, and at the University of Syracuse in early 1986. An earlier version was delivered by him at Michigan State University in May 1985. This version of the paper was presented by him at Cleveland State University in June 1988, and jointly by both authors at the Katholieke Universiteit Leuven (Belgium) in May 1989.

1. For his own account of the dichotomy of the objects of inquiry, see David Hume, *Enquiry concerning Human Understanding* (Indianapolis: Hackett Publishing Co., 1981), IV, 1, pp. 15–20. For an excellent presentation of the received view of the dichotomy, see the account of Hume's fork given by D. G. C. MacNabb in his entry "Hume, David" in *The Encyclopedia of Philosophy*, ed. Paul Edwards (New York: Macmillan, 1972), 4: 78–80.

2. Hume, *Enquiry*, XII, 1, p. 105.

3. See W. V. O. Quine, "Carnap and Logical Truth," in *The Philosophy of Rudolf Carnap*, ed. Paul Schilpp (LaSalle, Ill.: Open Court Publishing Co., 1963), 385–406.

4. *A Treatise of Human Nature* (Oxford: Clarendon Press, 1983), I, 3, xvi, p. 176.

5. Ibid., II, 1, xii, p. 327.

6. Ibid., I, 3, xvi, pp. 176–177.

7. In "Knowing Our Place in the Animal World," in her *Postures of the Mind* (London: Methuen and Co., 1985), 139–156, Annette Baier argues that, of the well-known theories of morality, only Hume's does justice to our uncontaminated intuitions about the proper treatment of animals. In effect, by emphasizing the similarity of humans and beasts in Hume's system with respect to the properties and abilities relevant to ethics, Baier does for Hume's moral philosophy what we try here to do for his theory of knowledge.

8. *Treatise*, I, 3, xvi, pp. 178–179.

9. *Enquiry*, IX, p. 72.

10. *Treatise*, I, 3, i, pp. 69–70.

11. *Enquiry*, IV, p. 17.

12. *Treatise*, I, 4, ii, p. 214.

13. See, for example, Noam Chomsky, Review of Skinner's *Verbal Behavior*, in *Language* 35 (1959): 26–58. For a fairly up-to-date report on the status of the debate, see Chomsky, *Rules and Representations* (New York: Columbia University Press, 1980), 40 ff., 100 ff., 244 ff.

14. Concerning the externalizing and the egoizing propensities, see Hume's *Treatise*, I, 4, ii, pp. 187 ff., and I, 4, vi, pp. 253 ff., respectively. Concerning cognitive propensities beyond those mentioned in the body of this paper, see, for example, Hume's mention of what we will call the *projection propensity* in ibid., I, 3, xiv, p. 167.

FIVE

Philosophy and the Exact Sciences

Logical Positivism as a Case Study

Michael Friedman

Much of modern philosophy developed in close association with the development of the exact sciences: the sciences of mathematics, optics, astronomy, and physics. Many modern philosophers—Descartes, Leibniz, and Kant, for example—took these exact sciences as paradigmatic of objective and rational knowledge and, moreover, took this conception of objectivity and rationality as the starting point of their philosophizing. In the present century this kind of conception has been championed by the logical positivists, who took mathematics and mathematical physics as paradigmatic not only of objective and rational knowledge but of objective or "cognitive" meaningfulness as well. Accordingly, they spoke disparagingly of the "cognitive meaninglessness" of ethical discourse, religious discourse, poetic discourse, and of course traditional philosophical ("metaphysical") discourse.

With the demise of logical positivism it has become fashionable to attack the ideal of scientific objectivity and rationality which they championed as well. Taking the exact sciences of mathematics, optics, astronomy, and physics as paradigmatic of objective and rational knowledge is now dismissed as vulgar "scientism," and we are now told that the world of modern mathematical physics, for example, is just one world picture among others—with no special claim to objective validity. In particular, the systems of representation embodied in the disciplines of art, literature, social science, or religion are equally legitimate and equally "objective." When such "relativistic" sentiments are expressed even by eminent philosophers of science, they become especially compelling and must certainly give one pause.

Nevertheless, I want here to oppose this new "relativism." I agree, of course, that logical positivism is a failed philosophical movement; but I think that the reasons for this failure have been very badly misunderstood. Indeed, contemporary critics of logical positivism operate with an extremely superficial and stereotypical characterization of that movement which misses entirely both its most distinctive aims and its real intellectual problems. As a result, the true nature of our current "relativistic" predicament remains hidden from us. I hope here to shed light on this predicament through closer attention to the actual history of logical positivism and, in particular, through closer attention to the intimate relationship between that history and the parallel developments taking place in the exact sciences themselves. My story will, I hope, lead to a renewed appreciation for the philosophical importance and centrality of the exact sciences.

I

Let me begin by briefly indicating the extent to which logical positivism has been seriously misrepresented and badly misunderstood. Recent critics—such as Kuhn, Hanson, Toulmin, and Feyerabend[1]—portray the logical positivists as both naively empiricist and naively ahistorical. Science is seen as the continuous accumulation of more and more accepted facts, facts that either record direct observations or generalize from such observations by a straightforward process of induction. It follows, then, that the logical positivists must have been inspired only by what Kuhn calls "normal science" and that they must have neglected entirely the fundamentally discontinuous transitions that occur during so-called "scientific revolutions"—where the most important example of the latter, for Kuhn, is the replacement of Newtonian physics by Einstein's theory of relativity.[2] Yet a brief examination of the actual history of logical positivism reveals that one of its most fundamental inspirations is precisely this Einsteinian revolution. The early writings of the logical positivists—of Schlick, Reichenbach, and Carnap, in particular—all focus on the theory of relativity, a theory whose revolutionary impact is explicitly recognized in the course of a polemic against their philosophical predecessors.[3] Specifically, the development of non-Euclidean geometry and Einstein's theory of relativity is taken by these writers to undercut decisively the conception of space and time bequeathed to them by the Kantian philosophy; and this, in fact, is the *starting point* of their philosophizing. So whatever else may be true, these philosophers can certainly not be accused of an ahistorical neglect of scientific revolutions.

What about the charge of naive empiricism? The logical positivists are supposed to have a crudely "atomistic" conception of scientific observation and experiment: observation is nothing but immediate contact with "the given" which, as such, can take place outside the context of any scientific theory whatsoever. Yet this naively empiricist conception of observation is, on the whole, explicitly rejected by the positivists. Thus, Reichenbach, in the introduction to his 1924 book on relativity theory, writes:

> Every factual statement, even the simplest one, contains more than an immediate perceptual experience; it is already an interpretation and therefore itself a theory.... We shall have to make use of the scientific theory itself in order to interpret the indications of our measuring instruments. Thus we shall not say, "a pointer is moving," but "the electric current is increasing." The most elementary factual statement, therefore, contains some measure of theory.[4]

This clear statement of what is now called the "theory-ladenness" of observation is virtually indistinguishable from any randomly selected statement of the doctrine from Kuhn or Hanson. Carnap, in his 1928 classic of positivist thought, *The Logical Structure of the World*—a work that is often taken as paradigmatic of the logical positivists' alleged naive empiricism—explicitly opposes an "atomistic" conception of experience or "the given" and instead endorses a "holistic" conception derived from Gestalt psychology.[5] Finally, the issue is subject to a spirited debate in the pages of the positivists' official journal *Erkenntnis* in the years 1932–1935.[6] The participants in this debate are Carnap, Schlick, Neurath, and Hempel: all but Schlick agree that there are no such things as pure or theory-independent observation-sentences ("protocol-sentences"); all but Schlick explicitly renounce the project of looking for an empiricist foundation of knowledge on the immediately "given" data of experience. Once again, the "naive empiricist" label simply does not fit.

II

As indicated above, the logical positivists begin their philosophizing by reacting against the Kantian system. But what in particular are they reacting against? Kant, like the positivists, views the exact sciences of mathematics and physics—and, specifically, the application of the former to the latter embodied in the brilliantly successful mathematical physics initiated by Newton—as paradigmatic of objective and rational knowledge. His fundamental problem is to explain how such knowledge is possible: How is it possible that mathematics, in its full precision, applies to the chaotic and apparently imprecise world of sense? Kant's solution to this problem is based on his theory of space and time: specifically, on his doctrine that space and time are "pure forms of our sensible intuition." It is this Kantian doctrine, above all, that the positivists are concerned to reject; and so, to understand their position, we have to say a few words about the meaning and significance of the doctrine.

First, Kant conceives pure mathematics as itself making essential reference to space and time. Geometry involves the construction or generation of figures in space—on the "blackboard of the imagination," as it were; arithmetic involves the successive addition of unit to unit in time. This conception, which is liable to seem either quaint or ridiculous to a sophisticated modern mathematician, actually makes extremely good sense in the context of the mathematics of Kant's day. For the proof structure of Euclid's *Elements*—unlike that of modern formulations of Euclidean geometry such as Hilbert's, for example[7]—does essentially involve a definite process of spatial construction: the procedure of construction with straightedge and compass. Moreover, the new calculus that is just being developed at the time, especially in the form of Newton's so-called theory of fluxions, makes an even more essential appeal to spatiotemporal intuition—in particular, to the intuitive idea of motion. As Newton himself puts it in a well-known passage from "The Quadrature of Curves":

> Mathematical Quantities [are] *generated by a continual motion.* Lines are described, and by describing are generated ... by a continual motion of Points. Surfaces are generated by the motion of Lines, Solids by the motion of Surfaces, Angles by a rotation of their Legs, Time by a continual flux, and so in the rest.[8]

In other words, for Kant, as for Newton, the only way even to conceive or represent mathematical quantities is by an intuitive process of spatiotemporal construction.

Lying behind this Kantian conception of pure mathematics is a fundamental difference between the Aristotelian subject-predicate logic that dominated Western thought until the latter part of the nineteenth century and the modern "symbolic" or "mathematical" logic developed by Frege and Russell. For within Aristotelian subject-predicate logic it is impossible adequately to represent the idea of an infinite aggregate or structure—for example, the idea of the infinity of the points on a line or the idea of the infinite extendibility of the series of natural numbers. Since for Kant logic is subject-predicate logic, these ideas—which are of course essential to all mathematical thinking—cannot be captured or represented in an axiomatic or deductive system in the manner of modern mathematics. On the contrary, the only way even to think such ideas is via the indefinite extendibility of our spatiotemporal intuition: by the fact that there is always "room"—that is, space and time—for "one more" number in the series of natural numbers, "one more" extension of a given finite line segment, and so on . This is why, for example, Kant says in the *Critique of Pure Reason* that "I cannot represent to myself a line, however small, without drawing it in thought, that is gradually generating all its parts from a point" (B203).

In any case, it is this conception of the necessarily intuitive character of pure mathematics that enables Kant to explain how mathematics is applicable to the chaotic world of sense, to explain how mathematical physics is possible. For Kant argues that the space and time of pure intuition—the space and time underlying the constructive procedures of pure mathematics—is the very same space and time within which we perceive or experience nature through the senses. The idea is that, in the absence of a rigorous mathematical framework within which to order and interpret our sense perceptions, they would not amount to *experience* or *knowledge* in the full-blooded sense. Instead of objective experience and rational knowledge, we would be left with merely subjective association of representations. As Kant puts it in a well-known passage from the *Prolegomena to Any Future Metaphysics*, it is only the rigorous framework of mathematical physics that allows us "to spell out sensible appearances in order to read them as experience" (§30).

This Kantian explanation of the applicability of mathematics to sensible nature has one crucially important consequence. For Kant, there is only one spatiotemporal framework that can possibly play such an experience-constituting role: the spatiotemporal framework of *our* pure intuition. Indeed, as we have seen, in abstraction from our spatiotemporal intuition it is quite impossible even to think or represent spatiotemporal ideas. But our spatiotemporal intuition, for Kant, has a fixed and determinate structure: space is necessarily Euclidean, time is necessarily Newtonian (more precisely, *space-time* is necessarily Newtonian). As a result, the spatiotemporal framework underlying (Newtonian) mathematical physics is a priori fixed or determined independently of all empirical data. There can be no question of subjecting this framework to confirmation, refutation, or revision in the face of experience; on the contrary, it alone makes objective experience first possible.

Now it is precisely here, of course, that the Kantian system comes to grief. For the development of nineteenth- and twentieth-century mathematics and mathematical physics is notable for the creation of a wide variety of alternatives to the Euclidean-Newtonian framework. I need here only mention the development of non-Euclidean geometries by Gauss, Bolyai, and Lobachevsky in the first third of the nineteenth century and the very general frameworks for both Euclidean and non-Euclidean geometries later devised by Riemann and Klein. These developments culminate in Einstein's work on relativity theory in the early years of the present century, wherein the new non-Euclidean and non-Newtonian frameworks are actually applied to nature. In particular, Einstein's special theory of relativity (1905) makes use of Klein's ideas in articulating a non-Newtonian theory of time (more precisely, of space-time); Einstein's general theory of relativity (1915) draws heavily on Riemann's work in developing a very strongly non-Euclidean conception of both space and time (more precisely, of space-time).

In the face of these new developments, the Kantian conception of pure intuition can no longer be sustained. Indeed, during this same period, mathematicians are developing techniques that free pure mathematics from any dependence whatsoever on spatiotemporal intuition. Here I am referring to the so-called "rigorization" of the calculus initiated by Bolzano and Cauchy in the early eighteenth century that culminates in the "arithmetization" of analysis by Weierstrass. As a result of this work, the calculus is purged of all reference to intuitive ideas of motion and change and is instead given a purely "formal" foundation on the modern ideas of function, convergence, and limit. Moreover, what makes this "formal" conception of mathematics itself possible is the new perspective on logic and mathematical reasoning first adequately formulated by Frege. For, as suggested above, it is only this new logic that allows us to represent ideas involving infinity (which of course are especially basic to the calculus) in a "formal" or nonintuitive manner. In other words, it is the development of the new mathematical logic, above all, that makes possible the modern picture of mathematics as based on deductive systems involving strict logical inference from explicitly stated axioms—axioms which therefore stand in no need whatever of an intuitive interpretation.

III

But what about the development of logical positivism? As I have said, the logical positivists are in clear agreement with Kant about the paradigmatic status of mathematics and mathematical physics as exemplars of objective and rational knowledge. Further, the positivists also agree with Kant on the underlying reason for this privileged status. Mathematics and mathematical physics are paradigmatic of objectivity and rationaliaty because it is only by ordering, interpreting, and structuring our sensory perceptions within a rigorous mathematical framework that we can first "objectify" them—that is, transform them from mere *appearance* into objective *experience*. In other words, it is mathematical physics alone that makes possible a full-blooded notion of objective knowledge in the first place. Thus, for example, Schlick in his *General Theory of Knowledge* draws a sharp distinction between knowledge or cognition (*erkennen*) and acquaintance with (*kennen*) or experience of (*erleben*) the immediately given. The latter, since it is momentary or "atomistic," cannot possibly yield knowledge. On the contrary, knowledge is possible only when we embed such momentary perceptions within a rigorous *system* of interconnected judgments of which the systems developed by mathematical physics are paradigmatic.[9] Similar themes are dominant in the early writings of the other logical positivists.[10]

It should be clear, on the one hand, how far we are from a naively empiricist conception of knowledge and experience. In particular, the "theory-ladenness" of observation is rigorously articulated and explicitly defended—and defended for fundamentally Kantian reasons. Yet, on the other hand, it is also clear that the Kantian system as a whole is no longer tenable. In particular, Kant's doctrine of pure intuition has collapsed completely. Pure mathematics no longer requires a basis in spatiotemporal construction but can instead proceed purely "formally" via strict logical deduction within an axiomatic system. As a result, pure mathematics has no intrinsic connection whatever with either spatiotemporal intuition or sense experience, and it is no longer possible to maintain that *any* mathematical theory has a necessary relation to our experience of nature. Similarly, there is no longer a single, privileged spatiotemporal framework—the Euclidean-Newtonian framework—lying at the basis of mathematical physics. Many such frameworks are now possible, and some of them have been already successfully applied to nature in Einstein's theory of relativity.

This situation constitutes the philosophical context within which logical positivism develops. The attempt to preserve a basically Kantian conception of knowledge and experience in the face of the collapse of Kant's doctrine of pure intuition creates fundamental, and ultimately unresolved, intellectual tensions. The underlying problem can perhaps be expressed as follows. We wish to follow Kant in insisting upon the need for a general theoretical framework in order to confer objectivity and rationality on our sense experience. We also wish to follow Kant in maintaining the privileged position of mathematics and mathematical physics. Yet there is no longer a single spatiotemporal framework that alone can perform this "objectifying" function. On the contrary, each of the many possible frameworks appears to exemplify its own particular standards of objectivity and rationality. Are we not forced, therefore, into a position of epistemic and conceptual "relativism" which undermines the very notions of objectivity and rationality that we are trying so hard to preserve?

This problem can be best appreciated, I think, if we juxtapose the philosophical efforts of the logical positivists with the so-called Marburg Neo-Kantianism of Cohen, Natorp, and especially Cassirer. These thinkers agree with the logical positivists in their assessment of the significance of Kant's philosophical achievement: Kant's achievement consists precisely in clearly recognizing and articulating the "objectifying" function of mathematics and mathematical physics. These thinkers—especially Cassirer—also agree with the logical positivists that Kant's doctrine of pure spatiotemporal intuition can no longer be maintained in the context of modern mathematics and mathematical physics.[11] But from these two ideas Cassirer draws explicitly "relativistic" conclusions: a doctrine which he calls "logical idealism." Since there is no longer a single, privileged framework for objective and rational thought, mathematical-physical thinking as such provides only one such framework among others. Thus, art, religion, myth, and metaphysics provide equally good rational frameworks—or what Cassirer calls "symbolic forms"—for each supplies its own characteristic standards of truth and hence objectivity.

The logical positivists refer to this "relativistic" doctrine as the Coherence Theory of Truth, for it views coherence and consistency within a particular symbolic framework as sufficient for objective truth—truth *relative to that framework*, of course—and supplies no means whatever for adjudicating disputes between such frameworks. Since the positivists wish to follow Kant in maintaining the privileged status of mathematics and mathematical physics, this doctrine is anathema to them; and they therefore do everything they can to distance themselves from it. Yet, at the same time, this proves to be no easy task; for, as we have seen, the positivists agree completely with the Marburg School on their underlying premises. This is the basis for the ensuing dialectic.

The problem of adjudicating between competing theoretical frameworks arises for the logical positivists in their earliest writings on relativity theory—most clearly, perhaps, in Schlick's 1915 paper on relativity theory. The trouble begins when Schlick explicitly acknowledges that there are alternative theories equally capable of accounting for the data that are explained by Einstein's new theory (e.g., and especially, the famous Michelson-Morley experiment of 1887). There is Einstein's theory itself, of course, which explains the anomalous data by radically revising the classical conceptions of space and time. But there is also the so-called "aether" theory of Lorentz, Fitzgerald, and Poincaré, which explains the very same data by retaining the classical conceptions of space and time and invoking compensatory disturbances—contractions and retardations—in the rods and clocks we use to measure space and time. The two theories lead to all the same empirical predictions—they are "empirically equivalent"; and so the choice between them is radically underdetermined by all the empirical facts. This kind of "theoretical underdetermination" is a dramatically new phenomenon in the history of science which, for example, is simply not possible in the context of the Newtonian physics of Kant's day.[12]

How, then, can we adjudicate the dispute between the two theories? How, in particular, can we rationalize our preference for the Einsteinian framework? In 1915 Schlick frankly admits that he has no satisfactory answer. It appears, to be sure, that Einstein's theory is "simpler" and less "ad hoc" than the competing "aether" theory. Yet we have no clear account of what such "simplicity" really comes to nor, more importantly, any assurance that "simplicity"—whatever it may be—is a reliable guide to truth. Why in the world should nature respect *our*—merely subjective—preference for "simplicity"? Once again, therefore, the objectivity of physical theory is subject to doubt.

Throughout the 1920s Schlick and the other logical positivists—Reichenbach, in particular—attempt to solve this epistemological problem by means of the doctrine of "conventionalism" which they derive from Poincaré.[13] The idea here is that two theories agreeing on all empirical data—two theories such as relativity theory and the "aether" theory that truly are "empirically equivalent"—are not really two *conflicting* theories at all. Their disagreement is only apparent, and so there is no need rationally to adjudicate the choice between them. The situation is precisely analogous, in fact, to two different coordinate systems or two different systems of units (the metric system and the English system, say). Rather than a substantive disagreement over objective truth, we are faced with a merely pragmatic question of convenience. In this sense, the choice is a purely conventional one.

Now this doctine, when consistently thought through, does in fact lead to a kind of radical empiricism. Since we wish to hold that two "empirically equivalent" theories are therefore completely equivalent descriptions of the same objective facts, we are committed to the view that the empirical facts—that is, the observable facts—are all the objective facts there are. We are committed to the view that the entire content or meaning of a scientific theory is lodged in its consequences for actual and possible observations. And, in fact, around 1930 this view hardens into a kind of dogma for the logical positivists in the form of the notorious Verifiability Principle.[14] The "cognitive meaning" of all discourse is declared to consist in its implications for actual and possible observations; and this principle is ruthlessly wielded both to solve the problem of underdetermined theory choice and to question the "cognitive meaningfulness" of all nonscientific discourse—of art, religion, myth, and metaphysics in particular. In this way, the positivists hope to divorce themselves from the "relativistic" and "idealistic" doctrines of the Marburg School once and for all.

Yet this kind of radical empiricism could not be consistently sustained. In the first place, it proves to be impossible to articulate a conception of "cognitive meaning" that can support the Verifiability Principle. In particular, it proves to be impossible to view advanced theories such as Einstein's theory of relativity as mere summaries of actual and possible observations; and this fact is explicitly acknowledged, with characteristic honesty and rigor, by the positivists themselves.[15] Second, and perhaps even more fundamentally, the notions of observation and empirical fact are subject to more weight than they can possibly bear. For, given the Neo-Kantian context of positivist thought, theory is supposed to give meaning to observation rather than the other way around, and an empiricist foundation for objective knowledge on supposedly pure or "theory-neutral" observation reports is quite impossible. As I indicated above, this fact is also explicitly acknowledged in the pages of the positivists' official journal *Erkenntnis* in the years 1932–1935,[16] wherein all parties except Schlick explicitly reject an empiricist foundation for knowledge—and reject such a foundation precisely on the grounds of the "theory-ladenness" of all observation. (Schlick, by contrast, perceptively but vainly warns that such a conception leads inevitably to the Coherence Theory of Truth.)

At this juncture, Carnap, who is clearly the deepest and most rigorous of the logical positivists, writes perhaps his greatest work: *The Logical Syntax of Language*. In this book the empiricist tendencies of logical positivism shrink to the point of vanishing, and Carnap instead rigorously articulates an explicitly "relativistic" viewpoint that is very close indeed to the Marburg School, on the one hand, and to much contemporary "relativism," on the other. Carnap's "relativistic" attitude is encapsulated in his famous Principle of Tolerance:

> *In logic, there are no morals.* Everyone is at liberty to build up his own logic, i.e., his own form of language, as he wishes. All that is required of him is that, if he wishes to discuss it, he must state his methods clearly, and give syntactical rules instead of philosophical arguments.[17]

But what does this principle really say?

First, Carnap views rules of logic—and hence criteria for meaningfulness and truth—as embodied in one or another language system or linguistic framework. Moreover, many such systems—many such linguistic frameworks—are possible, and all are equally legitimate. Indeed, since criteria for meaningfulness and truth—and hence criteria for objective knowledge—are internal to particular linguistic frameworks, there can be no question whatever of rationally adjudicating disputes between such frameworks. The only substantive questions are those that can be formulated within a given framework, and the choice of one framework rather than another—as a choice external to the frameworks under consideration—can only be made on the basis of pragmatic criteria of convenience. In other words, disputes within a single framework (internal questions) can be adjudicated by rational and objective criteria relative to that framework; disputes between different frameworks (external questions) cannot be so adjudicated.[18]

Second, however, Carnap sees the articulation and elaboration of the logical rules definitive of this or that linguistic framework as taking place within a definite and precise metadiscipline—a discipline he calls logical syntax.[19] Building on earlier logical-mathematical work of Hilbert and Gödel, Carnap views this discipline as itself a branch of pure mathematics. Indeed, in light of Gödel's so-called "arithmetization of syntax," this discipline can be viewed as a particularly neutral and uncontroversial branch of mathematics—a fragment of elementary arithmetic. Yet within this neutral and uncontroversial metadiscipline we can still describe the linguistic rules or logical syntax of much stronger and more controversial frameworks. In particular, given any such linguistic framework, we can, from the standpoint of our syntactic metadiscipline, draw a clear and precise distinction between those sentences definitive of the rules of that framework—the so-called logical or *analytic* sentences—and those sentences expressing substantive truths formulated within that framework—the so-called factual or *synthetic* sentences. We thereby give clear and precise content to the distinction between external and internal questions. Moreover, although the notion of truth *simpliciter* has indeed been relativized, the resulting notion of true-in-a-given-framework is "absolute." For this latter notion can itself be precisely and rigorously characterized within the *framework-neutral* metadiscipline of logical syntax. In this way, Carnap hopes to avoid the tendency toward vicious circularity inherent in the Coherence Theory of Truth; and it is here, rather than in any radical empiricism, that Carnap makes his last stand against the Marburg School.

More specifically, Carnap sets himself apart from the Marburg School in continuing to give pride of place to the exact sciences; and he does this, in fact, in two distinct yet interrelated ways. On the one hand, Carnap is able to show that, in an appropriately designed linguistic framework, the sentences of classical mathematics—and even some of the basic principles of classical physics such as physical geometry—turn out to be *analytic* truths in the above sense.

These sentences and principles are therefore constitutive of objectivity and rationality relative to this given framework, and Carnap has thus captured an important part of the traditional Kantian conception of the sciences. On the other hand, Carnap's metadiscipline of logical syntax itself takes place within the most exact of the exact sciences—namely, elementary arithmetic. This gives Carnap a fixed and exact place to stand from which he can articulate his thoroughgoing "relativism"—that is, his distinction between sentences that are analytic relative to a given framework and those that are synthetic, and thus his relativized notion of true-in-a-given-framework.

Alas, however, it was not meant to be. For it turns out to be impossible, in most cases of interest, to characterize even this relativized notion of true-in-a-given-framework in such an "absolute" or framework-neutral way. In particular, it is a consequence of Gödel's celebrated Incompleteness Theorem (1931) that, for any linguistic framework embodying a significant portion of classical mathematics, such a characterization can only be drawn within a still richer and more controversial framework.[20] The metadiscipline of logical syntax is in no way framework-neutral, and Carnap's dream of a truly objective and impartial notion of rationality—albeit one that is considerably weakened and explicitly relativized—is not to be had. As a result, we must question the objectivity and meaningfulness of the very distinction that motivates Carnap's program in the first place: the distinction between change of framework (or external questions), on the one hand, and change of substantive theory within a framework (or internal questions), on the other. In other words, the general notion of linguistic or theoretical framework is itself thrown into doubt.

IV

My story has been a story of failure. In particular, the positivists have failed to develop an adequate alternative to the Coherence Theory of Truth: the explicitly "relativistic" doctrines of the Marburg School. Does it follow that this Marburg "relativism" survives intact and, accordingly, that our contemporary "relativist" tendencies are on the right track after all? I think not. The underlying idea of such "relativism," I take it, is that our ordinary notion of truth *simpliciter* is to be replaced with a relativized notion of true-in-a-given-framework or true-in-a-given-symbolic-form. But if this move is to have any point, the notion of true-in-a-given-framework should have a different status from our old "naive" notion of truth *simpliciter*. Specifically, this new notion should not require further relativization; it should itself be "absolute." Compare the situation in relativity theory—which, for Cassirer at any rate, was always the model for his relativizing move. Relativity theory, as is well known, replaces the Newtonian notion of absolute simultaneity with a relativized notion of simultaneous-relative-to-a-given-inertial-frame. But this latter notion is itself absolute—once we specify the relevant frame.

Carnap's *Logical Syntax*, as I understand it, is an attempt to make clear sense of just this kind of relativizing move. In particular, it is an attempt to articulate a neutral metaperspective—logical syntax—from which we can survey all possible linguistic frameworks and within which we can develop a precise notion of true-relative-to-a-framework. This notion, since it is defined within our *framework-neutral* metaperspective, will itself have the desired "absolute" status. (This is what I had in mind when I said that Carnap hopes to avoid the tendency toward vicious circularity inherent in the Coherence Theory of Truth.) Gödel's Theorem then undermines this Carnapian project by showing that there is no such framework-neutral metaperspective. Yet it certainly does not follow that "relativism" emerges triumphant. On the contrary, the one possible standpoint from which we could hope coherently to articulate such a thoroughgoing "relativism" has been pulled out from beneath our feet.

Nor does it follow that the exact sciences have been in any way diminished in philosophical importance or centrality. Here we should remember that Gödel's Theorem is itself a theorem of elementary arithmetic. Under the Gödel numbering the theorem says that a certain number—the Gödel number of Gödel's unprovable sentence—is *not* in a certain set of numbers—the set of Gödel numbers of provable formulas. Moreover, this latter set of numbers can itself be defined in the language of elementary arithmetic—that is, in terms, ultimately, of addition and multiplication. In these terms, Gödel's Theorem merely expresses a rather arcane fact of elementary arithmetic: if you subject numbers with certain properties to certain arithmetical operations (a sequence of additions and multiplications in a definite order), you do not get a certain other number. The point is that Gödel's Theorem is itself as exact as exact can be: in principle, it is a proposition of the same kind as $2 + 2 = 4$.

Now this last result of the exact sciences has, I have argued, the most profound consequences for our philosophical understanding of the exact sciences. In particular, it shows that the logical positivists' attempt to give a Neo-Kantian explanation for the special status of the exact sciences cannot succeed; for it shows that the neutral metaperspective that alone could support their attempted explanation does not exist. As a result, we cannot, from a peculiarly philosophical vantage point—from a transcendental vantage point, as it were—explain the special status of the exact sciences at all. Yet it does not follow that the exact sciences do not have this special status. On the contrary, in precisely this failure of the positivist program the exact sciences have shown their special status in a completely unexpected and unprecedented way. We—as philosophers—cannot answer a question we have long desired to answer. But we now know exactly why we cannot answer it, and we know this on the basis of the most exact truths of elementary arithmetic. In other words, the exact sciences have themselves shown, and have shown exactly, the *limits* of our philosophical knowledge.[21] Such precise knowledge of the limits of our knowledge must inevitably strike a philosopher with Kantian sympathies as just the kind of defense of objectivity and rationality toward which the modern philosophical tradition has been aiming all along.

NOTES

Earlier versions of this paper were presented at the University of Wisconsin at Milwaukee, the University of Virginia, the University of Pittsburgh, Boston University, the University of Western Ontario, and the Ohio State University. I would like to thank Philip Catton, Graciela De Pierris, Cora Diamond, Arthur Fine, Bernard Goldstein, Peter Heath, William Howard, Richard Kraut, Thomas Kuhn, Penelope Maddy, Richard Rorty, Wesley Salmon, Robert Schwartz, and Matti Sintonen.

1. I should point out that Feyerabend presents a much more historically nuanced account of the logical positivists than do the other recent critics. See, in particular, his discussion of the positivists' "pragmatic theory of observation" (arising during the "protocol-sentence" debate in 1932–1935) in §1 of "Explanation, Reduction, and Empiricism," in *Scientific Explanation, Space, and Time*, ed. H. Feigl and G. Maxwell, Minnesota Studies in the Philosophy of Science, vol. 3 (Minneapolis, 1962). Yet even Feyerabend errs, it seems to me, in portraying the positivists as naive empiricists in the periods before and after the "protocol-sentence" debate.

2. See, for example, T. Kuhn, *The Structure of Scientific Revolutions* (Chicago, 1962), 97–102.

3. See M. Schlick, "Die philosophische Bedeutung des Relativitätsprinzips," *Zeit. für Phil. und phil. Kritik* 159 (1915): 129–175, translation by P. Heath in Moritz Schlick, *Philosophical Papers*, ed. H. Mulder and B. van de Velde-Schlick, vol. 1 (Dordrecht, 1978); M. Schlick, *Raum und Zeit in der gegenwärtigen Physik* (Berlin, 1917), translation by H. Brose in Schlick, *Philosophical Papers*; H. Reichenbach, *Relativitätstheorie und Erkenntnis Apriori* (Berlin, 1920), translation by M. Reichenbach (Berkeley and Los Angeles: University of California Press, 1965); H. Reichenbach, *Axiomatik der relativistischen Raum-Zeit-Lehre* (Vieweg, 1924), translation by M. Reichenbach (Berkeley and Los Angeles: University of California Press, 1969); M. Reichenbach, *Philosophie der Raum-Zeit-Lehre* (Berlin, 1928), translation by M. Reichenbach and J. Freund (New York, 1958); R. Carnap, *Der Raum: Ein Beitrag zur Wissenschaftslehre* Kant-Studien Ergänzungsheft, no. 56 (Berlin, 1922).

4. P. 5 of the English translation.

5. See R. Carnap, *Der logische Aufbau der Welt* (Berlin, 1928), §§67f., translation by R. George (Berkeley and Los Angeles: University of California Press, 1967).

6. See O. Neurath, "Protokollsätze," *Erkenntnis* 3 (1932): 204–214, translation by R. Cohen and M. Neurath in Otto Neurath, *Philosophical Papers* 1913–1946, ed. R. Cohen and M. Neurath (Dordrecht, 1983); R. Carnap, "Ueber Protokollsätze," *Erkenntnis* 3 (1932): 215–228, translation by R. Creath and R. Nollan in *Noûs* 21 (1987): 457–470; M. Schlick, "Ueber das Fundament der Erkenntnis," *Erkenntnis* 4 (1934): 79–99, translation by P. Heath in Schlick, *Philosophical Papers*, vol. 2; C. Hempel, "On the Logical Positivists' Theory of Truth," *Analysis* 2 (1935): 49–59.

7. D. Hilbert, *Grundlagen der Geometrie* (Leipzig, 1899), translation by L. Unger (La Salle, Ill., 1971).

8. In *Mathematical Works of Isaac Newton*, ed. D. Whiteside vol. 1 (New York, 1964), 1: 141.

9. See M. Schlick, *Allgemeine Erkenntnislehre* (Berlin, 1918), §§3–12, translation by A. Blumberg (New York, 1974).

10. See especially Reichenbach's 1920 book on relativity theory and Carnap's *Aufbau*.

11. See E. Cassirer, "Kant und die moderne Mathematik," *Kant-Studien* 12 (1907): 1–49; *Substanzbegriff und Funktionsbegriff* (Berlin, 1910); *Zur Einsteinschen Relativitätstheorie* (Berlin, 1920); latter two translated together by W. Swabey and M. Swabey (New York, 1953).

12. It might appear obvious that such "theoretical underdetermination" is not at all a new phenomenon in the history of science and, in fact, that even pre-Newtonian theories are subject to it: consider, for example, the choice between Ptolemaic and Copernican astronomy. It is precisely here, however, that the Kantian system (together with Newtonian physics) shows its greatest strength. In order for there to be an issue between Ptolemy and Copernicus, we need first to give clear sense to the notion of true or absolute motion; and how, independently of Newtonian physics itself, can this possibly be done? For Kant, there is no preexisting absolute space nor absolute motion. Newton's Laws of Motion, rather than asserting facts, as it were, about absolute motion, instead serve to make the idea of such motion first possible. More precisely, Newton's laws of motion, as employed in the argument for Universal Gravitation of *Principia*, Book III, serve to pick out a privileged frame of reference—the center-of-mass frame of the solar system—relative to which the notion of true or absolute motion is first defined. And, since this center-of-mass frame turns out to be centered very close to the center of the sun, the Copernican system is closer to the truth. Thus, in the context of the only procedure we possess for giving objective meaning to the idea of true or absolute motion in the first place—Newton's procedure—the Ptolemaic system is definitively ruled out. Moreover, for Kant, any possibility of "theoretical underdetermination" here is eliminated by the fact that Euclidean geometry and Newton's laws of motion (together with certain properties of gravitation as a "fundamental force") are themselves counted as a priori: there can be no question of subjecting *them* to refutation or revision in the light of experience. What is then dramatically new about relativity theory, in this context, is that it subjects just these features of Newtonian physics to empirical revision. For more details on Kant's reading of Newton see M. Friedman, "The Metaphysical Foundations of Newtonian Science," in *Kant's Philosophy of Physical Science*, ed. R. Butts (Dordrecht, 1986).

13. See especially H. Poincaré, *La science et l'hypothèse* (Paris, 1902), translation by W. Greenstreet (New York, 1915).

14. See especially M. Schlick, "Positivismus und Realismus," *Erkenntnis* 3 (1932): 1–31, translation by P. Heath in Schlick, *Philosophical Papers*; R. Carnap, *Scheinprobleme in der Philosophie* (Berlin, 1928), translation by R. George (Berkeley and Los Angeles: University of California Press, 1967).

15. See R. Carnap, "Testability and Meaning," *Philosophy of Science* 3 (1936) and 4 (1937); C. Hempel, "Problems and Changes in the Empiricist Criterion of Meaning," *Revue intern. de phil.* 11 (1951): 41–63.

16. See n. 6 above.

17. R. Carnap, *Logische Syntax der Sprache* (Vienna, 1934), §17, translation by A. Smeaton (London, 1937).

18. The internal/external distinction is explicitly formulated in R. Carnap, "Empiricism, Semantics, and Ontology," *Revue intern. de phil.* 4 (1950): 20–40.

19. As Carnap explicitly acknowledges, his conception of logical syntax is inspired by, and at the same time radically transforms, the ideas of Wittgenstein's *Tractatus Logico-Philosophicus* (with translation by C. Ogden [London, 1922]).

20. In brief, the problem arises in the following way. Carnap's linguistic frameworks are individuated by their "formation rules" (their grammar) and their "L-rules" or analytic sentences—for these latter, as we have seen, are definitive of the logical rules of the framework. These L-rules or analytic sentences are in turn characterized on the basis of a distinction between "logical" and "descriptive" expressions. This, in fact, is how logical rules like the sentences of arithmetic are distinguished from "physical" rules like Maxwell's equations: both are provable in an appropriate framework for classical physics, but the former contain only logical expressions essentially (*Logical Syntax*, §51). But how do we distinguish logical signs like the primitive signs of arithmetic from descriptive signs like the electromagnetic field functor? The logical signs are those signs such that *every* sentence built up from them alone is either provable or refutable in the given framework. By contrast, in the case of descriptive signs like the electromagnetic field functor, there will be *some* sentences—sentences ascribing particular values at particular space-time points to the electromagnetic field, for example—that are not either provable or refutable in the given framework: their truth can be determined only a posteriori, as it were (*Logical Syntax*, §50). It is clear, however, that this distinction requires a *nonrecursive* (in fact, nonarithmetical) consequence relation for the case of classical elementary arithmetic, and it follows that it cannot be drawn within the neutral (primitive recursive) metaperspective of logical syntax. For more details concerning the relevance of Gödel's Theorem to the program of *Logical Syntax* see M. Friedman, "Logical Truth and Analyticity in Carnap's *Logical Syntax of Language*," in *Essays in the History and Philosophy of Mathematics*, ed. W. Aspray and P. Kitcher (Minneapolis, 1987).

21. Here I am particularly indebted to conversations with Graciela De Pierris.

SIX

Language and Interpretation

Philosophical Reflections and Empirical Inquiry

Noam Chomsky

In the philosophical literature of the past forty years, there have been several influential currents that seem to me problematic in important, even essential, respects. I have in mind, in the first place, approaches that take as their point of departure certain conceptions of how language is studied, or should be studied, by the empirical scientist—or the "field linguist," to use the terms of Quine's familiar paradigm. One can include here Quine,* Donald Davidson, and others who have moved toward a form of pragmatism and "naturalized epistemology," incorporating questions thought to be of philosophical significance within their conception of empirical science, but also others who adopt a different starting point: Michael Dummett, and many of those influenced by Wittgenstein and ordinary language philosophy, for example.

To illustrate the flavor of these ideas, take some comments of Richard Rorty in his article in the Davidson volume.[1] He writes that "Davidson is surely right that Quine 'saved philosophy of language as a serious subject' by getting rid of the analytic-synthetic distinction. Quine's best argument for doing so was that the distinction is of no use to the field linguist."

As for the "field linguist," all that he "has to go on is his observation of the way in which linguistic is aligned with non-linguistic behavior in the course of the native's interaction with his environment, an interaction which [the linguist] takes to be guided by rules of action," specifically, the "regulative principle" that "most of the native's rules are the same as ours, which is to say that most of them are true" ("rules" here apparently referring to beliefs). We need not be concerned about "a conceptual scheme, a way of viewing things, a perspective (or . . . a language, or a cultural tradition)," because "the field linguist does not need them," so "therefore philosophy does not need them either." Quine and Davidson agree that "a theory of meaning for a language is what comes out of empirical research into linguistic behavior," when this is properly pursued, in accord with the doctrines of "holism and behaviorism."

This line of thought, Rorty continues, leads to a form of pragmatism that he espouses and attributes to James and Davidson, including crucially the denial of any relations of "'being made true' which hold between beliefs and the world." Rather, "We understand all there is to know about the relation of beliefs to the world when we understand their causal relations with the world."

Putting aside the conclusions that Rorty reaches,[2] consider his assumptions. If the best argument for dispensing with the analytic-synthetic distinction is that it is of no use to the field linguist, then virtually everyone who actually works in descriptive semantics, or ever has, must be seriously in error, since such work is shot through with assumptions about connections of meaning, which will (in particular) induce examples of the analytic-synthetic distinction. One would be hard put to find studies of language that do not assign structures and describe the meaning of 'kill', 'so', and so on, in such a way that there is a qualitative distinction, determined by the language itself, between the sentences 'John killed Bill, so Bill is dead' and 'John killed Bill, so John is dead'. Or to take another case, it would be difficult to find a study of referential dependence in natural language that does not conclude that the language itself determines that the relation holds between 'Mary' and 'herself' in

(1) Mary expects to feed herself

but not when the same expression is embedded in the context 'I wonder who—,' yielding

(2) I wonder who Mary expects to feed herself

Such syntactic-semantic properties will induce cases of the analytic-synthetic distinction; thus they will yield a distinction between 'Mary expects to feed herself, so Mary expects to feed *Mary*' (analytic, with the three occurrences of 'Mary' taken to be coreferential) and 'I wonder who Mary expects to feed herself, so I wonder who Mary expects to feed *Mary*' (not analytic, under the same interpretation). But what Quine is alleged to have demonstrated goes beyond the matter of analyticity, reaching to the conclusion that there are no semantic connections that can be attributed to the language faculty itself as distinct from our general systems of belief; elsewhere, Rorty takes this to be one of the two fundamental discoveries that undermine a traditional world picture.

As is well known, Quine and others have offered their own account of these distinctions. I will return to these proposals and how they might be evaluated in accordance with the canons of inquiry of the natural sciences, but will merely note here that reference to "the field linguist" can surely not be understood as reference to those who actually do linguistic work. Rather, it has a normative character, referring to the way such work ought to be done, keeping to the conditions of "holism and behaviorism" legislated by the philosopher but not followed in practice by the errant scientist. While it might turn out on investigation that this stance is justifiable, those with an appreciation of the history of the discipline might be pardoned some initial skepticism.

To select another example to illustrate the flavor of these discussions, consider Dummett's argument in the same volume that the "fundamental sense" in which we must understand the concept of language is the sense in which Dutch and German are different languages (he gives a different example, but the point is the same), each of them a particular social practice "in which people engage," a practice that "is learned from others and is constituted by rules which it is part of social custom to follow." Thus Dutch and German exist in this "fundamental sense," "independently of any particular speakers"; every individual speaker "has" such a language, but typically has only a "partial, and partially erroneous, grasp of the language." The intended import of Dummett's proposal is far-reaching. He is telling us what notion of "language" is essential for philosophical purposes, for the theory of meaning in particular; and also, as he makes clear, it is this concept of language that is in his view required for explaining the use of language, specifically, for understanding "what long-range theory someone brings to a first linguistic encounter with another." It is, therefore, a proposal that bears on the empirical study of language, of people, of what they know and what they do. Perhaps he means to allow that linguists may follow some different course for their special concerns, but clearly these proposals bear on the proper practice in empirical inquiry into language and its use.

Here the paradoxical flavor is of a somewhat different order. It lies in the conflict between Dummett's proposal and the commonplace assumption in empirical practice that there is no useful general sense in which we can characterize "language" so that Dutch and German are two distinct "languages," which people know only "partially" and "erroneously." This is so whether we are studying language structure, psycholinguistics, language change, typology, problems of communication, or whatever. People who live near the Dutch border can communicate quite well with those living on the German side, but they speak different languages in accordance with the sense of the term that Dummett argues is "fundamental"; and those on the German side of the border, with their "partial knowledge" of the language German, may understand nothing spoken by people living in some other region, who "have" a different "partial knowledge" of the language German in Dummett's sense. It is for such reasons as these that no such concept plays any role in empirical inquiry into language or psychology. Such terms as 'English' and 'Japanese' are used for general expository discourse, but with the understanding that their commonsense usage, which Dummett rather uncritically adopts, is to be abandoned when we turn to actual study of language, behavior, and communication.[3] If Dummett's concept is indeed fundamental for empirical inquiry and for philosophical purposes, then either philosophy, or the empirical study of language and behavior, or both, are in deep trouble, for reasons that should be familiar. The concept of language that Dummett takes to be essential involves complex and obscure sociopolitical, historical, cultural, and normative-teleological elements, which may be of some interest for the sociology of identification within various social and political communities and the study of authority structure, but which plainly lie far beyond any useful inquiry into the nature of language or the psychology of users of language.

To take one example, consider the study of language acquisition. In ordinary usage, we say that a child of five and a foreign adult are on their way toward acquiring English, but we have no way to designate whatever it is that they "have." The child, in the normal course of events, will come to "have" English (at least partially and erroneously), though the foreigner probably will not. But if all adults were suddenly to die and children were somehow to survive, then whatever it is they are speaking would be a human language, though one that does not now exist. Ordinary usage provides no useful way to describe any of this, since it involves too many disparate and obscure concerns and interests. This is one reason why the concept of language that Dummett adopts is useless for actual inquiry. This matter is of some importance when we consider the reliance on notions of "misuse of language," "community norms," "social practice," and "rule following" that are often adopted as if they are sufficiently clear; they are not.[4]

In this connection, it is perhaps worthwhile to recall some further truisms; in rational inquiry, in the natural sciences or elsewhere, there is no such subject as "the study of everything." Thus it is no part of physics to determine exactly how a particular body moves under the influence of every particle or force in the universe, with possible human intervention, and so on. This is not a topic. Rather, in rational inquiry we idealize to selected domains in such a way (we hope) as to permit us to discover crucial features of the world. Data and observations, in the sciences, have an instrumental character; they are of no particular interest in themselves, but only insofar as they constitute evidence that permits one to determine fundamental features of the real world, within a course of inquiry that is invariably undertaken under sharp idealizations, often implicit and based on common understanding, but always present. The study of "language" in Dummett's sense verges on "the study of everything" and is therefore not a useful topic of inquiry, though one might hope, perhaps, to build up to a study of aspects of such questions in terms of what comes to be understood about particular components of this hopeless amalgam.

The conception of language as a "social practice" that Dummett and others propose raises further questions, as becomes clear when it is applied to concrete examples. Consider again the examples (1) and (2):

(1) Mary expects to feed herself

(2) I wonder who Mary expects to feed herself

In (1), 'feed herself' is taken to be predicated of Mary, but in (2) it is predicated of some (female) person distinct from Mary; thus from (2) it follows that I wonder which female person Mary expects to feed that very person, but not that I wonder which person Mary expects to feed Mary herself. The example raises many pertinent questions, among them, how we know these facts. The answer seems to be that the initial state of the shared language faculty incorporates certain principles concerning referential dependence (Binding Theory), and when certain options left undetermined in the initial state are fixed by elementary experience, then we have no more choice as to how to interpret (1) and (2) than we have about whether to perceive something as a red triangle or as a person. Social custom appears to have nothing to do with the matter in such cases, though early experience helps set certain details of the invariant, biologically determined mechanisms of the mind/brain. The same seems to be true rather generally. Taken literally at least, the proposals of Dummett and others concerning "social practice" appear to be false, as a matter of empirical fact. At the very least, some argument would be required to show why they should be considered seriously.

If language is construed as a social practice in the manner of these discussions, then it is tempting to understand knowledge of language as the learned ability to engage in such practices, as Dummett suggests, or more generally, as an ability that can be exercised by speaking, understanding, reading, talking to oneself, and so on: "to know a language just is to have the ability to do these and similar things" (Anthony Kenny).[5] The temptation is reinforced by a common construal of knowledge more generally as a kind of ability. This view contrasts with the conception of a language as a generative procedure that assigns structural descriptions to linguistic expressions, knowledge of language being the internal representation of such a procedure in the brain (in the mind, as we may say when speaking about the brain at a certain level of abstraction). From this point of view, ability to use one's language (to put one's knowledge to use) is sharply distinguished from having such knowledge. The latter conception has two primary virtues: (1) it seems to be the right way to approach the study of human knowledge, knowledge of language in particular, within the general framework of the natural sciences, and it has proven a highly productive approach; (2) it is in accord with normal preanalytic usage, a secondary but not entirely insignificant matter. In contrast, the approach in terms of practical ability has proven entirely unproductive and can be sustained only by understanding "ability" in a way that departs radically from ordinary usage.

To see why this is so, suppose that Jones, a speaker of some variety of what we call "English" in informal usage, improves his ability to speak his language by taking a public-speaking course, or loses this ability because of an injury or disease, then recovering that ability, say, with a drug. Note that a speaker of Japanese, under the same circumstances, would recover *Japanese*, not English, with the same drug, and plainly recovery in such cases differs radically from acquisition; a child could not acquire English or Japanese without any evidence. In all such cases, something remains constant, some property K, while ability to speak, understand, and so on, varies. In ordinary usage, we say that K is knowledge of language; thus Jones's knowledge remained constant while his ability to put his knowledge to use improved, declined, recovered, and so on. The account in terms of internal representation of a generative procedure accords with informal usage in this case. Note further that other evidence (say, from autopsy, were enough known about the brain sciences) might lead us to conclude that Smith, who never recovered English, not having taken the drug, nevertheless retained his knowledge of English intact after having completely lost his ability to speak and understand.[6]

If knowledge is ability, then the property K must be a kind of ability, though plainly not ability in the quite useful normal sense of the word, since ability varied while K remained constant. We must therefore contrive a new technical sense of the term 'ability': call it *K-ability*. Then K-ability remained constant while ability varied.[7] K-ability is completely divorced from ability, has the properties of the old concept of knowledge, and might as well be called 'knowledge', doctrinal matters aside.

It is rather ironic that these moves should be presented as in the spirit of the later Wittgenstein, who constantly argued against the practice of constructing artificial concepts, divorced from ordinary usage, in defense of certain philosophical doctrines. In fact, the Wittgensteinian construal of knowledge as a species of ability seems to be a paradigmatic example of the practice that Wittgenstein held to be a fundamental source of philosophical error.

Notice that similar considerations show that *knowing-how*—for example, knowing how to ride a bicycle—cannot be analyzed in terms of abilities, dispositions, and so on; rather, there appears to be an irreducible cognitive element. Notice finally that an account of knowledge in terms of ability, taken in anything like its normal sense, has proved utterly unproductive. One might try accounting for the simple examples (1) and (2) in terms of Jones's abilities, for example. No such endeavor has ever been undertaken, and a close look at the problems makes it reasonably clear why it would have no hope of success.

The paradoxical flavor of ideas in the range I have been sampling becomes clearer when we look more closely at some of the specific injunctions. Take again Rorty's observation, taken as obvious without discussion, that "all the linguist has to go on is his observation of the way in which linguistic is aligned with non-linguistic behavior in the course of the native's interaction with the environment," apart from the "regulative principle" that the native informant is generally speaking truly. This conception, he notes, is drawn from Quine and Davidson. Thus in Quine's familiar paradigm of "radical translation," "field linguists" observing Jones must support their hypotheses *entirely* in terms of observation of Jones's behavior (or that of members of the "Jungle community," taken to be homogeneous; if it is not homogeneous, none of the arguments will go through, and if it is homogeneous, we may dismiss the community in favor of Jones without loss for these purposes, as I will do). I should note that in referring to Quine, textual questions arise, since in response to queries and criticism he has given many different versions of his paradigm, and these are not consistent;[8] but it is the one just cited, which Davidson and Rorty adopt, that is necessary if we are to be able to draw from Quine's paradigm any of the conclusions that are held to be important.

Before proceeding, let us note again that these prescriptions are radically different from the actual practice of the "field linguist." They are also completely foreign to the standard methods of the natural sciences. In the philosophical literature, the issues are generally discussed with regard to the theory of meaning, and in particular, with regard to aspects of the theory of meaning about which little is known (not, say, in connection with such matters as referential dependence, about which a good deal is understood). This is dubious practice, because it means that controls on speculation by empirical knowledge and theoretical understanding are very slight. But if the doctrine has any validity, it should hold with regard to all of our attributions of linguistic competence, and Quine, at least, has sometimes held that this is so. Thus he has argued that the same considerations hold when his "field linguist" alleges that in the sentence 'John contemplated the problem' there are two phrases, the noun phrase 'John' and the verb phrase 'contemplated the problem,' not, say, the two phrases 'John contemplated' and 'the problem' or 'John contemp' and 'lated the problem'. According to Quine, at least when he is keeping to the assumptions required for his well-known conclusions to follow, this attribution of some property (knowledge, or whatever we choose to call it) to the informant Jones must be based exclusively on evidence about *Jones's behavior*—in fact, evidence used in accord with highly restrictive canons that he outlines. And the same would be true in the study of sound structure, the relation of a reflexive to its antecedent, or whatever.[9]

It is worth noting that no linguist, or empirical scientist generally, would ever agree to be bound by such strictures. A comparable assumption in biology would be that in testing hypotheses about embryological development of humans, we cannot consider evidence obtained from the study of E. coli, or fruit flies, or apes, or physics. To mention one crucial case, in actual practice, every linguist approaches the study of a particular language on the basis of assumptions drawn from the study of other languages. Thus any linguist operating by the norms of the sciences would readily use evidence derived from the study of Japanese to help ground assumptions about Jones's knowledge of English. The logic is straightforward, and quite correct. There is overwhelming empirical evidence that people are not genetically "tuned" to acquire one rather than another language; rather, the "initial state" of their language faculty may be assumed to be uniform to a very good approximation. Presented with an array of evidence, the child acquires a specific language, making use of the resources of the initial state that determine a substantial part of the knowledge (competence) acquired; the initial state can be regarded as a fixed, biologically determined function that maps evidence available into acquired knowledge, uniformly for all languages.[10] Study of Japanese may, of course, provide us with evidence, perhaps compelling evidence, about the initial state, namely, by means of a comparison between what comes to be known and what is presented, the two being mediated by the resources of the initial state. If speakers of Japanese employ some formal property of language structure (say, *c-command*) in interpreting referential dependence, and the evidence available to the Japanese child does not somehow "compel" or is not even conducive to this uniform result, we are entitled to attribute to the initial state a version of Binding Theory, incorporating this property and relevant principles involving it, and thus to explain the facts observed. But the initial state is shared by the English speaker Jones, and hypotheses about his initial state will of course have consequences as to the proper description of the cognitive state he attains. The conclusions derived from Japanese concerning Jones's knowledge of English might be far-reaching. Thus evidence about referential dependence in Japanese might prove relevant for determining the position of phrase boundaries in English.[11]

All of this is just standard scientific practice, never questioned—or even discussed, because it is so uncontroversial—in the natural sciences. But Quine and those influenced by his paradigm are enjoining the "field linguist" to depart radically from the procedures of the sciences, limiting themselves to a small part of the relevant evidence, selected in accordance with behaviorist dogma; and also to reject the standard procedures used in theory construction in the sciences. The point is not academic; the normal practice of descriptive linguists crucially exploits these assumptions, which again should be the merest truisms.

We may put the point differently. The linguist and the child face radically different tasks. The child, endowed with certain innate capacities, acquires knowledge of a language—automatically, and with little if any choice in the matter. The linguist is trying to find out what knowledge the child acquires, and what innate properties of the mind/brain are responsible for this process of growth of knowledge (trying to find out what the child knows in advance of experience, to use a locution that seems to be quite appropriate). The linguist will quite properly use conclusions about innate properties, however derived, for the description of the knowledge attained—in particular, for the study of meaning, this domain having the same status as any other.

In fact, Quine's injunctions, consistently applied, would be still more extreme than this example indicates. Thus evidence from language pathology, or genetic variation, or neural structure, or biochemistry, or in fact evidence from any source, would be regarded by any scientist as potentially relevant in principle to determining the nature of the initial state or the state of knowledge attained, since these are simply elements of the natural biological world; Quine too insists on this point with regard to study of the natural world, apart from the study of humans above the neck when undertaken by "linguists," in his sense of this term. If it could be shown that some facts about the neural structure of the brain provide a natural realization of rule systems of one kind (say, with the breakdown of 'John contemplated the problem' into the two phrases 'John' and 'contemplated the problem'), but not other kinds, then this line of argument would be acceptable in the sciences to help settle the question of what is the correct description of Jones's knowledge—the cognitive state attained by John (the question of the choice of constituent structure, in the case in question). The same is true with regard to the theory of meaning, or any empirical inquiry. But all of these paths, familiar in the natural sciences, are excluded by fiat under the Quinean conditions on the work of the "linguist" in accord with the paradigm that is widely adopted in the philosophical literature.

Quine has qualified these doctrines in interesting ways. A closer look at these qualifications reveals more clearly the arbitrary character of the stipulations imposed and the persistent misunderstanding of the empirical issues. As an example of arbitrary stipulation, consider Quine's discussion of the evidence that might lead us to assign one or another constituent structure to the sentences of Jones's English.[12] If this evidence derives from psycholinguistic experiments on perceived displacement of clicks,[13] then it counts; if the evidence derives from conditions on referential dependence in Japanese or on the formation of causative constructions in numerous languages, then it does not count—though this is evidence interpreted in the normal manner of the natural sciences, along the lines discussed a moment ago. Perhaps Quine might be interpreted as holding that evidence of the former type (so-called "psychological evidence") is in fact more powerful and persuasive than the so-called "linguistic evidence"; if so, this would simply be another error, since the opposite is the case, for the present at least. In fact, Quine appears to hold that the evidence differs in its epistemological character, a notion that is completely untenable. Evidence does not come labeled "for confirming theories" ("psychological evidence") or "for purposes of 'simplicity and general translatability'" ("linguistic evidence"). It is just evidence, good or bad, compelling or noncompelling, given the theoretical frameworks in which it can be interpreted for the purposes of sharpening or confirming hypotheses.

As an example of misunderstanding of empirical issues, consider Quine's discussion of the so-called "coordinate structure constraint," a descriptive generalization that covers, for example, the radical difference in status between the interrogative expressions derived by questioning "Mary" in the sentences 'John saw Bill and Mary' and 'John saw Bill with Mary': that is, the difference between 'who did John see Bill and?', 'who did John see Bill with?'. Quine concludes that the "striking uniformity" exhibited in this constraint is not "a hint of a trait of all language" but "a hint of genetic kinship of the languages that seem most readily grammatized in these terms."[14] This conclusion, however, is based on a serious misunderstanding of the empirical issues at stake. The problem is to explain how each child knows the relevant difference between 'who did John see Bill and?' and 'who did John see Bill with?' It cannot be that the child relies on evidence from the history of language, and the child typically has no relevant experience to determine (by "induction," or whatever) that the simple rule "Front *wh*-phrase" is somehow blocked in the expression 'John saw Bill and who' but not in 'John saw Bill with who' (in colloquial English). Children do not, for example, produce 'who did John see Bill and?', then to be informed by their parents that this is not the way it is done; and languages have not "drifted" to incorporate this "simplification" of the rule of question formation over many millennia.[15] The problem, in short, is one of poverty of stimulus, and speculations about genetic kinship of languages have nothing whatsoever to do with it, in this and innumerable other similar cases.[16]

A similar refusal to permit the study of language to be pursued in the manner of the natural sciences is illustrated in other connections. Consider Donald Davidson's article "A Nice Derangement of Epitaphs" in the volume cited earlier.[17] Davidson considers the thesis that the goal of the descriptive study of meaning is to construct "an explicit theory" that "is a model of the interpreter's linguistic competence," a "recursive theory of a certain sort," and that we can "describe what an interpreter can do" only by appeal to such a theory. He then proceeds: "It does not add anything to this thesis to say that if the theory does correctly describe the competence of an interpreter, some mechanisms in the interpreter must correspond to the theory." Similar points have been made by Dummett and others.[18]

For anyone approaching these problems from the standpoint of the natural sciences, the final comment quoted is utterly wrongheaded. If it had any validity, the analogous comment would apply in the study of visual perception, or chemistry. As elsewhere, it adds a great deal to the thesis to say that "some mechanisms in the interpreter ... correspond to the theory." That is, natural scientists who construct a theory that "describes what an interpreter can do" will proceed to attribute to the subject certain fixed and explicit mechanisms that would have the properties assumed in this descriptive account, not others. The attribution might be at an abstract level, in terms of mentally represented rule-systems, or in terms of other abstract entities such as neural nets, or in terms of cellular structure, or whatever; all of this is just standard natural science. Having proceeded to attribute specific structure and mechanisms to the person's mind/brain—often at some remove from unknown "more elementary" physical mechanisms—the natural scientist is then in a position to test the theory in terms of a wide array of evidence, for example, evidence drawn from other languages in the manner just illustrated, or evidence from pathology or the brain sciences or biochemistry. Davidson's injunction blocks these efforts to employ the methods of rational inquiry in the sciences to determine whether the postulated account of the interpreter is indeed true, and to modify it if (as is likely) it is not.

The same problem arises when Quine, David Lewis, Dummett, and many others object that some philosophical problem arises when linguists attribute to a speaker-hearer a specific internalized rule-system, and then seek to determine whether this theory of the person is true by the standard methods of the sciences. Perhaps this is even pure "folly," as Quine has argued, to be overcome by proper reflection on methodology. The perceived problem is that for a fixed array of observed behavior, or a fixed infinite set of utterances selected on some obscure basis and taken by the philosopher to be "the language," it is of course possible to construct infinitely many different theories that are consistent with this evidence ("grammars," as they are sometimes called); it is therefore held to be an unwarranted move to postulate that one of them is "true" and others "false"—unless, Quine sometimes holds, there is "psychological evidence," with its mysterious properties that "linguistic evidence" lacks, to support one or another hypothesis. The argument is often buttressed by an analogy to the study of formal languages, which are completely irrelevant and highly misleading in this connection. If valid, the argument would hold throughout the sciences; in fact, it is nothing more than a form of skepticism that no one takes seriously in the study of the natural world for reasons that were clear by the seventeenth century, as Richard Popkin observes.[19] The natural scientist will attribute to the subject a specific system, not some other one (a "grammar," to use a misleading term), and will then proceed to determine whether this assumption is correct by seeking evidence of as wide a variety as possible, including crucial evidence from other languages, along the lines just discussed. Of course, there will always remain empirical indeterminacy, since this is empirical science, not mathematics, but that is all there is to say about the matter. A considerable literature exists arguing the contrary, but it is based on fundamental fallacies of reasoning.[20] Among these fallacies are the mistaken assumptions just discussed: that evidence about Jones's competence can only be drawn from Jones's behavior (interpreted in terms of the regulative principle about truth) and that it adds nothing to a description of Jones's behavior to attribute to Jones a specific internal mechanism, perhaps a particular system of rules or some form of neural organization that realizes them.

The point can be illustrated, again, with the matter of phrase-structure boundaries. Suppose we have two kinds of evidence for the placement of the major boundary after the subject in 'John—contemplated the problem', evidence from referential dependence in Japanese ("linguistic evidence") and evidence from perceptual displacement of clicks ("psychological evidence"). The first kind of evidence is subject to the familiar sort of indeterminacy.

So is the second. Suppose that under experimental conditions established to yield the right results (typically, after many attempts that go wrong), clicks will be perceptually displaced to the subject-predicate boundary, not the verb-object boundary. These results can be interpreted as supporting the conclusion that the structure is [NP—V NP], not [NP V—NP] or [NP—V—NP]. But it is easy to apply Quine's argument to show that there is "no fact of the matter" in this case. Plainly, there are many other interpretations of the experimental results. Perhaps clicks are perceptually displaced to the middle of a constituent, not its boundary; or perhaps the subject is responding by identifying the phrase-structure boundary directly below the major one. All other relevant experiments could be reinterpreted along similar lines, as can certainly be done in principle—though it is not so simple in practice, in the case of either the "psychological" or the "linguistic" evidence. The issues are the same throughout; or rather, there are no issues relevant here, since they hold of empirical inquiry generally.

When conclusions are drawn about phrase boundaries or other aspects of language on the basis of "linguistic evidence," Quine is reluctant to accept them "without further light on the nature of the supposed equipment,"[21] but when the same conclusions are based on "psychological evidence," these qualms do not arise. This epistemological dualism makes no sense whatsoever; it is a long step backward from traditional metaphysical dualism, which was a rational reaction, on assumptions now known to be faulty,[22] to perceived empirical problems. The qualms, such as they are, are in principle the same, whatever the evidence on which conclusions are based, and are simply features of empirical inquiry. As for the "supposed equipment," it raises no problems of principle that differ from those characteristic of all theory construction in the empirical sciences.

Yet another paradox arises within this framework. Linguists, it is argued, are not permitted to attribute one particular language system rather than others to the individual or idealized community that they are studying;[23] they are not permitted to explore what is true of the brain, described at the level at which we construct rule systems and the like. But something is true of the brain; there is something about my brain that is more or less like yours and crucially different from the brain of a speaker of Swahili. Therefore someone should be permitted to study these aspects of the real world, but not linguists, who are restricted to inquiry into Jones's behavior and may not proceed to attribute specific mechanisms to Jones's mind/brain and to use evidence from other languages (or from any domain, in principle) to verify the accuracy of their conclusions about these mechanisms. Accepting these terminological strictures about what the linguist must do, the rational step is to abandon linguistics (including the study of meaning in accord with the conditions stipulated in the Quinean paradigm). Having abandoned these pointless pursuits, we may now turn to this other subject, where we are permitted to attribute specific mechanisms to Jones's mind/brain and to investigate these hypotheses by the methods of the sciences, using whatever evidence is at hand—in fact, the actual practice of linguists that is condemned in this curious, though extremely influential tradition in modern philosophy, which, in a final irony, prides itself on its "naturalism" and adherence to the methods of the sciences.

In his most recent effort to justify the strictures he imposes, in the January 1987 issue of the *Journal of Philosophy*, Quine offers the following argument.[24] For the linguist, he argues, "the behaviorist approach is mandatory." The reason is that in acquiring language, "we depend strictly on overt behavior in observable situations.... There is nothing in linguistic meaning, then, beyond what is to be gleaned from overt behavior in observable circumstances," and the same holds true, by parity of argument, for the study of pronunciation, phrase structure, or whatever aspect of language we choose. Furthermore, as he makes explicit once again, the relevant behavior for the linguist is that of the natives to whom he/she is imputing knowledge of language: "If translators disagree on the translation of a Jungle sentence but no behavior on the part of the Jungle people [tacitly assumed to be homogeneous] could bear on the disagreement, then there is simply no fact of the matter," and the linguist who holds that there are facts to be discovered, and that some theories (grammars) are correct and others not, is guilty of serious methodological error or pure "folly" (recall that the "translator" stands for the language learner as well[25] and that the same argument holds for pronunciation, phrase structure, etc.).

Consider now the following analogous argument. In reaching its final physical structure in the passage from embryo to mature state, the organism depends strictly on nutrition provided from outside (including oxygen, etc.). There is nothing in the physical structure of the mature organism, then, beyond what is to be gleaned from the nutritional inputs. The student of human development and its outcome, then, must limit attention to these inputs; for the biologist, "the nutritionist approach is mandatory." The argument is the same as Quine's, and we see at once why it is untenable. True, the embryo "depends" on the nutritional environment just as the language learner "depends" on overt behavior. But what does the term "depends" include? Here we turn to the structure of the organism, which we may think of abstractly as a mapping M of external inputs into mature state. In the absence of such structure, observed behavior will lead to no knowledge of language and nutrition will lead to no growth. Quine of course recognizes this. Thus Quine's field linguist, pursuing the path of the language learner, "tentatively associates a native's utterance with the observed concurrent situation" and is permitted to make use of other hypotheses that allegedly correspond to capacities with which the language learner is endowed. If clarified, these hypotheses would constitute a theory of the innate structure of the organism and the mapping M.

As is agreed on all sides, without innate structure there is no effect of the external environment in language (or other) growth; in particular, without innate structure Jones could not have developed in a specific way from embryo to person, and his language faculty could not have assumed the state of mature competence that underlies and accounts for Jones's behavior. The child is endowed with this innate structure and therefore grows to maturity along a course that is largely inner-directed; the task of the scientist is to discover what the innate endowment is and what is the nature of the state attained. Currently, the best theory is that the initial state of the language faculty incorporates certain general principles of language structure, including phonetic and semantic principles, and that the mature state of competence is a generative procedure that assigns structural descriptions to expressions and interacts with the motor and perceptual system and other cognitive systems of the mind/brain to yield semantic and phonetic interpretations of utterances. A vast range of empirical evidence is relevant in principle to determining just how this proposal should be spelled out in detail. Again, all of this is normal science, yielding theories that are true or false[26] regarding Jones's competence and his initial state, part of the human biological endowment. Perhaps this approach should be abandoned in terms of some other conception, now unavailable, but to establish this conclusion it does not suffice to demand that the linguist abandon the methods of the sciences.

As in his earlier formulations of these ideas, Quine's specific stipulations about the innate structure (hence the mapping M) are completely arbitrary, apart from their historical antecedents, here irrelevant. There is no reason to accept them in the case of language, just as comparable dogmatism about "dependence" would be rejected out of hand in the study of other aspects of the growth of organisms. Furthermore, there is compelling evidence that they are false, insofar as they are explicit. As in the study of physical development generally, the rational investigator will dismiss these dogmatic assumptions about the nature of "dependence" (i.e., about innate structure) along with other doctrines such as those just sketched, and will use whatever evidence can be found concerning the structure of the organism, the mapping M, and the nature of the states attained in particular cases. The conclusions that Quine, Davidson, Rorty and many others draw remain unargued. Nothing can be resurrected from the Quinean picture with regard to these matters, so far as I can see, though some of his conclusions, in particular, with regard to "meaning holism," may well turn out to be correct, at least in large part.

Let us return now to the "analytic-synthetic" distinction, and the Davidsonian argument that by "getting rid of it," Quine "saved philosophy of language as a serious subject." Recall that what is at issue here is not simply this distinction but the question of language-determined semantic connections generally. As I mentioned, we cannot appeal to Rorty's argument, attributed to Quine, that the "field linguist" finds the distinction "of no use." In practice, semantic structure is regularly attributed to lexical items in descriptive work and theoretical studies on the semantics of natural language, and from these and other structural properties, semantic connections of various kinds are derivable, including analytic connections. There are good reasons for these standard assumptions about lexical structure. Acquisition of lexical items poses what is sometimes called "Plato's problem" in a very sharp form. As anyone who has tried to construct a dictionary or to work in descriptive semantics is aware, it is a very difficult matter to describe the meaning of a word, and such meanings have great intricacy and involve the most remarkable assumptions, even in the case of very simple concepts, such as what counts as a nameable thing. At peak periods of language acquisition, children are acquiring ("learning") many words a day, perhaps a dozen or more, meaning that they are acquiring words on very few exposures, even just one. This would appear to indicate that the concepts are already available, with much or all of their intricacy and structure predetermined, and that the child's task is to assign labels to concepts, as might be done with limited evidence given sufficiently rich innate structure. And these conceptual structures appear to yield semantic connections of a kind that will, in particular, induce an analytic-synthetic distinction, as a matter of empirical fact.

To the extent that anything is understood about lexical items and their nature, it seems that they are based on conceptual structures of a specific and closely integrated type. It has been argued plausibly that concepts of a locational nature, including goal and source of action, object moved, and so on, enter widely into lexical structure, often in quite abstract ways. In addition, notions like actor, recipient of action, instrument, event, intention, causation, and others are pervasive elements of lexical structure, with their specific properties and interrelations. Consider, say, the words 'chase' or 'persuade'. They clearly involve a reference to human intention. To chase Jones is not only to follow him but to follow him with the intent of staying on his path, perhaps to catch him. To persuade Smith to do something is to cause him to decide or intend to do it; if he never decides or intends to do it, we have not succeeded in persuading him. Furthermore, he must decide or intend by his own volition, not under duress; if we say that the police persuaded Smith to confess by torture, we are using the term ironically. Since these facts are known essentially without evidence, it must be that the child approaches language with an intuitive understanding of concepts involving intending, causation, goal of action, event, and so on, and places the words that are heard in a nexus that is permitted by the principles of universal grammar, which provide the framework for thought and language, and are common to human languages as systems that enter into various aspects of human life. These elements also appear to enter into an integrated "conceptual scheme," a component of the initial state of the language faculty that is fleshed out in specific ways, with predetermined scope and limits, in the course of language growth, one aspect of cognitive development. There may be revision and restructuring of such conceptual schemes,[27] but care must be taken to separate out the various factors that enter into the course of development, including, quite possibly, genetically determined maturation that yields effects perceived only in late stages of cognitive growth.

Notice again that we appear to have connections of meaning in such cases as these; we have a rather clear distinction between truths of meaning and truths of fact. Thus, if John persuaded Bill to go to college, then Bill at some point decided or intended to go to college and did so without duress; otherwise, John did not persuade Bill to go to college. Similarly if John killed Bill, then Bill is dead (though John may or may not be, depending on the facts). These are truths of meaning, not of fact. The a priori framework of human thought, within which language is acquired, provides necessary connections among concepts, reflected in connections of meaning among words, and more broadly, among expressions involving these words, as in the example of referential dependence mentioned earlier. Syntactic relations provide a rich array of further examples. For example, there seems to be a clear distinction between the sentence 'everyone who lives upstairs lives upstairs' and 'everyone who lives upstairs is happy.' Quine appears to believe that this distinction is more problematic and obscure than his distinction between "grammatical" and "ungrammatical," which he regards as somehow crucial for the linguist's investigations.[28] The opposite is the case. In fact, an absolute distinction between "grammatical" and "ungrammatical" appears to have little if any significance. It can be established one way or another, or perhaps better, not at all, since it is doubtful that the concept, in Quine's sense, plays any role in the theory of language. The reasons were discussed in the earliest work in generative grammar, actually the only work in which an effort was made to develop such a concept in some manner that might be relevant to linguistic theory, but in terms that were long ago understood to be inappropriate.[29]

It appears, then, that one of the central conclusions of modern philosophy is rather dubious: namely, the contention, often held to have been established by work of Quine and others, that one can make no principled distinction between questions of fact and questions of meaning, that it is a matter of more or less deeply held belief. This conclusion has been supported by reflection on an artificially narrow class of examples, among them, concepts that have little or no relational structure. In the case of such sentences as 'cats are animals', for example, it is not easy to find evidence to decide whether the sentence is true as a matter of meaning or fact, or whether there is an answer to the question in this case, and there has been much inconclusive controversy about the matter. When we turn to concepts with an inherent relational structure such as 'persuade' or 'chase', or to more complex syntactic constructions such as those exhibiting referential dependence or causative and relative constructions, then it seems that semantic connections are readily discerned. Contrary to what

Rorty and others assert, this is the common assumption of empirical work in the study of linguistic meaning, and, furthermore, it seems to be a reasonable assumption.

The status of a statement as a truth of meaning or of empirical fact can only be established by empirical inquiry, and considerations of many sorts may well be relevant; for example, inquiry into language acquisition and variation among languages. The question of the existence of analytic truths and semantic connections more generally is an empirical one, to be settled by inquiry that goes well beyond the range of evidence ordinarily brought to bear in the literature on these topics. Suppose that two people differ in their intuitive judgments as to whether I can persuade John to go to college without his deciding or intending to do so.[30] We are by no means at an impasse. Rather, we can construct conflicting theories and proceed to test them. One who holds that the connection between 'persuade' and 'decide' or 'intend' is conceptual will proceed to elaborate the structure of the concepts, their primitive elements, the principles by which they are integrated and related to other cognitive systems, and so on, and will seek to show that other properties of language and other aspects of the acquisition and use of language can be explained in terms of the very same assumptions about the innate structure of the language faculty, in the same language and others, and that the same concepts play a role in other aspects of thought and understanding. One who holds that the connection is one of deeply held belief, not connection of meaning, has the task of developing a general theory of belief fixation that will yield the right conclusions in these and numerous other cases. Suppose one holds, with Paul Churchland for example, that the connection is based on the "semantic importance" of sentences relating 'persuade' and 'decide' or 'intend' (i.e., that these sentences play a prominent role in inference, or serve to introduce the term 'persuade' to the child's vocabulary, and thus are more important than others for communication).[31] One then faces the task of showing that these empirical claims are in fact true. The first tack, in terms of innate conceptual structure, seems far more promising to me, and is the only approach that has any results or even proposals to its credit, but it is a matter of empirical inquiry, not pronouncements on the basis of virtually no evidence. Specifically, arguments against the first (conceptual) approach in terms of indeterminacy, unclarity, open issues, and so on, establish nothing unless it is shown that alternative approaches in terms of some (now unavailable) theories of belief fixation or semantic importance are not subject to these problems.

The whole matter requires extensive rethinking, and much of what has been generally assumed for the past several decades about these questions appears to be dubious at best. There is, it seems rather clear, a rich conceptual structure determined by the initial state of the language faculty (perhaps drawing from the resources of other genetically determined faculties of mind), waiting to be awakened by experience. All of this is much in accord with traditional rationalist conceptions and even, in some respects, the so-called "empiricist" thought of James Harris, David Hume, and others.

Many have found such conclusions completely unacceptable, even absurd; the idea that there is something like an array of innate concepts and that these are to a large degree merely "labeled" in language acquisition, as the empirical evidence suggests, certainly departs radically from many common assumptions. Some, for example Hilary Putnam, have argued that it is entirely implausible to suppose that we have "an innate stock of notions" including *carburetor* and *bureaucrat*.[32] If he were correct about this, it would not be particularly to the point, since the problem arises in a most serious way in connection with simple words such as 'table', 'person', 'chase', 'persuade', 'kill', and so on. But his argument for the examples he cites is not compelling. It is that to have given us this innate stock of notions, "evolution would have had to be able to anticipate all the contingencies of future physical and cultural environments. Obviously it didn't and couldn't do this."

Notice that the argument is invalid from the start. To suppose that in the course of evolution, humans come to have an innate stock of notions including *carburetor* and *bureaucrat* does not entail that evolution was able to anticipate *every* future physical and cultural contingency—only these contingencies. But that aside, notice that a very similar argument had long been accepted in immunology: namely, the number of antigens is so immense, including even artifically synthesized substances that had never existed in the world, that it was considered absurd to suppose that evolution had provided "an innate stock of antibodies"; rather, formation of antibodies must be a kind of "learning process" in which the antigens played an "instructive role." But this assumption may well be false. Niels Kaj Jerne won the Nobel Prize for his work challenging this idea, and upholding his own conception that an animal "cannot be stimulated to make specific antibodies, unless it has already made antibodies of this specificity before the antigen arrives," so that antibody formation is a selective process in which the antigen plays a selective and amplifying role.[33] Whether or not Jerne is correct, he certainly could be, and the same could be true in the case of word meanings, the argument being quite analogous.

Furthermore, there is good reason to suppose that the argument is at least in substantial measure correct even for such words as 'carburetor' and 'bureaucrat', which, in fact, pose the familiar problem of poverty of stimulus if we attend carefully to the enormous gap between what we know and the evidence on the basis of which we know it. The same is often true of technical terms of science and mathematics, and it surely appears to be the case for the terms of ordinary discourse. However surprising the conclusion may be that nature has provided us with an innate stock of concepts, and that the child's task is to discover their labels, the empirical facts appear to leave open few other possibilities. Other possibilities (say, in terms of "generalized learning mechanisms") have yet to be coherently formulated, and if some day they are, it may well be that the apparent issue will dissolve.

In fact, it is not clear what thesis is being proposed by Putnam and others who reject what they call "the innateness hypothesis"; I should add that though I am alleged to be one of the exponents of this hypothesis, perhaps even the arch-criminal, I have never defended it and have no idea what it is supposed to be. Whatever the truth may be about antibody formation, it is based on the innate resources of the body and its immune system, and the task of the scientist is to find out what these resources are. Exactly the same is true of concept formation and language acquisition. For this reason, people who are supposed to be defenders of "the innateness hypothesis" do not defend the hypothesis or even use the phrase, because there is no such general hypothesis; rather, only specific hypotheses about the innate resources of the mind, in particular, its language faculty. General arguments against some unformulated "innateness hypothesis" have no bearing on actual hypotheses about innateness, in the case of growth of language and conceptual systems or other forms of physical growth.

Putnam offers a counterargument to the one just sketched on analogy to the immune system. He points out that concepts "often arise from *theories*," and the number of possible theories (or perhaps even "theory *types*") is so immense, even for "short" theories, as to make "the idea that evolution exhausted all the possibilities in advance wildly implausible." The argument is correct, but again irrelevant. In the first place, we are considering what humans are capable of acquiring, and there is no reason to believe that "all theories" can be learned or constructed by humans, nor is it even clear what sense this thesis has.[34] Furthermore, Putnam's original argument was supposed to bear on the specific words 'bureaucrat' and 'carburetor', and no cardinality argument is relevant to these cases, or to any substantive empirical hypothesis about innate structure. In other words, his argument that "evolution couldn't have done that" simply does not hold in the cases for which it is offered. The argument that evolution couldn't have done "everything"—even what is beyond human capacity—might hold if one could make some sense of it, but such an argument would not be relevant here, even if it could be given in a coherent form.

In the same connection, Putnam argues that the thesis of "meaning holism," with the Quinean principle that "revision can strike anywhere," contributes to undermining certain conclusions concerning the innate structure of conceptual systems and language generally. But this line of argument is questionable. Suppose that the thesis of "meaning holism" is correct in the sense that, as Putnam puts it, there are no "'psychologically real' entities which have enough of the properties we preanalytically assign to 'meanings' to warrant an identification," and reference is fully determined only on holistic grounds. Nevertheless, it does not follow that semantic connections cannot be completely fixed and stable as a matter of biological endowment. Thus certain relations may remain stable as other considerations lead to various choices about fixing of reference. Furthermore, empirical considerations of the kind discussed earlier bear on the question of whether it is indeed true that "revision can strike anywhere." The point cannot be established for natural language by reference to the practice of the natural sciences from which Putnam draws many of his examples; these arguments, assuming them to be correct, do not suffice to show the absence of intrinsic semantic and conceptual structure based on fixed properties of the human mind. The thesis of "holism" may be correct in some measure or form, but the questions of semantic connections in natural language remain to be settled by empirical study, and for the present at least, the evidence appears to support their existence—rather strongly, it seems to me.

Let us pursue further Davidson's argument in his paper "A Nice Derangement of Epitaphs," in which he purports to show that the study of actual communication undermines a "commonly accepted account of linguistic competence and communication" and shows that "there is no such thing as a language, not if a language is anything like what many philosophers and linguists have supposed. There is therefore no such thing to be learned, mastered, or born with." This conception of language, which Davidson believes to be refuted, is founded on three basic assumptions concerning what he calls "first language" or "prior theory," a "complex system or theory" shared more or less by speaker and hearer. The assumptions are (1) that the prior theory is "systematic" in the sense that the *interpreter* who has this theory is able to interpret utterances on the basis of properties of their parts and the structure of the utterance; (2) that this method of interpretation is shared; and (3) that the component elements of the system are governed by learned conventions or regularities. The third of these assumptions is untenable for other reasons, but instead of delaying on this matter, let us present it in the form required for Davidson's argument: the component elements of the system are available, as he puts it, "in advance of occasions of interpretation"; it is a fixed element in communication situations, for interpreters at a fixed state of language knowledge.

To refute this conception, Davidson observes that in ordinary communication situations the interpreter makes use of all sorts of conjectures and assumptions about what the speaker may have in mind, relying on properties of the situation, the speaker's presumed intentions, and so on. The interpreter thus "adjusts his theory," modifying the "prior theory" to a "passing theory" that is "geared to the occasion." But this "passing theory cannot in general correspond to an interpreter's linguistic competence." This "passing theory is not a theory of what anyone (except perhaps a philosopher) would call an actual natural language," Davidson continues, and "'Mastery' of such a language would be useless, since knowing a passing theory is only knowing how to interpret a particular utterance on a particular occasion." Furthermore, communication can proceed quite well when the prior theory is not shared by speaker and hearer, and the prior theory too is not what "we would normally call a language" since it is a psychological particular, specific to the speaker-hearer with features that are not shared through the "community." The interpreter has some kind of "strategy," a "mysterious process by which a speaker or hearer uses what he knows in advance plus present data to produce a passing theory," and for communication, what two people need "is the ability to converge on passing theories from utterance to utterance." Given these facts, there is no longer any use for "the concept of a language," for "shared grammar or rules," for a "portable interpreting machine set to grind out the meaning of an arbitrary utterance"; rather, we need something more evanescent, mysterious and "holistic," "the ability to converge on a passing theory from time to time." We thus are led to "abandon ... not only the ordinary notion of a language, but we have erased the boundary between knowing a language and knowing our way around in the world generally." "In linguistic communication nothing corresponds to a linguistic competence" based on the three principles just mentioned, because "there are no rules for arriving at passing theories." At the conclusion of the discussion, however, Davidson asserts that a passing theory is derived somehow "from a private vocabulary and grammar," that is, from a "prior theory" meeting the first and perhaps a version of the third condition, but possibly not shared in the "community"; there is then a "prior theory" and there are surely certain methods, not others, "for arriving at passing theories," whether or not one wants to call these methods "rules."

The various parts of the argument are largely correct, but they do not seem to show very much. In particular, no reason has been offered to doubt that there is a "prior theory" in the usual sense of the study of language and knowledge of language—that is, a specific generative procedure incorporated in a specific mature state of the language faculty. Of course, this "prior theory" will be quite different from what is called "a language" in ordinary usage, but this is because no such concept plays a role in empirical inquiry into language and mind, as already noted.

In the face of Davidson's arguments, we may continue to suppose that there is, to very good first approximation, a fixed and invariant language faculty that maps presented evidence onto a system of rules and principles (or whatever turns out to be correct with regard to the cognitive state attained) that assign interpretations to utterances. Call this acquired system a "generative procedure." To know a language is to have an internal representation of this generative procedure, which we will express at various levels of abstraction from "more elementary" mechanisms and will seek to relate to such mechanisms, in the normal manner of the natural sciences.[35] Proceeding in accord with normal practice, we may also seek to construct a "parser," a device, also attributed to the mind/brain, which incorporates the generative procedure attained along with other specified structures and properties,[36] and maps presented utterances into structural descriptions that are interpreted by other components of mind. So far, we are dealing with feasible questions of empirical inquiry.

There is also a further problem, which we can formulate in vague terms but which cannot be studied in practice: namely, to construct an "interpreter" that includes the parser as a component along with all other capacities of the mind, whatever they may be, and accepts nonlinguistic as well as linguistic inputs. This interpreter, presented with an utterance and a situation, assigns some interpretation to what is being said by a person in this situation. The study of communication in the actual world of experience is the study of the interpreter, but this is not a topic for empirical inquiry, for the usual reasons: there is no such topic as the study of everything. Similarly, science does not investigate other phenomena of the world as presented to us in everyday experience. The interpreter, as Davidson correctly observes, includes everything that people are capable of doing, which is why it is not an object of empirical inquiry, and why nothing sensible can be said about it. We might hope to learn something about various elements of the interpreter, proceeding by the normal methods of the sciences, beginning with the "private vocabulary and grammar" that constitute the language attained, proceeding to the parser, then perhaps, to the extent feasible, turning to other elements of the mind and of situations that enter into normal human life. But if we begin with the demand for a theory of everything, we will find nothing; it is unnecessary to construct elaborate arguments to establish this point.[37] The situation is no different in the far more advanced sciences. The proper conclusion is not that we must abandon concepts of language that can be productively studied, but that the topic of successful communication in the actual world of experience is far too complex and obscure to merit attention in empirical inquiry, except as a guide to intuitions as we pursue research designed to lead to some understanding of the real world, communication included. These observations have no bearing on whether or not there is a "prior theory," an internalized generative procedure, in the normal sense of empirical practice.

Davidson's "passing theory" is not a useful notion; about this, he is surely correct. The interpreter will construct all sorts of "passing theories" (though, crucially, not *any* sort), changing moment to moment, because the interpreter as Davidson conceives it includes everything available to human intelligence; but it makes no sense to call its transient states "theories" or to consider them a subject of direct inquiry. Crucially, nothing in Davidson's argument bears on the assumption that the "prior theory" (though not understood quite in his terms) remains a fixed and invariant element of the "interpreter" (as of the narrower idealized parser) and that it enters into the functioning of the interpreter.

In this discussion, Davidson focuses attention on malapropisms and so-called "misuse of language" more generally. Here some care is necessary. Let's again take Jones, a speaker of a variety of what we informally call "English." Jones has mastered a generative procedure that associates with utterances structural descriptions, including semantic properties, and has other capacities of mind that allow him to produce and interpret linguistic expressions making use of these structural descriptions. Let us call this generative procedure his "I-language," where *I* is to suggest "internalized" (in the mind/brain) and "intensional" (in that the procedure is a function enumerating structural descriptions, considered in intension with a particular description);[38] here we are referring to specific postulated mechanisms of the mind/brain, considered abstractly.

Jones may speak in a way that is not in accord with his I-language, or may offer judgments inconsistent with his I-language; judgments about ourselves, like others, can be mistaken, and much more than I-language is involved in behavior. This is an uninteresting case of misuse of language; call it the "individual sense."

Suppose that Jones, like most of us, normally says such things as 'hopefully, we'll be able to solve that problem', or uses the word 'disinterested' to mean uninterested. Various authority figures tell us that this is "wrong," a "mistake," not in accord with the "rules of English." Jones is "misusing his language," namely, English, a language of which he has only a partial and perhaps distorted knowledge, as in Dummett's "fundamental sense" of language. Even if 95 percent of the population, or for that matter everyone but William Safire and a few others, were to behave in the manner of Jones, these cases would still constitute "misuse of language." Or Jones may try to adapt to the practice of some community for some reason, or perhaps for no reason at all, and may fail to do so, in which case people observing Jones may speak informally of a misuse of the language of this community. These concepts of "misuse of language," which we may call "the community sense," may be of interest for the study of the sociology of group identification, authority structure, and the like, but they have little bearing on the study of language, so far as we know. We understand this perfectly well in the case of pronunciation. Thus to say that one variety of English is "right" and another "wrong" makes as much sense as saying that Spanish is right and English wrong; and the same is true, though for some reason the point seems more obscure, with regard to other aspects of language.

Another possible sense of the concept "misuse of language" derives from Hilary Putnam's notion of "the division of linguistic labor." Thus in the lexicon represented in my mind/brain, the entry for 'elm' and 'beech', or 'mass' and 'kinetic energy', may include an indication that the reference for these terms is to be determined by experts to whom I defer. Then I might apply the terms inaccurately, in the sense that the reference is not in accord with the determinations of these experts. In this case, I might be said to be "misusing my own language."[39] Let us call this the "expert sense" of misuse of language. Again, nothing of great moment appears to follow, surely nothing relating to the approach to language within the framework of individual psychology sketched earlier, and typically followed in practice.[40] Notice that no useful concept of "language" or "community" emerges from these considerations. Thus my expert for 'elm' and 'beech' may be an Italian gardener who speaks not a word of English, and who corrects my usage through reference to the technical Latin names that we share; and my expert for 'mass' and 'kinetic energy' may be a monolingual German physicist. But we would not conclude that German and Italian are included in English, or that all of us form a "community" in any useful sense of the term.

Is there any other concept of "misuse of language"? I am aware of none. If so, the concept plays no important role in the study of language, meaning, communication, or whatever. To take some examples of the kind that Tyler Burge has discussed, suppose that Jones uses the term 'arthritis' to refer to a pain in the thigh. Suppose this is the usage of his village, but not the usage of the outside community. Jones is not misusing his language in the individual sense; his usage is true to his I-language. In his village, he is not misusing his language in the community sense, but outside its borders, he is. Depending on how 'arthritis' is represented in Jones's mental lexicon, he may or may not be misusing his language in the "expert sense." How should we attribute beliefs about arthritis to Jones? Here intuitions differ, and it may be that evidence is too slim, for the moment, to settle the point satisfactorily. Putting aside the "expert sense," suppose we use the term 'I-belief' to refer to the concept that is like belief, except that Jones has the same belief within his village and in the wider community, namely, the belief that we would express, in our I-language, by saying that he has some kind of body pain.[41] This may or may not be the same as the concept of belief in our ordinary language, but it is the concept that seems to be required for the study of what is misleadingly called "the causation of behavior"—misleadingly, because it is unclear that behavior is "caused" in any useful sense of the term. Clearly, there is no reason to suppose that the concepts of general psychology will be those of ordinary usage, just as the concepts of physics, or of the subbranch of psychology called "linguistics," typically are not. Nor is it at all obvious to me that there is a reasonable branch of science (or to be more accurate, human science, meaning the kind of scientific inquiry that humans, with their particular cognitive capacities, are capable of undertaking) that deals with questions of this nature.

It has not, I think, been established that there is anything more to say about the matter. In particular, reference to "misuse of language," to "norms," to "communities," and so on, seems to me to require much more care than is often taken. These concepts are obscure, and it is not clear that they are of any use for inquiry into language and human behavior. Any argument that relies on these notions merits careful scrutiny, and I doubt that familiar arguments can withstand it. Communities are formed in all sorts of overlapping ways, and the study of communities and their norms quickly degenerates into the study of everything. The fact remains that Jones speaks and understands the way he does on the basis of the I-language he has acquired in the course of language growth; and if Jones does or does not follow what we choose, for some transient purpose, to call "community norms" or "social practice," it is on the basis of this internalized I-language (along with much else). Boris, a monolingual speaker of some variety of Russian, has a different I-language, and follows different "norms." I can understand Jones, within limits, because my I-language is not too different from his, and because he and I more or less share other unknown properties that enter into the full interpreter; this is not a topic of empirical inquiry as it stands, in its unanalyzed complexity. That seems to me the way we should approach these questions.

In these terms, we can develop a concept of "knowledge of language" that is appropriate for the inquiry into language and mind; namely, mastery and internal representation of a specific I-language. The linguist's grammar is a theory of the I-language, and universal grammar is the theory of the initial state of the language faculty. Jones's I-language is one particular mature state—or output, regarding the language faculty as a function that maps evidence into I-language. What about the concept language? We might simply understand languages as I-languages, thus taking a language to be something like "a way of speaking," the "finite means" that provide for "infinite use" in the terms of Wilhelm von Humboldt's characterization of language, also an effort to capture his concept of language as a "process of generation" rather than a set of "generated objects." We thus take language to be, in effect, a "notion of structure" that guides the speaker in forming "free expressions," in Otto Jespersen's terms. For empirical inquiry, I think that is an appropriate decision, though obviously not for ordinary discourse. Or we might want to construct a concept of language divorced from cognitive states, perhaps along lines suggested by James Higginbotham. Taking knowledge of language to be a cognitive state, we might construe the "language" as an abstract object, the "object of knowledge," an abstract system of rules and principles (or whatever turns out to be correct) that is an image of the generative procedure, the I-language, represented in the mind and ultimately in the brain in now-unknown "more elementary" mechanisms. Since the language in this sense is completely determined by the I-language, though abstracted from it, it is not entirely clear that this further step is motivated, but perhaps it is.

In these terms, it seems to me that the questions about language and its use that can be subjected to empirical inquiry can readily be formulated and, as far as we now know, best addressed. There may well be many other questions that are not subject to empirical inquiry in the manner of the sciences, and perhaps never will be, if humans are themselves part of the natural world and thus have specific biological capacities with their scope and limits, like every other organism. We must be careful not to succumb to illusions about evolution and its adaptive miracles. There is nothing in the theory of evolution that suggests that we should be able to answer questions that we can pose, even in principle, even if they have answers, or that we should be able to pose the right questions. To the extent that we can, we have empirical science, a kind of chance convergence of properties of the mind and properties of the extramental world. There is nothing surprising about this; we take for granted that something similar is true of rats and bees, and should not be surprised to learn that humans are biological organisms, not angels. But within the limits of human science, it seems to me that the best guess as of the present is that the framework I have just briefly outlined is a proper one for inquiry into the empirical questions about language and mind; and within it, there are some notable successes and many intriguing prospects.

NOTES

* Editor's note. Readers may be puzzled by Chomsky's reference to Quine's most recent effort unless they realize that Chomsky's paper was written in March 1988. The delay in publication is to be regretted, but nothing which has happened in the intervening years would require any substantial revision in his argument.

1. E. LePore, ed., *Truth and Interpretation: Perspectives on the Philosophy of Donald Davidson* (Oxford and New York: Blackwell, 1986).

2. Thus from the last statement quoted, it follows that if I believe that it is raining because I heard it over the radio, so that the complete account of the causal relation of my belief with the world is this interaction, then there is nothing more to know about the relation of my belief that it is raining to the fact that it is or is not raining; there is no further question as to the relation between my beliefs and the world.

3. Though one may, of course, choose to ignore one or another distinction for the purposes of some particular inquiry. The point is that there is no general interpretation of Dummett's "fundamental sense" (no narrower interpretation, for example) that overcomes problems of the kind noted, or any known way to construct such a general concept as a useful idealization, or any reason to try to do so. Note that not every idealization is worth constructing. This one, whatever exactly is intended, apparently is not.

4. I know of only one attempt to come to grips with these problems: Trevor Pateman, *Language in Mind and Language in Society* (Oxford: Oxford University Press, 1987). Pateman develops a notion of language as a "social fact" in a way that seems plausible but has no relevance to the issues I am discussing here. In his sense, a person who is aware of some of the elementary facts about language and society will speak a great many languages, changing from moment to moment, depending on how he or she chooses to identify with one or another community; and a person unaware of such facts will have a considerable range of beliefs (and typically, illusions) about what he or she is doing, beliefs that may play some social role in certain communities.

5. *The Legacy of Wittgenstein* (Oxford: Blackwell, 1984). On Kenny's misunderstand-

ing of my rejection of these views, and the consequent irrelevance of his response to it, see my paper "Language and Problems of Knowledge," ms, 1986; Linguistic Agency,University of Duisburg, March 1987, series A, no. 181 (Duisburg: Duisburg University, 1987); *Synthesis Philosophica* 5, vol. 3, no. 1 (1988).

6. For more extensive discussion of these matters, and of possible alternative accounts, see my *Rules and Representations* (New York: Columbia University Press, 1980); *Knowledge of Language* (New York: Praeger, 1986).

7. This is, in fact, just the tack taken by Kenny, *Legacy*, in the face of conceptual considerations of this sort, though he does not recognize that a substantive change in the understanding of 'ability' or 'capacity' has been introduced. See my paper cited in n. 5 for further discussion.

8. See my *Reflections on Language* (New York: Pantheon, 1975), 187 f., 198 ff.

9. I return directly to some of Quine's qualifications, with regard to these curious doctrines.

10. To focus the discussion, I put aside further complexities—for example, the fact that the resources of the initial state also play a role in determining what counts as evidence and how it is used (or disregarded). Introduction of such further factors would simply strengthen the conclusions.

11. The example is, in fact, a real one. See *Knowledge of Language*, 61.

12. This and the next paragraph refer to Quine's "Reply to Gilbert H. Harman," in *The Philosophy of W. V. Quine*, ed. Edward Hahn and Paul Arthur Schilpp (La Salle, Ill.: Open Court, 1986).

13. He suggests also studies of uniformities in language acquisition; the same considerations apply in this case.

14. We might note, incidentally, that the latter phrase is appropriate only insofar as one might refuse to speak of theories as true in physics, only as being useful for some purpose over some domain of phenomena; Quine might reject this conclusion on the grounds of his stipulations with regard to the study of the mind/brain by the "linguist," in which the normal canons of natural science are (implicitly) held to be unacceptable, as discussed in the text.

15. I place "simplification" in quotes, since the concept is highly misleading. The rule "Front *wh*-phrase," not subject to the coordinate structure constraint and other locality conditions, would indeed be simpler than the actual rule, which is subject to these conditions, for an organism that lacked the conditions (or more properly, the principles from which they derive) as part of its innate structure; for humans, the opposite is true. Whatever sense there may be to the concept "absolute simplicity," independent of the structure of the system under investigation, it is not relevant here. For discussion of these matters, see my *Logical Structure of Linguistic Theory* (1955–56; New York: Plenum, 1975; Chicago: University of Chicago Press, 1985).

16. Quine supposes that the coordinate structure constraint is tied to translatability, assuming that to determine whether it holds in some language we must determine which expressions count as semantic counterparts of English coordinate constructions. The constraint, however, has to do with structures, independent of their semantic relation to coordinate constructions in some other language, and may well derive, at least in significant part, from much more general conditions on locality of grammatical operations that are construction-independent altogether; surely many examples of constraints raising the same issues are of this nature, perhaps all.

17. LePore, *Truth and Interpretation.*

18. For discussion of Dummett's version, see my *Knowledge of Language.* Note that Davidson is apparently limiting attention here to what is called "observational adequacy," not "descriptive adequacy," in the linguistic literature; if the theory of linguistic competence were understood in the latter sense, then it would attribute specific mechanisms (at an abstract level, to be sure).

19. See Richard Popkin, *The History of Skepticism from Erasmus to Spinoza* (Berkeley, Los Angeles, London: University of California Press, 1979); see my *Knowledge of Language,* 240, for discussion. Roger Gibson attributes to me the belief that "neither physics nor linguistics has a fact of the matter" (*Philosophy of Quine,* ed. Hahn and Schilpp), a conclusion that I do not accept and that is not suggested by the argument, to which he refers, that the study of language faces no problem of indeterminacy that does not arise throughout the natural sciences. His further effort to establish a difference on ontological grounds, endorsed by Quine in response, fails for the reasons given in the references he cites. We can certainly insist, loudly if we like, that there just *are* chemical elements and (unknown) physical configurations that determine the course of sexual maturation, and there just *aren't* lexical meanings, connections of referential dependency, and phrases, and perhaps this conclusion will someday be shown to have merit; but what is required is an argument. To say that "two conflicting manuals of translation can both do justice to all dispositions to behavior" and are "compatible with all the same distributions of states and relations over elementary particles" (Quine) makes as much sense as saying essentially the same thing about two theories of chemistry or physical maturation; and in the nineteenth century, one could have added, with equal irrelevance, that neither chemical theory could be accommodated within "an already accepted naturalistic-physicalistic theory" (Gibson), if by the latter we mean "fundamental physics," which had to be significantly modified to incorporate the chemist's discoveries. From such considerations, epistemological or ontological, nothing follows with regard to language or anything else.

20. For discussion, see my article in *Mind and Language,* summer 1987, from which some of these remarks are drawn, and sources cited there.

21. "Reply to Harman."

22. The basic assumption was that the theory of body could be given fairly sharp bounds, essentially those of Cartesian contact mechanics. This was undermined by Newton, and since that time it has been impossible to formulate a coherent mind/body problem in anything like Cartesian terms, or any others, as far as I can see, there being no fixed concept of body.

23. For Quine, grammars differ "extensionally" if "they diverge in net output" ("Reply to Harman"). This familiar usage is seriously misleading, because it is combined with stipulations as to what constitutes "net output" for a grammar. Recall again that Quine is not considering the empirically significant concept of "strong generation" of structural descriptions, but rather "weak generation" of some class K of expressions selected on a basis that seems quite arbitrary. It is K that is the "net output," but however K may be selected, its properties appear to be of no empirical significance. On these matters, see my *Logical Structure of Linguistic Theory* and *Aspects of the Theory of Syntax* (Cambridge, Mass.: MIT Press, 1965). Quine has always taken the question of "grammaticality" to be essentially that of "having meaning" and believes that this concept, "for all its shortcomings, is in far better order than" the concept "alike in meaning"

("Reply to Harman"). But insofar as we have any understanding of "grammaticality," it has little to do with "having meaning," and unlike the various semantic notions that Quine finds problematic, his concepts of "grammaticality" and "having meaning" appear to lack any moderately clear sense, or any status in the study of language.

24. "Indeterminacy of Translation Again," *Journal of Philosophy*, January 1987.

25. An erroneous assumption, since as noted earlier, the tasks of the child and linguist are radically different.

26. Insofar as any scientific theories merit this appellation. We may put aside here any questions that apply to scientific inquiry generally. It makes little sense to raise such questions with regard to the "soft sciences." If one is interested in finding answers to questions, rather than just harassing emerging disciplines, one will turn to domains in which answers are likely to be forthcoming, in this case, domains in which there is sufficient depth of knowledge and understanding to guide inquiry in a serious way.

27. See Susan Carey, *Conceptual Change in Childhood* (Cambridge, Mass.: MIT Press, 1985).

28. For recent reiteration of this idea, see his "Reply to Harman." Here he describes a "brilliant idea" of W. Haas concerning a criterion to establish the distinction he appears to have in mind; the criterion, such as it is, provides a distinction of no known significance for inquiry into the study of language. The widespread belief to the contrary is based in part on a mistaken analogy to formal languages, where the issues are entirely different, and may have been fostered by expository passages in early work in generative grammar that evidently were misleading, though appropriate qualifications were in fact expressed.

29. See *Logical Structure of Linguistic Theory*, where the issues were discussed in terms that seem to me still accurate, and an attempt was made to define such a concept in terms of the principles for assignment of derived constituent structure, but along lines soon shown to be inappropriate.

30. See Gilbert Harman, commentary, *Behavioral and Brain Sciences* 3 (1980).

31. *Scientific Realism and the Plasticity of Mind* (Cambridge: Cambridge University Press, 1979, 1986), 51 f.

32. See Putnam, "Meaning and Mentalism," chap. 1 of Putnam, *Representation and Reality* (Cambridge, Mass.: MIT Press, 1988).

33. For discussion in a linguistic-cognitive context, see *Rules and Representations*, 136 f.; Jerne's Nobel Prize lecture, "The Generative Grammar of the Immune System," *Science* 229 (13 September 1985): 1057–1059; and for more extensive discussion, Massimo Piattelli-Palmerini, "The Rise of Selective Theories: A Case Study and Some Lessons from Immunology," in *Language Learning and Concept Acquisition: Foundational Issues*, ed. William Demopoulos and Ausonio Marras (Norwood, N.J.: Ablex, 1986).

34. Nor are "short theories" necessarily theories attainable by humans, or recognizable as intelligible theories by humans, given their specific biologically determined intellectual capacities.

35. Again, we are assuming familiar idealizations, as discussed elsewhere.

36. Strategies, memory structure, etc. Note that a parser, as conceived in current research, is postulated, rightly or wrongly, to be a real component of the mind/brain, a coherent subsystem of some sort including certain elements of the full interpreter, not others. As throughout, these assumptions are subject to exactly those general questions that arise in all empirical inquiry. The study of the parser is often thought to be some-

how immune to general problems that arise in the study of linguistic competence (that is, study of the generative procedure that is taken to be one component of the parser), but this is an error. It is sometimes argued that since evidence is always from performance, we have no justification for using it to determine the nature of underlying competence. By the same (fallacious) argument, we could conclude that we are not justified in using such evidence to determine the nature of the idealized parser, and we would have no basis for supposing that physics is the study of anything beyond meter readings. Data do not come labeled as "evidence for X, not Y."

37. Related considerations help explain why the efforts in AI about which Daniel Dennett is so enthusiastic are so barren of consequences (see the article by Hilary Putnam, discussing this matter, and Dennett's response in *Daedalus*, Winter 1988). Dennett believes that there are or might be substantive results falling under something he calls "engineering," but it is not clear what he has in mind, and his report of informal discussion several years ago, on which his account is in part based, seems to me rather misleading, to say the least. Note that the notion "study of everything" dismissed here has nothing to do with the "theory of everything" sought in contemporary physics.

38. Note again that there is no reason to suppose that the I-language "weakly generates" some set of well-formed expressions, so that it would make sense to speak of I-languages ("grammars") as "extensionally equivalent" or not in Quine's terms; even if this concept is found to have some sense or significance, now unknown, there is no reason to suppose that formal properties of this set would be of any interest for the study of language structure, meaning, learning, communication, parsing, etc. See my *Aspects of the Theory of Syntax*, chap. 1. There has been vast confusion about these matters, which I will not pursue here.

39. In an odd sense, however. In this case, I am applying a word lacking certain evidence that is relevant to its application, as specified by my internal lexicon. We would not say that Jones is misusing his language when he refers to an object before him as a sphere, not knowing that the hidden part has some different shape.

40. Even by sociolinguists and others who sometimes allege that they are not following this practice. On this matter, see my *Knowledge of Language*, 17–18.

41. Suppose that Jones's lexicon includes deference to some expert, say some speaker of German, in the entry for 'arthritis'. Then attribution of "belief" to Jones may involve further circumlocution, or we might want to abandon the concept as useless in anything like its familiar sense for psychology. But no matter of much import appears to be at stake. For more on the questions touched on here, see Akeel Bilgrami, "An Externalist Account of Psychological Content," *Philosophical Topics*, Spring 1987; Gabriel Segal, "In Deference to Reference" (Ph.D. diss., MIT, 1987).

PART II

Theories and Explanation

SEVEN

Constructivism, Realism, and Philosophical Method

Richard Boyd

1. INTRODUCTION

1.1. Constructivism and Realism

Post-positivist philosophy of science has gone in three directions: toward more sophisticated versions of empiricism (e.g., van Fraassen 1980), toward social constructivism (e.g., Kuhn 1970), and toward scientific realism (Boyd 1983, 1990a; Putnam 1972, 1975a, 1975b). Defenders of the latter positions affirm, while sophisticated empiricists continue the tradition of positivists by denying, that the typical product of successful scientific research embodies knowledge of unobservable phenomena—that scientists routinely do "metaphysics" in the positivists' pejorative sense of the term. Realists and constructivists differ in that the former hold, while the latter deny, that the phenomena studied by scientists exist and have the properties they do independently of our adoption of theories, conceptual frameworks, or paradigms. Thus, while realism and constructivism are both antiempiricist positions, constructivism shares with later positivism a tendency largely absent from realism of treating large-scale theoretical claims in science as in some important sense conventional. In the present essay I will be concerned with the dispute between constructivism and realism. I have three aims: to articulate the best arguments for realism against sophisticated versions of constructivism, to explore the implications of those arguments for our understanding of the issue of conventionality generally, and to explore some broader issues of philosophical method which are raised by the dispute between realists and constructivists.

1.2. Versions of Constructivism

The target of my arguments will be constructivist conceptions of science of the sort whose influence was guaranteed by Kuhn's *The Structure of Scientific*

Revolutions (1970). The general slogan "Science is the social construction of reality" and similar expressions of constructivist sentiment have a variety of interpretations, more than one of them suggested by Kuhn's own insights into scientific practice, and I will be concerned here with just one among them. Sometimes when students of science portray science as the social construction of reality, they mean to emphasize the extent to which the actual production of scientific texts, instruments, institutions, and so on is a social enterprise subject to the same sorts of analyses—political, sociological, literary, anthropological, and so on—as any other social enterprise whose output includes texts or other cultural artifacts (let us call this doctrine science-as-social-practice constructivism, SSP constructivism). Sometimes they mean to offer a debunking critique as well: perhaps that the content of scientific theories is determined almost exclusively by facts about power both within the scientific community itself and within the broader society (let us call this debunking constructivism).

The constructivism with which I will be concerned here (let us call it "Neo-Kantian constructivism," "N-K constructivism," by way of indicating something of its motivation but without prejudice regarding questions of Kant scholarship) is different. According to Neo-Kantian constructivism, consideration of, for example, the theory-dependence of scientific observation and methods, or the existence of mutually irreducible conceptual schemes or of mutually incommensurable paradigms in the sciences, indicates that there is something misleading, but not literally false, about the claim that in scientific work scientists *discover* what *the world* is like. The implicatures of that way of describing science reflect a conception according to which the structures which scientists discover are, independently of any scientific activity, "out there" in "the world" available for "discovery." This conception the Neo-Kantian constructivist denies: in some deep sense the structures studied by scientists are imposed on the world, in the sense of being reflections of the conceptual schemes they employ.

But according to N-K constructivists, it would be misleading (indeed, a straight-out error) to say, with a certain debunking tradition, that the internal politics of the scientific community or external pressures *and not the world* determine the content of scientific theories. While the phenomena of political determination identified by debunking constructivists sometimes determine the content of scientific theories, the sort of social construction which N-K constructivists emphasize is supposed to be a universal feature of scientific investigation, and it is not appropriately described by denying that "the way the world is" can determine the content of scientific theories. Two considerations indicate to N-K constructivists that scientific theories are often brought into approximate conformity with "the way the world is." First, the successful establishment of a scientific research tradition (or "paradigm") requires the cooperation of nature: research traditions are viable only if they allow their participants to succeed in actual experimental practice by, for example, predicting unexpected results or predicting expected ones with increasing numerical precision.

Just as important is the N-K constructivists' more general (and "Kantian") epistemological conception according to which social construction of reality is a necessary condition for systematic investigation. It is a consequence of the alleged ubiquity of social construction that the socially constructed reality which scientists study is as real as studiable things can get. There is no more real set of things in themselves for us to study, and thus no debunking of scientific investigation is entailed by the insistence that the reality scientists study is socially constructed.

Each of the three (or more) conceptions of science as a matter of social construction is worthy of serious elaboration and criticism. I focus here on N-K constructivism for two reasons. In the first place, it seems right to think of logical empiricism, scientific realism, and social constructivism as competing conceptions of the nature and of the limits of scientific knowledge, corresponding to broader empiricist, realist, and "Kantian" traditions in epistemology and metaphysics. If logical empiricism and scientific realism are thought of as theses about genuine knowledge in science (and not, for example, about how frequently such knowledge is produced by actual institutionalized scientific practice), then each is compatible with SSP constructivism and each is compatible with all but the most extreme version of debunking constructivism. That is, each is compatible with any versions of debunking constructivism which do not deny that some genuine scientific knowledge—in the sense of beliefs controlled in a suitable way by the way things actually are—is *possible*, however rarely (if at all) it is produced by institutionalized scientific practice. By contrast, both logical empiricism and scientific realism are incompatible with N-K constructivism, and it is reasonable to see N-K constructivism as the manifestation of a "Kantian" epistemological and metaphysical conception in contemporary philosophy of science. It is the version of social constructivism we want to look at if we are to see how significant general philosophical tendencies are played out in the philosophy of science.

There is another reason for focusing on N-K constructivism. One feature of the literature, both within professional analytic philosophy of science and in related areas of history, sociology, and literary theory, has been a tendency to conflate the three conceptions of social construction. For example, especially in the literature outside professional philosophy of science, it is often taken for granted that a demonstration of SSP constructivism precludes a realist or empiricist interpretation in favor of debunking constructivism or N-K constructivism.

There is likewise a tendency, in the professional philosophical literature as well as in the literature in other intellectual disciplines concerned with science as an object of study, to fail to distinguish clearly between debunking and N-K constructivism. Each of these tendencies, it seems to me, makes it harder for researchers to assess the merits of the three different doctrines. One of the consequences, I believe, is that a central problem facing debunking constructivists has been inadequately examined. It is, moreover, a problem whose solution at least arguably depends on an assessment of the philosophical merits of N-K constructivism.

Here is the problem: For all but the most extreme debunking constructivist it will seem important to distinguish between those cases in which the actual structure of the world plays some important role in determining the content of scientific doctrines, so that some genuine knowledge is achieved, and those cases in which it does not. If a realist (or, for that matter, an empiricist) conception of scientific knowledge is appropriate, the intended contrast can be straightforwardly defined. If, in contrast, an N-K constructivist conception of genuine scientific knowledge is correct, the moderate debunking constructivist will need to provide some formulation of the distinction between those episodes of "social construction of reality" in which the relevant social processes of consensus formation in science are to be thought of as *really* constructing reality and those episodes in which the establishment of consensus is to be debunked.

This problem is an especially acute one for the many thinkers who seem to have adopted both debunking and N-K constructivism in response to a recognition of the ideological role frequently played by scientific doctrines and the associated ideological determination of their content. If episodes of consensus formation in science cannot be so nicely categorized, then such thinkers run the serious risk of having, in consequence of their N-K constructivism, to treat as true the findings of just those episodes of theory construction which they otherwise seek to debunk.

I am inclined to doubt that a principled solution to this problem is available to the N-K constructivist. I am thus concerned to provide an adequate justification for the adoption of a realist rather than an N-K constructivist conception of genuine scientific knowledge, not merely to advance our understanding of foundational issues in the epistemology of science but to provide a basis for drawing the required distinction between genuine scientific knowledge and the sort of social construction worthy of debunking. It seems to me that the insights of many debunking constructivists are too important—politically and morally as well as intellectually—to be muddled by N-K constructivism. In "socially constructing" racial differences, nineteenth-century biologists did not construct a world in which those of African descent are biologically suited to a subordinate role, however much they constructed theories to that effect, nor have their latter-day followers done so—any more than those same biologists (or we) have socially constructed a world in which the place of women is determined by biological necessity.

1.3. The Need for a New Realist Critique of Constructivism

It might seem that mounting a defense of realism against N-K constructivism is not timely. After all, the articulation of distinctly realistic and naturalistic conceptions of reference and of kind definitions (e.g., Kripke 1972, Putnam 1975a) has significantly undermined the N-K constructivist arguments of Kuhn and Hanson, as has the articulation of distinctly realistic accounts of the appropriateness of theory-dependent methods (e.g., Putnam 1972, Boyd 1983). Arguably the realist's concern should now be with SSP and debunking constructivism and her task should be to show that the plausible versions of each of these positions are compatible with (and perhaps even entail) a realist conception of genuine knowledge.

I agree about the importance of the latter task, but it seems to me that there are reasons to believe that the available realist critiques of N-K constructivism are inadequate. In recent years "pluralist" or "relativist" conceptions closely related to the social constructivism of Kuhn and Hanson (e.g., Goodman 1978) have grown in influence, and I am inclined to think that these conceptions and other sophisticated versions of N-K constructivism are not adequately addressed by the extant realist critiques of views like those of Hanson and Kuhn. In brief, what I will argue is that there are plausible versions of constructivism which are not committed to the semantic or methodological conceptions to which anticonstructivist arguments grounded in naturalistic theories of definition and reference provide an adequate rebuttal, and whose epistemological and metaphysical claims are not fully rebutted by realist accounts of theory-dependent methods. What these versions of constructivism have in common is that they reflect ways of understanding conventionality which are more complex—and more plausible—than those which underlie earlier debates about constructivism. I will put forward here what I think to be the strongest arguments against the more plausible versions of constructivism. While these arguments have not, so far as I know, been made so fully explicit as I intend to make them, they do, I hope, capture the considerations that incline many philosophers of science to reject constructivism without fully exploring its more sophisticated variants.

The arguments in question are methodologically interesting—at least I find them interesting—because, while not in any obvious way entailing a naturalistic conception of philosophical method, they involve a certain kind of a posteriori scientific assessment of constructivist claims. I will explicate the relevant sort of scientific assessment and compare its operation with that reflected in the traditional logical-empiricist concern to hold philosophical accounts subject to the requirement that they offer a "rational reconstruction" of actual science. One outcome of this investigation is the articulation of a conception of the dialectics of philosophical argumentation which indicates how distinctly philosophical considerations properly interact with considerations arising from other disciplines.

2. CLASSICAL NEO-KANTIAN CONSTRUCTIVISM

2.1. Two and a Half Traditional Arguments for Constructivism

In this and succeeding sections of part 2, I propose to lay out and evaluate the classical arguments for and against N-K constructivism—those arguments which have commanded the interest of philosophers from the first articulation of contemporary N-K approaches by Hanson and Kuhn. Although I will cite the work of many of the key figures, I do not intend to be providing a historical survey of arguments for and against constructivism. Instead, I will try to identify the best and most plausible features of the arguments and considerations, explicit or tacit, that have influenced philosophers' views on these matters. I turn first to the classical arguments for constructivism.

All of the traditional arguments for (N-K) constructivism rest on the important observation that all of the fundamental methods of science, from the most basic observational procedures to the most elaborate standards for the assessment of evidence, are deeply and irretrievably theory-dependent. They differ in the extent to which they depend as well on special alleged historical consequences of theory-dependence. The following typology sorts the traditional arguments into two and a half basic categories.

The Basic Epistemological Argument from Theory-Dependence. Into this category fall the various arguments that justify an N-K constructivist conception of scientific knowledge by appealing to the fact of deep theory-dependence of scientific methods and exploring its epistemological implications. These are the key Neo-*Kantian* epistemological arguments for constructivism. They reason that the methods of actual science are so deeply theory-dependent that the only sort of reality for whose discovery they would be appropriate would be a reality partly constituted by the theoretical tradition within which scientific research takes place. Since, in my view, it is important not to underestimate the force of such arguments, I want to indicate something of the origins of their persuasive force.

In the first place, it is important to see that the methods of scientific research are not merely deeply theory-dependent, they appear to be such that their application would not be rationally justifiable except on the assumption of the truth or the approximate truth of the theories upon which they depend. Thus, insofar as we take (some) scientific research to be a basically rational activity, we, like the scientists who engage in that research, must be taking for granted the (perhaps approximate) truth of the theories that underwrite their methods.

Second, the theory-dependence of scientific methods is not somehow restricted to *derived* rather than *fundamental* methodological principles. It is, of course, no surprise that in developed sciences some (or most) of the methods scientists employ are justified by appeal to features of previously established theories. It might seem, however, that if the development and confirmation of theories in the relevant scientific traditions are fully explored, then it will turn out to be true, either in fact or in an appropriate rational reconstruction, that the traditions can be seen as having been first established by the application of theory-independent fundamental methods to theory-independent observations and as subsequently developing by the application at any given time of only those theory-dependent methods ratified by earlier theoretical discoveries. Were such a story true, then "in principle" we could take inductive inferences in sciences as governed by the underlying theory-independent methodological principles, treating theory-dependent methods somewhat on the model of derived inference rules in deductive logic.

What Hanson, (especially) Kuhn, and others have shown is that this picture cannot be sustained. When recognizably scientific methods emerge within a discipline, they emerge as part of a package that includes theoretical conceptions necessary to ratify them, rather than as initially theory-independent principles that ground the initial adoption of theoretical conceptions.

Moreover, not only are methodological principles deeply dependent on theories, the theories they depend on are often deep. I mean by that that the theoretical presuppositions of scientific methods are not, generally, almost unproblematical, if still a posteriori, propositions like "like causes have like effects," "every event has a cause," or "there is order in nature." Instead, the methods within a scientific discipline are typically grounded in foundational theoretical principles peculiar to that discipline's special concerns. As Kuhn suggests, scientists' judgments about the nature of the problems to be solved and the forms of acceptable solutions (that is, their judgments of projectibility) are typically determined by a metaphysical picture of what the world they study is ultimately like.

In consequence, the methodology of science will seem, with respect to the testing of fundamental assumptions at least, disturbingly *circular*. We may make precise both the nature and depth of the circularity, and the seriousness of the disturbance it creates, by examining with some care the recent fate of foundationalist conceptions of knowledge. Modern epistemology has been largely dominated by positions that can be characterized as "foundationalist": all knowledge is seen as ultimately grounded in certain foundational beliefs that have an epistemically privileged position—they are a priori, or self-warranting, or incorrigible, or something of the sort. Other true beliefs are instances of knowledge only if they can be justified by appeals to foundational knowledge. Similarly, the basic inferential principles that are legitimate for justifying nonfoundational knowledge claims can themselves be shown a priori to be rational.

We may fruitfully think of foundationalism as consisting of two parts, *premise foundationalism*, which holds that all knowledge is justifiable from a core of epistemically privileged foundational beliefs, and *inference-rule foundationalism*, which holds that the principles of justifiable inference are ultimately reducible to inferential principles that are a priori justifiable.

Recent works in naturalistic epistemology (see, e.g., Armstrong 1973; Goldman 1967, 1976; Quine 1969a, 1969b) indicate that foundationalism cannot be entirely correct. For the crucial case of perceptual knowledge, there seem to be (in typical cases at least) neither premises (foundational or otherwise) nor inferences; instead perceptual knowledge obtains when perceptual beliefs are produced by epistemically reliable mechanisms. Even if this analysis is challenged and it is insisted that justification of some sort is crucial in cases of perceptual knowledge, it is clear that there will be nothing like the traditional foundationalist's vision of knowledge of the external world grounded in premises as secure as, for example, those about sense data, and justified by appeal to a priori defensible inference principles.

Even where premises and inferences are unproblematically relevant, the notion of justification does not appear to be as epistemically central as traditional foundationalists thought: it seems to be the reliable production of belief that distinguishes cases of knowledge from other cases of true belief. Justification appears to be relevant because of the causal role which the seeking and giving of justifications play in reliable belief production (or regulation; see Boyd 1982).

Despite these setbacks, it might seem that some appropriate version of foundationalism provides us with an approximately correct picture of knowledge. If we think of ordinary perceptual beliefs, obtained under appropriate conditions, as suitably privileged, for example, and if we tolerate inference rules whose presuppositions only "the skeptic" would challenge, then a modest foundationalism might seem to capture pretty well the intuitive notion that knowledge claims must be noncircularly or non-question-beggingly defensible, however poorly it underwrites the refutation of skepticism.

We are now in a position to see just how and why the "circularity" with respect to fundamental principles unearthed by constructivists is so disturbing. What it suggests is that even modest foundationalism fails, even as a good first approximation to a theory of knowledge, not because the most basic available premises are insufficiently privileged but because inference-rule foundationalism appears to be profoundly mistaken. The basic inferential principles that are reflected in scientific methodology rest on deep and sometimes controversial theoretical principles which someone could reject—and which some have rejected—without the slightest hint of philosophical skepticism.

Now foundationalism is an especially plausible philosophical position, especially if it is understood in the proposed modest way and as an analysis of the notion of non-question-begging justification rather than as part of a scheme for refuting the skeptic. Thus the discovery of the deep theory-dependence of methods appears to threaten an especially plausible and central part of our conception of knowledge.

It poses a closely related problem as well. We are used to thinking of the establishment of the first successful research traditions within the various scientific disciplines as, in the first instance, insofar as internal factors are concerned, the result of the adoption of appropriate scientific methods. It is the reliability of those methods which we expect will explain the successes of researchers in obtaining an approximately correct theoretical picture of the relevant phenomena. This explanation is apparently precluded by a recognition of the deep theory-dependence of scientific methods. Indeed, it seems to get things more or less backward. Since methods possessing the reliability characteristic of those of recent successful science rest upon approximate theoretical knowledge rather than on a priori or commonsensical principles, the emergence of epistemically successful scientific methods must have depended upon the logically, epistemically, and historically contingent emergence of a relevantly approximately true theoretical tradition rather than vice versa. It is not possible to understand the initial emergence of such a tradition as the consequence of some more abstractly conceived scientific or rational methodology which itself is theory-independent. There is no such methodology.

Thus the theory-dependence of methods poses the *start-up problem*—how are we to explain the first emergence of approximately true theories within a research tradition, and thus the emergence of the reliable methods they determine, if not by reference to the prior establishment of noncontingently reliable methods? What seems to be indicated is a sort of *radical contingency* in the epistemology of science: not only does the reliability of scientific methods rest on highly contingent presuppositions but it is, in a philosophically important (*and nonskeptical*) sense, an *accident* that in the early stages of a successful scientific tradition relevantly approximately true theories and the associated reliable methods emerge at all (for further discussion see Boyd 1982, 1990a).

Modest foundationalism is extremely plausible, and solving the start-up problem by appealing largely to accident or luck seems implausible. No doubt these facts explain part of the attractiveness of debunking constructivism: if scientific methods are circular in such a way that scientific knowledge claims cannot be accepted without rejecting modest foundationalism, and without treating the first systematic successes of scientific research as accidents, then so much the worse for scientific knowledge claims.

What is important for our purposes is that the N-K constructivist interpretation of scientific knowledge to a significant extent ameliorates these difficulties and restores the possibility of a modest foundationalism. If basic laws of nature are to be seen as, in some deep sense, imposed on nature by our social conventions and practices, then the most basic theory-dependent methods may well be justified, if not a priori, then at any rate by appeal to principles that have a distinctly privileged epistemic standing. Other more specific methods that depend on plainly a posteriori theoretical considerations might then be treated as reflecting derived inference rules just as the foundationalist project requires. Similarly, the start-up problem will seem somewhat more tractable: at least part of the explanation of how the first successfully established paradigmatic theories came to approximate the truth about natural phenomena will lie in the fact that the acceptance of those theories *constitutes* the reality of the phenomena in question.

It is these considerations which, I suggest, make it plausible that the theory-dependence of scientific methods is such that if they are to be understood as discovery procedures, the reality they are used to discover must be thought of as constituted by the adoption of the relevant theories and methods. Only such an interpretation preserves a modest foundationalism in the philosophy of science and (thereby) permits an epistemically satisfying solution to the start-up problem.

One final point about the basic argument from theory-dependence is important here. I have suggested that the thrust of the argument should be understood as an attempt to preserve an eminently plausible version of foundationalism in the light of potentially embarrassing facts about the actual history of science. Of course this argument for constructivism would be unconvincing if it were possible by other more modest means to avoid the rejection of modest foundationalism. I believe that it is not. I have argued (Boyd 1989, 1990a, 1991) that scientific realism entails—given overwhelmingly plausible scientific and philosophical assumptions—just the sort of antifoundationalism from which N-K constructivism saves us.

It might seem that an empiricist conception of scientific theories would fare better in this regard, given the centrality of foundationalist assumptions in empiricist epistemology. I have argued elsewhere (Boyd 1990a, 1991) that this is not the case. So deeply theory-dependent are the actual methods of science that the most plausible *empiricist* treatment of them will treat their reliability as an empirical matter and their justification as consequently a posteriori. Instead of portraying theory-dependent methods as presuming the approximate truth of the background theories upon which they depend, the plausible empiricist position will treat them as grounded in a second-order induction about the reliability of inductive methods in science of the sort suggested by Quine (1969a). Since the conclusions of such inductions about induction are just about as unobvious and subject-matter-specific as the background theories whose methodological import they reconstruct, the plausible empiricist will reach as pessimistic a conclusion about inference-rule foundationalism as will the realist. Only the N-K constructivist saves modest foundationalism.

I conclude, therefore, about the basic argument from theory-dependence that, when properly formulated, it rests on the correct assessment that only N-K constructivism can reconcile the recognition of such genuine scientific knowledge as we appear to have with the acceptance of a modest and independently plausible version of foundationalism.

One and a Half Arguments from Incommensurability. In this category I place the arguments, anticipated in Hanson 1958 and developed in Kuhn 1970 and elsewhere, which seek to establish that the methodological and conceptual distance between successive stages in certain central scientific traditions is so great as to preclude any interpretation according to which they have a common subject matter. If the traditions are historically central enough (and Kuhn's candidates certainly are), the demonstration of such incommensurability would make impossible any defense of scientific realism along any currently developed lines and would almost certainly compromise the position of any empiricist who adopted the response to theory-dependent methods suggested above.

It is useful to distinguish between two components of the alleged incommensurability between such stages, *semantic incommensurability* (the doctrine that the conceptual gap between the relevant stages precludes a common reference for the terms they employ in common) and *methodological incommensurability* (the doctrine that no rational methods acceptable within each of the two relevant stages are sufficient for the resolution of the dispute between them). Central to the defense of the first of these doctrines has been the conception that the most fundamental laws containing a theoretical term, and perhaps the most central methodological principles governing its use, should be thought of as providing its definition so that changes in such laws and such principles represent a change in subject matter.

The arguments for methodological incommensurability have been more complex, but they all revolve around demonstrations that certain changes in theoretical conceptions (or "paradigms") have departed from plausible models of scientific rationality in important ways: There are never "crucial experiments" whose relevance is accepted by proponents of the earlier and later paradigms and whose outcome is decisive by the standards of each group. Instead, the results of individual experiments are always subject to significantly differing interpretations. Decisions of scientists to adopt the new paradigm have the character of changes in allegiance or outlook or career commitment more than that of a measured response to decisive evidence. Equally rational and distinguished scientists make different judgments about which allegiance to adopt. Full acceptance of the new paradigm often waits until the holdouts (who are often older scientists) have largely died or retired rather than being occasioned by some especially convincing body of experiments. The "textbook" picture according to which the new paradigm is decisively confirmed by the available data emerges only after the victors write new textbooks; it does not describe the process of transition between paradigms.

All of these (and similar) features of revolutionary transformation in science, the constructivist argues, fail to fit the picture of progress leading to increased knowledge of a theory-independent world. We might ask, "What must the world be like if the procedures of normal science are to be discovery procedures?" Since, according to the constructivist, scientific revolutions cannot be construed as episodes of discovery, we must think of the periods of normal science which they delimit as involving the investigation of quite different sets of socially constructed phenomena. A constructivist interpretation is necessary if we are to understand each of the episodes of normal science which precede and succeed a scientific revolution as involving the establishment of genuine knowledge: N-K constructivism emerges as the only alternative to debunking constructivism.

It seems to me that these two arguments are not best understood as providing independent considerations favoring N-K constructivism; each, by itself, makes at best a rather weak case for constructivism. Consider the case of the argument from semantic incommensurability. Even without the development of sophisticated realist (or empiricist) alternatives to the underlying theory of the definitions of theoretical terms, a number of considerations cast doubt on the conclusion that changes in fundamental laws must be taken as indicating a shift in reference or in subject matter. In the first place, the range of examples of apparent reference by (or in the face of) misdescription outside science is considerable so that one's confidence that fundamental laws must fix reference by exact and essentially analytic description should be limited.

There are, moreover, numerous examples within science in which changes in the most fundamental laws involving less "fundamental" entities or magnitudes do not seem to have involved a change in subject matter. We are not, for example, inclined to think that an apparent discovery that a disease has a dietary rather than a bacterial cause must be diagnosed as a change in subject matter, nor are we at all inclined to think that apparent disputes about the mechanisms of speciation must always reflect instead changes in the extension of the term "species." Such examples suggest that even in scientific cases fundamental laws are not always to be thought of as providing analytic or otherwise unrevisable definitions of their constituent terms. These considerations do not *entail* that the semantic theory underlying the argument from semantic incommensurability is mistaken for the sorts of cases involved in scientific revolutions, but they do cast doubt on its plausibility.

There are likewise reasons to doubt that the argument from methodological incommensurability is sound. There are a number of models of the ways in which the rationality of the scientific community supervenes on the rationality of individual scientists, and of dialectics of rational assessment of experimental evidence, which can accommodate the troubling facts about the epistemology and politics of scientific revolutions to a realist or empiricist conception of scientific progress. Such models can easily portray both the idiosyncratic and programmatic features of scientists' shifts in allegiance during "revolutions" and the dialectical complexity of the assessment of novel data as generally contributory to the epistemic success of scientists in studying the (theory-independent) world. Thus any successful deployment of the argument from methodological incommensurability would require rebuttals to these alternative models of revolutionary episodes.

Despite these weaknesses, the arguments from incommensurability have played a very serious role in recent philosophy of science. In part, that is so because they indicate fundamental weaknesses or difficulties in the deeply influential empiricist conceptions of scientific knowledge and of the semantics of scientific terms. But it would be a mistake to see their impact as exclusively negative. Instead, I suggest, while neither argument is by itself especially convincing, taken together they spell out in a mutually reinforcing way the details of an important nondebunking alternative to realist and empiricist conceptions of progress in science (hence: one and a half arguments from incommensurability).

2.2. *Two and a Half Classical Rebuttals*

Realist rebuttals to the classical arguments for N-K constructivism can likewise be classified into two broad categories embodying responses to the basic epistemic argument and to the arguments from incommensurability.

Realist Treatments of the Epistemology of Theory-Dependent Methods. In seeking to identify classical realist rebuttals to the basic epistemic argument from the theory-dependence of methods it is important to remember that both N-K constructivism and contemporary scientific realism arose largely as commentaries on the inability of traditional empiricist conceptions of science to take adequate account of the theory-dependence of actual scientific methods. Far from defending realism against difficulties raised by theory-dependence, realist philosophers of science are probably better understood as embracing the fact of theory-dependence as the basis of an argument for realism.

Against the epistemological argument for constructivism, I suggest, the classical realist rebuttal (I have in mind here the lines of argument represented in, for example, Putnam 1962, 1975a) is best thought of as involving a strategy for seeing theory-dependent methods, realistically interpreted, as *guarantors of*, rather than *obstacles to*, knowledge of a theory-independent reality. Here the crucial idea is that such methods should be seen as establishing the basis for scientists' *epistemically relevant causal contact* with their subject matter. The clearest illustration of this conception is that provided by a realist treatment of the theory-dependence of measurement procedures (see, e.g., Byerly and Lazara 1973) according to which scientists employ available approximate knowledge of "theoretical entities" in order to devise procedures for measuring or detecting them and their properties, thereby providing the basis for improvements in theoretical knowledge and in subsequent measuring procedures.

In general an account of the epistemology of science developed so as to sustain the realist conception of the positive contribution of theory-dependent methods in this way will portray theory-dependent methods (which is to say, in fact, all the methods of science) as reflecting a theory-dependent theory-modification strategy in which, if things go well (partial and approximate) theoretical knowledge is exploited to develop methods for the acquisition of new (partial and approximate) knowledge, in turn leading to better methods, and so on. Such an account then envisions a dialectical interaction between theoretical and methodological developments producing, under favorable circumstances, mutually reinforcing progress in both arenas (Boyd 1982, 1990a).

It is important to understand the strengths and weaknesses of this classical rebuttal. It answers the puzzling question "How might methods as theory-dependent as those of science provide knowledge of a theory-independent world?" by offering an epistemically favorable but realist account of the operation of those methods, one according to which their operation systematically guides researchers toward (approximate) truth. Insofar as the epistemic challenge to realism is seen as arising from the threat of radically contingent conception of the epistemology of science, the situation is different. The classical rebuttal in no way avoids the radical contingency that seems to plague (or at any rate to accompany) a realist or empiricist treatment of deeply theory-dependent methods. The theory-dependent theory-modification strategy embodied in scientific methods is portrayed as a theory-improvement strategy only when the method-determining background theories are relevantly approximately true, so that inference-rule foundationalism is abandoned and a radically contingent solution to the start-up problem is entailed. The realist who, like the constructivist, asks, "What must the world be like if the procedures of normal science are to be discovery procedures?" must answer, "A world in which, as a highly contingent matter of fact, suitably approximately true theories arose whose acceptance established reliable methods rather than being a consequence of their operation." (For an alternative diagnosis of the situation of the realist with respect to this issue see the challenging analysis in Miller 1987.)

Insofar as the classical realist rebuttal responds to the challenge of radical contingency (rather than just to the question of how theory-dependent methods can be seen as contributing to knowledge of a theory-independent world), it is almost certainly best understood as justifying radical contingency in the epistemology of science by assimilating it to a broader naturalistic antifoundationalism justified independently by appeal to naturalistic conceptions of perceptual knowledge, everyday natural knowledge, "folk" psychological knowledge, moral knowledge, and so on. Thus, to a far greater extent than has been widely recognized, scientific realism must be thought of as a component of a general naturalistic and antifoundationalist epistemology. (I develop this theme in part 5.)

The Classical Rebuttals to Incommensurability Arguments. Against the arguments from incommensurability, the classical realist rebuttals to constructivism can be seen, with certain important qualifications, as resting on two conceptions: (a) causal or naturalistic theories of reference and of kind definitions (Putnam 1975a, Kripke 1972, Boyd 1979) which provide the resources necessary to defend, in a fashion appropriate to the actual history of science, the denial that conceptual changes during "scientific revolutions" entail changes in subject matter, and (b) arguments to the effect that, for the actual episodes in the history of science identified as revolutionary by defenders of incommensurability, there obtained, to a relevantly good approximation, *pairwise theory-neutrality of methods.* According to arguments in this second class, although there are no general and theory-independent methods adequate to resolve the differences between pre- and postrevolutionary theoretical conceptions (or to do anything else interesting for that matter), there have always been methods whose justification is neutral between the conflicting claims of the pre- and postrevolutionary conceptions which rationally dictate the choice of the latter conception in most or all of its relevant details. (I have it in mind that an appeal to approximate pairwise theory neutrality of methods captures central argumentative strategies of, e.g., Putnam 1962, Shapere 1964, and Scheffler 1967.)

Now for the qualifications. In the first place, the theories of reference and of kind definitions which have classically been advanced against arguments from semantic incommensurability have displayed a mix of naturalistic or causal elements on the one hand and descriptivist or conventional elements on the other. What almost all such conceptions share with the positions of, for example, Kripke (1972) and Putnam (1975a) is that they acknowledge the important role, in fixing the reference of scientific terms and in defining scientific kinds (properties, magnitudes, etc.), of nonconventional (non-"nominalist") features of linguistic and scientific practice—features that reflect a strategy of deferring to the actual causal structure of the world in classificatory, inductive, and explanatory practice (for a general account of the relation between such deference and scientific practice see, e.g., Putnam 1975a, 1975b; Boyd 1979, 1990a, 1990b). Even among philosophers who are critical of "pure" causal theories of reference, there is near consensus in favor of "mixed" theories recognizing such deference and near consensus about the appropriateness of such theories for rebutting (many) claims of semantic incommensurability.

Qualifications are also required with respect to the claim that classical realist rebuttals to arguments from methodological incommensurability posit pairwise theory neutrality of methods. As I suggested earlier, the ways in which rationality of the scientific community supervenes on the rationality of individual scientists is complex, and one of the complexities is that, without compromising either individual or collective rationality, scientists within a tradition may differ significantly in their methodological standards and conceptions. Indeed it is arguable (from almost any philosophical perspective) that such divergence of methodological perspectives and the similar divergence on theoretical matters which sustains and follows from it are essential to collective scientific rationality. In consequence, it would be mistaken to think of a plausible realist rebuttal as resting, for example, on the claim that all of the principal methods that underwrite the acceptance of a new theoretical perspective or paradigm are acceptable to all of the serious or rational defenders of its predecessors. What realists are best understood as claiming is that all or most of the evidential considerations which persuade those who adopt the new conception are certified as evidentially relevant by theoretical and methodological considerations rationally accepted by a substantial fraction of the opposition and that, over time, the evidence which has accumulated becomes persuasive by all or almost all of the evidential standards which the earlier conception underwrites. This pattern of overlapping methodologies stretching over "revolutionary" episodes, the realist argues, makes a realist historical explanation of such episodes as reflections of the growth of knowledge about a common world preferable to any explanation that invokes wholesale semantic and methodological discontinuity.

It is almost certainly also essential to this classical realist rebuttal to claim that the pattern of overlapping methodologies reflects a convincing pattern of *mutual ratification* between consecutive stages in the development of the relevant scientific disciplines. It is routine in the case of theoretical innovations that (a) the new and innovative theoretical proposal is such that the only justification scientists have for accepting it, given the relevant evidence, is that it resolves some scientific problem or question *while preserving certain key features of the earlier theoretical conceptions* and (b) the new proposal ratifies the earlier conceptions as approximately true in just those respects which justify their role in its own acceptance. Moreover the patterns of mutual ratification are characteristically seen to be *retrospectively sustained*: although later theoretical innovations typically require a revision in scientists' estimates of the degrees and respects of approximation of both the earlier innovative proposals and their predecessors, the initially discernible relation of mutual ratification is typically sustained as a very good first approximation to the evidentially and methodologically important relations between the innovation and its predecessor theories. It is the ubiquity of this sort of *retrospectively sustained mutual ratification*, even in cases of "scientific revolutions," which, the realist will argue, justifies our accepting the realist conception of justification reflected in (a) and (b) (see Boyd 1988, 1990a); it will also be important for the realist's case to insist that the qualified methodological commensurability which the historical record exhibits is all the commensurability that a realist should expect (see Boyd 1988, part 5).

Importantly, the classical rebuttals to semantic and to methodological incommensurability are closely related. On the one hand, the sorts of referential continuity endorsed by the former are just those required to sustain the latter. On the other hand, the reference-sustaining mechanisms—causal or descriptive—and the conceptions of kind definitions for particular cases posited by naturalistic semantic conceptions are just those which are apparently indicated by the picture of the growth of knowledge offered in rebuttal to the argument from methodological incommensurability. They, like antirealist arguments from incommensurability, should be thought of as mutually supporting components of single philosophical conception offered as an alternative to the constructivists' conception of scientific revolutions, rather than as independent criticisms of it (hence, one and a half rebuttals to constructivism on the issue of incommensurability).

One more point about the classical rebuttals to constructivism will prove to be important to our consideration of the second-generation options open to sophisticated constructivists and their realist critics. The details of the classical realist rebuttal to incommensurability, I suggest, are important for a full articulation and development of scientific realism *but not for establishing a prima facie case against the incommensurability arguments*. Instead the largely example-rather-than-theory-driven considerations that so much reduced philosophers' confidence in the analytic-synthetic distinction, especially with respect to scientific propositions, operated in the case of semantic and methodological incommensurability as well, so that, even in the absence of definitive and fully articulated realist semantic and methodological conceptions underwriting an appropriately qualified finding of pairwise theory neutrality of methods, there still existed good, if not entirely compelling, reasons to suppose that such conceptions would be forthcoming. Indeed, the number of plausible semantic and epistemological conceptions that underwrite an appropriate finding of commensurability is so large, and the arguments from incommensurability are so dependent on rigid positivist caricatures of the semantics and epistemology of theoretical inquiry, that it has been for a long time reasonable to doubt the cogency of those arguments.

By contrast, I suggest, the case for realism against the basic epistemological argument for constructivism does really require something like the articulation of an alterative realist *theory* of confirmation and of the foundations of the epistemology of science. This is so because accepting a realist conception of scientific knowledge over either an empiricist or a constructivist conception requires the rejection of extremely plausible epistemological principles. In order to reject key empiricist arguments against the possibility of knowledge of "unobservables," the realist must abandon even the most plausible versions of the extremely plausible position that empirically equivalent theories are always equally well supported or refuted by any given body of experimental evidence (see Boyd 1983, 1989). Rebutting the constructivist conception of scientific knowledge requires the realist to abandon not only the evidential indistinguishability thesis just mentioned but an extremely plausible version of modest foundationalism as well.

In consequence, an adequate defense of scientific realism against the basic epistemological argument really requires the articulation of a distinctly realist (and naturalistic) epistemological theory adequate to justify the abandonment of these two plausible epistemological theses. I have argued elsewhere (Boyd 1982, 1989, 1990a) that an appropriate epistemological theory is available. Nevertheless, neither the theory I propose nor any other version of epistemological naturalism is uncontroversial, and—as I have indicated earlier—a naturalistic epistemology adequate to underwrite scientific realism will need to reject modest foundationalism in a way in which, for example, a naturalistic conception of everyday knowledge might well not. I conclude therefore that the basic epistemological argument for N-K constructivism is considerably more powerful than the arguments from incommensurability and hence that versions of N-K constructivism which do not posit the sorts of incommensurability anticipated by those latter arguments would pose a serious and interesting challenge to scientific realism.

3. SOPHISTICATED NEO-KANTIAN CONSTRUCTIVISM

3.1. Three and a Half Arguments for Sophisticated Constructivism

A sophisticated N-K constructivism that avoids positing semantic and methodological incommensurability across scientific revolutions is, I shall presently argue, certainly possible and is thus certainly a potential rival to empiricist and realist conceptions of scientific knowledge. The defender of such a constructivism will have available the argumentative resources of the basic epistemological argument without the burden of defending apparently refuted claims of incommensurability. In assessing sophisticated constructivism it will, of course, be important to examine realist rebuttals to the basic epistemological argument—that is, to assess the relative merits of realist naturalism and constructivism as epistemological theories. It will also be important, however, to take account of the less technical considerations which philosophers and others have thought of as favoring constructivism and to see to what extent these considerations may favor or compromise sophisticated constructivism or its realist alternatives.

I have claimed that the arguments from incommensurability for N-K constructivism are weak and that the variety of plausible rebuttals to them is great. Still it remains true that the primary arguments for constructivism discussed in the literature are the arguments from incommensurability and that constructivist conceptions of science, and closely related relativist conceptions, continue to exercise considerable (and perhaps growing) influence. It is reasonable to ask what explains this continued influence. Several explanations suggest themselves. In the first place, the distinction between N-K constructivism and other doctrines affirming the "social construction of reality" has not always been sharply drawn, and N-K constructivism has no doubt gained some support that properly belongs to the more plausible versions of those other doctrines.

I am inclined, however, to think that there is another important reason for the continued influence of constructivism. Many people, I believe, are convinced that, however well or badly the technical arguments from incommensurability may fare, broader philosophical considerations favor constructivism. The more general considerations favoring constructivism, I believe, are those which suggest that constructivism is required in order to account adequately for a variety of important features of science and of the relations between scientific inquiry and other human activities, even when recognition of those features may be logically compatible with the affirmation of an alternative conception of scientific knowledge.

One especially clear case of the latter sort of consideration is almost certainly the tacit recognition of the force of the basic epistemological argument discussed earlier. The revolutionary episodes in the history of science which underwrite claims of incommensurability do indicate quite clearly the profound theory-dependence of scientific methods, so it is reasonable to suppose that those who advance, or are persuaded by, arguments from incommensurability are also tacitly influenced by the more persuasive basic epistemological argument from theory-dependence.

In addition to the considerations captured by the basic epistemological argument there are, I believe, considerations of two other sorts which are widely thought to support constructivism.

Consideration of Unobvious Conventionality or Historicity in Representation. Here I have in mind the suspicion (linked to concerns about ontological pluralism discussed below) that there may well be, and probably are, features of our scientific picture of the world which appear to reflect fundamental features of nature but which are, in fact, artifacts of conventional or otherwise merely historically determined features of our conceptual schemes. I have in mind the sort of thing that is true of most of our conception of taxa above the species level if cladists are right. Such possibilities raise questions in general about the cogency of the distinction between features of our representational apparatus and genuine features of a representation-independent reality.

Consideration of Two Sorts of Pluralism. *Ontological Pluralism.* Here I have in mind the (justly) influential idea that the conceptual scheme necessary for adequately describing the world is underdetermined by the task of matching theory to causal structure so that there will be several different ways of "carving up" the world which are equally scientifically legitimate. This point can be amplified by indicating two dimensions to the pluralism thus identified.

In the first place it is true that *between* different scientific disciplines there will be different ways of carving up the world answering to the different interests and concerns of the various disciplines. It is also true that even *within* a single discipline there will be a plurality of adequate conceptual schemes. Especially in a dialectical situation in which it is widely held that realism entails both the interest-independence of natural kinds and categories, and the existence of a single true theory (with a single appropriate conceptual scheme), these considerations of ontological pluralism make constructivism seem an attractive option.

Since, where the phenomenon of ontological pluralism obtains within disciplines, it will be in some sense a conventional or merely historical matter which conceptual scheme scientists employ, such pluralism is perhaps best seen as a particularly striking and philosophically provocative case of unobvious conventionality in scientific representation. Similarly, the interest-and-discipline-dependence of kind definitions makes kind definitions determined in part by historical factors, so that this phenomenon too may be viewed as an important special case of unobvious historicality.

Cultural Pluralism. Here I have in mind the analogous, but in a way deeper, point that the theories and practices of cultures different from one's own are likely to embody strikingly different conceptual schemes and apparent ontological commitments without thereby being shown to be irrational. In taking considerations of this sort to tell in favor of constructivism, philosophers and others are participants in what is by now a long and deeply influential tradition of relativism in the name of tolerance.

The most important fact about these latter considerations favoring constructivism is that, like the basic epistemological argument from theory-dependence and unlike the arguments from incommensurability, none of them has been decisively rebutted by arguments which all or almost all realists would now accept. At least arguably an adequate realist response to the concerns about unexpected conventionality and ontological pluralism would require the adoption of a distinctly realist and non-Humean conception of causation, of reduction, and of supervenience which would not be fully acceptable to many scientific realists (see Boyd 1985b, 1989). Similarly, a cogent realist response to the concerns about cultural pluralism may well ultimately depend on the naturalistic and anti-(modest) foundationalist realist rebuttal to the basic epistemological argument (Boyd 1989, 1990a, 1991). I conclude that in assessing the relative merits of realism and sophisticated N-K constructivism we need to take seriously three and a half arguments for constructivism: the basic epistemological argument from theory-dependence and two and a half less-technical arguments—the argument from cultural pluralism and the (one and a half) closely related arguments from considerations of unexpected conventionality and historicality and of ontological pluralism.

3.2. Constructivism without Analyticity: How to Be a Sophisticated Constructivist
Insofar as the available rebuttals to the arguments from incommensurability rest on recent developments in philosophical theory, they rest primarily on the articulation of alternatives to the traditional empiricist conception that the definitions of general terms should be provided by analytic sentences or "L-truths." It is the ease with which one can articulate and defend alternatives to this conception that explains the ease with which such rebuttals can be developed.

It might seem that any version of N-K constructivism, however little committed to incommensurability, would be vulnerable to the refutation in the light of recent critiques of analyticity. After all, we are by now used to thinking of social conventions regarding cognitive matters as being reflected in the analyticity or truth by convention of some body of sentences. The constructivist, in treating certain features of reality as matters of social convention, must, it would seem, treat certain theoretical claims or other scientific principles as analytic or otherwise true by convention. The burden of proof would then lie with her to show that the relevant claims of conventionality are not as vulnerable as others have so often been.

It is important to recognize that what really matters to the thesis of conventionality or social construction in science is not analyticity or linguistic conventionality but rather a sort of *historicality*. What matters is whether fundamental factual descriptions in science represent structures whose existence and properties are in the relevant sense independent of the historical development of the research or practical traditions in which they are studied, or whether instead what is true about the world scientists study is determined in relevant ways by features of the conceptual structure which, as a matter of historical fact, has developed within those traditions. Is truth a matter of being faithful to the world "out there" or is it instead a matter of being faithful to certain traditions *and thus to the only studiable world there is*?

If constructivism is understood as the affirmation of the latter answer, then the commitment to anything like analyticity of some set of theoretical statements or other principles is, I suggest, entirely dispensable. Consider what sort of conventionality the constructivist must posit as operating within a tradition of inquiry if she is to retain the ontological thrust of N-K constructivism with respect to that tradition while avoiding implausible commitment to the unrevisability of any particular theoretical principles or other doctrines. What she requires is that the metaphysical picture represented in the relevant theories or other doctrines within the tradition be *in broad outline* a matter of convention but that the conventionality involved be such that the rules of rational inference internal to the tradition itself permit quite radical revisions in laws or other principles as a result of new data, theoretical innovations, or other developments acknowledged as epistemically relevant within the tradition itself.

Let us call the required sort of conventionality or historicality *dialectically complex conventionality*. It is all but certain that dialectically complex conventionality is not only possible but actual. Consider for example the wide range of traditions of theological inquiry which we would now describe as mythological (I think that all theological traditions should be so classified, but nothing in my use of this example depends on such an assumption). It is profoundly unlikely that all such traditions possess a tradition-independent subject matter. Almost equally unlikely is the historical thesis that each such tradition is founded on a set of analytic or otherwise unrevisable principles. Indeed, given the extent to which such traditions are known to be influenced by changing cultural, philosophical, scientific, political, and diplomatic factors, it would be an unlikely historical thesis that any such tradition is so founded. Thus it is reasonable to suppose that our understanding of the semantics of any such tradition involves the recognition of just the sort of conventionality which the N-K constructivist requires. Of course, the question will remain whether or not the constructivist can defend the thesis that relevant instances of this sort of conventionality are world-constituting in the relevant metaphysical sense, but—given the actual history of intellectual and practical inquiry—it seems that dialectically complex conventionality is a better candidate for this role than conventionality grounded in anything like analyticity.

It might be objected that the judgment that the required sort of dialectically complex conventionality is possible is philosophically premature since we do not have a secure theory of univocity for terms governed by such conventionality. Perhaps no account of univocity for complex traditions of the sort in question will underwrite the required judgments of continuity of subject matter, and we will be forced to recognize that only dialectically simple conceptions of conventionality grounded in notions like that of analyticity will support diachronic judgments of univocity.

It is true, of course, that there is no single theory of univocity for (as a realist would put it) nonreferring terms. But here, as in the case of the search for semantic theories to ground a rebuttal to arguments from semantic incommensurability, we suffer from an embarrassment of riches. Almost any theory one can think of, from a "property cluster" account to an account that mimics causal theories of reference by emphasizing continuities in referential intent, will ground a quite plausible first approximation to the required theory of univocity. We have every reason then to expect that an appropriate theory is possible.

Dialectically complex conventionality is almost certainly a real phenomenon, and it is not theoretically intractable. It follows that a sophisticated constructivist conception of science may be understood as asserting that such conventionality characterizes the ontological commitments of even the most mature sciences and that such conventionality has metaphysical import. Such a constructivism need not be burdened with the assumptions regarding analyticity and semantic and methodological incommensurability which make classical constructivism vulnerable to decisive refutation.

3.3. Sophisticated Constructivism and Commensurability

If sophisticated N-K constructivism can avoid just the conclusions about incommensurability which embarrass the classical version, it is reasonable to ask just what conclusions about commensurability and incommensurability sophisticated constructivism can accommodate. Two conclusions seem clear from the considerations rehearsed above.

With respect to the question of semantic commensurability the sophisticated constructivist can certainly accept any philosophically and historically plausible diagnosis to which a realist might be attracted. *Indeed, and this is the important point, the constructivist can appropriate the causal theory of reference as an account of the ground of judgments of coreferentiality made within any given research tradition, so that she can say and defend anything about the referential semantics of actual scientific theories which a realist can say and defend.* Of course she will hold that the reference-determining causal relations are themselves social constructs, but since that is something she says about all causal relations, no special problems need infect her conception of semantic commensurability.

Moreover, precisely because the sophisticated constructivist need not be burdened with implausible judgments of semantic incommensurability, she may similarly make and defend any judgment about methodological incommensurability which a realist could make and defend.

One qualification to theses conclusions may be necessary if we focus our attention on a special notion of *long-range commensurability*. Consider the situation of two different theoretical or practical traditions which, rather than enjoying the relation of predecessor to successor, have developed in relative independence but which have to some extent overlapping subject matters. Neither realism nor constructivism, nor sophisticated empiricism for that matter, predicts methodological commensurability between two such traditions. The mixes of insight and error which they embody may be so mismatched that there are no common methodological principles adequate to resolve the differences between them. Nevertheless there may be the prospect of long-range methodological commensurability: subsequent theoretical developments within the two traditions, perhaps in response to their interaction, may lead to a situation in which methodological commensurability obtains. There are reasons to believe that realism makes a certain extremely qualified prediction of long-term commensurability in circumstances in which sophisticated constructivism need not. After all, if both traditions study the same (socially unconstructed) world, then the world itself can be seen as a causal factor enhancing the likelihood of sufficient theoretical convergence to underwrite methodological commensurability. The difference here is, I believe, important both to the constructivists' treatment of issues of ontological and cultural pluralism (see section 3.4) and to corresponding realist rebuttals (see sections 5.4, 5.6), but it does not diminish the sophisticated constructivist's capacity to mimic plausible realist treatments of more standard questions of commensurability between successive stages in a single research tradition or between components of closely interacting traditions.

3.4. The Virtues of Sophisticated Constructivism

I now propose to indicate those virtues of sophisticated constructivism which, in my view, make it the version of constructivism to have if you are going to be a constructivist and (thus) the version of constructivism to refute if you are going to defend realism. Of course the obvious virtue of sophisticated constructivism is that it does not entail semantic or methodological incommensurability for those key historical cases upon which the most successful features of the classical rebuttal to traditional constructivism rest.

Just as important is the fact that sophisticated constructivism is just as well supported by (an appropriate version of) the basic epistemological argument as traditional constructivism is. Recall that the argument in question portrays constructivism as superior to realism (or sophisticated empiricism) because constructivism alone among these positions allows for the preservation of a modest foundationalism in the light of the actual historical facts about scientific knowledge. The standard constructivist's response to the irremediable theory-dependence of scientific methods should be understood, I have already suggested, as a proposal that the theory-dependent methods of science be seen as falling into two categories. The most basic rules are to be seen as grounded in theoretical principles that are true by social construction and thus a priori or otherwise epistemically privileged. Other theory-dependent inference rules are to be seen as "derived" rules justifiable ultimately by appeal to observational data interpreted according to the epistemically privileged basic rules. Modest inference-rule foundationalism is thus sustained.

Plainly this picture cannot be taken over unchanged by the sophisticated constructivist since where dialectically complex conventionality operates, any one theoretical principle could be rejected in the light of empirical evidence and any potentially basic inference rule thus undermined.

Nevertheless, sophisticated constructivism does seem to restore a modest version of inference-rule foundationalism. While no single theoretical principle and thus no single principle of inductive inference is portrayed as a priori justifiable, we are provided with an a priori or otherwise epistemically elevated justification for the broad theoretical and metaphysical picture that underwrites scientific methods, and thus for the broad methodological strategy of employing theory-dependent methods in the expectation of their general reliability and with the expectation that their subsequent refinement with the development of new knowledge will enhance their reliability. Two considerations suggest that inference-rule foundationalism this modest is appropriate as a component in a general modest foundationalism. In the first place, for most if not all scientific findings there are available converging confirmation strategies that reach the same conclusion on the basis of a variety of different methodology-determining theoretical presuppositions, and for most if not all findings the relevant methods presuppose only the approximate truth of the theoretical principles that underwrite them. Thus the epistemic warrant which sophisticated constructivism envisions for particular scientific findings will be even stronger than the epistemic warrant for the theoretical principles that underwrite the methods employed in any particular experimental or observational confirmation of it.

Moreover, that warrant is, at least arguably, as strong as any modest foundationalist should want. It seems reasonable—especially in a post-Humean world—to be suspicious of any philosophical theory of the ground of inductive inferences which makes the methods employed in making such inferences out to be more secure than they are seen to be by philosophically uncritical scientists and other inductive-inference makers. But even scientists who have forgotten their Hume in their enthusiasm for scientific methodology recognize that particular "fundamental" methods, and the theories they are based on, are revisable.

Sophisticated constructivism positing a dialectically complex conventionality in the ontological commitments of scientific theorizing has excellent prospects as well for availing itself of the other two and a half promising arguments for constructivism. Consider first the argument from the possibility of unobvious conventionality. The argument gets its force from the judgment about certain actual cases in the history of science that they involve(d) undiagnosed conventionality and from the conception that the difficulty in diagnosing such conventionality is in fact explained by its unexpected ubiquity. Whatever the merits of this argumentative strategy, it clearly will not work unless the initial diagnoses of unexpected conventionality can be sustained. If we understand conventionality as grounded in analyticity, then familiar arguments of a Quinean sort will profoundly undermine any such diagnoses. Only a conception positing dialectically complex conventionality could provide the basis for the required historical judgments.

Consider for example the very important claims of cladists that many of the features of traditional taxonomy above the species level are arbitrary or conventional. What is important to cladists' claims is that the sorting of species into higher taxa displays a large measure of historicality—that it is largely the history of classificatory practices and not the fitting of taxonomic categories to actual causal structure which determines the boundaries of higher taxa.

Analyticity of the definitions of higher taxa is not entailed, and it would be entirely inappropriate to offer in rebuttal to cladism a demonstration that no proposed definition of a higher taxon is in principle immune from empirical refutation; even cladists acknowledge that such refutation is possible since they hold proposed taxa to a posteriori standards like strict monophyly. The whole scientific and methodological point of cladism is lost if conventionality is understood as entailing analyticity and so is the pro-constructivist philosophical force of cladists' claims.

Similar conclusions follow with respect to the very similar argument from ontological pluralism. The philosopher who offers Quinean arguments to the effect that more than one scheme of ontological commitments can equally well fit the data and all of our justifiable methodological norms will be most ill-advised to hold that whatever choices a particular scientific community adopts are irrefutable in principle or otherwise rest on analytic foundations.

In the case of the argument from cultural pluralism the superiority of sophisticated constructivism has an additional dimension. Of course the philosopher concerned to advance an N-K constructivist conception of knowledge in order to combat cultural chauvinism will not want to have to hold about her own culture or others that their fundamental conceptions are so rigid as to render basic principles unrevisable in principle. She will, however, want to be able to diagnose semantic and (consequent) methodological incommensurability in those cases in which chauvinism is a serious possibility. We need to see whether the sophisticated constructivist strategy contemplated here will afford her that opportunity.

I have argued that the sophisticated constructivist, employing a dialectically complex notion of conventionality, can mimic the realist with respect to issues of commensurability in the history of science and can thus avoid the prima facie refutation of her position by the actual history of science which threatens the traditional constructivist. With respect to issues of commensurability between divergent cultural traditions, however, she is free to reach diagnoses of semantic incommensurability which a realist, especially a realist who is also a materialist, might reject. Recall that the sophisticated constructivist will posit conventionality within a tradition with respect to just those broad features of its conception of the world which seem so central as to define its epistemology: its basic methods and standards of evidence. In consequence she will treat two traditions as reflecting distinct episodes of the construction of reality—and as manifesting semantic incommensurability—just in those cases in which the case for methodological incommensurability is strongest: in those cases in which there seems to be no prospect for resolving the apparent disagreements between the traditions by appeal to "fair" (that is, tradition-neutral) methods. But, of course, these are just the circumstances in which a concern to preclude the possibility of cultural chauvinism will seem most pressing, and in which a diagnosis of unobvious conventionality and the social construction of reality will be most plausible.

I conclude therefore that sophisticated constructivism avoids decisive refutation by extant realist arguments while optimally satisfying the motives that often underwrite constructivist analyses.

4. DIAGNOSING THE CHALLENGE TO REALISM

4.1. Hidden Conventionality and a Kind of Supervenience

It is an obvious truism that social constructivists and logical empiricists posit unobvious conventionality or historicality in their analyses of scientific theories and research traditions more often than do scientific realists. It is just as obvious why this is: Let us call a methodological practice strongly theory-dependent just in case that practice is dictated by previously accepted claims about unobservable phenomena in such a way that its justification would require treating such claims as embodying approximate knowledge of "unobservables." There are lots of cases of sound methodological practices in the sciences which appear to be strongly theory-dependent. While empiricists and constructivists differ systematically in their response to apparently strongly theory-dependent methods, a common thread of appealing to the conventional characterizes each approach.

Empiricists have traditionally denied that apparent theory-dependence of scientific methods survives "rational reconstruction." They have typically subscribed to some version of inference-rule foundationalism and thus they have often denied (or failed to consider) even the weaker form of theory-dependence which would obtain if some rational methods in science depended irreducibly on a posteriori premises about observables. Of course empiricists have necessarily rejected strong theory-dependence, and one especially attractive strategy for providing the required empiricist reconstruction of cases in which rational methods seem irreducibly to depend on theoretical premises is to grant the dependence but to portray as conventional (as L-truths in Carnap's sense) some of the theoretical principles upon which the rationalization of methodological practices depends, so that no unreduced appearance of strongly theory-dependent methods survives reconstruction. In no case will the posited conventionality be in any sense obvious.

Similarly, but for different reasons, social constructivists respond to apparent strong theory-dependence of methods by treating fundamental theoretical assumptions as reflections of conventionality (or "social construction"). They treat many cases of apparent strong theory-dependence as genuine—as involving methods with deep and irreducible metaphysical presuppositions—but, for the sorts of reasons indicated in the preceding sections, they see the metaphysical reality that is the real subject of those presuppositions as socially constructed. Like empiricists whose response to apparent strong theory-dependence theirs resembles, they typically portray the most basic theoretical principles as conventional or socially constructed, treating less fundamental principles as empirically justified, given the methods justified by the deeper social construction. Thus for constructivists too, in no case will the posited conventionality be in any sense obvious.

Realists, by contrast, typically embrace apparent strong theory-dependence at approximate face value without conventionalist reconstruction. They are thus much less inclined to posit unobvious conventionality than either empiricists or N-K constructivists. What is important for our purposes is that, although conventionalists diagnose hidden conventionality more often than realists, it is denied neither by realists nor by those empiricists who reject the strategy of rational reconstruction just discussed that there are possible (indeed actual) episodes in the history of science in which features of well-confirmed theories which were rationally taken to reflect real features of the world turned out instead to reflect historically contingent (and in that sense conventional) features of the conceptual scheme of the relevant community. Indeed, cases abound in which such a diagnosis would be plausible for any realist or empiricist. If the theoretical justification which Guyot (1987) provides for cladism is convincing, then the cladist diagnosis of a high level of conventionality in the definitions of higher taxa provides a spectacular example. So do some other less inspiring examples from the history of biology. Certainly many nineteenth- and early-twentieth-century discussions of the biology of race and nationality rest on schemes of classification of human populations which turn out to be, from the point of view of biology, conventional, historically contingent, or "socially constructed" in ways that were unexpected by those who employed them, and it would be wildly optimistic to hold that there are no similar cases of undiagnosed conventionality in current biological work on, for example, human social structures.

Thus the difference between realists, empiricists, and constructivists is not over whether hidden conventionality is possible or actual but over, among other things, when (and hence how often) it should be diagnosed. But there is another important question about hidden conventionality, one with respect to which realists and (as I shall presently argue) empiricists find themselves in agreement against N-K constructivists. I have in mind the question of whether or not unexpectedly conventional features of well-confirmed theories should be thought of as—in the relevant sense—reflections of the *reality* which scientists study.

The *agreement* between the three major conceptions of scientific knowledge that hidden conventionality is a real phenomenon is a reflection of general agreement on two points: first, the unproblematical claim that in every case in which a statement in a language is true (or false) its truth (or falsity) supervenes to some extent on the social practices and conventions of the relevant linguistic community, and, second, the almost equally unproblematical claim that the semantics of actual languages is complex enough that the extent and nature of that partial supervenience will not typically be entirely obvious. The *disagreements* between the three conceptions are much subtler. In particular if we focus, as we should in the present case, on the disagreement between realists and empiricists, on the one hand, and constructivists on the other, over whether unexpectedly conventional features of good scientific theories should be thought of as, in the relevant sense, *corresponding to reality*, then what emerges is an abstruse metaphysical issue about the nature of the partial supervenience relation between the truth of the statements those theories embody and the social practices within the communities that accept and employ them. It is with this issue that we must deal if we are to assess the relative merits of realism and sophisticated constructivism.

4.2. Philosophical Packages

If sophisticated constructivism can mimic realism in its treatment of episodes in the history of science even to the extent of availing itself of causal theories of reference, and if the disagreements between these positions revolve around relatively speculative issues regarding long-term commensurability and relatively esoteric issues about supervenience relations, it is reasonable to wonder what philosophical methods are appropriate for evaluating the relative merits of the two approaches. In this section I address this question, developing the notion of a *philosophical package*, which I have introduced in several earlier papers (Boyd 1988, 1990a, 1990b).

We are all familiar with detailed and specific arguments advanced in defense of or against philosophical conceptions: realism is epistemologically unsound because theoretical conceptions are underdetermined even by all possible observations, phenomenalism fails because the proposed definitions of physical objects in the sense-datum language must in fact incorporate a posteriori claims about the causal operation of the senses, we must accept a noncognitivist account of moral statements because there is a logical gap between statements of fact and conclusions about duty or obligation . . . (where each of these arguments is to be thought of as spelled out and elaborated). Much of what we do—and ought to do—in philosophy takes the form of the articulation and criticism of such arguments.

It is nevertheless no surprise that single arguments of this sort are rarely (or never) thought to be decisive. Philosophical theses get modified in the light of criticisms, and their defenders may offer revisions in our understanding of related philosophical (or other) matters in order to rebut a criticism or articulate a positive argument. Thus, for example, phenomenalism can be given a respite from the argument just sketched by a defender who adopts an entirely different conception of the semantics of the imagined sense-datum language according to which its terms might be thought of as referring *causally* to naturally occurring regularities in patterns of sensation. Since there is no real sense-datum language, this approach would have to be spelled out in terms of a suitable thesis about the semantics of thought, together with a suitable conception of the connection between thought and actual languages. The phenomenalist who makes the required modification in her account and accepts the associated semantic theses will have a version of phenomenalism which requires no analytic definitions at all.

Here we have a Duhem-Quine phenomenon in philosophical methodology. Scientific theories face the results of observation in bunches; philosophical theories face whatever-it-is-that-philosophical-theories-face in bunches, too. I have argued elsewhere (Boyd 1988, 1990a, 1990b) that, in response to this complication, there is a methodological conception tacitly at work in all of the philosophy of science (and in the rest of philosophy for that matter) according to which the case for any given philosophical position, like scientific realism, logical empiricism, or constructivism, consists not just in the arguments explicitly advanced on its behalf but also in the broader range of conceptions about epistemological, metaphysical, semantic, and other matters that are either necessary to its defense or plausible developments of it. Rational choices between competing philosophical conceptions are in turn based on assessments of the relative merits of the "philosophical packages" thus associated with them.

Thus, for example, the case for an empiricist conception of scientific knowledge rests not only on the primary verificationist arguments in its favor but also on the success of related empiricist treatments of issues of the semantics of theoretical terms, the nature of explanations, the analysis of materialism, and so forth. Similarly the case for realism rests not only on arguments designed to establish realism as the appropriate account of theory-dependent scientific methods but also on the development of distinctly realist conceptions in semantic theory and metaphysics. A rational assessment of the relative merits of these conceptions requires an evaluation of the relative merits of the associated philosophical packages.

What I propose is to employ this explicit formulation of commonsense philosophical methodology in analyzing the relative merits of realist and constructivist conceptions of scientific knowledge.

4.3. *Two and a Half Constraints on Conventionalism(s)*

In a certain sense all philosophical analyses of science, even realist ones, aim at what positivists called "rational reconstruction": they aim at identifying and highlighting as central those features of science which are most fully rationally justified and at distinguishing these from less rational features that are diagnosed as inessential. In this section I formulate some rational constraints on theories of conventionality in science, thinking of such theories as components in rational reconstructions of scientific knowledge, and thinking of those reconstructions in turn as components in broader philosophical packages. I suggest that we can glean from sound practice in the philosophy of science two and a half constraints on rational reconstructions which have a special bearing on accounts of conventionality in science. In each case what is crucial is that acceptable rational reconstructions must, in a sense to be explained, reconstruct *actual* science. I propose that any adequate rational reconstruction must meet two conditions, one of which has, as a special case, an important constraint on the supervenience relation between truth and (among other things) social practices discussed in section 4.1. Here they are:

Coherence with Actual Science. I have in mind here two closely related constraints on proposed reconstructions. The first requires that, prima facie, the reconstructed versions of scientific theories must be consistent with the apparently best-supported findings arising from actual scientific practice, where the standards of evidence are those prevailing in the apparently best examples of such practice. This requirement is not absolute both because it is permissible for philosophers to make philosophical or scientific criticisms of prevailing methodology and prevailing theories and because philosophical or other cogent reasons may dictate rejecting an apparently well-supported part of current science. Nevertheless, it has been an important and rational feature of practice in the philosophy of science and elsewhere to impose a burden of proof on philosophers whose reconstructions require abandoning apparently sound scientific findings. One example of the operation of this constraint has been the universal acknowledgment among empiricist philosophers that their denial of the possibility of knowledge of unobservables is in greater need of philosophical defense given the apparent success of chemists, using the best available chemical methods, in discovering features of the (unobservable) microstructure of matter.

The closely related constraint is that the specifically philosophical claims that are components of a proposed reconstruction (or are central to its defense) must prima facie also be coherent with (suitably reconstructed) findings of actual science. The most obvious example of the application of this constraint is probably the challenge to early logical empiricists' phenomenalism which arose from the difficulty in assimilating causal theories of perceptual experience, understood as empirical theories, to the phenomenalist conception that physical objects themselves are to be thought of as constructs out of sense data.

This example also illustrates a special case of the two constraints just discussed which is especially important for our present purposes: the constraint of *supervenience relation 'reduction'*. Whenever a theory, philosophical or otherwise, has the consequence that phenomena of one sort supervene on phenomena in some other class, rational methodology requires that, prima facie, the theory should be acceptable only if it is possible, given the best available theories of the relevant sorts of phenomena, to understand how phenomena of the first sort and their causal powers could be appropriately related to phenomena in the proposed supervenience base. What is required is that, in some weak sense of the term "reduction," it be possible to establish an appropriate reduction of the allegedly supervenient phenomena and their properties to the properties and interactions of the phenomena in the alleged supervenience base.

This requirement has two aspects. The first, illustrated in the case of critiques of phenomenalism, is that when it is maintained that phenomena in one class supervene only on phenomena in some second class, it should be possible to explain how the causal powers and properties of phenomena in the first class can be fully accounted for by the powers and properties of phenomena in the second class. The second aspect is more important for our present investigation. Suppose that it is proposed that phenomena in one class are essential components of any supervenience base for phenomena in some second class. Then it must be possible to make scientific sense of the posited necessity. It must be possible to understand why, were phenomena of the first sort relevantly absent or different, phenomena of the second sort would be absent or different. It is this aspect of the supervenience reduction requirement which is tacitly invoked when it is objected to a particular version of behaviorism that some psychological state or other could exist even if the behaviors said to be from a necessary component of any supervenience base are absent. Note that we can recognize a plausible appeal to the supervenience reduction constraint—or any other similar constraint—even if we hold that the resulting challenge to a supervenience claim is ultimately unsuccessful.

Of course this 'reductionistic' requirement applies in the special case in which the supervenience in question is an alleged eliminative or constructivist supervenience of the truth of various factual claims on features of linguistic or conceptual conventions or other aspects of social practice or mental life. When it is claimed that truths about some sort of phenomena supervene largely or exclusively on such matters of linguistic or other convention, and when, according to the best available science, the supervening phenomena have certain causal powers or effects, it must prima facie be possible to offer a scientifically acceptable account of how those powers and effects are realized by the causal capacities of the phenomena in the alleged supervenience base in such a way as to sustain the intended metaphysical (or antimetaphysical) conclusions. It is precisely this requirement which the phenomenalist eliminativist analysis of truths in the "physical object language" was apparently unable to meet.

Closely related to these constraints is another, the requirement of *ratification of reconstructed methods* which has been central in disputes in the philosophy of science. Scientific methods are (often if not always) theory-dependent and we prima facie require of a proposed reconstruction of well-established scientific theories that the reconstructed theories ratify (suitably reconstructed versions of) the actual methods of science. Of course this requirement significantly constrains the acceptance of conceptions of conventionality in science. Thus, for example, the operationalist doctrine that theoretical terms should be thought of as conventionally defined in terms of fixed laboratory procedures failed as a reconstruction precisely because there proved to be no plausible way of accommodating within an operationalist reconstruction the ways in which rational methods in science permit the relevant sorts of laboratory procedures to be revised and improved in the light of new theoretical developments.

It is important to see that these requirements are both stronger and weaker than a requirement that philosophical theories and the methods they would rationalize be *consistent* with the apparent findings and methods of the best science. On the one hand the requirements set weaker standards than consistency since sufficiently strong philosophical considerations might well justify abandoning apparently well-established findings or methods. Thus logical empiricism is not immediately refuted by the observation that it requires us to abandon the apparently scientifically appropriate methodological judgments that countenance the confirmation of propositions about the unobservable.

On the other hand, more than consistency with the ordinary findings of science is sometimes required. Where, for example, philosophical theses involve supervenience claims of a sort not contemplated in any of the (other?—see below) sciences, the "reductionist" requirement requires that we assess the coherence with the best science of claims which no scientist would ordinarily consider. If we reach an adverse verdict regarding a proposed supervenience claim, the reason will be that it does not make good scientific sense, all things considered, rather than that it is inconsistent with a finding of some scientific discipline or other.

A Naturalistic Note on Method. The methodological role played by these constraints illustrates an important methodological point about the "philosophical packages" that represent contending positions in the philosophy of science. One way to formulate this point is to say that such packages are not to be thought of as subject only to purely philosophical criticism: they are subject to additional requirements of appropriate coherence with the findings and methods of the various sciences. An alternative formulation is that philosophical packages should be thought of as including, in addition to distinctly philosophical doctrines, suitable versions of the findings of the various other disciplines with which philosophical inquiry overlaps. The latter formulation is almost certainly better: it is, after all, appropriate relations to suitably reconstructed scientific findings and methods which philosophical doctrines are required to achieve, and the suitability of a reconstruction of scientific findings is partly determined by the philosophical project in whose aid the reconstruction is proposed—that is, by the rest of the philosophical package with respect to which it is formulated. It will thus be more fruitful to think of philosophical packages as incorporating proposed reconstructions of the relevant findings from other disciplines. On this formulation, the two and a half constraints just discussed are to be thought of as reflections of broader requirements of coherence applicable to philosophical packages generally.

However the issue is formulated, what is important is that, quite independently of any general commitment to philosophical naturalism, we must recognize that good philosophical methodology requires of proposals in the philosophy of science an appropriate coherence with the empirical investigation of the natural and social world. Methods in the philosophy of science must be at least to that extent naturalistic.

It remains to see how these naturalistic considerations and other standards for assessing philosophical packages apply to the choice between realist and N-K constructivist packages when the latter packages reflect a dialectically complex conception of conventionality. It is to that question that we now turn our attention.

4.4. Diagnosing the Differences: How to Tell Carnap from Kuhn and Other Interesting Questions

N-K constructivists agree with realists that scientists routinely obtain and employ knowledge of unobservables, "metaphysical" knowledge of the sort logical empiricists thought impossible. They agree as well that the truth of the statements that articulate this knowledge supervenes to some extent on linguistic conventions and other social practices, but they disagree with realists in subtle but nonetheless crucial ways about the nature of that supervenience relation: they differ about the philosophical import of (at least some) conventions. If we are to examine the relative merits of constructivist and realist philosophical packages, we need to have a deeper understanding of the difference in their conceptions of conventionality. One possible approach is suggested by the dispute between realists and traditional constructivists like Kuhn. Traditional constructivists hold that fundamental scientific laws are sometimes (exactly) true by convention whereas it is unlikely that any scientific realist would treat any fundamental law as unrevisably conventional, and this seems to be a deep fact about realism: the realist's naturalistic and Quinean commitments will make her doubt that terms used in any dialectically complex inquiry will possess analytic definitions. We might hope, therefore, to distinguish realists' from constructivists' conceptions of conventionality in terms of the sorts of features of conceptual systems which they think can in principle be conventional: the kinds of things which rationally acceptable conventions can dictate that we accept or do.

Sadly this approach is unlikely to be helpful in the present case. The reason is that the defender of sophisticated constructivism is equipped with a dialectically complex notion of conventionality. Such a conception has two features. In the first place, of course, it avoids the commitment to analyticity and can in fact be incorporated into a semantic theory which *very* closely mirrors that of the realist with respect to actual cases in the history of science. More importantly, the sorts of features of conceptual systems which sophisticated constructivism treats as conventional in science (roughly: broad features of a metaphysical picture) are the sorts of features which the realist must hold can be (indeed are) matters of convention in some cases of dialectically complex inquiry. Thus, while the almost complete rejection by realists of analyticity may provide a clue to the difference between realist and constructivist conceptions of conventionality, a simple extrapolation of that rejection will not help us to distinguish realists from sophisticated constructivists.

What would be nice to examine would be a case in which realists and sophisticated constructivists agreed exactly about what the conventional features of a tradition of inquiry were but regarding which they differed about the philosophical import of the conventionality they both accepted. Such a case would be provided, for example, if realists and sophisticated constructivists agreed—as they well might—about the conventional elements in, say, ancient Greek theology but differed in that constructivists took the relevant conventionality to be *world-constructing*, in the philosophically relevant sense of that notion. Of course we have no such example to examine: sophisticated constructivism is a position that has yet to be fully articulated, and thus we are not yet in a position to see just what instances of conventionality the sophisticated constructivist would have to take as world-constructing. Instead of using examples of the sort in question to clarify the differences between realists and sophisticated constructivists regarding conventionality, we need to do something like the opposite: to use an understanding of the different conceptions of conventionality to clarify differences in the conceptions of the philosophical applications of that notion.

In consequence I propose to approach the problem of characterizing constructivist-realist differences over conventionality indirectly, by examining a case in which a traditional constructivist and a traditional empiricist do agree almost exactly about what the conventional elements are in a scientific research tradition while differing about the philosophical import of the conventionality they both acknowledge. I propose to ask how to tell Carnap from Kuhn. The question arises because, on the one hand, the later Carnap (of, say, "Empiricism, Semantics, and Ontology," 1950) accepts, in a certain sense, the constructivists' and realists' claim that scientific knowledge extends to knowledge of, for example, electrons, and, on the other hand, Kuhn in *The Structure of Scientific Revolutions* (1970) avoids the apparent realist implications of this conclusion by adopting a conventionalist conception of the semantics of scientific language which is almost exactly that advanced by Carnap in order to avoid the same realist conclusions. Each takes the fundamental laws involving a theoretical term to constitute that term's conventional definition. How, then, is Carnap different from Kuhn? If we understand the basis of the deep differences in philosophical import of two conceptions of conventionality as similar as Carnap's and Kuhn's, I suggest, it will help in diagnosing other deep but subtle differences regarding conventionality.

Insofar as they are taken to be describing (rather than philosophically analyzing) scientific practice, Kuhn may be seen as in large measure persuasively working out the historical, social, and psychological details of the adoption, in a natural-language context, of the sorts of theoretical conventions mirrored by the "L-truths" of the formalized languages appealed to by Carnap. Pretty plainly this conception of the descriptive content of Kuhn's work leaves unaddressed the philosophical features of Kuhn's analysis which result in its distinctive challenge to empiricist (and realist) conceptions of scientific knowledge. What we need to know is what features of Carnap's and Kuhn's positions make the first distinctly empiricist and the latter distinctly (antiempiricist and) social constructivist.

An obvious candidate (and perhaps a point of difference in their descriptions of scientific practice) lies in Kuhn's emphasis on the theory-dependence of observations. There must be something right in focusing on this issue, but recognizing their differences over the theory-dependence of observations by itself is not likely to allow us to fully understand the difference between Carnap and Kuhn or—since this is our ultimate aim—the difference between the treatments of conventionality appropriate to realist, empiricist, and constructivist philosophical packages. The reason is this: There is a variety of ways in which the empiricist can acknowledge the theory-dependence of observations in scientific practice without abandoning hope of a suitably empiricist rational reconstruction of observational practice in science. We have already seen that an appeal to the pairwise theory-neutrality of methods generally (and of observation in particular) may play a role in such a reconstruction. In fact, all that would be needed for an empiricist or a realist reconstruction would be an account according to which the theory-dependence of the methods and vocabulary of observation in science does not preclude our understanding observations and observation reports as providing for science epistemic access to its theory-independent subject matter. What is important is that somehow the N-K conception of scientific conventionality is supposed to obviate the need for such a reconstruction: epistemic access to theory-dependent reality is what scientists are to be seen as achieving.

If we move to the consideration of the structure of philosophical packages, what we see then is that the constructivist philosophical package à la Kuhn is to be equipped so that it treats socially constructed observation of, for example, a socially constructed planet as playing roughly the same role which an empiricist (or realist) package assigns to the (unconstructed) epistemic access to an (unconstructed) planet which it attributes to astronomical observation. Plainly more is going on than just the recognition of the theory-dependence of observation. Whatever else is going on must provide the answer to the question of how, given that both Kuhn and Carnap hold that fundamental laws are true by convention, their conceptions of conventionality differ in such a way that Carnap's position is empiricist while Kuhn's is antiempiricist and N-K constructivist.

Pretty obviously the difference lies in whatever is expressed by Kuhn's claim that scientists who work within different and competing paradigms study "different worlds": the constructivist conception of (certain) conventions in science treats them as world-constituting or something of the sort whereas the empiricist conception does not. Of course N-K constructivists' talk about "different worlds" or the "social construction of reality" is plainly metaphorical. If such talk is without genuine metaphysical and epistemological import—if it is just a vivid way of indicating some of the sociological and psychological consequences of the theory-dependent and socially organized character of scientific practice—then constructivists turn out to be empiricists, or to be realists, albeit realists with an inadequate semantic theory for theoretical terms. So we need an interpretation of "different worlds" and related metaphors which gives them metaphysical and epistemological import and which distinguishes Kuhn's conception of conventionality, for example, from that of the later Carnap.

One idea might be to say that Kuhn's and Carnap's conceptions of conventionality differ in that Kuhn affirms whereas Carnap denies that conventional truths can have ontological import. For Kuhn and for Carnap the question of, for example, the existence of free electrons is to be understood within a context determined by certain fundamental laws about electrons which are themselves to be understood as constituting the conventional definition of "electron." But, it might be argued, for Kuhn the content of those conventional laws has ontological import, which the question of the existence of free electrons inherits, whereas for Carnap ontological import is absent. Something like this must be right, but the notion of ontological import does not do the right job: after all, the point of "Empiricism, Semantics, and Ontology" is precisely that it is the "internal" existential questions about theoretical entities like electrons which capture all the ontological import there really is. Still, we can certainly say that, according to Kuhn, but not according to Carnap, the theoretical conventions that fix the meanings of theoretical terms have metaphysical import. Carnap's position is empiricist rather then realist (or constructivist) in large part because his drawing the distinction between internal and external questions is designed to permit him to treat the former as nonmetaphysical components of scientific inquiry and the latter as nonmetaphysical pragmatic questions.

As the differences between empiricist and constructivist treatments of the theory-dependence of observations indicates, "different worlds" and related metaphors are supposed to have epistemological as well as metaphysical implications. One thing that seems clear about Kuhn's position is that the fundamental tenants of a paradigm are supposed to be research-guiding in an epistemically central way. Paradigm articulation consists in developing and testing problem solutions suggested by the previous achievements of the paradigm, and this pattern of reasoning defines scientific rationality.

It is important to seeing the relation between paradigm articulation and rationality that we recognize that, in exploring those problem solutions suggested by the paradigm, the scientist is to be understood as exploiting previously acquired *knowledge* of the world. Solutions to new problems are explored just in case they fit the metaphysical picture represented by the paradigm in its current stage of development, and this research strategy is rational (indeed defines rationality) precisely because that metaphysical picture represents knowledge of the world the scientist studies. A proposed problem solution that "fits" existing paradigmatic achievements is appropriate for scientific investigation precisely because it is supported by a kind of inductive inference at the theoretical level: from previously acquired theoretical knowledge the scientist infers a nontrivial likelihood that the proposed solution is correct, and that is what justifies her experimental investigation of it. It is precisely this that is the import of Kuhn's (and the realist's) claim that rational scientific investigation is guided by a metaphysical conception of the phenomena studied.

Here, I think, is the clue to the epistemological difference between the constructivist's and the empiricist's conception of conventionality in science. Although Carnap, for example, must agree that scientists know the theoretical claims that constitute the definitions of their theoretical terms, the nonmetaphysical empiricist interpretation of the relevant conventions precludes a rational research-guiding role for that knowledge. Inductive reasoning from conventionally adopted theoretical principles to (nonconventional) theoretical conclusions ("All hitherto posited charged particles have unit charge [where this is a matter of conventional definition], therefore we are inductively justified in believing that all fundamental charged particles have unit charge [where this is nonconventional]") is not acceptable on the empiricist conception. I do not mean that the empiricist need deny that such reasoning plays a pragmatic role in theory-invention, but merely that acknowledging the epistemic legitimacy of this sort of theoretical-level induction is precisely the mark of a metaphysical understanding of the relevant theoretical premises. It amounts to acknowledging them as reflections of the way in which (unobservable aspects of) the world, rather than mere convention, constrains rational scientific description at the theoretical level. There is, after all, no logical contradiction or semantic anomaly in positing a new particle with charge 1/2 even though all those previously posited have had unit charge; there is only an inductive risk, and that only if one sees the earlier posits as corresponding to a reality which scientists attempt to discover.

We have been examining two special cases of empiricism and constructivism which share a common (and nondialectical) conception of the conventions that govern scientific investigation, but nothing in the considerations we have employed to diagnose the differences between them depends on the details of that conception. I conclude that if we are to understand the distinction between empiricist and constructivist conceptions of conventionality in science, then we should should look for conceptions of the metaphysics and epistemology of conventionality which—even when they agree about what the conceptual truths are—differ about the import of conventionality in the way suggested by the following chart:

Doctrine	Metaphysical import?	Inductive Import?
Empiricism	No	No
Constructivism	Yes (sometimes)	Yes (sometimes)

(I qualify "yes" with "sometimes" for the constructivist since presumably she will hold that not all conventions are world-constituting.)

What then of realism, whose position on the philosophical map we are trying to locate? Once we have sorted out empiricism and constructivism, there are very good reasons for holding that the realist's conception of conventionality, if it differs from the empiricist's at all, must agree with the empiricist's on these matters. Recall that the realist holds that neither the empiricist's nor the constructivist's conventionalistic treatments of theory-dependent methods in science is adequate because, according to the realist, neither approach adequately reconstructs the metaphysical import of the way in which inductive appeals to past theoretical achievements rationally regulate scientific practice (Boyd 1985a, 1989, 1990a). So the map we are looking for situates empiricism, constructivism, and realism as follows with respect to the import of conventionality:

Doctrine	Metaphysical import?	Inductive Import?
Empiricism	No	No
Constructivism	Yes (sometimes)	Yes (sometimes)
Realism	No	No

Realism and empiricism thus agree against constructivism in affirming the *metaphysical innocence of conventionality*, which they treat as entailing a corresponding *epistemic infertility*. It is to the implications for philosophical packages of these competing conceptions of conventionality that we now turn our attention.

4.5. *Metaphysical Innocence and Philosophical Packages*

A Quasi-naturalistic Constraint. An N-K constructivist philosophical package must reject, while a realist package must honor, the metaphysical-innocence and epistemic-infertility principles. Our understanding of the relative merits of the two sorts of packages would be enhanced by a clearer understanding of the implications of those constraints for the packages that must meet them. Fortunately developments in the history and philosophy of science which we have already explored in understanding the case for constructivism permit us to identify an additional quasi-naturalistic constraint which any plausible philosophical package must meet. If we restrict our attention to philosophical packages that meet the quasi-naturalistic constraint, I will argue, there emerges a simple, elegant even, characterization of the difference between packages that honor innocence and infertility and those that do not.

We have already seen that realist, constructivist, and sophisticated empiricist accounts of scientific knowledge represent three quite different responses to an initially surprising discovery—that the theory-dependence of scientific methods cannot be made to go away. All of the rational inductive methods of the sciences are theory-dependent in the sense that their scientific justification rests on an appeal to established background theories. Theory-dependent methods resist rational reconstruction; they cannot be portrayed as "derived rules" obtained in the first instance through the application of theory-independent methods. Nor do they honor the traditional empiricist's distinction between the scientific and the "metaphysical": the methodological dictates of the prevailing background theories depend on the theoretical structure of those theories and not just on their observational consequences. If we use positivist terminology and describe as "surplus meaning" those features of theories which go beyond their empirical content, then what has been discovered is that the methodological dictates of background theories depend on their surplus meaning.

What is important for our present purposes is that each of the quite different responses to ineliminable theory-dependence is appropriately seen as a response to the requirement discussed earlier that, prima facie, a philosophical package in the philosophy of science must accommodate the well-confirmed findings of the various special sciences. We can see this by understanding more clearly the nature of the theory-dependent rationales which background theories provide for methodological practices.

Recall that the standard arguments for scientific realism (Putnam 1962, 1972; Boyd 1983, 1990a) are abductive: they portray realism as a component of the best explanation for the success of scientific methods. Whether or not such arguments are successful in defending realism as a philosophical thesis (for critical discussions see Fine 1984, van Fraassen 1980), they rest on important facts about the nature of the theoretical rationale for scientific methods: For any scientifically justifiable theory-dependent method M, the theoretical rationale for M will take the form of a *well-confirmed* explanation of its reliability in terms of the (typically unobservable) causal mechanisms and processes posited in the relevant background theories. The explanation for the reliability of M will characteristically invoke the prevailing theories of those mechanisms and processes to explicate the ways in which the employment of M establishes reliable epistemic contact between scientists' practices and the causal mechanisms or processes that determine the relevant properties of their subject matter. Thus an apparently *naturalistic* explanation for the reliability of M— one that presupposes the (approximate) truth of the relevant background theories—provides the scientific rationale for M. The science's "own story" of the reliability of its methods seems to presuppose knowledge of "unobservables." It is this fact, together with the impossibility of reconstructing all such methods as derived rules, which creates the challenge to empiricism and provides a case for realism or constructivism: it appears that empiricist's anti-metaphysical commitments will prove incompatible with her articulation of a philosophical package that accommodates highly well-conformed naturalistic accounts of the reliability of rational scientific methods themselves.

Of course realists and constructivists must also prima facie accommodate the same apparently naturalistic theories and, of course, they do, realists by accepting the naturalistic explanations "at face value," constructivists by accepting the explanations while reconstructing their metaphysical content along Neo-Kantian lines (thereby attenuating their philosophical naturalism and preserving modest foundationalism). It will be important for our purposes to have a more abstract and metaphysical formulation of the conception of the epistemology of scientific methods which realists and constructivists thus come to have in common. Each of the particular naturalistic explanations for the reliability of a theory-dependent feature of scientific practice portrays that feature as reliable (and thereby justifies it) by indicating that the method in question is appropriate to the underlying causal structures of the relevant phenomena. For each such justified methodological feature, the role of the relevant background theories in providing its justification is to provide an (approximately) accurate account of those causal structures. Since both realists and constructivists accept this conception of the reliability and the justification of inductive methods in science generally, they should be thought of as accepting a *quasi-naturalistic* two-part *accommodation thesis*: (i) inductive methods are reliable to the extent that they are accommodated to the causal structures of the phenomena under study and of the systems (including humans) used to study them, and (ii) background theories reliably govern methodology to the extent that they provide a relevantly approximately accurate account of those structures. Good scientific method is a matter of theory-determined accommodation of practice to the actual causal structures of the relevant phenomena.

I have argued (Boyd 1990a, 1991) that the appropriate empiricist response to the challenge of theory-dependence, "sophisticated empiricism," should be thought of as accepting the conclusion that theory-dependent methods are justified by, and their reliability explained by, knowledge reflected in the "surplus meaning" in the relevant background theories while rejecting a metaphysical understanding of that knowledge. Instead of metaphysical knowledge, the relevant surplus knowledge is knowledge of inductive methods of the sort suggested in Quine's "Natural Kinds" (1969a). The theoretical structure of our background theories represents the accumulated results of second-order induction about induction. (I argue in Boyd 1990a that the consistent empiricist must portray such structures as reflecting the results of n-th order induction about induction, for all n, but that point need not concern us here.)

What we have just learned about the way in which theory-dependent methods are theoretically justified permits us to describe this sophisticated empiricist position more precisely. When background theories T justify a method M, they do so by entailing that M is reliable. Thus, in accepting well-confirmed background theories as repositories of knowledge about the reliability of inductive methods, the empiricist is simply accepting a somewhat broader conception of their empirical content: one that counts as part of the empirical content of a body of scientific theories their (conjoint) predictions about the instrumental reliability of methodological procedures. Thus, for example, theories in biochemistry would be seen as having—together with other well-confirmed scientific theories—implications not only about the observable behavior of chemical, cellular, and ecological systems but also about the reliability of methods in chemistry, cell biology, and ecology. Since the implications about the instrumental reliability of such methods represent predictions about *observable* phenomena, the traditional empiricist stricture against acknowledging metaphysical knowledge is maintained: all scientific knowledge is instrumental knowledge. The sophisticated empiricist accepts the apparently naturalistic scientific explanations for the reliability of particular methods and interprets them in just the same instrumentalist way she interprets any other scientific findings. What is untraditional about the sophisticated empiricist position is just its naturalistic and antifoundationalist treatment of scientific knowledge.

What, we may now ask, is the sophisticated empiricist assessment of the accommodation thesis? The sophisticated empiricist agrees with realists and constructivists in taking the apparently (on the empiricist's interpretation *actually*) naturalistic explanations for the reliability of scientific methods to constitute the full story of their reliability and their justification. Thus she accepts it that (i) inductive methods are reliable to the extent that they are accommodated appropriately to lawlike patterns in the relations between observable features of scientists, the objects of their study, and the equipment they employ, and that (ii) background theories reliably govern methodology to the extent that they provide a relevantly approximately accurate account of those patterns. But, of course, on the empiricist analysis causal structures *just are* lawlike structures in the relations between observables, so the sophisticated empiricist accepts precisely the (appropriate empiricist rationally reconstructed version of) the accommodation thesis. Thus, we have seen that an appropriate response to the depth of theory-dependence of scientific methods requires of empiricist as well as of realist and constructivist philosophical packages that they incorporate an appropriate version of the accommodation thesis. Since realism, empiricism, and constructivism represent the serious contenders in the philosophy of science, we may conclude that, in the current dialectical setting, any plausible philosophical package must include a version of the accommodation thesis. This is the quasi-naturalistic constraint on philosophical packages which permits us to formulate the metaphysical-innocence thesis with greater precision.

Recall that we are looking for an understanding of the metaphysical-innocence thesis which, when we attribute it to empiricists and to realists but not to constructivists, will ratify the convictions of realists and empiricists that conventional truths lack metaphysical import and that *for that reason* they lack inductive import. If we restrict our attention to philosophical packages incorporating the accommodation thesis, then in the packages we consider, it will be held that a feature of scientists' theoretical conception of their subject matter properly has inductive import *if and only if* it represents knowledge of the causal structures of the relevant phenomena. Realist and empiricist philosophical packages satisfying the quasi-naturalistic constraint must, therefore, incorporate the claim that when (or to the extent that) such features of scientific theories are true by convention, they fail to describe causal structures, whereas constructivists must hold that *some* conventional features (those implicated in the social construction of reality) do represent knowledge of causal structures.

Here then is the insight necessary to an understanding of the metaphysical-innocence thesis: the sense in which realists and empiricists hold, while constructivists deny, the metaphysical import of conventionality in science is that constructivists affirm whereas realists and empiricists deny that in the relevant sense social conventions in science determine the causal structure of the phenomena scientists study. I add "in the relevant sense" because, of course, scientific (and other) conventions are a matter of human social practice and human social practices themselves have *causal* effects including *causal effects on the causal structures scientists study*. Since this claim is philosophically uncontroversial, we should understand realists and empiricists as affirming and constructivists as denying *the No Noncausal Contribution thesis* (2N2C): the thesis that human social practices make no noncausal contribution to the causal structures of the phenomena scientists study. If the accommodation thesis is accepted, then 2N2C exactly expresses the metaphysical-innocence doctrine whose acceptance differentiates realists and empiricists from constructivists.

A point about this interpretation of N-K social constructivism is in order here. I am of course about to go on to argue *against* constructivism in part by arguing *for* 2N2C, so it will be important to my argument that that thesis is what distinguishes plausible realist and empiricist philosophical packages from plausible constructivist ones. My experience has been that philosophers' reactions to 2N2C and the analysis of constructivism in terms of it are quite varied.

Some have thought that a demonstration that constructivists must deny 2N2C would amount to a *reductio ad absurdum* of constructivism while others have thought the interpretation of constructivism offered here entirely fair to the philosophical intentions of constructivists. I want to emphasize that I am not offering the denial of 2N2C as an analysis of the authorial intentions of defenders of N-K constructivism nor as an analysis of the meaning of any of the various claims that express N-K constructivist theses. Instead I am arguing that philosophical insights regarding theory-dependence of scientific methods, insights which constructivists helped to establish, dictate acceptance of the accommodation thesis and that it is this thesis in turn which dictates that metaphysical innocence be diagnosed in terms of 2N2C. Thus those who find 2N2C obvious should take what has been said here so far as a *reductio* rather than as an uncharitable interpretation of authorial intent or of meaning.

That said, it is worth remarking that the denial of 2N2C has considerable independent merit as an interpretation of the meaning or the intent of N-K constructivism. Neo-Kantian constructivism is, after all, supposed to be Neo-*Kantian*, and it is hard to think of an interpretation more in keeping with that understanding. Moreover it is by no means impossible to offer arguments in favor of the denial of 2N2C besides the general arguments for N-K constructivism. For example, Putnam (1983) argues against a realist conception of the "total cause" of an event that no such notion of cause is available *because the notion of explanation is prior to that of cause* (and presumably because there is no explanatory context in which an appeal to an event's total cause is appropriate). I do not mean to speculate here about how Putnam understands the relation between the concepts of causation and explanation nor about the relation between his pragmatism and N-K constructivism. What is important is that his claim of the conceptual priority of the notion of explanation is philosophically plausible and that it could be easily articulated along lines that would entail the denial of 2N2C.

5. DEFENDING REALISM

5.1. Defending Innocence, Part 1: Innocence as a Scientific Hypothesis

Let C be any statement whose truth or falsity is determined by certain causal structures and let S be any set of human social practices. If the members of S contribute to the truth or falsity of C, then we may think of their contribution as factorable into two components: the contribution which elements of S make to determining the relevant causal structures and the contribution the members of S make to establishing the semantics of the language in which C is expressed. We have seen that the dispute between realists (and empiricists) and constructivists is over the possible extent of the first component. Prima facie philosophical packages must accommodate well-confirmed scientific theories, so one approach to assessing the relative merits of realism and constructivism is to assess 2N2C as a scientific hypothesis. A number of considerations suggest that we should take it to be extremely well confirmed and to conclude, in consequence, that the plausibility of constructivism is seriously compromised.

In examining the status of 2N2C as a scientific hypothesis, we face an interesting problem. If either scientific realism or a naturalistic version of empiricism is accepted, then one should probably think of philosophy itself (or at least the philosophy of science) as a scientific discipline, whereas no similar conclusion follows from constructivism. Moreover, in any science philosophical considerations operate in determining answers to questions about confirmation. How then are we to understand the question of how well confirmed 2N2C is as a scientific hypothesis? To what extent should philosophical considerations enter into that judgment?

I have no general solution to the problem of philosophical method raised here, but I propose for present purposes to ask how well confirmed 2N2C is by scientific standards not directly affected by philosophical considerations regarding N-K constructivism and closely related issues. If 2N2C fares well by those standards, I will take that to be a prima facie problem for constructivist philosophical packages but one that could be overcome (from the points of view of both science and philosophy) if the distinctly philosophical arguments for constructivism prove sufficiently powerful.

If we approach the issue in that way, then the scientific case for 2N2C seems quite strong, if a bit hard to state. Suppose that we first ask whether anything in our current understanding of human beings or their social practices suggests that 2N2C could be false. Is such a possibility suggested by what we know of the biology, psychology, sociology, anthropology, or history of human social practices, or by what we know from linguistic theory? Different N-K constructivist packages will portray different features of the scientific picture of the world as social constructions, but, for example, do the findings of any of these disciplines provide us with any reason to suppose that there are features of human social practice which necessarily lie in any supervenience base of the causal structures that reflect the atomic composition of matter? I take it that if we exclude from consideration findings of sociologists and anthropologists whose work is quite directly influenced by—or part of—the philosophical case for N-K constructivism, the answer is plainly "no." In particular, if we examine the best available empirical theories of how social practices determine the truth or falsity of statements in natural languages, they provide every reason to accept the picture of the factorization of that determination suggested by 2N2C.

Similarly we may ask whether findings in any of the other sciences provide any reason to suppose that 2N2C is false. Do the findings of chemistry and physics, for example, give us reason to suppose that social practices of, for example, chemists and physicists are necessary components of any supervenience base of the causal structures they study? Here again of course the answer is "no." But, someone might object, the fact that none of our scientific theories give us any reason to believe that a hypothesis is false provides us with no reason to suppose that it is well confirmed, thus the failure of our background theories to endorse the denial of 2N2C is irrelevant to the issue at hand.

Complex general issues are raised here about the relation between theoretical considerations and confirmation, but three things are important in the present case. In the first place, there *is* positive evidence for 2N2C, since it underwrites our best current conceptions of how human social practices determine the truth values of statements. Moreover, the fact that violations of 2N2C are not contemplated in our best theories of human social practices itself has evidential significance, if the scientific practice that gives rise to those theories is taken to be even approximately sound. The reason is this: if people live in worlds whose causal structure is determined noncausally by their beliefs and practices in the ways contemplated by N-K constructivism, then the laws governing the relations between social practices and other conditions of human life are quite different from what they would be were 2N2C true. A research methodology that does not even countenance the possibility of failures of 2N2C would be as inadequate under such conditions as one that failed to acknowledge the important ways in which theoretical practices and concepts *causally* determine causal structures—self-fulfilling prophecies for example, or the social effects of ideologically determined theories. Thus, 2N2C may be appropriately viewed as a presupposition of methodology in social inquiry (cases directly influenced by social constructivism aside), so the philosopher who accepts the methods of social scientific inquiry as in this regard sound has reason to accept 2N2C with respect to the noncausal influences contemplated in social constructivism.

Still one might not be sufficiently confident about methods in the relevant social sciences to find the case just outlined convincing, so it is important to realize that the claim that certain practices necessarily lie in any supervenience base of certain causal structures entails that were the practices relevantly different, the causal structures would be too. Whatever the final word on the analysis of counterfactuals, they are the sorts of propositions which we can often evaluate by scientific standards. We may reasonably ask, in the light of the best available scientific theories, whether or not, for example, the general causal structures of matter would be different if chemists and physicists engaged in different social practices. The answer is "no," and the answer would be "no" for any of the alleged cases of social construction appropriate to N-K constructivist philosophical packages. *That* is evidence for 2N2C, or at least (what is enough) against those denials of 2N2C essential to the constructivist's project.

Finally it must be noted that it is in general difficult to say precisely why loopy proposals are scientifically unacceptable. Consider for example the hypothesis that social practices in gem-cutting noncausally contribute to the determination of crop yields in Missouri. That is scientifically silly, but it is hard to say exactly why. I suggest that constructivist denials of 2N2C are, scientifically speaking, equally silly, so that the distinctly philosophical arguments for constructivism must be quite strong indeed if the constructivist's philosophical package is not to prove less plausible than the realist's.

A somewhat different sort of objection might at this point be offered against the strategy of scientifically assessing the constructivist's denial of 2N2C. It might be argued that both 2N2C and its denial are philosophical rather than scientific hypotheses and that treating them as scientific hypotheses begs the question against the philosophical arguments in their favor. In support of this contention it might be argued that the dependence of causal structures on social practices posited by constructivists is supposed to be noncausal and that, therefore, scientific considerations of supervenience relations are irrelevant to its assessment.

Against the second and more specific of these objections it must be replied that whatever the nature of the presumed determination, to say of some processes that they are necessarily part of any supervenience base for some structures entails that those structures would not obtain, or would be relevantly different, if the processes did not themselves go on. The counterfactuals of this sort which would follow from plausible N-K constructivist accounts of science do certainly seem to be the sorts of counterfactuals that are assessable scientifically, and they seem deeply disconfirmed. I conclude that there is a strong burden of proof on the constructivist to deny that her position entails such counterfactuals or to provide for them an interpretation that makes them immune from scientific criticism.

Against the more general objection it must be insisted that the special cases of the accommodation thesis relevant to any particular N-K constructivist account of actual episodes in the history of science *are* scientific hypotheses, as are the scientifically dubious counterfactuals entailed by that account in the light of those special cases. Thus it appears that the details of any particular constructivist package will be vulnerable to the charge of inconsistency with well-established science whatever the status of the most general formulations of constructivism.

It might be thought that even particular cases of 2N2C are too philosophical to be well confirmed as scientific theses and that the embarrassing counterfactuals are likewise too philosophical to be evaluated by scientific standards. Even so, the prima facie requirement that philosophical packages be articulated so as to cohere with well-confirmed science is a central methodological standard in the philosophy of science, and the supervenience reduction constraint is an unproblematical special case of that requirement. What our investigation of the relation between 2N2C and well-established science indicates is that—although it is easy to see how the truth of causal claims depends in part on social practices—we have, scientifically speaking, not the foggiest idea of how causal structures themselves could depend on social practices except in mundane causal ways. Precisely because of the scientific inexplicability of the violations of 2N2C which it entails, the constructivist's account of the role of scientific conventionality in determining the truth or falsity of scientific statements fails to meet this constraint, which is clearly met by competing realist (and empiricist) accounts. Thus principles of the unity of philosophical and scientific knowledge which seem central to methodology in the philosophy of science are violated by the details of any N-K constructivist account of actual scientific episodes.

Indeed, there are a number of other considerations which suggest that N-K constructivism may cohere poorly with scientific findings. For example, we have scientific reasons grounded in evolutionary theory to suppose that our capacities are continuous with those of nonhuman animals. Do *they* socially (or otherwise) construct the causal structures of the things they know about? If not, then do we construct those structures, and how are our constructs related to their perceptual abilities? If their causal world is unconstructed, how is it that ours requires construction? . . . (You get the idea.)

Similar concerns arise about the coherence of N-K constructivism with the best-established findings of historians of science. There is a long tradition of holding that Kuhn's acknowledgment of the historical phenomenon of ineliminable *anomalies* within paradigms compromises any metaphysical understanding of his metaphorical claim that scientists who accept different paradigms study different worlds. We are now in a position to make that criticism precise and to show that it is applicable to dialectically complex versions of N-K constructivism as well as to less complex versions.

What seems evident historically is that not every effort at world construction can succeed. Certain conceptual frameworks, metaphysical conceptions, and methodological approaches will not result in the successful establishment of a tradition of inquiry because, in some sense or other, the world fails to cooperate: problem solutions of the anticipated sort are not found which are experimentally successful, anticipated success in developing predictive laws is not forthcoming, the results of efforts to articulate explanations for relevant phenomena do not result in a coherent picture of how they work, . . . Similarly, as anomalies show, apparently successful world construction can hit snags: new discoveries can pose challenges insoluble within an established paradigm.

Now, different degrees of dialectical flexibility in one's account of world-constituting conventionality will affect just which cases of world construction one would have to diagnose as failing in one or the other of these two ways, but no one thinks that scientists or others can impose just any metaphysical picture (however dialectically flexible) on the world. Feyerabend (1989) has termed the constraints which the world imposes on paradigms "resistance."

Now resistances have interesting properties. They seem to be independent of human social practices at least in this sense: that such practices seem to make no noncausal contribution to them. They appear to underwrite counterfactuals: it is not just true that some episodes of attempted world construction have met with resistance, others would meet resistance if they were attempted. Finally, successful theory construction and successful methodology require accommodation to the structure of resistances. Resistances, that is, are a lot like the theory-independent causal structures posited by realists and empiricists: the only obvious difference seems to be that N-K constructivists believe in them.

Resistances are an apparently well-confirmed feature of the history of science, and they pose a challenge to any N-K constructivist package that acknowledges them. Why, given that human social practices can construct, in broad outline, the causal relations scientists study, do they leave unaffected resistances, which look so much like causal structures? Indeed, what is the justification for denying that resistances *are* theory-independent causal structures, and for denying that, in accepting it that scientific theories and methods must be accommodated to resistances, a philosopher has already accepted a realist (or empiricist) interpretation of the accommodation thesis?

I am inclined to hold that causal structures—or at any rate the causal structures accessible in scientific investigation—*just are* the resistances which history teaches us to acknowledge; or perhaps that the causal structures scientists study are the substrate of such theory-independent resistances. Whether or not this particular analysis can be sustained, the fact remains that anomalies and other resistances represent apparent features of scientific practice which are enough like unconstructed causal structures and which play a role enough like that assigned by realists and empiricists to such structures as to pose the question of whether or not N-K constructivism coheres with the results of empirical inquiry in the history of science. It is worth remarking that one reservation which someone might have with the identification of causal structures with resistances (or their substrate) is that there would remain the question of how to distinguish between those features of established scientific theories which reflect the structure of resistances and those which are reflections of conventionality in the broad dialectical sense. N-K constructivism might be seen as gaining some support from a recognition of the difficulty of detecting such conventionality. I discuss the connection between constructivism and the problem of hidden conventionality below (see section 5.4).

I conclude that there are good reasons to hold that N-K constructivism fails to meet adequately the criterion of coherence (or perhaps even consistency) with the findings of the various special sciences and of the history of science and that the philosophical arguments in its favor would have to be very strong indeed in order to overcome the resulting philosophical implausibility. I suggested at the beginning of this paper that N-K social constructivism is often conflated with debunking constructivism. Here is an additional reason to suspect such a conflation: it seems possible to maintain, even from a realist (albeit not a *scientific* realist) perspective, the debunking conclusion that scientific "truth" is merely a social construction; it is much harder indeed to maintain, with the N-K constructivist, that scientific *truth* is a social construction. I suspect that one reason why the depth of the difficulties facing the latter position have not always been recognized has been a failure to distinguish clearly enough between the claims of debunking and N-K constructivism.

5.2. Defending Innocence, Part 2: Conventionality and the Equifertility of Methods
I have argued that constructivism fails to meet the constraint of coherence with well-established science. Turning now to the other fundamental constraint identified in section 4.3, I propose to argue that the rejection of 2N2C undermines the possibility of rationalizing a central and ubiquitously applicable methodological principle having to do with the methodological import of conventional or arbitrary features of scientific description. Recall that it is uncontroversial that there can be instances of unobvious conventionality in scientific practice and that the accommodation thesis dictates that theoretical considerations properly govern inductive practice only to the extent that they reflect knowledge of relevant causal structures. It will be useful therefore to ask what good scientific method dictates when features of well-established scientific theories are shown to be unexpectedly conventional or otherwise arbitrary.

Let us say that the choice between two theoretical conceptions is *arbitrary, or conventional in the broad sense,* just in case what would count for the appropriateness of choosing one over the other would be facts about the history and current practice of the relevant scientific community rather than anything that obtains independently of that history or practice. Simple or dialectically complex conventionality in science, whether obvious or not and whether "world-constituting" or not, will be reflected in there being a possible alternative to the actually accepted conception such that the choice between them is conventional in this sense. What is the methodology appropriate to the discovery of unexpected conventionality in a body of scientific research? I suggest that the principle that is actually central to scientific practice is the following:

The Methodological Equifertility Principle. Suppose that the choice between two conceptions is conventional in the broad sense. Then the only methodological practices which will be properly justified by the acceptance of one of these conceptions will be those practices which would also be justified by the acceptance of the other.

Corollary. Suppose that two conceptions are sufficiently different that they appear to provide competing accounts of some phenomena and to have, in consequence, different methodological import. Suppose further that the choice between them is in fact conventional in the broad sense and that this fact comes to be known. Then, the methodological import of those conceptions must be reevaluated according to the principle that the only methodological practices that will be properly justified by the acceptance of either will be those practices which they dictate in common. Practices which, prior to the discovery of the unexpected conventionality, were taken to be justified by one of the conceptions and not the other must be understood to be justified by neither.

Two examples will illustrate the application of the equifertility principle. According to Lewontin (1976), Jensen (1968) presents as evidence for the genetic determination of individual differences in intelligence the fact that the distribution of IQ scores in typical human populations is a normal distribution. Since a normal distribtion is characteristic of certain polygenically determined traits, the normality of score distributions for IQ is taken as evidence that intelligence is such a trait. A number of criticisms can be made of this line of reasoning; one is that the normality of IQ score distributions is an artifact of practice of test designers: they design batteries of test questions in order to obtain normal score distributions. Once this fact is recognized, the normality of such score distributions ceases to have evidential bearing no matter what relations normal distributions may ordinarily have to underlying genetic facts. Operative here is the equifertility principle: the standard conception of how to measure intelligence is shown to be one of several conceptions between which the choice is conventional in the broad sense, but the proposed strategy for establishing evidence about genetic determination of intelligence differences is ratified by only some of these conceptions.

Consider now the case of alleged unobvious conventionality mentioned earlier in this paper. According to cladists, there is a deep level of conventionality in the definitions of higher taxa of which traditional systematists were unaware. Some cladists put this claim in an especially strong way by maintaining that the only nonarbitrary constraint on the erection of higher taxa is that the taxa themselves be monophyletic. Consider now research strategies in the study of macroevolution. Researchers interested in how the pace of evolutionary change has varied between different intervals in geological time have often proposed to assess such variation by estimating, for such intervals, the number of higher taxa at various levels which have either emerged or have become extinct during them.

Suppose now for the sake of argument that the strong cladist claim about the arbitrariness of higher taxa is true. In that case, of course, calculations of the rates of emergence and extinction would produce entirely arbitrary results and would thus be irrelevant to the study of evolutionary forces. Again the operative methodological principle is equifertility: different classificatory conceptions between which the choice is conventional in the broad sense would dictate entirely different numerical measures of the rates of evolutionary change.

Equifertility seems to be a fundamental methodological principle regarding conventionality or arbitrariness in scientific descriptions. Indeed, we can use it to provide a kind of methodologically relevant "measure" of the extent to which features of such descriptions are arbitrary. By the *methodological spectrum* of a theory let us mean the class of methodological judgments which (given prevailing background theories) it properly underwrites. The equifertility doctrine entails that two theories between which the choice is conventional in the broad sense will have the same methodological spectrum. In consequence, the claim that a theory is unexpectedly arbitrary in particular respects entails that its methodological spectrum is narrower than prevailing methods would suggest; competing claims regarding respects of arbitrariness will thus entail different conceptions of a theory's methodological spectrum, and these differences provide a measure of sorts of the methodological import of the differing estimates of arbitrariness (see Boyd 1990b).

Moreover, there do not seem to be any limitations to the applicability of the equifertility principle: good scientific method seems to dictate that we reject methods that are artifacts of social convention or other idiosyncratic features of our community's history. Nevertheless, if the accommodation thesis is accepted, then it follows that the acceptability of any instance of equifertility is equivalent to the acceptability of the corresponding special case of 2N2C. Thus the constructivist appears to be in the position of being unable to provide an account of scientific knowledge which ratifies a central principle of scientific methodology. She must acknowledge exceptions to 2N2C and thus corresponding exceptions to equifertility.

On no plausible account can all social conventions in science be world-constituting, and thus the constructivist will have to distinguish between cases in which 2N2C holds and cases in which it fails. Given the scientific inexplicability of any such failures, the prospects are dim that she will be able to offer a satisfactory account of the difference between the two sorts of cases. The fact that the constructivist must also rationalize a corresponding distinction between applications of equifertility makes the prospects for her success even fainter.

I conclude, therefore, that N-K constructivism fails pretty spectacularly to satisfy the requirement of coherence with the findings and methods of the best science. One additional concern about authorial intent is raised by the arguments I have offered for this conclusion. Some philosophers have objected to those arguments on the grounds that the authors of Neo-Kantian conceptions of social construction clearly *intended* to appeal to a kind of social construction that is prior to scientific theorizing about causation or about method in a way that would make scientific critiques inappropriate.

I agree that authorial intent has been correctly assessed here, but the question we have been addressing is whether or not there is a sort of social construction with the features N-K constructivists require. After all, phenomenalists intended to appeal to a conception of the reducibility of physical objects to sense data which would not compromise our ordinary conception of the causal relations involved in perception nor compromise methodological commitments that rest on a notion of independent observation of the same object by several researchers. Recognition of that intent does not, by itself, give us any reason to reject the arguments that suggest that no such reduction exists. A similar situation exists with respect to N-K constructivism. Constructivists make claims about the metaphysical import of human practices that—when taken together with other claims about science with which they agree—appear to contradict 2N2C. That gives us a good reason to doubt that the sort of social construction they posit happens. The burden of proof lies with the constructivist either to indicate a flaw in the arguments about 2N2C or to provide other philosophical (or scientific) reasons why we should find its rejection acceptable.

5.3. Assessing N-K Constructivism as Epistemology: Philosophical Integration and Species Chauvinism

Pretty plainly the denials of 2N2C entailed by N-K constructivism deeply compromise its capacity to meet well-established requirements of unification with the findings of the sciences; so serious is the shortfall, in fact, that the N-K constructivist's position has much in common with debunking constructivism. Still, coherence with established science and its methods is not the only standard by which philosophical packages are properly assessed, and there is a nontrivial epistemological argument *for* constructivism: that it permits the preservation of a plausible version of inference-rule foundationalism. We need to know whether or not this advantage outweighs the apparent epistemological failings of constructivism, so that it would be appropriate to rethink our understanding of the epistemology of science so as somehow to accommodate (nondebunkingly) the oddities of constructivism.

That the answer is "no" is suggested by three considerations. In the first place, of course, the depth of the failure of N-K constructivism to reconstruct actual science is profound, and this strongly suggests that it is on the wrong track epistemologically.

Moreover, the failures of foundationalism implied by the rejection of inference-rule foundationalism are independently suggested by other naturalistic developments in epistemology. The whole thrust of reliabilist accounts of more commonplace cases of knowledge is that what is decisive in distinguishing cases of knowledge from other cases of true belief is not the operation of some privileged principles of justification but the reliability of the operative mechanisms of belief regulation. While such an account of, for example, perceptual knowledge does not entail the falsity of modest inference-rule foundationalism, it does enhance the plausibility of its rejection, especially since the naturalistic account of inductive reasoning in the sciences which is apparently provided by the sciences themselves assigns to theory-dependent justificatory methods and procedures a crucial causal role in ensuring that reliability, thus corroborating the traditional intuition that justification is somehow essential in most cases of inductive knowledge. I conclude that a philosophical package that includes a realist and naturalistic account of scientific knowledge has the virtue that its rejection of inference-rule foundationalism coheres well with the results of independently developed naturalistic research in epistemology and the further advantage that it affords us a naturalistic account of the important role of justificatory arguments in induction.

These advantages are supplemented by another that is suggested by our earlier consideration of the peculiar relation of constructivism to evolutionary theory. It has proved very fruitful in contemporary epistemology and philosophy of mind to consider the ways in which psychological and epistemic descriptions can be appropriately applied, either literally or metaphorically, to nonhuman animals or to nonliving information-processing systems. Two things seem clear. First, there is almost no doubt that we should literally attribute knowledge to a variety of different nonhuman animals, not all of them intelligent primates. Second, when we attribute knowledge metaphorically to much simpler animals and simple nonanimal information-processing systems, our extension of epistemic concepts is well motivated: there is much in common between the "knowledge" of such systems and knowledge in humans and more complex animals. Now for none of these nonhuman systems is it plausible to suppose that their knowledge (or "knowledge") rests on their being able to deploy the resources of a priori justifiable inductive methods or anything of the sort. We thus have philosophical as well as evolutionary reasons to be concerned about a kind of species chauvinism in our epistemological thinking: what reason have we to think that for us alone knowledge is to be understood in terms of epistemically privileged principles of induction? I suggest that the answer is "none."

I do not mean to suggest that if apparently adequate inductive rules of this sort were discovered—or if their existence were strongly suggested by examinations of scientific practice—then we should reject the proposal that they should set epistemic standards for creatures like us capable of understanding them. Nor do I suggest that we should leave unexplored the hypothesis that approximate adherence to those rules explains the special inductive successes of the sciences. What I do suggest is that, in the absence of any evidence that such rules exist, we should favor philosophical packages that incorporate a scientifically grounded naturalistic and anti-(inference-rule)-foundationalist treatment of scientific knowledge over packages that salvage foundationalism at the expense of scientific plausibility. I conclude that when we weigh the case for N-K constructivism provided by the basic epistemological argument against the contrary case arising from considerations of the quasi-naturalistic constraint and the plausibility of 2N2C, the case against constructivism is quite strong. I suggested in section 3.1 that there were three and a half arguments for constructivism of which the fundamental epistemological argument was the first. It is time to turn our attention to the other two.

5.4. Hidden Conventionality and the Case for Constructivism

It is unproblematic that there could be—and all but unproblematic that there are—features of our current scientific conception of the world that are conventional in the broad sense but that appear to us to represent discoveries about causal structures. We lack altogether certain methods for ferreting out such hidden conventionalities, and this fact seems to underwrite N-K constructivist convictions for at least some students of the philosophy and social studies of science. In a way this might seem strange since fallibilism regarding questions of social construction hardly justifies social constructivism, especially of the Neo-Kantian variety. Still, there is a point to the concern: scientific realism is, characteristically, a position of those who are inclined to accept the findings of the various sciences "at face value," and the arguments for it turn on accepting for the most part the naturalistic accounts of the reliability of scientific methods which are confirmed by the application of those very methods. A serious enough skepticism about our ability to uncover hidden conventionality would cast doubt on the realist's case. We need more than mere fallibilism, however—all the more so because realist approaches provide some resources for distinguishing mere conventions from real "maps" of causal structures (for example, count as probably nonconventional those features of received background theories which clearly seem implicated in reliable methodology: see Boyd 1990b). We need some special reason to suppose that philosophers generally, or at any rate realist philosophers, will tend to make significant mistakes about what is conventional or merely historical and what is not. I believe that those who worry about hidden conventionality typically have one or both of two different special concerns of this sort in mind. One is a matter of assessing the prospects for *experimental metaphysics*, the other a matter of concern over *hidden politics*.

Experimental metaphysics first. Positivists called "metaphysics" any theorizing about the unobservable, and they held that experimental knowledge of "metaphysics" is impossible. If realism is true, then scientists routinely do experimental "metaphysics," and they often do it successfully. What about experimental metaphysics (without the quotation marks)? Plainly it has been an influential view among realists that scientists do successful experimental metaphysics as well: witness the widespread view among realist philosophers of science that materialism has been confirmed as a scientific hypothesis. One plausible concern with this enthusiasm for experimental (no quotes) metaphysics might plausibly be that we run the risk of treating as metaphysically informative features of scientific theories which are in fact merely artifacts of the conceptual history of the relevant scientific communities. If we hold, with the realist, that *physical* scientists—biochemists, molecular geneticists, and pharmacologists, let us say—have discovered something(s) unobservable and important about the biological and even the mental world, and if we agree that they have done so by employing a materialist research strategy, one that could be and is defended by claiming that all phenomena—mental as well as biological—are physical, *still* need we conclude that it is the materialist theoretical formulation of their perspective which captures their insights about the relevant causal structures? Could not the materialistic thesis that these scientists, or our rational reconstructions of them, affirm be conventional? Could there not be a rationalization of the same methods for studying (admittedly partly unobservable) causal structures which had no materialist philosophical implications? Might a sort of *scientism* not blind *scientific* realists regarding this question?

I think that questions such as these pose interesting problems for the defender of experimental metaphysics but that N-K constructivism is the inappropriate position for the philosopher who has the concerns in question. The worry, after all, is that we may not be able to determine reliably just which elements of our best-confirmed scientific theories are really conventional in the broad sense. But the proposed solution is to adopt a general solution to that difficulty: to hold that it is *always* the features of our theories which define the basic metaphysical picture which are conventional (that is, after all, what N-K constructivists hold). Moreover, this solution seems to have the opposite of the desired methodological import with respect to experimental metaphysics. If we are always justified in taking the basic metaphysical picture presented by the sciences as reflecting socially constructed *reality* (which is supposed to be, of course, as real as things get), then we *are* justified in, for example, taking materialism to be a well-established scientific finding. What the critic of experimental metaphysics raises is the possibility that the metaphysical-looking doctrines reflected in scientific theorizing are *merely* conventional, where that status deprives them of real metaphysical import. Since the defining feature of N-K constructivism is that it attributes metaphysical import to just the sorts of conventions at issue, we have again a case in which N-K constructivist doctrine is invoked where a limited sort of debunking—of just the sort precluded by N-K constructivism—is needed instead. As we shall see, this pattern continues.

On to politics. A central concern of many scholars (not just professional philosophers) who are attracted to N-K constructivism is to elucidate the often hidden role of ideology in science. When scientific ideology is effective, it is invisible: a hidden political element determining the content of scientific theorizing. It is effective, that is to say, because there are features of social practice whose influence on the content of scientific theories is unobvious. Struck by the overwhelming evidence that such hidden politics is a standard feature of much of scientific life, many scholars have been led to adopt an N-K constructivist conception of scientific knowledge. Once again, the oddity of the position is evident when it is recognized that their aim is a critical one.

Consider a case of ideological factors in science, say the "social construction of gender." It was an all but uniform feature of nineteenth-century biological thinking to affirm the intellectual inferiority of women; that is ideology in science. How will adopting an N-K constructivist view of nineteenth-century biology help us criticize this ideology? Well, first, it is clear that the principal explanation for the uniformity with which this doctrine was accepted involves the operation in science of historically determined social practices toward which the critic has an unfavorable attitude. The influence of these practices is hard to detect—just like the influence of world-constituting conventions in science. Are the social practices that determined the doctrine of the inferiority of women themselves to be thought of as world-constituting? If not, then it is hard to see why an N-K constructivist conception should be especially important to their criticism, since the standards for the epistemic and political criticism of non-world-constituting social practices are presumably the same for the realist and the N-K constructivist.

Suppose, then, instead that the social practices are to be understood as world-constituting. In that case, the critic will be obliged to hold that it was true (by social construction—but that is as true as things can be) that nineteenth-century women were intellectually inferior in the way indicated by the relevant biological theories. Now, this is a conclusion which someone independently committed to N-K constructivism might be obliged to accept, but it could hardly be taken to indicate that N-K constructivism facilitates the criticism of ideology. Here again, thinkers who have adopted an N-K constructivist conception seem to have been looking instead for a conception of the relevant conventions which denies them metaphysical import. It is a debunking constructivist treatment, if not of nineteenth-century biology in general, then of nineteenth-century biology of sex differences, which is recommended here, not N-K constructivism.

One remaining political application of N-K constructivism needs to be discussed here. In some cases of the ideological role of science—the social construction of gender is an example—the subject matter of the relevant sciences is *us*, and it is important to understand the extent to which scientific practices in such areas may determine what we are like. Theories of sex differences frame social and educational expectations, self-images, legal and economic possibilities, and so on, so that the nature of men and women is in a deep sense *socially constructed*. Some thinkers, struck by this fact, and concerned to emphasize its importance, understand the social construction of gender, for example, on the N-K model of the social construction of reality. Two considerations suggest that this is a mistake.

In the first place, of course, the social construction of gender roles facilitated by, among other things, sexist ideology in science, is *causal*: social practices in science are among the factors that cause other social patterns that cause men and women to exhibit certain psychological dispositions more often than others which they would exhibit under different circumstances. In the absence of an entirely independent argument, there is no reason to assimilate these causal relations to the model of noncausal determination of causal structure by theoretical practices.

Moreover, noncausal social construction—even of the dialectically complex sort—*cannot fail*: the whole idea is that certain social practices *impose*, in something like a logical or conceptual way, a certain general causal structure on the world. But social constructions of the causal sort often fail spectacularly at particular historical junctures. The social construction of the inferiority of colonial subjects (which was, of course, accomplished more with troops, guns, whips, and courts than with scientific theories) eventually produced rebels, not persons genetically suited to be ruled. Although no one doubts this, thinking of *causal* social construction on the model of Neo-Kantian *noncausal* construction focuses attention on its successes rather than on the conditions of resistance. It is hard to see how that would enhance the prospects for a critique of ideology.

I conclude that general considerations of the unobviousness of the influence of (some) social practices in science, although important, do not tend to support N-K constructivism.

5.5. Scientific Pluralism and Nonreductionist Materialism

Two quite specific forms of the social determination of the structure of scientific theories are often cited as providing reasons for N-K constructivism. In the first place, it seems certainly true that for any given scientific discipline, there will be more than one conceptual scheme that could be employed to capture adequately the knowledge reflected in its theories. There is thus a significant measure of conventionality in the broad sense involved in the acceptance of whatever conceptual framework scientists in a given discipline employ.

Moreover, between scientific disciplines there are variations in the schemes of classification and description which are appropriate even when—in some sense—the same phenomena are under study: economists and sociologists must employ different explanatory categories even if they are both studying consumers. The naturalness of concepts and the appropriateness of methods seem to be interest-dependent—to depend on the interests of the investigators.

Each of these instances of pluralism in science has been taken to provide evidence for N-K constructivism or related positions. In the first case, the conventionality involved in choices of conceptual schemes is assimilated to world-constituting conventionality on the N-K constructivist model; in the second, the interest-dependence of kinds and methods is taken to indicate the sort of mind-dependence of reality congenial to constructivists but not to realists.

I have discussed these cases at some length elsewhere (Boyd 1980, 1985a, 1989). What is important here is that the plurality of conceptual schemes exemplified in the two sorts of cases, far from representing a challenge to realism, is predicted and fully explained by a realist conception of scientific knowledge. Consider first the plurality of conceptual schemes within a single discipline. It is a truism that when we employ a relatively small finite vocabulary to formulate descriptions of complex systems, the respects of similarity and difference which ground the definitions of the primitive terms we use will not exhaust the explanatorily or predictively important respects of similarity and difference. The remaining explanatorily important distinctions must be captured by more complex descriptions generated from the basic vocabulary. Thus there will always be some arbitrariness—some conventionality in the broad sense—in the choice of conceptual frameworks in any complex inquiry.

This truism is uncontroversial and it certainly poses no problem for the realist who holds that the respects of similarity and difference involved are reflections of socially unconstructed causal structures. (Perhaps it poses a problem for the constructivist—Why don't we just socially construct a simpler world?—but that's not the issue here.) Thus the conventionality of choice of conceptual schemes is apparently something which the realist can cheerfully acknowledge. It is true, of course, that such conventionality raises methodological problems for realist friends of experimental metaphysics: one must somehow be sure that one's metaphysical lessons are not drawn from features of scientific theories which are conventional in this way. But that is a problem for realists in their experimental-metaphysician moods, not a problem for defenders of 2N2C.

Consider now the interest-dependence of conceptual schemes. In a causally complex world the respects of similarity and difference in causal powers which are predictive or explanatory of one sort of phenomenon (or of certain aspects of a given sort of phenomenon) will not typically be those which are important for phenomena of different sorts or for different aspects of the same phenomena. Thus it is unsurprising that the vocabulary and conceptual schemes suited to one sort of inquiry will usually be unsuited to inquiry with different explanatory or predictive aims. Here again there is nothing to trouble the realist. The appropriateness of a scheme of classification depends on the purposes or interests in the service of which it is to be used, but there is nothing here to indicate that the causal structures which the various conceptual schemes map out depend noncausally on human interests and desires or on social practices. That conceptual schemes are "mind-dependent" in the way indicated suggests nothing Kantian or Neo-Kantian. There is no threat to 2N2C.

There remains one additional route to N-K constructivism along similar lines. Scientific realism does open up the possibility of scientific metaphysics, and most scientific realists are materialists—either materialists generally, or at least materialists about the subject matters of the various special sciences including psychology. It may be reasonably argued that in the present dialectical situation plausible realist philosophical packages will embody a commitment to materialism. If this is conceded, then it follows that the realist will be obliged to offer a materialist interpretation of each of the plurality of conceptual schemes appropriate to scientific inquiry. This requirement, it might be argued, fatally compromises the realist's endorsement of conceptual pluralism—a materialist interpretation of a theory or conceptual scheme must be reductive, so the realist must hold that the conceptual resources of any scientific discourse are ultimately reducible to those of some standard version of physical theory.

The objection is cogent just in case it is impossible for the realist to defend a nonreductionist understanding of materialism. There is a certain irony here. A nonreductionist understanding of materialism is available to the realist *but not to the empiricist or to the constructivist.* Here is why: Materialism asserts that all phenomena (or all phenomena in the relevant domain) are composed of physical phenomena. In particular it asserts that all causal powers and mechanisms are composite from physical causal powers and mechanisms. For the empiricist such causal talk must reduce to talk about the deductive subsumption of the relevant laws and lawlike generalizations under the laws of physics, and that in turn requires (in consequence of Craig's theorem) that the vocabulary of those laws and generalizations be reducible to that of the laws of physics.

Similarly, for the constructivist, physical (biological, psychological, historical ...) causation is socially constructed in the practices of physicists (biologists, psychologists, historians ...), so to say that the causal powers or mechanisms operating in some other discipline are composite from physical powers or mechanism is to say that there is a reductive relation of some sort between the concepts and practices of the other discipline and those of physics.

On a realist understanding, by contrast, causal powers, mechanisms, and the like are phenomena conceptually and metaphysically independent of our conceptual schemes, and the ways in which powers, mechanisms, particles, and so on aggregate to form composite phenomena is not a conceptual matter but a matter of the theory-independent causal structures of the relevant phenomena. Thus on a realist analysis materialism is not in need of, and does not possess, a reductionist analysis of the sort at issue (I develop this and related themes in Boyd 1985b, 1989).

Thus if realists should be materialists (despite the methodological difficulties with experimental metaphysics discussed earlier, I think they should), they are entitled to formulate and defend philosophical packages that provide a nonreductionist understanding of materialism, one compatible with a plurality of mutually irreducible scientific conceptual schemes. Incidentally, since both materialism and the mutual irreducibility of theoretical conceptions in science are independently attractive positions, the capacity of realism to accommodate them both when empiricism and constructivism cannot is an additional point in its favor.

5.6. Cultural Pluralism: Alternative Conceptions of Tolerance

Sophisticated constructivism reflecting a dialectically complex conception of conventionality will mirror realism in its treatment of semantic and methodological commensurability for standard cases in the history of science, but the sophisticated constructivist has an option not open to the realist. Whenever two traditions of inquiry are sufficiently different that there are no compelling arguments for methodological or semantic commensurability, the constructivist is free to diagnose a particularly deep form of methodological and semantic incommensurability: that which obtains between traditions involved in different episodes of world making. The availability of this option has often been taken as providing a justification for constructivism on the grounds that its exercise, in some or all cases of the sort in question, provides the appropriate remedy to cultural chauvinism. Where the "Western scientific outlook," say, conflicts with that reflected in the tradition of some preindustrial tribal culture, an analysis according to which the two traditions represent different episodes of world making precludes on our part any sort of condescension based on the conviction that participants in the other tradition are irrational or fundamentally wrong. Both rationality and truth are differently constructed in our two traditions.

It is important to see what is *not* at issue here. In the first place, it is not at issue that sometimes, when there is a translation scheme that appears to establish semantic commensurability between two traditions of inquiry, there will be a better semantic conception that diminishes the apparent disagreement between the traditions perhaps at the expense of semantic commensurability. It is fully compatible with realism to hold for example, about an apparent disagreement between a Western physician and a tribal medical practitioner, that the tribal terms initially translated as "disease" and "cure" really have different meanings *and different extensions* than the English terms offered as their translation, that their meanings and extensions are not expressible in English, and that when properly understood the tribal practitioner's views are more accurate than they appear to be on the initial translation.

Where the realist's and the constructivist's options differ here is that their accounts of the semantics of the relevant languages and of the accuracy of the different theories are subject to different constraints. The constructivist may cheerfully hold that some tribal term "d" means "conditions caused by demons," has as its extension the set of conditions that are so caused, and has a non-null extension—all of this in the world socially constructed by the relevant tribal practice. The realist could say the same things only if she could defend a philosophical package in which the existence of demons is somehow reconciled with the apparent scientific evidence against their existence—all this, of course, in the single world which she and both practitioners study. Thus while the strategy of attenuating apparent disagreements between traditions of inquiry by diagnosing appropriate failures of semantic commensurability is available to both realists and constructivists, its applications are considerably more constrained for the realist.

More importantly, there is no issue about the *cultural relativity of rational justification nor any issue about the extent of its applicability*. Here is why: Both realists and constructivists accept the accommodation thesis and the associated critique of the hope for theory-independent methods of empirical investigation. They must agree that, insofar as rationality is a matter of epistemic responsibility, rationality is exhibited by the conscientious application of culturally transmitted standards of reasoning and of epistemic practice. At least for a person with significant exposure to only one cultural tradition, there are no other possible standards for the assessment of her epistemic responsibility. Moreover, and this too is dictated by any rejection of the existence of theory-independent methods, even cosmopolitan agents with experience of more than one culture are obliged to assess conflict in cultural standards from a perspective somehow derived from their primary theoretical and practical commitments. There just are no other rational standards to apply.

Thus neither the realist nor the constructivist lacks the resources for explaining, in any case of conflicting cultural standards of rationality, why it would be inappropriate to take such a conflict as indicative of a failure of rationality—or of intelligence, or of any other cognitive or moral virtue—on the part of participants in the other culture. Only the empiricist who believes in a priori justifiable theory-neutral standards of rationality lacks such resources—and perhaps only a caricature of an empiricist, since any philosopher who believes that such standards exist will surely hold that their discovery would require developments in statistical theory of sufficient complexity that it is to no one's discredit as a rational agent not to have lived in a culture in which they have been achieved. Almost certainly the main antidotes to chauvinist diagnoses of the irrationality of other cultures are political rather than philosophical, but insofar as philosophical remedies are sought, they are as readily available to the realist as to the constructivist.

What the realist cannot do—as the constructivist can—is to offer an account of the relation between traditions of inquiry which guarantees that neither *could be* better than the other at mapping causal structures or metaphysical reality because they represent independent instances of world construction. Thus a certain sort of guarantee of tolerance is available only to the constructivist. Should this count in favor of the constructivist perspective?

Of course, if the availability of this sort of ontological tolerance is seen as advantageous, its advantages will have to be weighed against the numerous philosophical disadvantages of N-K constructivism already diagnosed. But it is not in any event obvious that there is an advantage at all. If being a constructivist is never having to say they're wrong, it is never having to say we're wrong either. If the basic metaphysical presuppositions of any framework of inquiry are taken to be basically correct by convention, then this is true of one's own framework, and a certain conception of open-mindedness—being willing to consider the possibility that others' conceptions are in some ways superior to one's own—is compromised.

The latter claim may be made precise. The following principle—call it the *insight thesis*—is a consequence of the accommodation thesis:

Suppose that a body of research practice within a research tradition has proved systematically successful in achieving some sort of knowledge. Then its success provides good evidence that the theoretical principles and methodological practices that have governed that research reflect an insight into *the causal structures of the phenomena under study*.

This thesis is common to constructivists, realists, and sophisticated empiricists, but its interpretation depends crucially on the philosophical perspective from which it is advanced. For either a realist or a sophisticated empiricist, the causal structures referred to are features of the unique actual world, whereas for the constructivist the reference to causal structures in the formulation of the insight thesis is reference to causal structures in the world socially constructed by the research tradition within which the successes in question occurred. In the light of these differences consider the following:

An Antichauvinist Principle for Projectibility Judgments within a Research Tradition T. Suppose that it is discovered about a tradition T′ other than T that (a) T and T′ share to some extent a common subject matter and (b) inquirers (or practitioners) in T′ possess skill or sophistication about some theoretical or practical issues concerning that common subject matter roughly comparable to that of inquirers and practitioners in T. Then, prima facie, the doctrine that the theories employed by workers in T′ in their successful endeavors embody an approximation to the truth about the causal structures of the phenomena that make up that common subject matter must be counted as projectible in T.

Corollary. The discovery of the relevant sort of commonality of subject matter with a sophisticated tradition makes relevant features of that tradition *internal* to the tradition within which the discovery of commonality takes place. The recognition of relevantly sophisticated traditions alternative to T sharing a common subject matter dictates a corresponding "open-mindedness" within T *even when the two traditions are such that methodological commensurability between them fails to hold.*

Each of these principles is entailed by the insight principle, but for constructivists—and not for realists or sophisticated empiricists—their application is restricted to those cases in which the traditions T and T′ are part of a common episode of the social construction of reality. In precisely those cases in which constructivism is supposed to provide an antidote to chauvinism—those in which the constructivist portrays the apparently competing traditions as embodying different episodes of world construction—the force of the openmindedness principle is lost. The cost of metaphysical insurance against treating other traditions as mistaken is immunity from the requirement that one take them seriously. Even if it were not for the deep technical difficulties with N-K constructivism, it is not clear that this would be the version of cultural tolerance to endorse.

5.7. Realism and Unity of Knowledge: Concluding Scientific Postscript

One line of argument in metaphilosophy has it that a generally naturalistic conception of the subject matter and methods of philosophy is appropriate. Naturalistic conceptions are correct in epistemology, semantic theory, metaphysics, and ethics, and the reason they are correct is that philosophy is one of, or at any rate is continuous with, the empirical sciences. (It usually goes with this position to remind the reader that the empirical sciences are not what empiricists thought they were.) I am inclined to think that *something* like this is right, but the interesting task is to say just what it is. The results of our inquiry into the relative merits of realism and N-K constructivism provide some indications of an answer.

In the first place, if inference-rule foundationalism is seriously mistaken, as it appears to be, then the accommodation thesis or its analogue will hold about all or almost all branches of knowledge. Whether this entails naturalism in epistemology or not, it certainly entails that the epistemology of inquiry in any field must be grounded to a significant extent either in the findings of that field or in a substantive critique of its findings and methods. (The epistemology of morals must be grounded to a significant extent in moral theory, or in a critique of moral theory and its methods, and similarly for social sciences, theology, aesthetics, etc.) Insofar as the various areas of human inquiry are interconnected, epistemological theories must satisfy a requirement of integration with the best-substantiated results of all of the various areas of inquiry.

Similarly, once the possibility of experimental metaphysics is acknowledged, any sort of human inquiry must be seen as potentially relevant to metaphysics, and thus metaphysical theories too must face the requirement of integration with the rest of our knowledge. What seems dictated is that philosophy—along with all other disciplines—is properly governed by a principle of unity of inquiry analogous to the principle of unity of science proposed by empiricist philosophers of science: the results of inquiry in any area are potentially relevant to the assessment of the results in any other.

This principle of unity of inquiry seems philosophically attractive; indeed, it seems to capture much of the motivation for philosophical activity. It has, however, the consequence that—even when the relations between disciplines are understood nonreductively—there is some limit to disciplinary autonomy. This fact has provided for some a motivation for a particular kind of N-K constructivism which portrays various contemporary disciplines as reflecting independent episodes of world construction. Often the aim is to save, for example, the social sciences, the arts, literature, history, morals, or religion from the threat of scientific criticism ("the imperialism of physics"). Reflection on the nonreductionist character of (realist) materialism will indicate, I believe, that neither the social sciences, nor the arts, nor literature, nor history, nor morals are in any way challenged by the sciences. (For the crucial case of morals see Sturgeon 1984a, 1984b; Miller 1984; Boyd 1988; Railton 1986.) In the case of most orthodox religion, by contrast, there does appear to be a conflict with apparently well-confirmed materialism.

Should N-K constructivism be accepted in order to save religion from scientific critique? The myriad metaphysical and epistemological difficulties facing the articulation of constructivist philosophical packages suggest that the answer must be "no." So too does the fact that constructivism seems in general ill-suited for the defense of open-mindedness. Finally, the denial of the full applicability of the principle of unity of inquiry seems especially inappropriate for the defense of traditions of inquiry with aims as synoptic as those of traditional theology. I conclude that a respect for the integrity of the aims of theology as well as other deep philosophical considerations precludes such a move. The scientific challenge to religion cannot be made to go away.

REFERENCES

Armstrong, D. M.

1973 *Belief, Truth and Knowledge*. Cambridge: Cambridge University Press.

Boyd, R.

1971 "Realism and Scientific Epistemology." Unpublished.

1972 "Determinism, Laws, and Predictability in Principle." *Philosophy of Science* 39:431–450.

1973 "Realism, Underdetermination, and a Causal Theory of Evidence." *Nous* 8:1–12.

1979 "Metaphor and Theory Change." In *Metaphor and Thought*, ed. A. Ortony. Cambridge: Cambridge University Press.

1980 "Materialism without Reductionism: What Physicalism Does Not Entail." In *Readings in Philosophy of Psychology*, ed. N. Block, vol. 1. Cambridge, Mass.: Harvard University Press.

1982 "Scientific Realism and Naturalistic Epistemology." In *PSA 1980*, ed. P. D. Asquith and R. N. Giere, vol. 2. East Lansing, Mich.: Philosophy of Science Association.

1983 "On the Current Status of the Issue of Scientific Realism." *Erkenntnis* 19:45–90.

1985a "Lex Orandi est Lex Credendi." In *Images of Science: Essays on Realism and Empiricism*, ed. P. M. Churchland and C. A. Hooker. Chicago: University of Chicago Press.

1985b "Observations, Explanatory Power, and Simplicity." In *Observation, Experiment, and Hypothesis in Modern Physical Science*, ed. P. Achinstein and O. Hannaway. Cambridge, Mass.: MIT Press.

1985c "The Logician's Dilemma." *Erkenntnis* 22:197–252.

1987 "Realism and the Moral Sciences." Unpublished.

1988 "How to Be a Moral Realist." In *Moral Realism*, ed. G. Sayre McCord. Ithaca, N.Y.: Cornell University Press.

1989 "What Realism Implies and What It Does Not." *Dialectica*

1990a "Realism, Approximate Truth, and Philosophical Method." In *Scientific Theories*, ed. Wade Savage. Minnesota Studies in the Philosophy of Science, vol. 14. Minneapolis: University of Minnesota Press.

1990b "Realism, Conventionality, and 'Realism About.'" In *Meaning and Method*, ed. George Boolos. Cambridge: Cambridge University Press.

1991 "Realism, Anti-foundationalism, and the Enthusiasm for Natural Kinds." *Philosophical Studies* 61:127–148.

Brink, D.

1984 "Moral Realism and the Skeptical Arguments from Disagreement and Queerness." *Australian Journal of Philosophy* 62(2):111–125.

1989 *Moral Realism and the Foundations of Ethics*. Cambridge: Cambridge University Press.

Byerly, H., and V. Lazara

1973. "Realist Foundations of Measurement." *Philosophy of Science* 40:10–28.

Carnap, R.

1928 *Der Logische Aufbau der Welt*. Berlin.

1934 *The Unity of Science*. Trans. M. Black. London: Kegan Paul.

1950 "Empiricism, Semantics, and Ontology." *Revue internationale de philosophie* 4:20–40.

Feyerabend, P.

1989 "Realism and the Historicity of Knowledge." *Journal of Philosophy* 87:393–406.

Fine A.

1984 "The Natural Ontological Attitude." In *Scientific Realism*, ed. J. Leplin. Berkeley, Los Angeles, London: University of California Press.

Goldman, A.

1967 "A Causal Theory of Knowing." *Journal of Philosophy* 64:357–372.

1976 "Discrimination and Perceptual Knowledge." *Journal of Philosophy* 73:771–791.

Goodman, N.

1973 *Fact, Fiction, and Forecast*. 3d ed. Indianapolis and New York: Bobbs-Merrill.

1978 *Ways of Worldmaking*. Indianapolis: Hackett.

Guyot, K.
1987 "What, If Anything, Is a Higher Taxon?" Ph.D. diss., Cornell University.

Hanson, N. R.
1958 *Patterns of Discovery*. Cambridge: Cambridge University Press.

Jensen, A.
1968 "How Much Can We Boost I.Q. and Scholastic Achievement? *Harvard Educational Review*.

Kripke, S. A.
1971 "Identity and Necessity." In *Identity and Individuation*, ed. M. K. Munitz. New York: New York University Press.
1972 "Naming and Necessity." In *The Semantics of Natural Language*, ed. D. Davidson and G. Harman. Dordrecht: D. Reidel.

Kuhn, T.
1970 *The Structure of Scientific Revolutions*. 2d ed. Chicago: University of Chicago Press.

Laudan, L.
1981 "A Confutation of Convergent Realism." *Philosophy of Science* 48:218–249.

Lewontin, R.
1976 "Race and Intelligence." In *The I.Q. Controversy*, ed. N. Bolck and G. Dworkin. New York: Pantheon.

Miller, R.
1984 "Ways of Moral Learning." *Philosophical Review* 94:507–556.
1987 *Fact and Method*. Princeton: Princeton University Press.

Putnam, H.
1962 "The Analytic and the Synthetic." In *Scientific Explanation, Space, and Time*, ed. H. Feigl and G. Maxwell. Minnesota Studies in the Philosophy of Science, vol. 3. Minneapolis; University of Minnesota Press.
1972 "Explanation and Reference." In *Conceptual Change*, ed. G. Pearce and P. Maynard. Dordrecht: Reidel.
1975a "The Meaning of 'Meaning.'" In *Mind, Language, and Reality*, by H. Putnam. Cambridge: Cambridge University Press.
1975b "Language and Reality." In *Mind, Language, and Reality*, by H. Putnam. Cambridge: Cambridge University Press.
1979 *Meaning and the Moral Sciences*. London: Routledge and Kegan Paul.
1981 *Reason, Truth, and History*. Cambridge: Cambridge University Press.
1983 "Vagueness and Alternative Logic." In *Realism and Reason*, by H. Putnam. Cambridge: Cambridge University Press.

Quine, W. V. O.
1961a "On What There Is." In *From a Logical Point of View*, by W. V. O. Quine. Cambridge, Mass.: Harvard University Press.
1961b "Two Dogmas of Empiricism." In *From a Logical Point of View*, by W. V. O. Quine. Cambridge, Mass.: Harvard University Press.
1969a "Natural Kinds." In *Ontological Relativity and Other Essays*, by W. V. O. Quine. New York: Columbia University Press.

1969b "Epistemology Naturalized." In *Ontological Relativity and Other Essays*, by W. V. O. Quine. New York: Columbia University Press.

Railton, P.
1986 "Moral Realism." *Philosophical Review* 95:163–207.

Scheffler, I.
1967 *Science and Subjectivity*. Indianapolis: Bobbs-Merrill.

Shapere, D.
1964 "The Structure of Scientific Revolutions." *Philosophical Review* 73:383–394.

Sturgeon, N.
1984a "Moral Explanations." In *Morality, Reason, and Truth*, ed. D. Copp and D. Zimmerman. Totowa, N.J.: Rowman and Allanheld.
1984b Review of *Moral Relativism* and *Virtues and Vices*, by P. Foot. *Journal of philosophy* 81:326–333.

van Fraassen, B.
1980 *The Scientific Image*. Oxford: Oxford University Press.

EIGHT

Do We Need a Hierarchical Model of Science?

Diderik Batens

According to hierarchical models of science, our scientific knowledge in the broadest sense, including descriptive as well as methodological and evaluative statements, forms a knowledge system or is embedded in a larger knowledge system that has two properties: (i) it is stratified, and (ii) the items of some layer are or should be justified in terms of items of a higher layer. Hierarchical models are deeply rooted in Western culture in general. They are both viewed as describing the natural order in a variety of domains and as outstanding problem-solving environments.[1] Most past philosophers explicitly or implicitly favored hierarchical models. The vast majority of those who view science as a rational enterprise will, if pressed, opt for a hierarchical model. Even those who reject hierarchical models often retain many of their aspects.

I hope to show, first, that hierarchical models are affected by a number of difficulties—I shall be brief on this well-known point—and, next, that we need not try to repair them because there is a much more attractive alternative which I shall try to spell out and argue for. The alternative is the "contextual" approach to meaning and knowledge, embedded in a relative-rationality view. I deal with only a few aspects of this approach here and refer to other publications where necessary, but I have tried to make the present text as self-contained as possible.[2]

I begin with a historical remark. In section 2, I indicate some major difficulties of the hierarchical (and the holistic) model with respect to justification. The third and fourth sections are devoted to two central features of the contextual model. For the sake of expository clarity, I postpone the discussion of some more fundamental problems to the final section.

1. HISTORICAL NOTE

With respect to the kinds of certainty that scientists and philosophers of science are considered to have available, one may distinguish three periods since the seventeenth century. In the first period, the general conviction was that certainty may be attained in at least three different domains: scientific method, observations, and scientific theories. In the second period, starting around 1820–1830, a fallibilistic view on theories is gaining ground, but people stay convinced that certainty is available in the two other domains. They have changed their view on the scientific method[3] but are convinced that the new view is the correct one. They became more critical about observation, as may be seen from the attention paid to the relation between observation and so-called sensations, but sensations became fashionable precisely because they were seen as absolutely reliable. At present we are in a third period: absolute certainty is given up in all three domains. Theory-ladenness has been decisive for the rejection of observational certainty, and many philosophers of science became convinced that methodological rules and methodological values may change and indeed have been changing in the past. More importantly, they are convinced that it is, and always will be, impossible to articulate *the* correct methodology of science. Some think this is so because this methodology is too complex to be known and to be spelled out. Marcello Pera (1988) is one of them. But most philosophers of science simply gave up the idea of a timelessly correct scientific methodology.[4]

In the first period, and even in the second, to adopt a hierarchical model of science was a most plausible move. The standard hierarchical model locates descriptive statements about the world, statements about facts and laws, at the lowest level, and methodological rules at the second level.

The force of hierarchical models lies essentially in the fact that decisions at the lower level derive directly from the items at the higher level. If we are certain about methods, we are able to understand the way in which we attain certainty about facts and theories, the reasons for our mistakes at these levels, and the ways in which we may correct them. Once direct certainty at the methodological level is given up, the hierarchical model requires us to find a higher level at which certainty is available and from which certainty about methods may be derived. When this failed, some moved to a meanwhile available alternative: the holistic model.

At least since the end of the nineteenth century a holistic view about science has been taking shape. We find it to some extent with Pierre Duhem, for whom it mainly concerns observations and theories. In the early writings of Quine it takes a quasi-universal form, applying also to logic and methodology. With Kuhn, a form of the holistic model is claimed to be historically accurate, and the model gains respect from there. According to that model there are two loci for justification: within the knowledge system (resulting in extensions of it) and about the choice between overall systems. In justificatory activities of the first type, the system as it stands is taken for granted, and extensions, perhaps even small modifications, are judged in terms of their consistency (in a weak sense) or coherence. In choices between overall systems, the only possible criterion seems again to be consistency or coherence; I return to this in the next section.

Both models may be combined, and in Kuhn 1962 they are in a specific sense; roughly, normal science follows a hierarchical model, paradigm shifts are holistic in nature.

2. PROBLEMS WITH THE TRADITIONAL MODELS

Both the hierarchical and holistic model lead to a number of well-known difficulties. Larry Laudan argues that both models are actually problematic from a descriptive as well as from an explanatory point of view. He mentions that influential proponents of hierarchical models arrived at the conclusion that disagreements on the level of cognitive values or aims—the apparently highest level—cannot be settled in a rational way. Notice that the holistic view leads to the same conclusion. Combining this with the global character of paradigm changes, "we are forced to say that the various shifts in the predominant goals in science are just part of the history of taste and fashion" (Laudan 1984, 50). Laudan offers substantial arguments to show, first, that cognitive aims are not in principle beyond the reach of cognitive decision and have indeed been changing in rational ways, and, next, that scientific change need not and did not proceed according to Kuhn's holistic model.

Apart from these difficulties, both models are deeply problematic as justificatory mechanisms. The hierarchical model is bound to lead either (i) to an infinite regress, or (ii) to a stable highest level at which absolute certainties are available, or finally (iii) to a merely instrumental justification that stops at the highest level. If the hierarchical model is to lead to justifications, then (i) is unacceptable even in principle, apart from epistemological difficulties, (ii) is unacceptable if the historical remark of the previous section is even roughly correct, and (iii) is unacceptable in view of the fact that, for any statement, one does actually find human beings that disagree about it. More importantly, we actually find disagreements about very "high-level" items, such as aims and values, among sensible people who are being serious and not in extreme situations (not enraged, drunk, etc.).

If absolute certainty fails at some level, the certainty available at lower levels is difficult to ascertain, however stringent the justification of the lower-level items in terms of the higher-level items. I think this is one of the main reasons for the recent discontent with hierarchical models. As soon as one accepts the fallibility of methodological rules, the justificatory chain is broken and the force of hierarchical models reduces to nil. As a result, some recurred to holistic models that had been developed by a minority. They have the advantage of not requiring that higher levels be always more stable than lower ones, and of admitting that the justification of the full systems is different in nature from justification within the system.

Nevertheless, the force of a justification deriving from a holistic model depends directly on the justification of the choice between overall systems. If this is not to be a matter of taste, we need a criterion or value superseding all possible overall systems and independent of each of them, and we again stumble upon the difficulty of resolving disagreements about this criterion or value. Many seem convinced that consistency or coherence is a sensible candidate, but this derives from a mistaken view on logic. There are different notions of consistency and coherence; they have to function as elements of overall systems and will take a different form and especially different weights in such systems. Other people recurred to pragmatic arguments, but these clearly cannot resolve all disagreements in a final way.

This is not the place to discuss the proposals by which adherents of hierarchical and holistic models have tried to overcome these difficulties.[5] I merely wanted to point out that the difficulties are there, both with respect to explanation and with respect to justification, and that they cannot be overcome unless by reaching absolute justification and rock-bottom certainty. In my view, we do not have to continue this unending quest, both because of the historical reasons sketched before and because of epistemological reasons (see Batens 1974, 1978).

Before leaving the matter, let me point out two things that are perhaps indications rather than arguments but nevertheless seem relevant. Hierarchical as well as holistic models presuppose that knowing subjects are able to deal with overall systems of knowledge, hierarchically ordered or not, that they are able to relate specific choices to such systems, and, at least for the holistic model, that they are able to arrive at a justified choice between them. It seems to me that humans do not have these capabilities. No human fully overviews even one substantiated overall system. No human disposes of a complete and detailed system of norms and values. We count ourselves happy to dispose of a few realistic alternatives now and then, and to have some arguments to choose one rather than the other. And even then we realize that other alternatives may be discovered in the future, and that new arguments may come up. Moreover, neither of the two models takes into account (i) that human beings necessarily perform a number of activities that are beyond their conscious control, and (ii) that human beings are subject to mechanisms belonging to the domain of the social sciences.[6] In other words, both types of models presuppose a model of man according to which knowledge acquisition, if not all human activity, is a matter of conscious deliberation—a model *known* to be false.

My conclusion is that we need a model of science which is both less pretentious and more realistic. The model we need should (i) be closer to actual justificatory processes, (ii) not require absolute certainties in any domain, (iii) allow in principle for changes in any part of our knowledge system, and (iv) not require that we ever move "above" our knowledge system and its known alternatives in order to choose between them.

3. CONTEXTUAL PROBLEM-SOLVING

In order to clarify the alternative approach, I shall consider two of its features. The present section concerns problem solving, the next deals with the structure of the knowledge system.

The basic idea is that problems are not solved with respect to the full knowledge system but *within specific problem-solving situations*, which I shall call *contexts* for short. A context consists of a number of elements which I briefly enumerate:

(i) The problem one tries to solve.

(ii) The participants. There may be one, but also more, for example if people cooperate to solve a problem or have an intellectual fight about something. In general the context will be different for each participant. To stipulate otherwise would lead to an unrealistic and simplistic approach and would result in sweeping a lot of important difficulties under the carpet.

(iii) The contextual certainties. These are statements that are relevant to the problem and are considered as contextually beyond discussion. They define the possible answers to the problem as well as the contextual meanings of the terms. Examples of contextual certainties are easily provided: a set of physical laws for an engineer designing a bridge; properties of the employed instruments for laboratory experiments; some properties of paper and pencils for me writing this text. I will argue later that no contextual certainty is common to all contexts.

(iv) The statements that are considered relevant to the problem and true or given within the context. By "relevant" I mean two different things. First, it matters with respect to the solution of the problem whether we include such a statement or not; for example, the position of the moon is irrelevant to a chemical experiment. Moreover, the truth of these statements should not be determined by the contextual certainties. In other words, they should be logically contingent; keep in mind that logical truth is a contextual notion, determined by the contextual certainties.

(v) The methodological rules or, in general, normative rules and evaluative statements that are judged appropriate for the solution of the problem. "Methodological rules" should be taken in the broad sense, including rules to handle measuring instruments as well as, for example, a specific inductive method in the sense of Carnap. Some or all of these rules may be heuristic.

The problem is defined by (ii), (iii), and (v). If a solution is possible within the context as it stands (and is a matter of reasoning, not, e.g., of observation or action), the solution is "derived" from (iv). It follows that the elements of a context are not independent of one another. We only know what the problem is if we have specified the constraints on its solution, and these are determined by the other elements of the context. Also, I already mentioned the dependence between (iii) and (iv).

One of the main advantages of the contextual approach is that problems are not solved "in the open" and not even with respect to some knowledge system, but with respect to something much more specific, which I called a context. It is important to point out at once that the certainties, truths, and methodological rules are all contextual. The fact that the properties of some instrument are considered beyond discussion within a given context does not prevent one from questioning and investigating these properties in another context. The fact that an engineer considers some physical law as certain in a given context does not even entail that it is a law of contemporary physics (it may actually be rejected).

Another point which I should stress is that contexts are very small and specific.[7] It may turn out that some piece of information necessary to solve the problem is missing; or that the setup of the context is incomplete and hence that the problem is not well-defined; or that the constraints contained in the context, whether certainties or methods, are inconsistent or incoherent. In all such cases new, *derived* problems are generated, the solution of which belongs to other contexts. These problems may include such questions as "What was wrong with the original context?" or "How likely is it that the derived problem may be solved?" or "How important was the original problem?" After the derived problems are solved—sometimes we decide to give up—one may return to the original problem. This does not mean, however, that one returns to the original context. The very fact that the derived problem has been solved will entail that the new context is different from the old.

A further proliferation of contexts will occur if more than one participant is involved. Disagreements of all kinds may lead to new problems that have to be solved before the original problem may be tackled. This obtains for disagreements about relevant truths, contextual certainties, and so on. Remember in this connection that contextual certainties are directly related to the meanings people attach to words.

I hope all this makes it clear that problem solutions may require considering a great number of related problems and moving through a great number of contexts.

I skip the discussion on the way in which problems may be generated. Let me just mention that the proliferation of problems is cut down by at least two mechanisms. First, one may choose between problems on the basis of their importance and the prospects for their solution. Next, one should not generate problems unless there is a good reason to do so. It is perfectly all right to reflect upon one's knowledge system, because this usually leads to quite good reasons to consider new problems, but it is not sensible in general to generate problems for their own sake. By all means, we are not short of urgent and important problems.

Let me summarize some further materials on contextual problem-solving by listing some theses. They are all specified and defended at length in Batens 1985, with the exception of thesis 8, which is dealt with in Batens 1983, and of thesis 9, to which I return in section 5.

1. There is no highest context. In general, one context cannot be said to be higher (in a transitive sense of the term) than another; see also section 5.
2. A contextual certainty, a relevant truth, or a methodological rule of a context C1 may be the problem of a context C2.
3. *A* may be certain or relevantly true in C1 whereas not-*A* is certain or relevantly true in C2.
4. No statement is contextually certain with respect to *all* problems. The idea of a *corpus* of accepted statements, as defended by Isaac Levi (1980), should be rejected.
5. All contextual certainties are *logical* certainties, and all logical certainties are contextual. This is related to thesis 1 and entails thesis 6.
6. Meanings vary from one context to another, and not only from one language to another or from one person to another.
7. Communication does not require that people assign the same meanings to words. Notwithstanding 6, communication may be defined in an adequate way: people that have completely different "worldviews" may nevertheless communicate perfectly on a number of problems.
8. This notion of communication enables us to solve a number of problems connected with incommensurability.
9. Some problems are solved in an unconscious way. This fact is not a difficulty for the present approach. Incidentally, if one were to deny it, one would have to define basic problems. The trouble with these is quite analogous to the one pointed out in connection with basic actions by Annette Baier (1979).

Here are some materials from the literature by which the present approach may be substantiated in a direct way:

(1) Philosophy of science: in the first place a large part of Larry Laudan's work; on more specific topics, work by Tom Nickles and others on scientific discovery and problem solving in general; remarks on question dynamics and question dialectics by Nicholas Rescher.

(2) Logic: a treasure of results may be found in Jaakko Hintikka's work on dialogues and questions; also relevant are results on the same topics by Lennart

Åqvist, Ruth Manor, and by Risto Hilpinen and other people from the "Hintikka school."

(3) Artificial intelligence: a lot of fascinating results on problem solving and heuristics are found in the work of Herbert Simon, the MIT group, and the Stanford group. The idea of heuristic programs that transform themselves is central for the contextual alternative.

Also, this approach fits in quite well with results evolving from cognitive science,[8] action theory, and other recent developments in the social sciences in general.

Although it is obvious that the view propounded in this section runs counter to hierarchical models of science, the reader may wonder how the information needed to set up contexts and resulting from problem solving is organized and stored. Do hierarchical models crop up in this connection? In the next section I will argue that the answer to this question is negative.

4. THE KNOWLEDGE SYSTEM

The knowledge system contains elements of many kinds: factual, nomological, normative, evaluative, and so on. From this system we take the items we need to set up contexts, and to the system we add results of problem solving and attempted problem solving. The elements of the knowledge system are accompanied by indices that point to the *function* of these elements with respect to the solution of problems or types of problems. Unlike what one might expect, the elements of the knowledge system may not in general be classified as certainties, truths, or methodological rules. Rather, an element may occur in the knowledge system with different indices that point to different functions with respect to different problems.

How do we set up a context for a particular problem? First of all, it is important to realize that a problem never comes "completely open" but is always specified to some extent. If the specification is insufficient, we first have to consider a derived problem. When we start solving a problem, we further supplement the incomplete context with elements of the knowledge system that are related by their indices to this problem or to problems of this type. If someone performs an experiment to obtain an answer to a specific question, he or she will take from his or her knowledge system the relevant data concerning the experimental setup, the actions to be performed, the measuring instruments, the rules governing these instruments, the number of measurements that warrant a reliable average result, and so on. Most of these data will pertain to a connected set of contexts rather than to a single context. If one is in doubt about the setup of the context, or if the context turns out to be incoherent or incomplete in some other way, one first moves to a derived problem.

Once a (derived or "primitive") problem is solved, we may add its solution to our knowledge system. Incidentally, if we decide to stop attempting to solve a problem—for example, because its solution seems beyond reach or not worth the trouble—this decision is itself a solution to a derived problem and may in that capacity be added to our knowledge system. Whether or not some solution will be added, and whether it will later be removed or replaced (or will be forgotten), depends to some extent on unconscious mechanisms.

Philosophers might worry about the origin of our very first knowledge system. Quite obviously, it is the result of a complex process that takes place during our youth. The process is to a large extent determined by mechanisms that remain beyond (our and others') conscious control. We can only hope our original system is sufficiently open to allow for justified improvements.[9] Apart from this, I think, there is nothing particular here that a philosopher should worry about. But remark that the answer suits the contextual model, whereas hierarchical models have a much harder problem here.

Hoping that the general picture is clear, I turn to the way in which the items of our knowledge system are ordered with respect to contexts. I maintain that we need (and actually introduce) only two kinds of order here. The first consists in the fact that some elements are linked to types of problems rather than to specific problems. For example, statements and rules about measuring instruments concern whole sets of problems. The same obtains for inductive methods and for deductive systems. The second kind of order derives from the fact that elements of our knowledge system may be joined into connected and coherent wholes. The two forms of order are related in that the latter appears to be a more elaborated and substantiated version of the former.

We appear to have a need for coherent subsystems, the reasons being now intellectual, then practical. I mention some examples that presumably occur in most people's knowledge systems.

Most of us have a general view of the world, which we try to make compatible with present-day scientific theories, and which should enable us to understand our environment. This general view should be more coherent than our knowledge system in general. To its statements we apply criteria for *truth*, at least if we are intentional realists, and to the connected methodological rules we apply criteria for correctness that are stronger than the correctness criteria applied to most other rules. This general view contains the solution to a number of problems and should form a suitable basis for the solution of a large set of potential problems. If we have to extend or modify our knowledge system in order to solve some explanatory problem, we shall try to extend or modify specifically this subsystem. Philosophers of science have concentrated too exclusively on this general explanatory theory and have erroneously identified it with the set of contemporary accepted scientific theories.[10] Sometimes they even identify it with the full knowledge system. For this reason, I stress that scientific theories form, separately and by sets, subsystems of the knowledge system which are mutually different as well as different from the general explanatory theory, and I at once give some other examples of connected and coherent subsystems.

We all handle a subsystem pertaining to the objects of everyday life: doors, typewriters, buses, hammers, and so on. We want it to contain more than just data about the usual functions of these objects. For example, we want not only data about hammers that guide us in hammering nails in a plank but also data that enable us to use a hammer for, say, lifting some object or keeping something from being blown away. Although these data clearly presuppose a lot of nomological order in the world, we do not need detailed scientific explanations for them. If you want other examples, consider the so-called context of pursuit: a relatively new theory may be doing a lot worse than one of its established competitors but may nevertheless be promising enough to be worked out further. Or think about the set of norms and values that are applied by a person who composes a piece of music.

Connected and coherent subsystems are, fortunately, not fully independent of one another. Some are contained in (form subsystems of) others. It is tempting to extend the inclusion to contexts. However, it rarely occurs that all certainties or all relevant statements of one context also belong to some other context, and hence inclusion seems not very helpful to systematize contexts. If I am right, the unification of the knowledge system will improve our capacity to set up contexts successfully, but contexts themselves are only indirectly related.

Sometimes, one subsystem is not included in another but is within certain limits supplemented with items from the other. For example, all statements derivable from the general explanatory theory will, insofar as they are relevant there, and unless there are explicit reasons not to do so, be added to the subsystem related to everyday objects. Another nice example is the subsystem formed while reading a novel. Specific statements from the novel are supplemented with items from other subsystems insofar as consistency allows. Among the other subsystems may be the one concerning everyday objects, but also the general explanatory system, some scientific theories (especially for science fiction novels), or subsystems of values. In one typical and interesting case, the subsystem under construction has to be restructured several times—a "trick" frequently used by Marquez; in another, the construction of the subsystem for the novel leads to changes in the subsystems from which supplementary information is taken—for example, if the reader's value judgments appear untenable with respect to the constructed system.

Other relations between subsystems play a role in increasing the order of our knowledge system. A connected methodological system *M* may be associated with a subsystem *S*. The elements of *M* will play a role in setting up contexts for problems the solution of which should be derivable from *S*, but usually *M* will be too poor to set up the fifth element of the contexts. The elements of *M* will rather pertain to the overall evaluation or extension of *S*.

Next, instructions about setting up derived contexts may be associated with a subsystem; for example, specific instructions for measurements are associated with most scientific theories. Moreover, the knowledge system may contain statements about the mutual relevance of the knowledge items of a subsystem; we have a large number of vague theories about the kinds of mechanisms that might obtain in reality, and such theories function, practically speaking, as theories about relevance.[11] An analogous but weaker mechanism may apply if knowledge items of one subsystem do not occur in another, or if their negation occurs in the other. If there is a discrepancy between the subsystem related to everyday objects and the scientific theories, a well-forged knowledge system should contain information about the reasons for it, and for the reliability of the scientific theory with respect to everyday objects.

The order in our knowledge systems is arrived at by rather simple means. If we are unable to set up an adequate context for a given problem, we will check whether the problem is of a specific type and will inquire whether elements of our knowledge system that are linked to other problems of the *same* type may be linked to *all* problems of this type. Or else we will check whether the problem belongs to the type for which some subsystem is relevant. If a solution was not derivable from the relevant statements of its (suitably constructed) context, the subsystem from which these derive is clearly incomplete. We will move on to derived problems, introducing the contextual requirement that the solution of the original problem should be compatible, and even in some stricter sense coherent, with the relevant subsystem. If this restriction has to be given up in order to arrive at a solution, we shall have to restructure the subsystem.

In the aforementioned cases, the order of our knowledge system is increased as a side effect of specific problem solutions. We may also purposefully introduce problems directed at increasing the order in our knowledge system. If we discover that our problem-solving capabilities are low for a given type of problem, we may start looking for knowledge elements that may be linked to all problems of this type, or we may try to subsume the problems under a subsystem or build a new subsystem for them. Conversely, if we discover a new knowledge element or subsystem that proves effective for the solution of some problem, we may look for types of problems to which this element may be linked. Finally, we may rely on relations between subsystems in order to extend or modify some of them.

Let me end this section with some remarks on unification. Without any doubt, the ideal state of our knowledge system would be that it form a single consistent and complete, perfectly connected system to which all subsystems are deductively linked. However, this ideal is clearly beyond the reach of ordinary mortals; whence we need a more realistic model for the justified change of our knowledge system, for solving specific problems, and for evaluating specific methods. Next, one should not exaggerate the importance of unification.

Many times it is better to dispose of relatively disconnected knowledge in many domains, rather than of unified knowledge about fewer domains. Finally, it is crucial that one is extremely careful about the point at which unification is desirable. The attempts to copy (presumed) methods from the so-called exact sciences in the social sciences is a well-known example where it went wrong. Given the differences between domains, unification should proceed in view of the general aims and take the differences into account. The contextual model quite naturally leads to such an approach.

Needless to say, we should strive to unify our knowledge system. Even if we are far away from the ideal state, we may have an idea about the extent to which certain theories and other subsystems will be unifiable after being extended or corrected. This will guide us in phrasing problems and evaluating solutions concerning the change of those subsystems.

5. CONCLUDING REMARKS

There are four points left that I need to touch upon: (i) relative justification, (ii) the fact that the present model avoids the difficulties that affect the hierarchical model, (iii) unconscious mechanisms, and (iv) the openness of the present model.

Unlike the hierarchical model, the present model does not require any absolute certainties or absolute justifications to which all decisions may in the end be "reduced." Justification is relative to the state of the knowledge system at a given moment, but one may improve this state and in this way arrive at more reliable justifications (both the improvement and the increase in reliability are themselves relative to the knowledge system and its history). I cannot defend the notion of relative justification within the confines of the present paper. Some of my older papers (Batens 1974, 1978) deal with this topic, including the relative improvement of our knowledge system. The relative justification defended there agrees with Nicholas Rescher's statement: "The issue of legitimation is thus settled in terms of a cyclic interdependence and self-supportiveness" (1984, 13–14). Traditionally this feature is regarded as undermining the claim on justification. The ultimate reply to the objection is that (i) indeed, relative rationality does not lead to any absolute warrant and clearly is not the optimal logically possible form of rationality, but (ii) it appears the best thing actually available, and (iii) it offers a true form of justification in that one relies upon the knowledge system to which one is committed and which one considers the most reliable, if not the only available, alternative.[12]

The contextual model avoids the difficulties that affect the hierarchical model. The main difficulty for the latter derives from the fact that, in order to escape infinite regress, there should be some highest level, and the items at this level should be absolute certainties. So let me show that we cannot sensibly introduce levels, let alone a highest level, and that we do not have such levels in the contextual approach.

Of course the certainties of a context are, in a sense and with respect to the context, at a higher level than the problem or the relevant truths. Given this, the following reasoning might be tempting: let the problem of C1 be at the lowest level; the certainties of C1 are at the second level; consider a context C2 in which a certainty of C1 is the problem; the certainties of C2 are then at the third level; and so on. This reasoning, however, is defective because it is quite possible that an item which, according to this reasoning, is at the first level functions as a relevant truth or even as a certainty in a context of which the problem belongs, always according to that reasoning, to a higher level. For the sake of example, consider a statement that functions as a methodological rule with respect to a set of descriptive problems. The justification of this statement may very well rely essentially on all kinds of descriptive statements, among others: (i) historical data about the methods actually used, (ii) considerations about the process that would have occurred if some other method had been used, (iii) descriptive statements about human beings—for example, about our senses, the complexity of the decision procedures we are able to apply,[13] or the kinds of knowledge at our disposal.[14] To see that this list is far from complete, remember that our observational methods should in part depend on the nature of the observed objects,[15] that the use of instruments involves all kinds of factual presuppositions, and that our ability to construct measuring instruments for some property, as well as the correctness, reliability, and precision of these instruments, depends among other things upon our knowledge about the world.[16] The reader may easily apply the same reasoning to contextual certainties.

My conclusions are that there are no levels in general, and no highest level in particular, and that there is no sense in which the methodological rules of all contexts form a set that is higher than, say, the set of descriptive statements.[17]

Incidentally, part of my objections also hold against Laudan's (1984) reticulated model. This model rejects the idea of a "privileged or primary or more fundamental" level and views the levels as mutually dependent. But I doubt that there are levels or even coherent sets of, respectively, theories, methods, and aims. On the one hand, these sets seem rather incoherent— compare the theories of physics with those of medicine, and do not be too optimistic about a clear-cut distinction between theoretical and applied sciences. On the other hand, the distinction between a methodological instruction and a descriptive statement reduces many times to a matter of grammatical form.

Unconscious mechanisms may play a role in the selection of problems, in their solution, in setting up contexts, in ordering our knowledge system, and so on. Some are psychological in nature, others sociological, neurological, and so on. If we compare humans to computers, we may say that unconscious mechanisms play a role in at least the three following respects. First, the *hardware* is beyond the reach of conscious mechanisms. We may study it and take the results into account, and we may try to externalize knowledge and decisions—for example, by putting things on paper and by computer simulation—but the hardware will never be modeled in full, and to change it is by definition impossible. Next, unconscious mechanisms play a role as *defaults*. There are activities that we may (learn to) perform in a conscious way, but that will be regulated by unconscious mechanisms whenever we do not make a special effort. Finally, unconscious mechanisms may *deform* or even direct conscious processes, and in extreme cases the latter may be mere rationalizations. To show the import of unconscious mechanisms acting as defaults, let me expand on an example. We may set up the context for some problem p in a conscious and controlled way by first considering the *derived* problem "Which elements form an appropriate context for p?" We may even bring the setup of the context for this derived problem under such control by moving on to a further derived problem, *but we cannot do so indefinitely*. At least some contexts will be set up by an unconscious mechanism.

I take it to be an essential advantage of the present model that unconscious mechanisms need not be in the way of sound justifications. Indeed, we may rely on the general argument deriving from evolutionary epistemology to consider at least our hardware as minimally adapted to our need for knowledge. We run into trouble if we try to apply evolutionary models to all knowledge acquisition, and we should even be careful not to exaggerate the import of the general argument. Nevertheless, the general argument does show that our hardware cannot be all that bad. Other unconscious mechanisms are easier to handle within the present model. Many of them are the result of learning, and a lot more may be studied, reflected upon, and changed, if this appears desirable. To see the impact of this remark, consider an example. A person who learned to observe through a microscope will most probably leave out conscious control from some point on. This does not preclude that the person is performing the act in a (locally) justified way and that he or she may change his or her habits if they prove erroneous. In more extreme cases the justification of some result will be considered dubious because of the lack of conscious control. No doubt this constitutes a difficulty; it undermines the justification of the solutions to a set of problems. But the difficulty is only a local one, not, as for other models, an insurmountable disaster.

I now come to the final point: the question whether the present model is not too open, whether it rules out at least some knowledge systems as unscientific and irrational. In one sense the model is very open: no element of the knowledge system is in principle excluded from critical examination and change. I suppose all will agree that this is a positive property. A second form of openness is equally desirable: a justificatory model (and its underlying rationality view) should not specify the knowledge elements themselves nor any methods, logics, or values. I may illustrate the point as follows. Some people try to demonstrate by general philosophical arguments that science is better off than, say, astrology or fortune-telling. I think this is a mistake. There is nothing wrong in principle with those "disciplines"; they are just no good for a hundred reasons that derive from the *contents* of our knowledge system. So, many things we want to reject are not and should not be excluded by the present model itself.

Precisely because of the absence of absolute justifications, the present model forces us to substantiate and confront our knowledge system with relevant information, to study sensible alternatives to parts of our knowledge system, and to enter into debate with adherents of such alternatives.[18] In view of the fact that the hierarchical structure of knowledge systems is rejected, methodological and epistemological questions, and philosophical questions in general, are rephrased as questions to which scientific results are relevant. In this way, the model enables us to view ourselves both as knowing and acting beings and as integral parts of the world.

NOTES

Part of the research for the present paper was done while I enjoyed a research fellowship at the Center for Philosophy of Science of the University of Pittsburgh, where a former version was delivered as a lecture. Part of the research was supported by a grant from the Belgian National Science Foundation (NFWO). I wish to thank James Child, John Forge, Ulrich Mayer, Helmut Pape, Lothar Shäfer, Anastassios Tsiadoulas, and especially Jerry Massey and Nicholas Rescher, for critical remarks and suggestions. Reading Larry Laudan's *Science and Values*, I realized the import of the hierarchical model.

1. Typically, all standard solutions of the paradoxes introduce a hierarchy.

2. Many recent results point in the direction of the contextual model and of relative rationality. Many contemporary philosophers of science implicitly adhere to something close to it. I hope the present paper contributes to render the model more explicit.

3. For a convincing analysis of the reasons see Laudan 1980.

4. Apart from methods, observations, and theories, one might consider cognitive values. The picture is more or less the same: during the first and second periods, philosophers and scientists many times disagree about specific values but are convinced that certainty may be attained in the domain; at present this certainty has been given up.

5. Much relevant information is contained in Laudan 1984.

6. See Batens 1987 for a paradoxical discrepancy between the traditional view on the social science and the equally traditional view on epistemology; both views actually belong to the same tradition.

7. Patrick Goes (1984) has analyzed part of a dialogue by Galileo and found, on the average, more than one context per page.

8. I warmly recommend Johnson-Laird 1988, an excellent account of the state of the art, clearly written, consistent with its basic principles, and full of excellent suggestions.

9. This statement concerns the justification of one's own knowledge system. However, the rationality view underlying the present paper has implications for the organization of societies and for education. Some are pointed out in section 9 of Batens 1974.

10. Moreover, philosophers of science erroneously took it for granted that this

theory was (bound to be) accompanied by a single and coherent set of methodological rules.

11. Without such theories, we would practically be unable to set up contexts because it is essential that the possibly relevant data are restricted (experiments form a good example).

12. I really never understood that there should be a fundamental objection to the following mechanism: one is committed to a set of beliefs but knows they are not absolutely reliable, and one successively relies on a subset to improve an element outside of this subset. Although this clearly cannot lead to *absolute* justification, it clearly leads to some form of justification—the only possible one in my view.

13. The complexity that humans are able to deal with is a strong argument against global induction as defended, e.g., by Rudolf Carnap (1968) and Yehosua Bar-Hillel (1968).

14. For example: we have no direct access to reality; we have no stable observational data; most of our theories are "falsified" most of the time; most scientific theories (in the strict sense of a particular formulation) remain accepted only for a relatively short period of time.

15. As a consequence our factual knowledge about humans is not only relevant with respect to all methods but also relevant in a specific way to the methodology of the social sciences.

16. The history of the thermometer is a good illustration of the difficulties involved in the design and actual construction of instruments. With a little reflection the reader will easily find the numerous factual presuppositions behind the use of thermometers. Measuring instruments are *not* conventionally accepted and are rejected if their factual presuppositions turn out false.

17. A different set of arguments, more theoretical in nature and also related to meaning, is presented Batens 1985.

18. These aspects could not be elaborated upon in the present paper; contextual problem-solving and the "structured" knowledge system are meant to be embedded in a relative-rationality view.

REFERENCES

Åqvist, Lennart

1965 *A New Approach to the Logical Theory of Interrogatives*. Uppsala: Filosofiska Föreningen.

Baier, Annette

1979 "The Search for Basic Actions." *American Philosophical Quarterly* 8:161–170.

Bar-Hillel, Yehosua

1968 "The Acceptance Syndrome." In *The Problem of Inductive Logic*, ed. I. Lakatos, 150–161. Amsterdam: North-Holland.

Batens, Diderik

1974 "Rationality and Justification." *Philosophica* 14:83–103.

1978 "Rationality and Ethical Rationality." *Philosophica* 22:23–45.

1983 "Incommensurability Is Not a Threat to the Rationality of Science or to the Anti-dogmatic Tradition." *Philosophica* 32:117–132.

1985 "Meaning, Acceptance, and Dialectics." In *Change and Progress in Modern Science*, ed. J. C. Pitt, 333–360. Dordrecht: Reidel.

1987 "Action Science and the Reunification of the Social Sciences and Epistemology." *Philosophica* 40: 109–134.

Carnap, Rudolf

1968 "On Rules of Acceptance." In *The Problem of Inductive Logic*, ed. I. Lakatos, 146–150. Amsterdam: North-Holland.

Goes, Patrick

1984 "Maten voor Informatie." M.A. thesis, Rijksuniversiteit, Ghent.

Hilpinen, Risto

1988 "On Experimental Questions." In *Theory and Experiment*, ed. D. Batens and J. P. van Bendegem, 15–29. Dordrecht: Reidel.

Hintikka, J., and F. Vandamme, eds.

1985 *The Logic of Discovery and the Logic of Discourse*. New York: Plenum Press.

Johnson-Laird, Philip N.

1988 *The Computer and the Mind: An Introduction to Cognitive Science*. Cambridge, Mass.: Harvard University Press.

Kuhn, Thomas S.

1962 *The Structure of Scientific Revolutions*. Chicago: University of Chicago Press. 2d enl. ed., 1970.

Laudan, Larry

1977 *Progress and Its Problems*. Berkeley, Los Angeles, London: University of California Press.

1980 "Why Was the Logic of Discovery Abandoned?" In *Scientific Discovery, Logic, and Rationality*, ed. Thomas Nickles, 173–183. Dordrecht: Reidel.

1984 *Science and Values*. Berkeley, Los Angeles, London: University of California Press.

Levi, Isaac

1980 *The Enterprise of Knowledge*. Cambridge, Mass.: MIT Press.

Manor, Ruth

1982 "Pragmatics and the Logic of Questions and Assertions." *Philosophica* 29: 45–95.

Nickles, Thomas

1988 "Reconstructing Science: Discovery and Experiment." In *Theory and Experiment*, ed. D. Batens and J. P. van Bendegem, 33–54. Dordrecht: Reidel.

Nickles, Thomas, ed.

1980a *Scientific Discovery, Logic, and Rationality*. Dordrecht: Reidel.

1980b *Scientific Discovery: Case Studies*. Dordrecht: Reidel.

Pera, Marcello

1988 "Breaking the Link between Methodology and Rationality: A Plea for Rhetoric in Scientific Inquiry." In *Theory and Experiment*, ed. D. Batens and J. P. van Bendegem, 259–276. Dordrecht: Reidel.

Rescher, Nicholas

1984 *The Limits of Science*. Berkeley, Los Angeles, London: University of California Press.

NINE

Theories of Theories

A View from Cognitive Science

Richard E. Grandy

Logical positivism is interred. And with it a conception of scientific theories that once dominated the philosophy of science scene (at least the English-, German-, and Polish-speaking portions). In its place we have a growing family of views of scientific theories. Whether the positivist view died of its own internal problems, of historicist criticisms, or of selective disadvantage with respect to the new, I leave to the historians of the philosophy of science. It was certainly not without problems, but any ongoing research program has problems; the question I want to address, with the advantage of some (probably not enough) hindsight, is: What was seriously wrong with the view?

Although this "Standard View" is now (almost) totally rejected, I want to delineate it explicitly, because in comparing new views with the old, it is important to be precise about what the differences are. Some of the essential characteristics of the Standard View of theories are said to be:

1) Theories are to be represented in first-order logic.

The expositors vary in the degree of their care on this. For example, Hempel says, "Formally, a scientific theory may be considered as a set of sentences expressed in terms of a specific vocabulary. . . . Henceforth, we will assume that theories are given in the form of axiomatized systems" (1958, 46). Notice the phrase "may be considered"—he does not say "is." Of course one often loses sight of the difference between the representation and the thing.

2) There is a fundamental distinction between observational and theoretical vocabulary.

Carnap for example begins his paper on the methodological character of theoretical concepts by saying, "In discussions on the methodology of science it is customary to divide the language of science into two parts, observational and theoretical" (1956, 38). He goes on to say, "The terms of V_O are predicates designating observable properties of events or things (e.g., 'blue,' 'hot,' 'large,' etc.) or observable relations between them (e.g., 'x is warmer than y,' 'x is contiguous to y,' etc.)" (p. 40).

3) Bridge principles or correspondence rules.

4) Theoretical postulates.

The theoretical postulates define the internal relations among the purely theoretical terms, and the bridge principles or correspondence rules relate the theoretical vocabulary to the observational. Much of this structure, especially the emphasis on and distinction between the last two components, is often traced back to N. R. Campbell (1920).

This view of theories grew up in the 1930s, went through various refinements as problems became obvious to its adherents, and came under external attack question in the 1950s. By the late 1950s and early 1960s it was criticized by a new group of more historically and holistically minded philosophers and historians of science, notably N. R. Hanson (1958), who was the first to have much influence, Thomas Kuhn (1962), who was the most influential in terms of the impact of his book, Paul Feyerabend (1965), and others.

I will not discuss this cluster of views at length. One of the main points of this approach, though, was to oppose or question the observational/theoretical distinction, and that is a point to which I will turn later. The view of theories, if there was one embedded here, is much less articulated than the Standard View. One analysis of the newly emerging Cognitive View of science (Giere 1988) is that it combines the significant insights of the historically oriented approach with the more elaborated view of theories of a third approach.

The proponents of this third approach differ, and, of course, their terminology varies. In some cases it is called the "Semantic View" of theories. In other cases it is called the "Model-theoretic View" of theories, the "Structuralist View" of theories, or the "Set-theoretic View" of theories. There are important differences, but they are irrelevant here, because I wish to contrast the Non-statement View with the Standard View and to articulate why in general terms the Non-statement View seems to be preferable. Thus I have chosen for now the rather obscure term, which is less specific than "Structuralist" and certainly much less specific than "Set-theoretic" or "Model-theoretic."

Under this general heading I include one of the founders, Evert Beth (1961); one of its proponents, Bas van Fraassen (1980); and, in a somewhat different but related form, Fred Suppe (1977) and Dudley Shapere (1984). Another genesis is Patrick Suppes (1967, 1969), and this leads to its most prolific form, Joseph Sneed (1971), whose work was taken up by Stegmuller (1976) and more recently by a host of workers, Balzer (1986), Moulines (1976), and Balzer, Moulines, and Sneed (1987). To a considerable extent, I am lumping together people who would not be happy about being lumped, but I believe a more global perspective has its value. Very roughly, then, the Non-statement View says that a theory should be thought of not as a set of statements describing the world but as a class of structures that are approximately isomorphic, under suitable interpretations, to parts of the world.

WHAT IS WRONG WITH THE STANDARD VIEW

It is often useful to know not only that a view is wrong but also why. If we are unclear about why a view is wrong, there is a considerable danger that later we will either incorporate some of the bad features or overlook some of the good ones. Thus I begin by discussing what is wrong with the Standard View and, for a start, taking a look at some of the more unconvincing criticisms.

One group of criticisms, some of them suggested by Stegmuller's own terminology, is that the Standard View's first-order presentation of theories makes a theory a set of sentences, and therefore makes the theory linguistic, rather than a more abstract language-independent object. That is not a very deep problem, because associated with each set of first-order sentences is a class of models. And those models are abstract and language-independent.

There is a potential problem if one confuses the representations of the theories with the theories, but as long as one makes that distinction, there seems to be no problem with giving linguistic formulations of theories. And in fact in many of these approaches, for example Sneed's (1971), one of the concepts that play an important role is a *theory formulation*. And a theory formulation is a set of sentences which picks out a class of structures.

For historical purposes, theory formulations are especially important. Two different formulations of a theory ex hypothesi have the same models, but they may have very different heuristic properties and may appear very different to scientists. For example, it would seem peculiar to say that Newton showed that in all models of planetary systems with inverse-square forces, all planetary orbits are ellipses. Rather he *derived* the elliptic orbit law from the inverse-square law.

Another objection that some people have raised against the Standard View is that it is merely first-order logic, that the logic is not rich enough. Brent Mundy (1987, 1988) has argued for reviving the Standard View using a second- or higher-order logic. If that were all that is wrong with Standard View, then only a stronger formal language would be required, whereas the terminology of the new approach contrasts it with the linguistic character of the Standard View. The objection seems not to be that the Standard View used the wrong language but that it was too language-oriented.

Another objection that is sometimes made is that the Standard View is based on the observational/theoretical distinction. While that may be why the historically orientated philosophers of science reject it, it cannot be why the

Sneed group rejects it because one of the developments coming out of that version of the Non-statement View is a more precise theoretical/nontheoretical distinction. So if such a distinction exists, the problem with the Standard View cannot be that it assumes one, although it can be that it assumes the wrong one or misdescribes its importance.

Let me make a first pass at articulating a deeper problem. I will then outline in more detail a particular version of the Non-statement View and then say a little more exactly what the differences are. What the apparatus of bridge principles / correspondence rules / dictionary is supposed to do is to provide a partial interpretation of the theory. The problem is set by the assumption that the theoretical postulates are taken as uninterpreted; with them is associated a class of models which would model that part of the language, but that class is highly unconstrained. Thus the dictionary principles are to provide more specification of the theory than was originally given by the theoretical postulates. They "hook it to the world," a phrase that is often used. Only partially, of course, because they by no means uniquely determine the interpretation of the theoretical postulates; if they did, the theoretical terms would be definable and would be eliminable. But the idea is that they are supposed to narrow it down. The question remains as to what is the empirical content of the theory?

One response, which was suggested in the 1920s by Frank Ramsey (1960), amounts to saying that the content of a theory T is the statement that there is some way of interpreting the theoretical postulates to produce a model of the theory. That turns out to be extremely weak: any consistent theory is going to have such a model—if nowhere else, at least in the natural numbers and in set-theoretic structures. If that is what it meant to say that a theory was true or described the world, then any consistent theory would be true and that is far too weak. What we want to say is that among the class of models of that theory is the Real World. But of course the Real World is not carved up into a nice structural set of relations, and there seems not to be any good way of picking out the Real World. A lot of the discussions that Hilary Putnam (1977) produced on metaphysical realism and its inarticulateness are really discussions about ways of picking out the real world in this spirit. That is a rather vague statement of what is wrong with the Standard View, that in the notion of partial interpretation the theory is trying to latch onto the world, and the problem is to get the latches to hold tighter.

What is the alternative in the Non-statement View? I will start with a little more background, and a little more technical terminology. One of the basic ideas comes from Patrick Suppes, who was very interested in axiomatization—semiformal axiomatization, not in first-order logic, but in a set-theoretic notation—of various physical theories. To be concrete, let me give an example: McKinsey, Sugar, and Suppes (1953). What they define is a set-theoretic predicate of quintuples of being a system of particle mechanics.

A system of particle mechanics is a quintuple: $\langle p,m,T,s,f \rangle$. The first component is a nonempty finite set—the particles. The second component is a function, which for any object in the set of particles assigns a positive real number—that is the mass of the particle. 'T' is an interval of real numbers. That serves as the background time for the interpretation. The function 's', applied to any of the particles and any time out of the relevant set, specifies a triple of real numbers. And that gives the spatial location, by specifying the coordinates. And finally, the 'f' is the force function, and f applied to a particle, a time, and an index (1, 2, 3, . . .) gives the first force, the second force, the third force. . . . Each force is specified as a triple of reals giving the components of the force vector in each dimension.

Intuitively f(1,x,t) specifies the effect of the first force acting upon x at time t. The one further stipulation is that the second derivatives of the space location in time (the second derivatives with respect to time) always exist. That is to say that we can always speak sensibly about the acceleration of the particle. Such a quintuple is a Particle Mechanics. It is a set of things that have roughly the role of particles, of assigning them masses, of giving them background time, of assigning them location, and of specifying the forces acting upon them.

We have characterized an entirely set-theoretic predicate. Some of the things that have this structure will include physical objects. Some of them will include natural numbers. This is a totally abstract description of a structure. There are many different interpretations of it, many ways of realizing this structure.

We can go a bit further if we wish and add a restriction if we want this not to be any old particle mechanics but one that is essentially Newtonian. If we write the second derivative of the spatial location as Axt for the acceleration of x at t, then the further condition we require is that for each particle its mass times its acceleration at a given time is equal to the sum of the forces acting on it. This will determine that the change in motion is the result of the forces.

Suppes was interested in this conception of the structures related to theories. It separates the roles of different assumptions to tease out the mathematics underlying the theory in different ways. He was not particularly interested in questions of observational/theoretical vocabulary, theoretical content, or reduction.

One issue that *was* of interest to him was the relation between theory and applications. If one looks at classical applications of particle mechanics, objects on an inclined plane, pendulums, objects in the situation of any traditional physics problems, these can be seen as specific instances of the general class of set-theoretic structures. The difference between Suppes's view of what a theory does and the Standard View is that Suppes saw a theory as providing a class of mathematical models which has many applications, not as a single description of the world which is specified by deducing new consequences from extra conditions.

Sneed, a student of Suppes, asked a question to which the Standard View had not been able to give a very good answer: what is the empirical content of a theory? Part of the empirical content of a theory, for example, a theory of particle mechanics, can be given by saying that pendulums are a type of instance of classical particle mechanics. That is, if one considers the set consisting of the particle, the restraints on it, its mass, its motion through time, the forces acting on it, one finds that it is an instance of this kind of structure. That is part of the content, but of course classical particle mechanics says more than that; it does not apply just to a few particular cases but should apply to many instances.

What Sneed added to the basic Suppes framework is the notion of intended applications. So the new conception of a theory—and now we are getting somewhat closer to a version of the Non-statement View—is that a theory consists of a Suppes-like structure, together with a specification of intended applications. In the intended applications, one has a much less formal object, in the sense that what you want to give for any live scientific theory is not simply a finite list (because you expect to extend that) but a more *intentional* characterization of where the applications are going to come from.

This part of the Non-statement View consists in wedding the Suppes-like structures to the somewhat amorphous notion of intended applications. To make two other connections with other approaches, I think that much of Shapere's work on scientific domains can be usefully seen, maybe appropriated, as a way of specifying the intended applications. In fact Shapere's notion of domain may be better for this purpose than Sneed's own characterization of intended application. It also has affinities with Kuhn's notion of an exemplar. There is an interesting relation between Sneed and Kuhn which I do not have time to explore (see Sneed 1977, Kuhn 1977). This approach gives you a different view of the relation between the theory and the world from what we have on the Standard View. On the new view, instead of a linguistically given theory statement we have a class of structures and a class of applications; the problems are to use the structures to make predictions, to give explanations about structures in the world, and to extend the class of applications.

Another element must be added before this will be at all satisfactory: so far, there is no constraint that relates the applications—one of the applications might be to explain the motion of the earth around the sun. To do that we need to assign a mass to the earth in the problem. Suppose we do that. Then later we want to make a different application, for example, to explain the motion of the moon and the earth, or perhaps the tides, and one assigns a mass to the earth for that problem. In a third case we want to calculate the escape velocity of a rocket, and you assign a mass to the earth for that problem. From what I have said so far, there is no reason why these assignments of a value to the mass of the earth have to bear any relation to one another, which clearly seems wrong. So

Sneed also added what he called "constraints," which require in this instance that whenever a particle appears in different applications, it has to be assigned the same mass.

That may seem too strict an assumption. We of course can use approximations, so that if we are doing a problem that involves me hanging from one side of a pulley, and a weight on an inclined plane on the other side of the pulley, and you want to know what is going to happen to me in the next two seconds, you can regard me as a particle because my mass does not change in the relevant amount of time even if I am on a very strict diet. Thus part of what Sneed has captured is that for particular applications approximations may be close enough. This is not all that Sneed added to Suppes: he also made a distinction between theories and theory cores that enabled him to talk about the same theory going through changes over time as a part of the relation by which he was trying to model some of the aspects of theory dynamics and the relation between theories that Kuhn was concerned about. The extent to which he succeeded is an interesting and controversial subject but is well beyond the scope of this paper.

I want to turn now to Norman Campbell's view of theories, which is usually said to be largely responsible for inspiring the Standard View. I do not want to question that as a *causal* historical claim, but I do wish to argue briefly that he should instead be thought of as one of the founders of the Non-statement View. I will say more about this shortly.

In presenting the molecular theory of gases he says:

> The hypothesis of the theory may be stated as follows:
>
> (1) There is a single independent variable t.
>
> (2) There are three constants, m, v, and l, independent of t.
>
> (3) There are 3n independent variables (x_s, y_s, z_s) $(s = 1 \text{ to } n)$ which are continuous functions of t. They form a continuous three-dimensional series and are such that $(x_s^2 + y_s^2 + z_s^2)$ is invariant for all linear transformations of the type $x' = ax + by + cz$. (This last sentence is merely a way of saying that (x,y,z) are related like rectangular coordinates; but since any definitely spatial notions might give the idea that the properties of the (x,y,z) were somehow determined by experiment, they have been avoided.)
>
> (4) $\frac{d(x_s, y_s, z_s)}{dt}$ is constant, except when (xyz) is 0 or 1; when it attains either of these values it changes sign.
>
> (5) $\frac{1}{n}\sum_{1}^{n}\left(\frac{dx}{dt}\right)^2 = v^2$, and similar propositions for y and z [Campbell 1920, 126–127]

This presentation of the theory is not in first-order logic, and to put it into such a formalism would require considerable background development to define 'continuous function', 'invariance', and the differential and summation notations. However, a Suppes type of reformulation would be straightforward

—a molecular gas model would be a quintuple ⟨t,m,v,l,n⟩ where t is a real valued variable, and m, v, and l are positive real constants and n a positive integer, and where the quintuple meets the conditions (1) through (5).

Consider now his description of the dictionary:

> The dictionary contains the following propositions:
>
> (1) l is the length of the side of a cubical vessel in which a "perfect" gas is contained.
>
> (2) nm is the mass of the gas, M.
>
> (3) $\frac{1}{\alpha} nm^2$ is T, the absolute temperature of the gas, where α is some number which will vary with the arbitrary choice of the degree of temperature[1].
>
> (4) Let $\Delta m \frac{dx_a}{dt}$ be the change in $m \frac{dx_a}{dt}$ which occurs when x_a attains the value l; let $\Sigma, \Delta m \frac{dx_a}{dt}$ be the sum of all values of $\Delta m \frac{dx_a}{dt}$ for which t lies between t and $t + \gamma$; let
>
> $$(p_a, p_b, p_c) \quad \mathrm{Lt}_{n-\alpha, \gamma-a} \sum_{n-1}^{n} \frac{1}{\gamma} \Sigma, \Delta m \frac{d(x_5, y_5, z_5)}{dt},$$
>
> then p_a, p_b, p_c are the pressures P_a, P_b, P_c on three mutually perpendicular walls of the cubical containing vessel.

Again first-order logic is not at all in evidence, and furthermore the concepts to which the theoretical variables are related are hardly observational in the Carnap/Hempel sense. The mass of the gas is hardly a simple perceptual qualitative property. The dictionary also relates the theory to temperature as one of the antecedently understood items—clearly a very theoretical concept compared to 'warm'. Thus if one goes back and rereads Campbell with fresh eyes, he appears to be working toward a semantic view.

There is still an element missing, of course; he does not emphasize the class of structures satisfying the theory, so his presentation is still a step short of Suppes's. Thus a more appropriate historical name for the view might be the Campbell-Suppes View of theories. And the Standard View was a distraction from Campbell's in that it emphasized formalizability and introduced a strong observational/theoretical distinction, in place of Campbell's distinction between concepts proper to the theory and those already extant. "Whatever the nature of the dictionary, all theories have this in common that no proposition based on experimental evidence can be asserted concerning the hypothetical ideas except on the assumption that the propositions of the theory are true" (Campbell 1920, 125).

In making these historical points, it is also important to add that another aspect of theories that Campbell regarded as indispensable is the analogical. This aspect has been almost totally ignored by both the Standard View and the Campbell-Suppes, although it has been developed at length by Hesse (1966) and others.

Let me return to my title. A difference between the Standard View and the Campbell-Suppes View as I have been describing it is that the Campbell-Suppes View provides models, and the problem is to find ways of applying those models in the world, to find approximate isomorphisms between physical systems and the abstract systems described by the theory (Moulines 1976). That may make it sound as though scientists are not really making statements about the world, that they are doing something rather different from what we do in our ordinary talk when we say things that are straightforwardly true or false. And this impression probably has some relevance as to why some structuralists have drawn antirealist conclusions from their views of theories, although one of the least realist structuralists, van Fraassen (1987), has observed that the view is compatible with all shades of realism and antirealism.

I want now to discuss some concepts that have been important to cognitive science. This is mostly in work in artificial intelligence and cognitive psychology when people are discussing memory, text processing, question answering, and other natural cognitive processes. The fundamental notion is that of a schema. The general accounts of schemas are unsatisfying. They usually say something like "a schema is a mental data structure for the generic properties of concepts." Thus Rumelhart explains:

> A schema, then, is a data structure representing the generic concepts stored in memory.... A schema contains, as part of its specification, the network of interrelationships that is believed to normally hold among the constituents of the concept in question.... That is, inasmuch as a schema underlying a concept stored in memory corresponds to the meaning of that concept, meanings are encoded in terms of the typical or normal situations or events that instantiate that concept. [1980, 34]

What does that mean more specifically?

For example, the schema associated with a concept like table will specify what are the parts of a table. The *obligatory* parts of a table are legs and a top. Optional parts of a table may be drawers, leaves to insert, and so on. That is one aspect of the schema. Another is the specification of some default values and ranges for some of the parts. Part of the information in the schema for a table is that the typical number of legs for a table is four. If you are reading a story that mentions a table and you know nothing else about the table, it is a reasonable assumption that it has four legs. You will also know that the actual number can be anywhere from one to some largish number. Another part of the schema will be the typical functions of a table.

Schemas can also characterize kinds of events. Young children in certain socioeconomic strata quickly acquire the schema for a birthday party. It is a series of events involving guests, an honoree, cake, candles, presents from the guests, party favors for the guests, and games. The schema prescribes relations among the various elements, as well as indicating additional optional items (ice cream!).

Schemas are related to actual episodes of reasoning, thinking, and getting around in the world, by providing a structure on which to base predictions, explanations, reasoning, and actions about the world more or less successfully. This suggests there are similarities—not identities, but similarities—between this notion of schema, which many cognitive scientists regard as ubiquitous and fundamental in our cognitive processing, and scientific theories. Of course, typically scientific theories are formulated much more explicitly, they are adopted more consciously, their applicability is tested more systematically. I do not want to overstate the relations between theories and schemas, I simply want to point out the significant similarities.

A second point is that in giving an account of reading, recall, or other phenomena involving schemas, cognitive scientists have come to distinguish "declarative" from "procedural" knowledge. That is more or less a relabeling of the old philosophical distinction between "knowing that" and "knowing how," so that knowledge which is in the schema amounts to knowing that, and knowing which schema to apply in a particular situation, knowing when to call in another schema, knowing when a schema is inappropriate, is procedural knowledge, or knowing how. Similarly, in the Campbell-Suppes View the theory formulates a certain kind of knowledge, but the application of it to particular cases is not something that is fully formalized and articulated as a part of the theory.

I see two important similarites between this view of theories and schemas as discussed by cognitive scientists. First, they are general descriptions of kinds of relational structures that are not immutably anchored to the world; applications must be found and evaluated. Second, the choice of an appropriate theory/schema is at least as much a matter of knowing how as knowing that. This suggests the not surprising thesis that scientific theories develop historically and psychologically out of familiar patterns of reasoning and are distinguished by the degree of the mathematization, explicitness, precision, and testing, but that they are not totally foreign cognitive creatures. Theories are to schemas as microscopes and telescopes are to the eye.

Let me turn now to a more specific range of topics beginning with a new version of the observational/theoretical distinction. Sneed, in his own account of theories, distinguished, not between absolutely observational and theoretical, but for a given theory, which of the terms appearing in it are T-theoretical, that is, are dependent upon the theory for meaning, as opposed to which are not. For example, Sneed would say that a function or a magnitude is CPM (classical particle mechanics) theoretical if and only if every assignment of a value to that function assumes the correctness of the theory. What Sneed had in mind is that one of these functions is CPM theoretical if and only if every determination of a value presupposes the theory. If there is any way of determining a value independently of this theory, then it is not CPM determined. So it turns out, at least on his account, that force is CPM theoretical. Another way of formulating the distinction is that it depends on whether one must presuppose that theory in every determination of the magnitude.

More recent work by others very consciously in the Sneed tradition, for example by Wolfgang Balzer (1986), differs. Balzer likes the general Sneed approach, but he dislikes Sneed's theoretical/nontheoretical distinction because, he says, it is a *pragmatic* one. It can vary from time to time depending on whether we have other means of determining the value, so he wants one that is more purely formal. He gives one; what it amounts to roughly is that a magnitude is theoretical with respect to a given theory if fixing the other values of the theory parameters determines the remaining ones. If you fix all the other quantitative magnitudes, and if that determines the remaining function, then that determined function is going to be theoretical within that framework. There are some details about change of scale which complicate the definition but need not concern us.

Balzer's is an absolute, nonpragmatic distinction, entirely a formal matter of theory, so it meets his goal for having a nonpragmatic criterion. The trouble is that if there is anything like an intuitive notion, then this is the wrong one. For example, one can formulate what I will call a system of planetary mechanics. $\langle P, \theta, D, T \rangle$ is a system of planetary mechanics if and only if

P is a nonempty finite set,

T a real interval,

θ a function (continuous in T) from pairs of members of T and P to angles,

D a continuous function from P and T to nonnegative reals.

Heuristically, P is the set of planets, $\theta(i, t)$ gives the angle of the i-th planet at time t, and $D(i, t)$ is the distance of the i-th planet from the sun at time t. The requirement of continuity on the functions θ and D represents the assumption that the planetlike objects move smoothly through space.

We can formulate a Suppes-like characterization of a Keplerian planetary theory. The constraints would be that the combination of angles and distances would produce elliptical planetary orbits that sweep out equal areas in equal times, and

$$\left(\frac{Ti}{Tj}\right)^2 = \left(\frac{Ri}{Rj}\right)^3$$

where Ri is the average of $D(i, t)$ and Ti is the period of planet i, that is, the smallest number x such that $\theta(i, t + nx) = \theta(i, t)$ for all integers n. This seems to me *a*, if not *the*, natural formulation of Keplerian theory. But in that formulation, unless I misunderstand Balzer's criteria, since the rates of change of the angles determine the periods, and the average distances are determined by the periods, the distances d of the planets are theoretical in Balzer's sense. They are determined by fixing the other parameter θ, so on Balzer's criterion the distance from the sun to the planets is theoretical.

But from the historical point of view, that is backward. Kepler arrived at his laws by having painstakingly accumulated evidence on the periods and distances and figured out, as far as anyone knows purely by trial and error, that the regularity fits. "The Third Law did not, in itself, change the theory of the planets, and it did not permit astronomers to compute any quantities that were previously unknown. The sizes and the periods associated with each planetary orbit were available in advance" (Kuhn 1957, 217). Although Balzer's may be an interesting *formal* distinction, it does not at all capture what interests us.

What has gone wrong here? I think that what went wrong with Balzer and also with Sneed and also long ago with the Standard View, was the attempt to draw a theoretical/nontheoretical distinction with respect to terms. I am not quite sure what the right unit is; it seems to me that it is something more like statements or assertions.

Why? Consider the question whether distance is theoretical or nontheoretical. After all, we can measure distances without much difficulty, at least some distances. Other distances have proved very elusive. To push the example to an extreme, one of the standard objections to the Copernican theory was that there is no observed annual parallax with respect to the fixed stars.

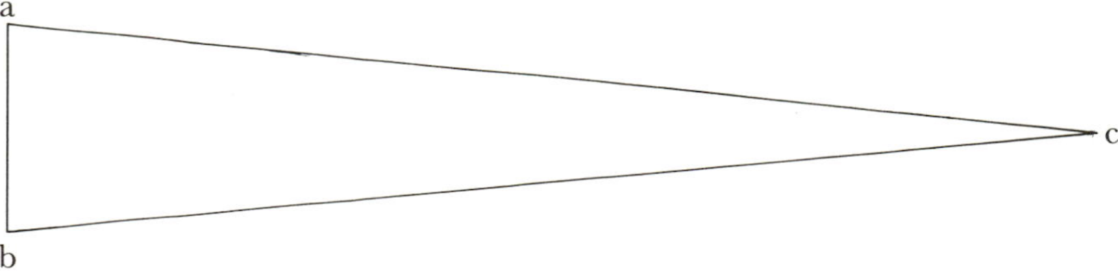

That is, where a and b are the positions of the earth six months apart and c is Sirius, the angles abc and bac are indistinguishable from 90°. Every Copernican knew the answer was that the fixed stars are too far to detect parallax. That answer was repeated even as the telescope was invented and ever finer measurements of parallax were made, with no observation of the parallax of the fixed stars. It became a matter of concern to at least some Copernicans to provide a more articulate answer than "Well, they're further out than we thought" and actually to give an estimate of the approximate distance of the fixed stars, to provide some degree of empirical commitment.

Huygens attempted to provide an estimate via optics. Utilizing a device that could restrict his view of the sun to a very small near-point, he judged the light seen through a small aperture to be approximately that of Sirius, which he took to be one of the nearest fixed stars. Making the large assumption that Sirius is about as bright as the sun, he calculated the distance to the nearest star. He did not come very close, but the process involves a difficult perceptual judgment. You have to observe the sun and remember what Sirius looked like the night before or vice versa, so a considerable memory component enters the comparison. It is surprising, and perhaps accidental, that he came as close as he did (van Helden 1985, 158).

Newton noted the difficulty for Huygens's method and saw that there was, in theory, a solution. If you could put an adjustable mirror in space, so that at night you could simultaneously observe Sirius directly and the sun in the mirror, and adjust the mirror so that the reflected brightness of the sun equaled that of Sirius, then, if you knew the size of the mirror and its distance from the sun, you could calculate an estimate of the distance to Sirius. Of course you could not—at least not then—put a mirror in space. So he used the next best thing to a mirror, a planet.

> . . . the disk of Saturn, which is only 17″ or 18″ in diameter, receives only about 1/2100000000 of the sun's light; for so much less is that disk than the whole spherical surface of the orb of Saturn. Now if we suppose Saturn to reflect about 1/4 of this light, the whole light reflected from its illuminated hemisphere will be about 1/4200000000 [?—R.E.G.] of the whole light emitted from the sun's hemisphere, and, therefore since light is rarefied inversely as the square of the distance from the luminous body, if the sun was 10000/42 times more distant than Saturn, it would yet appear as lucid as Saturn now does. [Newton 1728, 596]

This argument assumes that the nearest stars are the brightest, that the albedo of Saturn is 1/4, that the inverse-square law for brightness holds at astronomical distances, and that no significant amount of light is absorbed as it passes through space (an assumption he goes on to defend explicitly).

His result is fairly accurate, and it would probably have brought some minor fame to many other astronomers. The point of belaboring this example is that here we have a measurement of distance, and I think that measurement is highly theoretical.

The point I want to emphasize is that we should not ask whether the statement that a distance is 2.14×10^n meters is theoretical or not without qualification, for it seems clearly theoretical if n is +10 or −10. And the theories involved are, of course, quite different at the two ends of the scale.

What about middling distances? These judgments may seem nontheoretical, but only because the theory is transparent or familiar. For example, Descartes was apparently the first to note that our visual judgments of length depend not only on relative size and occlusion, which are available to monocular vision, but also on binocular cues. If in the diagram above on page 227 one takes a and b to be the two retinas, then information about the angles bac and abc provided by muscles controlling eye movements is computed by the visual system and provides a judgment about the distance to c. This is not a theory that is held by the viewer who is totally unaware of the process, but can be considered to be a theory assumed by the natural wiring of the visual system. If, for example, space were not locally Euclidean, then a different theory would presumably be wired into us. (The assumption that visual space is Euclidean is not beyond dispute; see Heelan 1983.)

Another way of regarding length is through the lens of foundational studies in measurement, according to which a magnitude is given an abstract characterization in terms of combinatory operations on a domain and mappings from that domain to some appropriate number system. Actual physical domains and operations can be investigated as approximate instances of the abstract characterization. The theory of length as measured by collinear concatenation of rigid bodies depends on applied geometry (to judge collinearity) as well as a theory rigidity.

Moreover the choice of collinear concatenation, rather than perpendicular concatenation (or any of an infinite family of others), is a choice that requires justification. Ellis (1966), who originally raised this point, believed the choice to be arbitrary since perpendicular concatenation satisfies all of the axioms of extensive measurement (as do infinitely many other choices). Practical convenience would probably dictate the use of collinear concatenation by itself, but there are stronger, more general theoretical grounds. Use of perpendicular concatenation as the basis of length measurement would lead to a system of physics in which the laws are not invariant under Galilean transformations of coordinate systems and in which Newton's first law does not hold unless we postulate Reichenbachian universal forces (Bozin 1989).

CONCLUSION

What was wrong with the Standard View?

I have argued that the root problems with the Standard View of theories stem more from the epistemology that its adherents brought to the study of theories than from their view of theories itself. They regarded science as starting from a set of true qualitative observation statements and moving through theory development and some version of confirmation to finding more theoretical true descriptions of the world. An alternative description is that they were concerned with giving a linguistic formulation that would anchor the meaning of theoretical terms in the observational (Hempel 1973). The presumption of first-order logic contributed to the distortion by making it much more difficult to formulate theories that related to quantitative data, thus reinforcing the conception of a qualitative foundation.

On the alternative Campbell-Suppes View, theories provide schematic descriptions of kinds of structures. These structures can be applied to provide approximate descriptions of processes, events, and quantities in the world via approximate isomorphisms. This approach emphasizes the procedural component of the application process, and the theoretical aspects of the descriptions of the processes, events, and quantities. The underlying conception of the Standard View was a Cartesian one of scientists following a godlike process from observed certainty toward higher truths. The alternative is a view of scientists moving from approximate descriptions using simple or implicit theories to more explicit schematic characterizations of underlying processes and variables which often lead to refinement or replacement of the original theories about the "data" themselves.

The image is one of proceeding from pretty good schemas to somewhat better ones, a more modest and perhaps more realistic goal. The epistemology of the new view is not yet a matter of consensus. Indeed there is a question how much epistemology is wanted, but it will be at most a naturalized epistemology of muddling through to better approximations of data that are themselves revisable (Giere 1988, Hull 1988).

What is not (yet?) right with the Campbell-Suppes View?

I have argued that more attention needs to be paid to the questions of which statements are theoretical and with regard to which theory. Here, as with some of the claims about theory reduction and succession, at least some versions of the new view seem to suffer from an inclination to prefer formal problems and definitions to historically realistic ones (Kuhn 1977).

Truesdell (1981) has argued vehemently that the new view is more concerned with mathematics than with mathematical physics, let alone with physics. He also has criticized the almost exclusive attention to particle mechanics as opposed to the large area of continuum mechanics, and has also criticized the McKinsey, Sugar, and Suppes formalization. These last complaints could presumably be remedied, while the first demands that more attention be paid to observation and measurement, as I too have argued.

A more serious open issue is whether justification can be given for the significant shift from Sneed's title *The Logical Structure of Mathematical Physics* to Stegmuller's sweeping *The Structure and Dynamics of Theories*. In the most mathematical of physical theories—relativity theory—physicists themselves formulate their theories in set-theoretic terms, for example, Hawking and Ellis's (1973) definition of a manifold. And many other physical theories can readily be cast in those terms. But whether such an account fits geology, biology, or psychology without serious distortion remains to be determined.

NOTE

Nader Chokr, Timothy Deibler, Richard Duschl, John Earman, and Patrick Suppes provided helpful comments on earlier versions.

REFERENCES

Balzer, W.
1986 "Theoretical Terms: A New Perspective." *Journal of Philosophy* 83:71–90.

Balzer, W., C. U. Moulines, and J. D. Sneed
1987 *An Architectonic for Science*. Boston: Reidel.

Beth, Evert
1961 "Semantics of Physical Theories." In *The Concept and the Role of the Model in Mathematics and Social Sciences*, 48–51. Dordrecht: Reidel.

Bozin, Dragana
1989 "An Inquiry into Fundamental Measurement. " M.A. thesis, Rice University.

Campbell, N. R.
1920 *Physics: The Elements*. Reprinted as *Foundations of Science*. New York: Dover, 1957.

Carnap, Rudolf
1956 "The Methodological Character of Theoretical Concepts." In *The Foundations of Science and the Concepts of Psychology and Psychoanalysis*, ed. H. Feigl and M. Scriven, 38–76. Minnesota Studies in the Philosophy of Science, vol. 1. Minneapolis: University of Minnesota Press.

Descartes, René
1984–5 "Optics." In *The Philosophical Writings of Descartes*, trans. John Cottingham et al. Cambridge: Cambridge University Press.

Ellis, Brian
1966 *Basic Concepts of Measurement*. Cambridge: Cambridge University Press.

Feyerabend, Paul
1965 "Problems of Empiricism." In *Beyond the Edge of Certainty*, ed. R. Colodny, 145–260. Pittsburgh: University of Pittsburgh Press.

Giere, Ronald N.
1988 *Explaining Science*. Chicago: University of Chicago Press.

Hanson, N. R.
1958 *Patterns of Discovery*. Cambridge: Cambridge University Press.

Hawking, S. F., and G. F. R. Ellis
1973 *The Large Scale Structure of Space-Time*. Cambridge: Cambridge University Press.

Heelan, Patrick
1983 *Space-Perception and the Philosophy of Science*. Berkeley, Los Angeles, London: University of California Press.

Hempel, C. G.
1958 "The Theoretician's Dilemma." In *Concepts, Theories and the Mind-Body Problem*, ed. H. Feigl, M. Scriven, and G. Maxwell, 37–98. Minnesota Studies in the Philosophy of Science, vol. 2. Minneapolis: University of Minnesota Press.
1973 "The Meaning of Theoretical Terms: A Critique of the Standard Empiricist Construal." In *Logic, Methodology and Philosophy of Science IV*,

ed. P. Suppes, L. Henkin, A. Joja, and G. Moisil. Amsterdam: North Holland.

Hesse, Mary

1966 *Models and Analogies in Science.* Notre Dame, Ind.: University of Notre Dame Press.

Hull, David L.

1988 *Science as a Process: An Evolutionary Account of the Social and Conceptual Development of Science.* Chicago: University of Chicago Press.

Kuhn, T. S.

1957 *The Copernican Revolution.* Cambridge, Mass.: Harvard University Press.

1962 *The Structure of Scientific Revolutions.* Chicago: University of Chicago Press.

1977 "Theory-Change as Structure-Change: Comments on the Sneed Formalism." In *Historical and Philosophical Dimensions of Logic, Methodology, and Philosophy of Science*, ed. R. E. Butts and J. Hintikka, 289–309. Dordrecht: Reidel.

McKinsey, J. C. C., A. C. Sugar, and P. C. Suppes

1953 "Axiomatic Foundations of Classical Particle Mechanics." *Journal of Rational Mechanics and Analysis* 2:253–272.

Moulines, C. U.

1976 "Approximate Application of Empirical Theories: A General Explication." *Erkenntnis* 10:201–227.

Mundy, Brent

1987 "Scientific Theory as Partially Interpreted Calculus." *Erkenntnis* 27: 173–196.

1988 "Scientific Theory as Partially Interpreted Calculus II." *Erkenntnis* 28: 165–183.

Newton, Sir Isaac

1728 *System of the World.* In *Sir Isaac Newton's Mathematical Principles of Natural Philosophy and His System of the World*, ed. F. Cajori. Berkeley: University of California Press, 1934.

Putnam, Hilary

1977 "Models and Reality." Reprinted in *Realism and Reason*, by Hilary Putnam, 1–25. Cambridge: Cambridge University Press, 1983.

Ramsey, Frank

1960 "Theories." In *The Foundations of Mathematics*, by Frank Ramsey. Paterson, N.J.: Littlefield, Adams and Co.

Rumelhart, David

1980 [illegible]hemata: The Building Blocks of Cognition." In *Theoretical Issues in Reading Comprehension*, ed. R. Spiro, B. Bruce, and B. Brewer. Hillsdale, N.J.: Erlbaum.

Shapere, Dudley

1984 *Reason and the Search for Knowledge.* Dordrecht: Reidel.

Sneed, Joseph

1971 *The Logical Structure of Mathematical Physics.* Dordrecht: Reidel.

1977 "Describing Revolutionary Scientific Change: A Formal Approach." In *Historical and Philosophical Dimensions of Logic, Methodology, and Philoso-*

phy of Science, ed. R. E. Butts and J. Hintikka, 245–268. Dordrecht: Reidel.

Stegmuller, Wolfgang

1976 *The Structure and Dynamics of Theories*. New York: Springer-Verlag.

1979 *The Structuralist View of Theories*. New York: Springer-Verlag.

Suppe, Frederick

1977 *The Structure of Scientific Theories*. Urbana: University of Illinois Press.

Suppes, Patrick

1967 "What Is a Scientific Theory?" In *Philosophy of Science Today*, ed. S. Morgenbesser, 55–67. New York: Basic Books.

1969 "Models of Data." In *Studies in the Methodology and Foundations of Science*, by Patrick Suppes, 24–35. Dordrecht: Reidel.

Truesdell, C.

1980/81 "Suppesian Stews." In *An Idiot's Fugitive Essays on Science*, by C. Truesdell, 504–572. New York: Springer-Verlag, 1984.

van Fraassen, Bas

1980 *The Scientific Image*. Oxford: Oxford University Press.

1987 "The Semantic Approach to Scientific Theories. In *The Process of Science*, ed. Nancy Nersessian. Dordrecht: Nijhoff.

van Helden, Albert

1985 *Measuring the Universe: Cosmic Dimensions from Aristarchus to Halley*. Chicago: University of Chicago Press.

TEN

Procedural Syntax for Theory Elements

Joseph D. Sneed

I. INTRODUCTION

I.1. The Keystone of the traditional logical empiricist account of empirical science is that scientific theories may plausibly be represented by sets of sentences in a formal language—usually some variant of first-order predicate logic. Over the last twenty years an alternative to this view—commonly called "the semantic view" [24] or "structuralism" [1], [17]—has developed. There are significant differences among common variants of this view. But what these variants all have in common is the view that identifying scientific theories with their semantic "models," rather than with the syntactic entities that characterize these models, provides a more fruitful starting point to address a number of traditional philosophical issues about the nature of scientific activity.

I.2. For one convinced of the fruitfulness of the semantic approach, it is tempting to conclude that "syntax" has become irrelevant to philosophy of science. But this would be rash, for several reasons. First, it is obvious that "model theory" cannot be totally separated from "syntax" for the simple reason that we must use *some* language (though perhaps not a formal one) to talk about models. Second, it has been recognized for some time that some traditional questions like eliminability and definability of theoretical concepts elude a purely semantic approach ([17], 196–197). Finally, the recent reappearance of "the context of discovery" ([6], [10], [13], [14], [19]) in the mainstream of philosophical discussion, together with the appearance of computer models of scientific discovery and problem solving, forces us to focus our attention on the "syntactic representation" of scientific theories.

I.3. One may be convinced that the syntactic aspects of scientific theories remain essential to the discussion of important problems without believing that first-order logic (or some of its common emendations—higher-order logics, many-sorted logics, modal logics) provides the most useful syntactic apparatus. Beginning with the view that model classes are the "essential" features of scientific theories, one may then look around for a "suitable" syntactic apparatus to characterize these model classes. 'Suitable' means here simply 'adequate to dealing with the philosophical questions of interest'. One might even countenance the possibility that there are a variety of approaches to syntax—each "suitable" for addressing different questions. Roughly, if model classes are the essence of scientific theories, then we may be pragmatic and even eclectic about the syntax used to describe these model classes.

I.4. The purpose of this paper is to sketch an approach to providing a syntax for structuralist reconstructions of scientific theories. This syntax is offered as an alternative to syntax based on first-order logic and its relatives. The motivation for this alternative approach to syntax is diverse. First, it is intended to provide an "intuitively natural" picture of how people (and machines) might represent model classes. Second, it is intended to provide a syntax adequate to expressing the structuralist conception of the "empirical claim" of a scientific theory. Finally, it is suggested as a means to deal with some specific philosophical issues. Among these are:

- the epistemological status of "theoretical concepts" and questions of their eliminability and definability;
- the concepts of "problem," "problem solution," and "problem solver" relative to a specific empirical theory;
- the role of the structuralist concept of "constraints" in problem solving;
- the concept of "conceptual innovation" as the discovery of theoretical concepts and the empirical laws containing them;
- criteria of success for automatic problem solving and theory discovery.

This paper is a report of "work in progress," not a sustained defense of a well-formulated view. It sketches an alternative approach to syntax and indicates how it might be expected to serve the purposes just mentioned. In no way are these claims supported by sustained argument or detailed examples. More explicitly, the apparatus sketched is illustrated by application to a very restricted class of theories—simple relational theories—and even here, important theoretical questions about the expressive power of the syntax are ignored.

I.5. The fundamental idea developed here is this. Classes of models appearing in structuralist reconstructions of empirical theories may be characterized syntactically by pairs of procedures $\langle P, P' \rangle$. Procedures are expressions in a formally specified language that describe functions on set-theoretic entities. The class of models characterized by $\langle P, P' \rangle$ is simply those models in which the value of P is a subset of the value of P′. It will be suggested that using procedural syntax allows us to denote and manipulate model-theoretic entities in a more explicit and transparent way than first-order logic. This makes it easier to provide syntactic descriptions of intuitively significant features of model-theoretic reconstructions.

I.6. In section II, I characterize a restricted class of set-theoretic structures—simple relational theories—that is the initial focus of the investigation. The semantic concept of "query"—a formal analogue of a kind of experiment—for these structures is introduced in section III. That the concept of "query"—drawn from the realm of data-base theory—has many features intuitively analogous to "experiments" is the basis for the claim that the syntactic apparatus sketched here is "intuitively natural." Roughly, it provides us with a way of viewing empirical laws as describing relations among the results of experiments. Arguably, this is much closer to the representation of laws actually used in the practice of empirical science than that provided by sentences in first-order logic. Procedure languages and their interpretation as queries are described in section IV. The languages are characterized rather abstractly in only enough detail to make plausible the intuitive idea that procedures interpreted as queries may be viewed as experiments on "empirical systems."

I.7. In section V, I sketch how the syntactic apparatus of section IV can capture the essential ideas of structuralist reconstructions. The main result of this discussion is to argue that procedural syntax can represent the structuralist conception of the "empirical claim" of a scientific theory. To arrive at this result, both empirical laws and constraints are represented as relations among the results of procedures—interpreted as queries, or more intuitively "experiments." The claim of theories involving theoretical concepts requires for its representation the use of a "generator procedure" that plays the role of query for theoretical concepts. In this way the quantification over predicates in a Ramsey sentence formulation of the empirical claim is replaced with a "generate and test" procedure that searches for instantiations of theoretical concepts that "work." In connection with this discussion, section V.3.3 indicates how the syntactic apparatus may be applied to traditional questions of eliminability and definability of theoretical concepts.

I.8. In sections VI and VII, I sketch how procedural syntax might be used to extend structuralist accounts of empirical science to areas of problem solving and theory discovery. Section VII sketches a general account of "search" for empirical laws, extending the work of Langley et al. ([10]) to discovery of laws containing theoretical concepts in models where these concepts are not explicitly definable.

II. POTENTIAL MODELS AS $M_p[U, r]$-RELATIONAL STRUCTURES

II.1. I begin by considering procedural syntax in a special case. The structuralist notion of theory element will be restricted in three ways. First, I consider only finite structures. Second, I consider structures in which only sets of tuples (relations) over a single domain appear, rather than more general set-theoretic constructions obtained from Bourbaki's echelon constructions ([1], sec. I.2). Finally, I do not consider structures containing auxiliary mathematical apparatus like the real numbers.

II.2. The basic semantic entities I will use are set-theoretic structures like the usual "models" for first-order logic. Consider a countably infinite set of "urelemente" U. For all $n \in \mathbb{N}$, $D \subseteq U$ and finite, let

$$R[U,D,n] = \{R \mid R \subseteq D^n\}; \qquad R[U,D] = \bigcup_{n \in \mathbb{N}} R[U,D,n]$$

$$R[U] = \bigcup_{[D \subseteq U \,\&\, \text{finite}]} R[U,D]$$

Members of the set $M_p[U,r]$—*$M_p[U,r]$-relational structures*—are all the finite relational structures of the same set-theoretic type $r = \langle r_1, \ldots, r_i, \ldots, r_n \rangle$ whose individuals are drawn from U. They are examples of what we have called *potential models* of an empirical theory ([1], [17]). For $m_p = \langle D, R_1, \ldots, R_n \rangle \in M_p[U,r]$, the notation $D(m_p) = D$ and $R_i(m_p) = R_i$ will be used.

III. $M_p[U, r]$-QUERIES

III.1. One may regard each member of $M_p[U,r]$ as a "data base" containing information about situations or systems treated by empirical science. Intuitively, "experiments" are viewed as queries and "empirical data" as the results of queries. To make this metaphor more precise, we introduce the concept of an $M_p[U,r]$-query.

III.2. An *$M_p[U,r]$-query* is simply a function:

$$Q: M_p[U,r] \rightarrow R[U]; \qquad Q(m_p) \in R[U, D(m_p)]$$

for all $m_p \in M_p[U,r]$. Intuitively, a query Q is a *kind* of experiment that may be done on members of $M_p[U,r]$, while $Q(m_p)$ is the *result* of doing an experiment of kind Q on the specific "system" m_p.

III.3. For $M_p[U,r]$'s representing empirical theories only Q's invariant under set-theoretic isomorphism are of interest. Also, we want to represent queries syntactically so that the syntactic representation is a description of an algorithm for computing their values. Thus, we may restrict our attention to partial recursive Q's. Such Q's we call *computable*. The set of all computable $M_p[U,r]$-queries I denote by '$Q[U,r]$' ([3], [5]). Queries whose values are the domain and relations in $m_p \in M_p[U,r]$ are of special interest. I use the notation QD and QR_i for queries so that, for all $m_p \in M_p[U,r]$, $QD(m_p) = D(m_p)$ and $QR_i(m_p) = R_i(m_p)$. For example, see Appendix A.1.

IV. PROCEDURE LANGUAGES AND THEIR INTERPRETATIONS

IV.1. *Procedure Languages.* The fundamental intuitive idea here is that $M_p[U,r]$-queries provide interpretations for (some) expressions in a formal language |L(G). The programming languages LISP ([11], [12]) and PROLOG ([16], [20]) may be viewed as examples of the kind of formal languages I have in mind. Other examples have been devised more specifically for expressing queries and addressing theoretical questions ([3]). I will sketch, very generally, how I propose to exploit this idea without being committed to any specific formal language.

IV.1.2. A *procedure language* is a formal language |L(G) generated by a context-free grammar G over some alphabet. |L(G) consists (in part) of a set of expressions |E to which interpretations will be assigned. |E will consist of two types of expressions—|E = |P ∪ |D—which, for present purposes, we may take to be disjoint. We think of the |P-expressions in |L(G) as "processes" or "programs" whose inputs and outputs are |D-expressions in |L(G) (partial recursive functions on |D). That is, for all P ∈ |P, we assume:

$$P: |D \rightarrow |D \cup \{\bot\},$$

where ⊥ is the value assigned to P for members of |D for which it is undefined. Intuitively, members of |P are "query" or "procedure" expressions, while members of |D are "data" expressions.

IV.1.3. I assume the grammar G works in such a way that the procedure expressions may be analyzed into component parts that are also procedure expressions. The notation

$$\{P_1, \ldots, P_n\} \, |G| - P$$

is used to indicate that procedure P is *generable* from procedures $\{P_1, \ldots, P_n\}$, together with "logical primitives" of |L, via the formation rules of G. The members of $\{P_1, \ldots, P_n\}$ need not be "primitive." Thus, P may be generable from more than one set of subprocedures.

IV.2. *Interpretations for Procedure Languages*. Members of |E will be assigned interpretations recursively using the production rules of |G. For the moment, we may abstract from the details of how members of |E are constructed and interpreted and simply think of an *interpretation for a procedure language* |*L*(*G*) as an ordered pair:

$$I = \langle ID, IP \rangle$$

so that ID assigns m-tuples of relations in R[U] to (some) data expressions in |D and IP assigns functions from these m-tuples to R[U] to (some) procedure expressions in |P. This works in such a way that P is always assigned a procedure that is "restricted to" a specific member of $M_p[U, r]$ and P (as a function on |D) "commutes" with I and the values of I. More precisely, ID and IP are functions such that

$$ID = \bigcup_m ID_m \qquad IP = \bigcup_m IP_m$$

$$ID_m: |D \rightarrow R[U]^m \cup \{\bot\}$$

$$IP_m: |P \times M_p[U, r] \rightarrow SET(R[U]^m, R[U]) \cup \{\bot\}$$

so that, for all $m_p \in M_p[U, r]$; D, D′ ∈ |D; P ∈ |P,

$$IP_m(P, m_p) \in SET(R[U, D(m_p)]^m, R[U, D(m_p)])$$

and, whenever

$$ID_m(D) \in R[U, D(m_p)]^m \quad \text{and} \quad ID_1(D') \in R[U, D(m_p)],$$

$$P(D) = D' \quad \text{iff} \quad IP_m(P, m_p)(ID_m(D)) = ID_1(D').$$

The notation 'SET(A, B)' means the set of all functions from A to B.

IV.2.2. Some procedures |P may be interpreted as queries—members of Q[U, r]. Recall that members of $M_p[U, r]$ are simply certain kinds of n + 1 tuples of relations from R[U]. Thus, $IP_{n+1}(P, m_p)$ will be a (perhaps improper) superset of a member of Q[U, r], provided only that it has a non-⊥ values (is defined) in $M_p[U, r]$ and isomorphism invariant. Here, we restrict our attention interpretations and P's so that, for all $m_p \in M_p[U, r]$,

$$IP_{n+1}(P, m_p) \in Q[U, r].$$

Where no confusion results, I will occasionally abbreviate '$IP_{n+1}(P, m_p)(m_p)$' by '$P(m_p)$'. Note that there may remain P ∈ |P that are not interpreted as queries.

IV.2.3. I assume that the interpretation I works in such a way that when

$$\{P_1, \ldots, P_n\} |G| - P$$

the value of P is determined by the values of $\{P_1, \ldots, P_n\}$. Roughly, this means that P may be analyzed (perhaps in several ways) into subprocedures whose values suffice to determine the value of P. When P is interpreted as a query, it is possible that all members of {P1, . . . , Pn} are also interpreted as queries, but we do not require this.

IV.2.4. Intuitively, $IP_{n+1}(P, m_p)$ is the query that procedure expression P computes *in the potential model* m_p. The same procedure expression P will generally compute different queries in different m_p's. That is, when $m_p \neq m_p'$,

$$IP_{n+1}(P, m_p) \neq IP_{n+1}(P, m_p').$$

For example, see Appendix A.1.

IV.2.5. In the contex of empirical science, we may think of a procedure expression P as something like an *experimental* procedure that has a limited range of applicability. The semantic entities in Q[U, r] characterize kinds of things experiments might measure or determine. The syntactic entities in |P characterize concrete experimental methods. The interpretation function tells us what specific experimental procedures do in fact determine in a given situation (potential model).

IV.2.6. These considerations motivate the following. Call pairs ⟨|L(G), I⟩ of procedure languages and their interpretations *interpreted procedure languages* for $M_p[U, r]$. For interpreted procedure language ⟨|L(G), I⟩ for $M_p[U, r]$,

$P \in |P$, $m_p \in M_p[U, r]$, $M \subseteq M_p[U, r]$ and $M_p[U, r]$-query $Q \in Q[U, r]$, we say that:

1) P *expresses* Q in m_p iff $IP_{n+1}(P, m_p)(m_p) = Q(m_p)$;
2) P *expresses* Q in M iff, for all $m_p \in M$, P expresses Q in m_p;
3) P *universally expresses* Q iff P expresses Q in $M_p[U, r]$.

For $P \in |P$ and $Q \in Q[U, r]$, we may define

$$M(P, Q) = \{m_p \in M_p[U, r] \mid P \text{ expresses } Q \text{ in } m_p\}.$$

Intuitively, M(P, Q) is all the members of $M_p[U, r]$ in which procedure P "works" for computing query Q.

IV.2.7. Viewing procedures expressing queries as experimental methods motivates us to to restrict our attention to procedures that are generable from procedures universally expressing queries for the relations appearing in members of $M_p[U, r]$ (relative to $\langle |L(G), I\rangle$). That is, we are interested in P so that

$$B|G| - P \qquad \text{and} \qquad V \subseteq \{PD, PR_1, \ldots, PR_n\}$$

where PD and PR_i universally express QD and QR_i respectively. I call P an *empirical procedure expression* and the set B an *empirical base* for P. This corresponds to the customary distinction between "intensional" and "extensional" database relations ([23], 100).

V. THEORY ELEMENTS

V.1. *Introduction.* In this section I will sketch how procedure languages may be used to provide syntactical expression for the essential model-theoretic entities appearing in structuralist reconstructions of empirical theories ([1], [17]). These include potential models and models (sec. V.2), partial potential models (sec. V.3), and constraints (sec. V.4). I will indicate how questions of eliminability and definability that elude precise semantic formulation might be handled with this syntax. I do not consider the structuralist concept of inter-theoretical link here, but I believe one might extend procedural syntax to this as well.

V.2. *Empirical Laws.* Clearly, M(P, Q) could be used to characterize empirically interesting classes of models. However, Q is a semantic entity. More appropriate, for our purposes, is a purely syntactic characterization. Consider pairs of empirical procedure expressions $\langle P, P'\rangle \in |P \times |P$ so that, relative to $\langle |L(G), I\rangle$, both P and P′ universally express queries Q and Q′. The pair $\langle P, P'\rangle$ characterizes a class of *models* M(P, P′)—a subset of $M_p[U, r]$—in the following way:

$$M(P, P') = \{m_p \in M_p[U, r] \mid IP_{n+1}(P, m_p)(m_p) \subseteq IP_{n+1}(P', m_p)(m_p)\}.$$

For empirical theories, M(P, P′) is just the class of potential models in which results of the experimental procedure P are a subset of the results of P′. Intuitively, we may say that, in M(P, P′), P "partially determines" the same observable of systems of kind $M_p[U, r]$ that P′ determines. For example, see Appendix A.2.

V.2.2. Generally, the "laws" for a theory T for $M_p[U, r]$ may be viewed as a finite set of procedure expression pairs

$$L = \{\langle L_1, L_1' \rangle, \ldots, \langle L_n, L_n' \rangle\}.$$

where all $L_i, L_i' \in |P$. The *models* for the theory are

$$M(L) = \bigcap_{[L_i \in L]} M(L_i, L_i')$$

Generally,

$$M(L) \subseteq M_p[U, r] \qquad \text{and} \qquad T = \langle M(L), M_p[U, r] \rangle$$

determined by the set of expression-query pairs L is an attenuated example of what we have called a *theory element* ([1]).

V.3. *Theoretical Concepts*

V.3.1. *Theoretical Structures.* Consider

$$M_p[U, r_1, \ldots, r_k, r_{k+1}, \ldots, r_l] = M_p[U, n, t];$$

$$M_{pp}[U, r_1, \ldots, r_k] = M_{pp}[U, n]$$

where

$$n = \langle r_1, \ldots, r_k \rangle; \qquad t = \langle r_{k+1}, \ldots, r_l \rangle.$$

Members of $M_{pp}[U, n]$ are k + 1, ..., kl "reducts" of members of $M_p[U, n, t]$. We call members of $M_{pp}[U, n]$ *partial potential models.* Intuitively, the relations in the places k + 1, ..., l are *theoretical relations* and those in places 1, ..., k are *nontheoretical relations.* $M_p[U, n, t]$ is the class of *theoretical structures* while $M_{pp}[U, n]$ is the class of *nontheoretical structures.*

V.3.1.2. Denote the "Ramsey functor" ([1], sec. II.4) from M_p onto M_{pp} by

$$\text{Ram}: M_p[U, n, t] \to M_{pp}[U, n]$$

so that, for all $m_p = \langle D, R_1, \ldots, R_k, R_{k+1}, \ldots R_l \rangle$ in M_p,

$$\text{Ram}(m_p) = \langle D, R_1, \ldots, R_k \rangle.$$

Queries for $M_p[U, n, t]$ and $M_{pp}[U, n]$ we will denote respectively by

$$Q_p: M_p[U, n, t] \to R[U] \qquad \text{and} \qquad Q_{pp}: M_{pp}[U, n] \to R[U].$$

V.3.1.3. Expression pairs $\langle L_p, L_p' \rangle$ for M_p determine sets of M_p-models in the manner described above. Via the Ramsey functor, they also determine sets of M_{pp}-models:

$$\overline{\text{Ram}}(M(L_p, L_p')).$$

Similarly, a theory L for M_p determines a set of M_{pp}-models which we have called *the nontheoretical content* of the theory element $\langle M_{pp}, M_p, M(L)\rangle$ ([1]). That is,

$$\text{Cn}(M_{pp}[U, n], M_p[U, n, t], M(L)) = \overline{\text{Ram}}(M(L)).$$

V.3.1.4. The motivation for calling M_{pp}'s nontheoretical structures is this. In the situations where the theories represented by these structures are actually used, all data to which we have "direct" empirical access is definable in terms of the M_{pp}-relations. By "direct" we mean roughly access that does not depend on assuming that we are dealing with a member of $\text{Cn}(M_{pp}, M_p, M(L))$. Thus, supposing we are "given" some $m_{pp} \in M_{pp}$, all the data we can obtain for m_{pp} is of the form $\langle Q_{pp}, R\rangle$ where $Q_{pp} \in Q_{pp}[U, n]$ and $R = Q_{pp}(m_{pp}) \in R[U]$.

V.3.2. *Theoretical Laws*. This intuitive understanding of the data available to the process L_p suggests that it must operate in a somewhat unusual way. Suppose L_p has an empirical base consisting of expressions for all relations in $M_p[U, n, t]$'s. In operating on a data expression D whose interpretation is m_p, L_p requires as intermediary steps the results of the queries expressed by PD, $PR_1, \ldots, PR_n, \ldots, PR_t$. However, L_p may have only the results of the nontheoretical queries $PR_1, \ldots, PR_n$ available. The results of the theoretical queries $PR_{n+1}, \ldots, PR_t$ may be totally unavailable. In effect, we are invited to consider a procedure expressing an $M_p[U, t]$-query operating on a data expression for a member of $M_{pp}[U, n]$. How could this work?

V.3.2.2. We may imagine L_p working with "generators" in place of expressions of theoretical queries. L_p marches along calling and evaluating nontheoretical subprocesses $PR_1, \ldots, PR_n$ until it reaches a call for PR_j, $j \in \{n + 1, \ldots, t\}$. At this point, instead of calculating PR_j from the given data expression (which cannot be done), L_p systematically generates (out of nothing) a "candidate" for the output of PR_j of the appropriate set-theoretic type and uses this output to complete its calculation. To make this precise, we need some concept of a *generator* procedure. A generator should take as input expressions for the domain of an m_{pp} and deliver as output a *sequence* of members of $R[U, D(m_{pp})]$ of a specific set-theoretic type. An L_p involving theoretical concepts is simply one that has generators, rather than query expressions at certain places.

V.3.2.3. This means that determining whether a given m_{pp} is in $\overline{\text{Ram}}(M(L_p, L_p'))$ becomes a "generate and test" process—repeatedly generating pairs $\langle L_p(m_{pp}), L_p'(m_{pp})\rangle$ and testing whether $L_p(m_{pp}) \subseteq L_p'(m_{pp})$. The first successful test is sufficient to legitimate m_{pp} as a member of the nontheoretical content of the theory whose single theoretical law is $\langle L_p, L_p'\rangle$.

V.3.3. *Eliminability and Definability.* Procedural syntax permits us to raise questions of eliminability and definability of theoretical concepts in a precise way. More important, it may prove possible, using this apparatus, to address these questions for theories that are not readily formalizable in first-order logic.

V.3.3.2. Given interpreted procedure language $\langle |L(G), I\rangle$ and the theory element $\langle M_{pp}[U, n], M_p[U, n, t], M(L_p)\rangle$ with the members of L_p in |P, we say that the theory

$$L_{pp} = \langle\langle L_{pp_1}, L_{pp_1}'\rangle, \ldots, \langle L_{pp_k}, L_{pp_k}'\rangle\rangle$$

for M_{pp} with all $L_{pp_i} \in |P$ is *Ramsey equivalent* to L iff

$$M(L_{pp}) = \overline{\mathrm{Ram}}(M(L)).$$

We then ask, Is the following true? RAMSEY ELIMINABILITY THESIS: For all theory elements $\langle M_{pp}, M_p, M(L_p)\rangle$, there is a theory L_{pp} for M_{pp} so that L_{pp} is Ramsey equivalent to L.

V.3.3.3. The question of definability of theoretical terms and its relation to model-theoretic eliminability may be raised in this way. Suppose

$$\{P_1, \ldots, P_n\} |G| - P$$

and relative to the interpreted procedure language $\langle |L(G), I\rangle$,

$$M(P, Q) \subseteq \bigcap_i M(P_i, Q_i)$$

then we say, relative to $\langle |L(G), I\rangle$, *Q is definable in terms of* $\{Q_1, \ldots, Q_n\}$ *in* $M(P, Q)$. Note that 'definability' applies to queries rather than to expressions for them. In the special case of queries QR_i we say that R_k *is definable in terms of* $\{R_{i_1}, \ldots, R_{i_n}\}$ *in* $M \subseteq M_p[U, r]$ when there exist P_k and $\{P_{i_j}\}$

$$\{P_{i_j}\} |G| - P_k$$

and

$$M = M(P_k, QR_k) \subseteq \bigcap_j M(P_{i_j}, QR_{i_j}).$$

Thus, for theory element $\langle M_{pp}[U, n], M_p[U, n, t], M(L_p)\rangle$ we may ask whether R_k, $k \in t$, is definable in terms of $\{R_{i_j}\}$, $i, j \in n$, in $M(L_p)$. Clearly, the answer to both eliminability and definability questions depends on |L.

V.4. *Constraints*

V.4.1. *Constraints and n-ary Queries.* Model-theoretically, a constraint is just a subset of $Po(M_p)$—the set of all subsets of M_p that satisfy the "constraint." A simple example of a constraint is the requirement that identical particles in different models of classical particle mechanics have the same mass values. This example is trivial in that it is equivalent to a requirement on the union of the constrained m_p's. However, examples of nontrivial constraints such as the "extensivity constraint" on mass in particle mechanics abound in empirical science. That representing nontrivial constraints is essential to representing empirical theories has been argued in detail in [1], section II.2.

V.4.1.2. Can procedural syntax be used to represent constraints? First, let us restrict our attention to constraints that are sets of two-member subsets of $M_p[U, r]$. We might think of a *binary queries* as functions:

$$Q: M_p[U,r] \times M_p[U,r] \rightarrow R[U]$$

so that, for all $\langle m_p, m_p' \rangle \in M_p \times M_p$, $Q(m_p, m_p') \in R[U, (D(m_p) \cup D(m_p'))]$. That is, Q maps pairs of potential models into relations on the union of their domains. A computable query of this type is (partial) recursive and consistent in a natural extension of the sense of section III above.

V.4.1.3. We may consider a *binary interpretation* for procedures in language |L as a function:

$$IP_m: |P \times M_p[U,r] \times M_p[U,r] \rightarrow SET(R[U]^m, R[U]) \cup \{\bot\}.$$

Relative to a binary interpretation, *P expresses the binary query Q in* $\langle m_p, m_p' \rangle$ iff $IP_{n+1}(P, m_p, m_p')(m_p, m_p') = Q(m_p, m_p')$. For P in |P and binary query Q we may define

$$K(P,Q) = \{\langle m_p, m_p' \rangle \mid P \text{ expresses } Q \text{ in } \langle m_p, m_p' \rangle\}.$$

Thus, an expression-binary query pair may be used to characterize a subset of $M_p[U,r] \times M_p[U,r]$, and this characterization may be rendered fully syntactic by replacing Q with P′ in the manner of section V.1. Clearly, we can generalize these ideas to n-ary queries without losing the capability of representing computable n-ary queries in a formal language.

V.4.1.4. Some additional conditions are needed to make the sets of n-tuples determined by procedure-n-ary-query pairs have the properties that constraints for real empirical theories usually have. This has been worked out in an unpublished manuscript ([18]). Whether all "interesting" constraints can be represented by sets of n-tuples is less clear. But the answer seems to be "yes," provided we restrict our attention to finite sets of potential models.

V.4.2. *Theories with Constraints.* As with the laws of a theory, we may regard the constraints C associated with a theory for M_p as a set of procedure pairs where the procedures will express multi-argument queries of the sort exemplified above. Let

$$K = \{\langle K_1, K_1' \rangle, \ldots, \langle K_k, K_k' \rangle\}$$

where $K_i, K_i' \in |P$ and, for some $n \in \mathbb{N}$, K_i universally expresses

$$Q_i: M_p[U,r]^n \rightarrow R[U].$$

$$c_i(K_i, Q_i') = \{s \in M_p[U,r]^n \mid IP_{n+1}(K_i, s) \subseteq IP_{n+1}(K_i', s)\}$$

$$C_i(K_i, Q_i) = \{S \in Po(M_p[U,r] \mid S^n \subseteq c_i(K_i, Q_i)\}$$

The intuitive idea is that subsets of M_p satisfy $C_i(K_i, Q_i)$ iff all n-tuples from them satisfy $c_i(K_i, Q_i)$. It is argued (inductively) in [18] that this is enough to represent all "interesting" constraints. The set of sets of models determined by K is:

$$C(K) = \bigcap_i C_i(K_i, Q_i).$$

V.4.2.2. We may now consider what we have called a *theory element* ([1]):

$$T = \langle M_{pp}, M_p, M(L), C(K) \rangle$$

where the L and K provide syntactic representations for the model and constraints M(L) and C(K). The nontheoretical content of T is

$$Cn(T) = \overline{\overline{Ram}}(Po(M(L) \cap C(K))).$$

The issue of eliminability of the theoretical components of the models can be raised for this more general concept of theory element in the same way as outlined above for the theory element without constraints.

VI. $M_p[U, r]$-PROBLEM SOLVING

VI.1. *$M_p[U, r]$-Problems and Their Solutions.* Problem solving in empirical science may be described in the vocabulary of queries to a data base. A "problem" is then: given the results of a series of queries to the same data base, predict the result of a further query. Viewed syntactically, a problem solution is a procedure constructed from procedures expressing the "data" queries which expresses the "unknown" query. Problem solving is then viewed as search in the graph of |P for a problem-solution process. It appears that conception of "problem solving" may provide a formally precise model of actual practice. Such a formal model might serve as the theoretical basis for computer-assisted instruction in empirical sciences analogous to that for theorem proving in first-order logic and set theory ([22]).

VI.1.2. Generally, an *$M_p[U, r]$-problem type is a pair* $\langle \overline{Q}, Q \rangle$ where $\overline{Q}$ is a vector of queries providing the "given data" for this problem type and Q is the query whose possible results are desired. Intuitively, a solution to the problem type $\langle \overline{Q}, Q \rangle$ is some general method of providing the possible results of query Q corresponding to any possible given results of queries Q. Since there may be more than one possible result for Q, this method should be viewed generally as producing a set of possible results or a set of minimum (wrt $\subseteq$) results.

VI.1.3. Assuming that we are dealing only with $M \subseteq M_p[U, r]$ in which the queries in the problem type are expressed by empirical procedures $\langle \overline{P}, P \rangle$, a solution may be conceived as a procedure $S \in |P$ such that

$$\overline{P}|G| - S,$$

that is, S is generable from $\bar{P}$, and so that, for all $m_p \in M$,

$$S(m_p) = P(m_p).$$

What makes S a "useful" solution is that $S(m_p)$ may be obtained only from the given results of $\bar{P}$ without "looking at" a full description of m_p. Since S is generable from $\bar{P}$, $S(m_p)$ can be computed from the values of the members of $\bar{P}$ in m_p (see sec. IV.1.3).

VI.1.4. With this concept of solution, the process of "problem solving" may be viewed syntactically as attempting to construct S from $\bar{P}$, using the formation rules G. Thus, "constructing a solution" becomes somewhat analogous to "constructing a proof" in first-order logic with the formation rules G playing the role of inference rules (see [8], esp. sec. 6). There is, of course, no guarantee that this will yield a suitable S.

VI.2. *Problem Solving with Empirical Laws.* Empirical laws conceived as pairs of procedures $\langle L, L' \rangle$ may be used in problem solving essentially as extensions to the formation rules G. They provide additional "substantive" principles for constructing new procedures from given procedures.

VI.2.2. The basic idea of using $\langle L, L' \rangle$ to construct new procedures is to exploit the fact that, for $m_p \in M(L, L')$, $L(m_p) \subseteq L(m_p')$. Clearly, if we may assume that the data for our problem comes from a model for a theory containing $\langle L, L' \rangle$, we may exploit this fact as a kind of "substitution principle" to construct new procedures from those providing the data for the problem. More precisely,

SUBSTITUTION PRINCIPLE: From

$$\langle L_1, L_2 \rangle \quad \text{and} \quad \{P_1, \ldots, L_2, \ldots\} |G| - P$$

construct

$$\{P1, \ldots, L1, \ldots\} |G| - P'.$$

This construction has the desirable property that, for $m_p \in M(L_1, L_2)$,

$$P'(m_p) \subseteq P(m_p).$$

VI.2.3. Substitution alone is not a very powerful inference principle. However, together with some principles for generating new laws from old it appears more interesting. First, note an obvious transitivity property of law-pairs:

$$\text{From } \langle L_1, L_2 \rangle, \langle L_2, L_3 \rangle \text{ construct } \langle L_1, L_3 \rangle$$

in appropriate model classes. Other principles depend heavily on the specific nature of |L(G). We can get some idea of how this might work by supposing that |L(G) contains as logical primitives the usual Boolean operations on sets. For example, suppose ',' and ';' are among the primitive symbols of |L(G) and work in the following way:

$$(P_1, P_1)(m_p) = P_1(m_p) \cap P_2(m_p)$$

$$(P_1; P_2)(m_p) = P_1(m_p) \cup P_2(m_p)$$

With this apparatus available, we have such principles as:

From $\langle L_1, L\rangle$, $\langle L_2, L\rangle$ construct $\langle (L_1, L_2), L\rangle$.

From $\langle L, L_1\rangle$, $\langle L, L_2\rangle$ construct $\langle L, (L_1; L_2)\rangle$.

VI.2.4. This suggests that, in appropriately chosen $|L(G)$, something like the symbolic manipulations associated with problem solving in physics and other empirical sciences may be modeled in a formally rigorous way. Further, it appears that semantically equivalent laws may perhaps be distinguished by relative "ease" with which they admit of these syntactic manipulations ([8], 380). Were this so, it would provide a new approach to some aspects of the traditional problem of "lawlikeness."

VI.3. *Problem Solving with Theoretical Laws and Constraints.* We may extend these ideas to theories with theoretical concepts and theoretical laws in the following way. Most generally, we may think of problems as any combination of theoretical and nontheoretical queries. First, consider completely nontheoretical problems—queries on the nontheoretical structures $\langle \overline{Q}_{pp}, Q_{pp}\rangle$ with corresponding expressions $\langle \overline{P}_{pp}, P_{pp}\rangle$. Again, a solution is some S such that:

$$\overline{P}_{pp}|G| - S \quad \text{and} \quad S(m_p) = P_{pp}(m_p).$$

Theoretical laws are pairs of procedure expressions $\langle L_p, L_p'\rangle$ that operate on the full theoretical structures. We view these procedures as constructed, in part, from "generators" rather than query procedures for theoretical concepts (sec. V.3.2). Generally, problem solving here is more complex just because there may be multiple values generated for theoretical concepts that make $L_p(m_p) \subseteq L_p'(m_p)$. The process of problem solving using the formation rules and laws in the manner sketched above will be essentially the same. However, we should expect the S arrived at to yield arrays of solutions corresponding to the multiple possible values of the theoretical concepts.

VI.3.2. Consider next the case in which the "data" queries are just those for the nontheoretical concepts $\overline{Q} = \langle QR_1, \ldots, QR_n\rangle$ and the "unknown" query is theoretical QR_t. This is a problem in determining the value of the theoretical concept R_t from complete data about nontheoretical concepts. The S that solves this problem will generally not yield unique solutions for specific values of $\overline{Q}$. But there may be some m_p's in which the solution is unique. These correspond to systems that provide "measurement" methods for R_t.

VI.3.2. Up to this point we have viewed problems and problem solving as having to do with a single member of $M_p[U, r]$. It has been argued at length in

[17], chapters 4 and 5, and in [1], section II.2, that this is an incomplete and seriously inadequate picture of the way empirical science is practiced. Problem solving essentially involves the "import and export" of information across different models of the same theory. A procedural version of this view is roughly this. The generators for values of theoretical concepts are replaced (supplemented) by procedures for "importing" these values from other members of $M_p[U, r]$—those in which the laws of the theory suffice to determine them uniquely. This suggests that, in practice, in "real-life" situations, the role of generators may be relatively insignificant. The procedures that effect the "importing" are essentially constraints on n-tuples of m_p's (sec. V.4). This suggests that a fully adequate account of problem solving will require n-ary queries and constraints.

VII. THEORY DISCOVERY

VII.1. *Introduction.* The conception of theory discovery as search is well known ([10]). Procedural syntax provides a precise, general method for bringing this conception to bear on empirical theories represented as model-theoretic structures. In addition it provides a characterization of conceptual innovation—the discovery of theories employing theoretical concepts—and suggests a way that "search" might be expected to yield conceptual innovation. This reformulates and extends the work of Langley et al. in [10]. The formulation sketched here opens the way to precisely addressing the question of whether there are computational limits on automatic (algorithmic) conceptual innovation. In what follows, I restrict the discussion to discovery of single laws in theories.

VII.2. *$M_{pp}[U, n]$-Data Presentations.* The conception of law discovery under consideration is "data-driven" in the sense that the discovery process is viewed roughly as a function from "*data presentations*" to "laws." The simplest (though not the only interesting) conception of "data" for $M_{pp}[U, n]$-structures (relative to an interpreted procedure language $\langle L(G), I\rangle$) is a sequence of data expressions interpreted as $M_{pp}[U, n]$-structures:

$$S: \mathbb{N} \to |D$$

so that

$$ID(S(i)) \in M_{pp}[U, n].$$

Our purposes require that we are able to speak partitions of a presentation S into n nonoverlapping parts. I do this with the formal device of a *data partition* π:

$$\pi: \mathbb{N} \to \mathbb{N}[n]$$

so that, for i, j $\in \mathbb{N}[n]$; i $\neq$ j and the inverse of π, $<\pi$,

$$\langle\pi(i) \cap \langle\pi(j) = \wedge.$$

VII.2.2. We may think of a law $\langle L_{pp}, L_{pp}'\rangle$ as "capturing" a *part* of a data presentation S when all m_{pp}'s in the part of the initial segment are in the model class determined by the law. Thus, relative to partition π, we say $\langle L_{pp}, L_{pp}'\rangle$ *$\langle m, n\rangle$-captures S* iff, for all i $\in (\mathbb{N}[m] \cap \langle\pi(n))$,

$$ID(S(i) \in M(L_{pp}, L_{pp}'\rangle.$$

VII.3. *Nontheoretical Law Discovery.* Intuitively, the objective in law discovery is to find the "strongest" law that captures all the data known at any point in time and continues to do this as more data are obtained. In our formalism, for data presentation S, we seek a procedure pair $\langle L_{pp}, L_{pp}'\rangle$ so that, relative to partition π, both:

A) for all m, n $\in \mathbb{N}$, $\langle L_{pp}, L_{pp}'\rangle$ $\langle m, n\rangle$-captures S;

B) for all $\langle P_{pp}, P_{pp}'\rangle$ so that A), $M(L_{pp}, L_{pp}'\rangle \subseteq M(P_{pp}, P_{pp}')$.

A) requires that all parts of all initial segments of S be captured by $\langle L_{pp}, L_{pp}'\rangle$, while B) says $\langle L_{pp}, L_{pp}'\rangle$ is the strongest procedure pair that does A), in the sense that it determines the smallest model class.

VII.3.2. Search for procedure pairs satisfying A) and B) might simply be conceived as search through a graph $\| P^2$ which is the cross product of the graph of $\| P = \langle |P, \langle\ \rangle$ of procedure expressions in $|L(G)$ with itself. The partial ordering of pairs $\langle P, P'\rangle$ in this graph will be determined by the formation rules G and may not have much intuitive relation to our objective. More useful to our enterprise would be a partial ordering $<_m$ having the property that

$$\langle P_1, P_1'\rangle \langle_m \langle P_2, P_2'\rangle \qquad \text{iff} \qquad M(P_1, P_1') \subseteq M(P_2, P_{2'}).$$

VII.3.3. Intuitively, search in $\langle |P^2, \langle_m\rangle$ may be viewed in this way. At some point i, as we march through our data presentation S, we are sitting at procedure pair $L_i \in$ in $|P^2$ knowing that L_i $\langle i, m\rangle$-captures S, for all m. Before examining S(i + 1), we move down $\langle_m$ to see if we find a stronger pair that still captures all our data. (How we choose the order of exploring downward paths remains unspecified.) We stop when we hit a pair that fails to capture the data and back up to the last successful pair—L_i*. Then we examine S(i + 1). If L_i* $\langle i + 1, m\rangle$ captures S, we examine S(i + 2). If not, we back further up $\langle_m$ until we reach a pair that captures all the data. Then we repeat the whole process. Here the $\langle_m$-ordering provides an "incremental" search in the sense of [15], [16]. It does not, of course, fully specify a search procedure. Rather, it appears to be a necessary condition on any reasonable search through procedure pairs. How one defines an $<_m$ ordering is clearly dependent on specific properties of |L(G). At this point, I do not know how to construct it for a specific example. However, there is work for clauses in first-order logic that suggests how one might start ([13], [14]).

VII.4. *Theoretical Law Discovery.* The preceding discussion ties model-theoretic representations of empirical theories to previous work in automated law discovery via procedural syntax. It does not suggest any essentially new ideas about discovery. However, Hempel ([6]) and others have maintained that a crucial question about the adequacy of this work as a model for scientific practice is whether it can be extended to automated discovery of "new vocabulary" or "new concepts" and laws containing them. Model-theoretic representations of theories with theoretical concepts do suggest what appears to be new insights into this question. Model-theoretic reconstructions of "real-life" examples ([17], chap. 3) reveal that theoretical concepts—while not definable in terms of nontheoretical concepts in *all* models of the theory—are so definable in *some* models. Automated methods have been developed for identifying theoretical concepts and laws containing them in those models where they are definable. Further, the "same" theoretical concept appearing in different laws may be identified ([10], 156; [19]). Procedural syntax for model-theoretic representation appears to afford the apparatus to reformulate and extend this work to situations where definability is not present in all models. Within this somewhat more abstract formulation it should become possible to formulate precisely (and settle) the question of whether discovery as search can yield genuine conceptual innovation.

VII.4.2. How can we recognize in a data presentation S that we are dealing with a phenomenon requiring a new theoretical concept? I suggest roughly the following. We "discover," by methods sketched above, a data partition π and k different nontheoretical laws

$$\langle L_{pp}^{1}, L_{pp}^{1'}\rangle, \ldots, \langle L_{pp}^{k}, L_{pp}^{k'}\rangle$$

so that, relative to π:

1) $\langle L_{pp}^{k}, L_{pp}^{k'}\rangle$ $\langle m, k\rangle$-captures S;

2) at some level, L_{pp}^{k}'s ($L_{pp}^{k'}$'s) have isomorphic parse trees;

3) L_{pp}^{k}'s ($L_{pp}^{k'}$'s) differ only in $P_k{}^*$ at isomorphic positions in their parse trees.

Property 1) is simply that different nontheoretical laws capture different parts of the initial segment m of the data. However, these different laws have the same form above a certain level; that is, they *use* data processed at a lower level in the same way—2). They differ only in the way presentation data is processed $P_k{}^*$ at lower levels—3).

VII.4.3. Intuitively, the different $P_k{}^*$'s correspond to different ways of measuring the value of the value of the *same* theoretical concept in different models of the theory. We recognize this as the *same* concept just in that the output of all P_k*'s is *used* in the same way by the laws. In fact, there is really just *one* law—once we have "identified" the different P_k*'s as outputting values of the *same* concept. Very roughly, what I am suggesting here is a way of turning old-fashioned "operationalism" around. Instead of identifying concepts by their methods of determination, I suggest we identify them by the further use we make of the results of (different) determination methods. Note that it is the procedural syntax that makes it possible to identify precisely the "uses" of results.

VII.4.4. I sketch here a process that might be turned into an algorithm for discovering the simplest kind of theoretical law—that containing only one theoretical concept. Assuming one thinks that such discoveries count as "interesting" conceptual innovation in empirical science, two kinds of things might be done with such a sketch. First, one might try to implement the sketch in some working procedural language and see how it fared on some nontrivial examples (e.g., momentum mechanics). Second, one might try to characterize the process in some more abstract way and investigate its computational properties. Success with the first would show that interesting conceptual innovation can be automated. Failing this, one might pursue the second line in the hope of showing that the kind of algorithm needed for conceptual innovation is computationally "hard" ([9], chap. 13), thus providing a kind of "impossibility" result. It is the need to represent and search (intelligently) through data partitions that suggests this might be the case.

VIII. APPENDIX

A.1. In the case of binary relational structures $M_p[U, \langle 2 \rangle]$, the "converse" function:

$$\hat{Q}: M_p[U, \langle 2 \rangle] \rightarrow R[U]$$

so that, for all m_p in $M_p[U, \langle 2 \rangle]$,

$$\hat{Q}(\langle D(m_p), R_1(m_p) \rangle) = \hat{R}_1(m_p)$$

is in $Q[U, \langle 2 \rangle]$. A procedure P that simply computes QR_1, that is,

$$IP_{n+1}(P, m_p)(\langle D(m_p), R_1(m_p) \rangle) = R_1(m_p)$$

will also compute $\hat{Q}$ in some members of $M_p[U, \langle 2 \rangle]$—namely, those in which R_1 is symmetric—but not in other members.

A.2. We may represent each $m_p \in M_p[U, \langle 2 \rangle]$ as PROLOG data base where "facts" of the form:

```
dom(a).

rel(a, b).
```

respectively describe $D(m_p)$ and $R_1(m_p)$. Taking PROLOG as our procedure language $|L(G)$, the queries "dom(X)" and "rel(X, Y)" form the empirical basis for theories about binary relational structures. Consider the PROLOG rules:

1_1(X) :- rel(X, X).

1_2(X, Y) :- dom(X), dom(Y).

1_3(X, Y) :- rel(X,_), rel(_, Y).

Via the PROLOG analog of set-theoretic abstraction (the "findall" function) each of these may be viewed as procedure that computes a function defined on $M_p[U, \langle 2 \rangle]$ whose value is a set. Procedure pairs formed from these and the basic queries correspond to properties of binary relation structures in the following way:

⟨rel(X, Y), 1_2(X, Y)⟩ $R_1 \subseteq D \times D$

⟨1_1(X), dom(X)⟩ reflexivity

⟨rel(X, Y), rel(Y, X)⟩ symmetry

⟨1_3(X, Y), rel(X, Y)⟩ transitivity

Note that since PROLOG expressions have both a denotational and a procedural interpretation, the class of models determined by the pair ⟨L, L′⟩ is the same as the class of models in which, in addition to the clauses defining L and L′, the clause L :- L′ is true.

REFERENCES

[1] Balzer, W., C. U. Moulines, and J. D. Sneed
1987 *An Architectonic for Science: The Structuralist Program*. Dordrecht: Reidel.

[2] Bauer, K.
1989 "Das strukturalistische Theorienkonzept: Ein Computermodell zu den intendierten Anwendungen einer Theorie der Geometrie." Master's thesis, University of Munich.

[3] Chasndra, A. K., and D. Harel
1980 "Computable Queries for Relational Data Bases." *Journal of Computer and System Sciences* 21:156–178.

[4] Gaifman, H.
1983 "Why Language?" In *Reduction in Science*, ed. W. Balzer, D. Pearce, and H.-J. Schmidt, 319–330. Dordrecht: Reidel.

[5] Gurevich, Y.
1988 "Logic and the Challenge of Computer Science." In *Trends in Theoretical Computer Science*, ed. E. Borger, 1–57. Rockville, Md.: Computer Science Press.

[6] Hempel, C. G.
1985 "Thoughts on the Limitations of Discovery by Computer." In *Logic of Discovery and Diagnosis in Medicine*, ed. K. F. Schaffner, 115–122. Berkeley, Los Angeles, London: University of California Press.

[7] Hindley, J. R., and J. P. Seldin
1986 *Introduction to Combinatorics and Lambda Calculus*. Cambridge: Cambridge University Press.

[8] Hogger, C. J.
1981 "Derivation of Logic Programs." *Journal of the Association for Computing Machinery* 28(2):372–392.

[9] Hopcroft, J. E., and J. D. Ullman
1979 *Introduction to Automata Theory, Languages, and Computation*. Reading, Mass.: Addison-Wesley.

[10] Langley, P., H. A. Simon, G. L. Bradshaw, and J. M. Zytkow.
1987 *Scientific Discovery: Computational Explorations of the Creative Process*. Cambridge, Mass.: MIT Press.

[11] McCarthy, J.
1960 "Recursive Functions of Symbolic Expressions and Their Computation by Machine, Part I." *Communications of the ACM* 3:184–195.

[12] 1963 "A Basis for a Mathematical Theory of Computation." In *Computer Programming and Formal Systems*, ed. P. Braffort and D. Hirshberg. Amsterdam: North-Holland.

[13] Plotkin, G. D.
1970 "A Note on Inductive Generalization." In *Machine Intelligence 5*, ed. B. Meltzer and D. Michie, 153–161. Edinburgh: University of Edinburgh Press.

[14] 1971 "A Further Note on Inductive Generalization." In *Machine Intelligence 6*, ed. B. Meltzer and D. Michie, 101–124. Edinburgh: University of Edinburgh Press.

[15] Shapiro, E. Y.
1981 *Inductive Inference of Theories from Facts*. Research Report 192, February. New Haven: Yale University, Department of Computer Science.

[16] 1982 *Algorithmic Program Debugging*. Cambridge, Mass.: MIT Press.

[17] Sneed, J. D.
1979 *The Logical Structure of Mathematical Physics*. 2d ed. Dordrecht: Reidel.

[18] 1983 "Constraints as Intertheoretic Relations." Unpublished manuscript.

[19] 1987 Review of *Scientific Discovery*, by Langley et al. *Science* `36: 1357–1358.

[20] Sterling, L., and E. Y. Shapiro
1987 *The Art of Prolog: Advanced Programming Techniques*. Cambridge, Mass.: MIT Press.

[21] Stoy, J.
1977 *Denotational Semantics: The Scott-Strachey Approach to Programming Language Theory*. Cambridge, Mass.: MIT Press.

[22] Suppes, P.
1981 "Future Educational Uses of Automatic Theorem Proving." In *University-Level Computer-Assisted Instruction at Stanford, 1968–1980*, ed.

P. Suppes, 165–182. Stanford, Calif.: Institute for Mathematical Studies in the Social Sciences, Stanford University.

[23] Ullman, J. D.
1988 *Principles of Database and Knowledge-Base Systems*. Vol. 1. Rockville, Md.: Computer Science Press.

[24] van Fraassen, B. C.
1976 "To Save the Phenomena." *Journal of Philosophy* 73:623–632.

ELEVEN

Why Functionalism Didn't Work

Hilary Putnam

Starting around 1960, I developed a view in the philosophy of mind based on the analogy between a mind and a digital computer. I gave my view the name "functionalism," and under this name it has become the dominant view—some say the orthodoxy—in contemporary philosophy of mind.

In my book entitled *Representation and Reality*[1] I argue that the computer analogy, call it the "computational view of the mind," or "functionalism," or what you will, does not after all answer the question we philosophers (along with many cognitive scientists) want to answer, the question "What is the nature of mental states?" That book was conceived as a single argument, and I obviously cannot give the entire argument in a brief discussion. But what I hope to do is to explain some of the leading ideas of the argument that led me to abandon my former position.[2]

The computational analogy was itself a reaction against the idea that our matter is more important than our function, that our *what* is more important than our *how*. My "functionalism" insisted that, in principle, a machine (say, one of Isaac Asimov's wonderful robots), a human being, a creature with a silicon chemistry, and, if there be disembodied spirits, a disembodied spirit, could all work much the same way when described at the relevant level of abstraction, and that it is just wrong to think that the essence of our minds is our "hardware." This much—and it was central to my former view—I do not give up in my new book, and indeed it still seems to me to be as true and as important as it ever did. What I try to do in the book is the trick attributed to adepts in jujitsu of turning an opponent's strength against himself: I try to show that the arguments for the computational view, in fact, the very arguments I formerly used to show that a simple-minded identification of mental states with physical-chemical states cannot be right, can be generalized and extended to show that a straightforward identification of mental states with *functional* states, that is, with computationally characterized states, also cannot be right. Functionalism argued that mental states cannot simply *be* physical-chemical states, although they are emergent from and supervenient on physical-chemical states; I now argue that mental states also cannot be computational states, or computational-cum-physical states (states defined using a mixed vocabulary referring both to physical and to computational parameters), although they are emergent from and may be supervenient upon our computational states.

Although this is not a historical essay, I would like to begin with a historical remark. I think that what we would really *like* to believe, if we could only square such a belief with our scientific consciences, is just what the ancients believed. Ancient philosophers held that things in the world have *Forms*—these are a kind of Reason-in-the-World—and that we have a mental faculty, the active intellect, which is precisely suited to figuring out the Forms of things. The beauty of Greek metaphysics was that *nous* (the Reason in us) and the Forms were made for each other. Since the appearance of modern science and philosophy in the seventeenth century, the notion of a Form and the notion of a special faculty for knowing Forms have ceased to meet our standards of clarity and explanatory value. We are no longer able to believe that Reason-in-the-World and Reason-in-Us fit together like the pieces of a jigsaw puzzle.

Instead, what many philosophers believe is that we have minds (with a small "m"—the "mind" no longer has a distinguished part, the "active intellect" or *nous*, which can be identified with Reason) and that what looks like Reason-in-the-World is produced by our minds by an act of "projection." This was Hume's line (and he has many contemporary successors). Hume, however, assumed that one mental power—the power of *referring*—was relatively unproblematical. In the simplest case, an idea refers to another idea or to an impression by *resembling* it. This "resemblance theory" of the semantic powers of the mind is long dead, and thus Hume's present-day successors have a more difficult task than Hume; if our ascription of Forms (i.e., of "natures," or "causal powers," or even of dispositions) to things is "projection," then they owe us an account of the faculty of Projection. Other philosophers say, in effect, that there is Reason "out there" (an objective relation of "bringing about" in the world, or objective "dispositions" or objective counterfactuals), and our minds simply have evolved with a propensity to "track" these sorts of facts. The problem is that neither intentional powers in us nor Reason out in the world fit into the world picture of reductive physicalism. Explaining how we can have the ability to refer and to think *if* there is a primitive and objective notion of Explanation built into external reality is of no real interest. Explaining how we can "project" a relation of Explanation into external reality *if* we assume a primitive and objective relation of *reference* is of no real interest. The circle connecting Explanation and Reference is too short. The task of the reductive physicalist is to show that it is possible to account for *both* Explanation and Reference starting from what he takes to be the ultimate "building blocks" of reality—the distribution of fundamental magnitudes over space-time points, or something of that kind. And this is what I contend he cannot do.

But enough for historical background; now for an account of the difficulties with functionalism.

The first difficulty I encountered with my functionalist views was that they were incompatible with the account of meaning that I myself put forward in "The Meaning of 'Meaning.'" According to the arguments of that essay, the content of our beliefs and desires is not determined by individualistic properties of the speaker but depends on social facts about the linguistic community of which the speaker is a member and on facts about the physical environment of the speaker and of the linguistic community. For example, I pointed out that the fact that experts (or other speakers on whom we rely) are prepared to count certain things as "real gold," certain things as "elm trees," certain things as "aluminum," and so on, helps to fix the extension of these terms. The fixing of extension depends on cooperation and linguistic deference. Reference is not fixed by what is "in the heads" of speakers.

Even experts need not have criteria (in the sense of necessary and sufficient conditions) that determine the extensions of our terms. Given a tradition of investigation into nature, a tradition of theory construction and experimentation that gives sense to such questions as "Is this the same metal as that?," "Is this the same liquid as that?," one can fix the referent of a term (perhaps with some vagueness, but vagueness need not be fatal) by deciding that it will apply to whatever is *of the same nature* as certain paradigms. (In the "Twin Earth" example that I used in "The Meaning of 'Meaning,'" the word 'water' on two different planets turned out to refer to two different liquids even though there was nothing "in the heads" of the individual speakers which was different.) What the nature of something is (not in the metaphysician's sense of "the nature," but in the scientist's or the artisan's) can determine the reference of a term even before that nature is discovered. What *chrysos* (gold) was in ancient Greece was not simply determined by the properties ancient Greeks *believed* gold to have (although many philosophers still make the mistake of thinking that a community's notion of a substance is the *definition* of the substance for that community). If the beliefs ancient Greeks had about *chrysos* defined what *it is to be* gold (or "chrysos") at that time, then it would have made no sense for an ancient Greek to ask himself, "Is there perhaps a way of telling that something isn't really gold, even when it appears by all the standard tests to be gold?" Remember that this is precisely the question Archimedes did put to himself! with a celebrated result. Archimedes' inquiry would have made no sense if Archimedes did not have the idea that something might appear to be gold (might pass the current tests for "chrysos") while not really having the same nature as paradigm examples of gold. Reference (and "meaning") depend upon the nonhuman *environment* as well as upon society.

The upshot of this new theory of reference for the philosophy of mind is that "propositional attitudes," as philosophers call them, that is, such things as *believing that snow is white*, *feeling certain that the cat is on the mat*, and so on, are not "states" of the human brain and nervous system considered in isolation from the social and nonhuman environment. *A fortiori*, they are not "functional states"—that is, states definable in terms of parameters that would enter into a software description of the organism. *Functionalism, construed as the thesis that propositional attitudes are just computational states of the brain, cannot be correct.*

One way of meeting this objection has been defended by Jerry Fodor and more recently by Ned Block.[3] This is to divide meaning into an individualistic component (often called "narrow content") and an external component (reference, or reference in possible worlds). The individualistic component *is* a computational state of the brain in the case of each "meaning" and each "propositional attitude," Block would argue. Against this I would argue (in company with Tyler Burge)[4] that there is no *one* physical state or *one* computational state that one must be in to believe that there is a cat on the mat. Speaking at the level of spontaneous phenomenology, it is undeniable that we preceive one another as "thinking that the cat is on the mat," or whatever. If we understand a foreign language—say, Thai—we may have such "perceptions" even when the person in question speaks a language very different from ours and comes from a very different culture. For example, I may know that a certain Thai peasant thinks that his cat is on a mat. But it does not follow that the Thai peasant who believes that his "meew"[5] is on a mat is in the same "psychological state" as an English speaker who believes a "cat" is on a mat in any sense of "psychological state" that can be explained without reference to what the Thai peasant and the English speaker *mean*. After all, the Thai peasant does not have the same perceptual prototype of a cat as the English speaker (the paradigmatic Thai cat is what we would call a "Siamese" cat, and the English speaker is unlikely to regard a Siamese cat as a stereotypical cat, even if she happens to have seen Siamese cats); the Thai speaker might have to rely on others to be sure that the English speaker's cat was really a "meew"; Thai beliefs about meews (especially in a village) could be quite different from English speakers' beliefs about "cats"; and so on. Block specifies that "narrow content" is to be a matter of speakers' beliefs and/or inferences that speakers make; yet, as this example illustrates, it seems impossible to specify *which* beliefs and inferences must be the same in order for the "narrow content" of a word to be that of the word 'cat'. Block and Fodor recognize that the enterprise of trying to produce necessary truths about what a speaker must think in order to mean a given thing by a given word is hopeless; yet they provide no alternative way of fixing the "narrow content" of a word.

GLOBAL FUNCTIONALISM

A different way of trying to reconcile functionalism with the non-individualistic theory of reference defended in "The Meaning of 'Meaning'" might be to extend the computer analogy to a larger system. Why not think of *the entire language community together with an appropriate part of its environment as analogous to a computer* rather than just the individual mind? (This was suggested to me by Richard Boyd.) If the content of a word depends on relations to other speakers, why not try to describe those relations computationally? If the content also depends on the nature of the objects the word refers to, why not try to characterize the relation of *reference*, which links the word to those objects, computationally? Perhaps one would have to use both computational notions *and* physical/chemical notions in the definition of reference; but the point is that one might, in some way, accept the chain of arguments that link meaning to reference and reference to entities (experts and paradigms) "outside the head" of the individual speaker without conceding that the intentional cannot be reduced to the nonintentional. *One can be a reductionist without being a methodological solipsist, after all.* Functionalism may have to become more complicated. We may have to speak of functional (and partly functional) properties of organisms-cum-environments and not just of functional properties of individual brains. But functionalism is not yet refuted.

Of course, the question is whether this can be done in principle, not whether it can really be done in practice. It is widely recognized that the interpretation of someone's language must always proceed simultaneously with the ascription of beliefs and desires to the person being interpreted. As the example of the Thai peasant illustrated, such an ascription will rarely, in practice, make the other's beliefs and desires come out exactly the same as ours. We construe one word as meaning *plant*, another word as meaning *water*, still another word as meaning *gold*, in spite of the fact that the beliefs of the speakers we are interpreting, as discovered by this very interpretation (by the "translation manual," as Quine calls it), disagree with ours—perhaps disagree over the nature of plants, the nature of water, the nature of gold. When we ought to count two words as having the same meaning in spite of the difference between *their* beliefs and *our* beliefs which the very interpretation we are constructing requires us to posit, and when the beliefs we are attributing as the result of our translation are so bizarre as to require revision of the translation, is a question of "reasonableness." *A functionalist definition of synonymy and coreferentiality would "rationally reconstruct" these intuitive judgments of reasonableness.* And there is no reason to think that it would be easier to do this than rationally to reconstruct inductive logic, or, indeed, human informal rationality itself.

Few philosophers are afraid of being Utopian, however. A philosopher might well insist that all this could be done *in principle*. The philosophical problem, such a philosopher will insist, is to evaluate the claim that a certain type of reduction is "possible in principle."

APPRAISING REDUCTION CLAIMS

Appraising reduction claims is something that analytic philosophers have a great deal of experience at doing. Thus, after Carnap's *Der Logische Aufbau der Welt* was published, a great deal of philosophical work went into examining (and, in the end, rejecting) the philosophical claim that "thing language is reducible to phenomenalistic language." Likewise, attempted reductions of mathematical to "nominalistic" language have been and continue to be studied (e.g., Hartry Field's *Science without Numbers*). Appraising the claim that the notion of reference can be reduced to computational or computational-plus-physical notions is a very similar enterprise to appraising these other reducibility claims.[6]

If this is not quite self-evident, it is because these other claims were claims about the *conceptual* or *necessary* relations between concepts, and my own functionalism was explicitly put forward as an empirical hypothesis (although Armstrong and David Lewis appear to regard some version of functionalism as conceptually necessary). But if one examines the famous arguments against the claim that thing language is reducible to sense-datum language given by Hans Reichenbach or by Wilfrid Sellars, one observes that what those arguments really showed was that there is no *nomological relationship* between such typical statements in thing language as 'There is a chair in the room' and any statement in phenomenalistic language. That is to say, the refutation of phenomenalism would have been exactly the same if phenomenalism had been put forward as an "empirical hypothesis" and not as a piece of "conceptual analysis"!

Thus, what we need to examine is the question that is perfectly analogous to the question Reichenbach considered in *Experience and Prediction*: Is there any strict nomological relation between arbitrary statements in the class to be reduced (in the present case, statements of the form X refers to Y) and statements in the reducing class (in the present case, statements in the computational-cum-physical vocabulary)?

From familiar considerations applicable to all reduction claims, we know that we must not say that reference has been reduced to some physical-cum-computational relation R (defined over organisms-cum-environments) unless: (I) reference is coextensive with R in all physically possible systems—coextensive for all physically possible organisms and environments such that those organisms are capable of using language, referring, and so on, in those environments: (II) R obeys (approximately) the "laws" that reference is supposed to obey in intuitive (or anthropological) belief about reference; and (III) the presence of R explains the effects (to the extent that they really exist) that the intuitive or anthropological notion of reference was supposed to explain. Merely finding a functional relation R that is coextensive with referring for those organisms which happen to refer (perhaps, by chance, there aren't any other than human beings) would not be enough.

The requirements (II) and (III) assume that the "definiens" in a reduction must be a property or relation which we can define in the vocabulary of the reducing discipline (allowing as parts of that vocabulary constants for appropriate mathematical objects, e.g., tensor or scalar constants, mathematical functions, etc.) where 'define' has the normal sense of *define in finitely many words*. (If such a requirement is not imposed, then the question of reducibility becomes trivial, since—if we happened to be blessed with omniscience—we could "define" *any* term that refers to any property or relation that is supervenient on physical facts by just listing all the infinitely many physically possible cases in which the property term applies or the relation obtains.)[7]

Analogues of these considerations were involved in the debate about the reducibility of thing language to sense-datum language. At first the phenomenalists were content to claim that material-thing sentences could be "translated" into *infinitely long* sense-datum sentences; however, it was very quickly pointed out that unless the translation were finite (or the infinitely long translation could be constructed according to a rule that was itself statable in finitely many words), then the issues over whether the translation exists, whether it is correct, whether it is philosophically illuminating, and so on, would be essentially undiscussible. The antiphenomenalists said, in effect, "Put up or shut up."

In the same way, I am saying to the functionalists (including my former self), "Put up or shut up." However, the antiphenomenalists did not put all the burden of proof on the phenomenalists. Reichenbach, Carnap, Hempel, and Sellars gave *reasons* why a finite translation of material-thing language into sense-datum language was impossible. Even if these reasons fall short of a strict mathematical-impossibility proof, they are highly convincing, and this is the reason why there is hardly a single phenomenalist left in the world today.[8] In the same spirit, I am going to give principled reasons why a finite reduction of intentional relations and properties in terms of physical/computational relations and properties is impossible—reasons which fall short of a strict proof, but which are, I believe, convincing.

THE SINGLE-COMPUTATIONAL-STATE VERSION OF FUNCTIONALISM

I am going to begin by considering an oversimplified version of functionalism. This is the theory that each state of believing something, desiring something, perceiving something, having a particular emotion, and so on, corresponds to one definite computational state. The identification is to be species-independent: *believing that snow is white* is to be the same computational state for all physically possible organisms capable of having that belief. While it is true that so simple a functionalism has never been defended by anyone, as far as I know, the theory that each propositional attitude, emotion, and so on, corresponds to one particular computational (or computational/physical) state *in the case of each particular organism* is a feature of all the familiar varieties of functionalism. For all of the familiar versions of functionalism—my own and David Lewis's[9] in particular—assume that a propositional-attitude term applies to an organism just in case that system is a model for an appropriate psychological theory, where something is defined to be a "model" of a psychological theory only if it has *nonpsychological*—physical or computational—states that are related as the psychological theory says the mental states are related. This clearly assumes that one can find one physical or computational state per propositional attitude in the case of a single organism. Where more sophisticated versions of functionalism differ from our oversimplified version is in allowing that the physical or computational states that serve as the "realizers" of a given mental state may be different (although "functionally isomorphic") in the case of *different* organisms and/or different species.

Consider the following model for a speaker-hearer of a natural language: the "organism" is an information-processing system (it could be a robot) that possesses a way of assigning "degrees of confirmation" to the sentences in its "language of thought," and a "rational preference function" that (together with the degrees of confirmation) determines how it will act in any given situation. Certain semantic distinctions must be marked in any such model: for example, we can tell when a word is *acquired* by the fact that the "*c*-function" of the organism (the function that calculates the degrees of confirmation) and the rational-preference function are *extended* to a new range of sentences. We can tell when a word is *ambiguous* by the fact that (in the underlying "language of thought") the word is marked by subscripts, or functionally equivalent devices, as, for example, 'nap_1' (short sleep) and 'nap_2' (nap of a rug). But if all we are given to go on is the current subjective probability metric (the current degrees of confirmation), the current desires (the current "utilities"), and the underlying prior-probability function by which the current subjective probability metric was formed by conditionalizing on the observations of the organism, then at least the first two of these will be different even in the case of speakers whose meanings we are prepared to count as the same. In short (this was the point of a paper I published a number of years ago),[10] there will be no discernible synonymy relation extractable from the model itself, nothing to mark the fact that when I say 'bureaucrat' and you say 'bureaucrat' we are uttering words with the same meaning.

The problem does not disappear even if we suppose (as Carnap did) that we should include information to the effect that certain sentences are marked *analytic* in the very description of a formal language. Even if certain sentences are marked *analytic* by the model, say 'bureaucrats are officials in large institutions', unless I have a criterion of synonymy to tell me that when I say 'official' and you say 'official' we mean the same thing, and that when I say 'institution' and you say 'institution' we mean the same thing, I cannot conclude that 'bureaucrat' has the same meaning for both of us from the fact that this *sentence* is analytic for both of us. (Moreover, the word may have the same meaning even if we have a *different* stock of "analytic" sentences. For example, someone who lives in a monarchy may have the sentence 'People appointed to high positions by the king are officials' in his stock of "analytic" sentences, while someone who doesn't know what a king is but who is acquainted with presidents will have different "analytic" sentences about officials in his language, but this is not what we count as a difference in the meaning of 'official'.)

Finally, Quine's celebrated "gavagai" example shows that problems of synonymy can arise even at the level of observation terms. Here is a little bit of evidence in support of Quine's claim. I recall that when I visited China in 1984 I lectured on Quine's views at Fudan University in Shanghai, and sophisticated Chinese told me that they did not think that the Chinese word 'mao' (cat) could be determinately translated into English as 'cat'/'cathood'. What they claimed was that "Are you saying there is a cat or that there is cathood exemplifying itself?" is the wrong question to put to a Chinese speaker. There is no special suffix in Chinese to distinguish "mao" from "maohood" ('mao' is used both in contexts in which we would translate it as 'cat' and in contexts in which we would translate it as 'cathood'), nor are there articles in Chinese. 'Cat there' and 'Cathood there' would go into the same sentence in Chinese. If my informants were right, then there may be no "fact of the matter" as to whether a certain Chinese character means 'rabbit' or 'rabbithood' or neither-of-the-foregoing. In fact, sameness of "stimulus meaning" is not even a necessary condition for synonymy, even in the case of observational terms. A Thai speaker may not associate the same stimulus meaning with 'meew' that I do with 'cat', but it is still reasonable to translate 'meew' as 'cat'. ('Elm' in English and 'Ulme' in German would still be synonyms even if 'Ulme' were an observation term for Germans—they all learned to distinguish elms—and not an observation term for English speakers.)

So far I have argued that, in the sort of model of linguistic capacity that seems reasonable given the insights of Quine's meaning holism, there is no way to identify a computational state that is the same whenever any two people believe that there are a lot of cats in the world (or whatever). Even if the two people happen to speak the same language, they may have different stereotypes of a 'cat', different beliefs about the nature of cats, and so on (imagine two ancient Egyptians, one of whom believes cats are divine while the other does not). The problems that arise "in principle" become much worse if the two "people" may be members of different "physically possible species."

Even in the case of a single species, the "functional organization" may not be exactly the same for all members. The number of neurons in your brain is not exactly the same as the number of neurons in anyone else's brain, and neurologists tell us that no two brains are literally "wired" the same way. The "wiring" depends on the maturational history and environmental stimulation of the individual brain.

Still, many thinkers would suppose, with Noam Chomsky, that there is some "competence model" of the human brain to which all actual human brains can be regarded as approximating. This model would determine the "space" of possible computational states that can be ascribed to humans. The problem in the case of two different species is that in this case there is no reason to assume that the space of possible computational states is the same or that either space can be "embedded" in the other.

Consider, for example, the crucial "belief fixation" component of the model. Even if we assume the species are ideally rational, this leaves an enormous amount of leeway for different inductive logics (as Carnap pointed out).[11] Carnap introduced the concept of a "caution parameter"—a parameter that determines how rapidly or slowly the logic "learns from experience," as measured by how large a sample size the logic typically requires before it begins to give significant weight to an observed sample mean. Different inductive logics can assign different caution parameters. Different inductive logics can also assign different weights to analogy and count different respects as respects of "similarity." In short, different inductive logics can impose different "prior probabilities." Granting that the need for survival potential will reduce the variability, we must remember that we are talking about all physically possible species in all physically possible environments—that is to say, about all the ways evolution (or whatever—some of these "species" will be artifacts, e.g., robots) might work to produce intelligent life, compatibly with physical law, not just about the way evolution actually happened to work in the one physically possible environment that actually exists.

For example, if the species is one whose members are very hard to damage, then they can afford to wait a long time before making an inductive generalization. Such a species might use an inductive logic with a very large "caution parameter." What properties it will be useful to count as "similarities" or respects of analogy will obviously depend upon the contingencies of the particular physical environment. Perhaps in a sufficiently peculiar physical environment a species that projected "funny" predicates (e.g., Nelson Goodman's famous predicate 'grue') would do better than a species with our inductive prejudices. Computers that have to compute very different "analogies" or employ very different caution parameters (caution parameters that can themselves be different mathematical functions of the particular evidence *e*, not just different scalars) may have totally different descriptions either in the Turing-machine formalism or in any other formalism. The number of states may be different, the state rules may be different, and there is no reason why either machine should have a table that can be mapped homomorphically into the machine table of the other machine.

For all of these reasons, members of different possible species (physically possible organisms with minds and language) who are sufficiently similar in their linguistic behavior in a range of environments to permit us to translate some of their utterances may nevertheless have computational states that lie in quite different machine tables—lie in, so to speak, different "spaces" of computational states. The fact that their way of reasoning is similar to ours in some situations (when we interpret that way of reasoning using a "translation manual" that we have succeeded in constructing) does *not* imply that their states or the algorithms in their brains are literally the same. The idea that there is one computational state that every physically possible being who believes a given proposition p must be in is false.

What about physical states? The reason for introducing functionalism in the first place was precisely the realization that we are not going to find any physical state (other than one defined by the sort of "infinite list" that we ruled out as "cheating") that all physically possible believers have to be in to have a given belief, or whatever. But now it emerges that the same thing is true of computational states. And (finite) conjunctions, disjunctions, and so on, of physical and computational states will not help either. Physically possible sentient beings just come in too many "designs," physically and computationally speaking, for anything like "one computational state per propositional attitude" functionalism to be true.

EQUIVALENCE

I already said that the one-computational-state version of functionalism is oversimplified and that it is a version that no one has ever actually held. Let me now describe a version which I have seriously entertained. This version still makes the assumption (which is made by all forms of functionalism) that each mental state corresponds to one computational (or computational/physical) state in the case of each single organism (or, in the case of "global functionalism," in the case of each language community of organisms), but it does not assume that different organisms (or different language communities) must be in the *identical* computational state when they have a given belief, desire, and so on. Rather, it assumes that they must be in computational states that are *equivalent* under some computationally definable equivalence relation. Let me explain what I mean by this.

Imagine some definite formalism for computational theory to be fixed—say, for definiteness, the Turing-machine formalism. Although each Turing machine has its own "space" of machine states, still one can mathematically describe the totality of these machines—indeed, this is just what Turing and his successors did. One can define predicates that relate the states of different machines in different ways, and the notion of *computability* has been defined for such predicates. What is true in this respect of Turing machines is equally true of any other kind of machine that might be taken as a model in computational theory. Thus, given an equivalence relation (or, indeed, any relation) that is defined on computational states of different machines, the question whether that relation is itself "computable" is well defined. (One can also define classes of predicates which, though not computable, are definable starting from the computable predicates—these form the so-called "arithmetic," "hyper-arithmetic," etc. hierarchies.) But why should one believe that there is a computable equivalence relation that connects the propositional attitudes of a person in one language community and the propositional attitudes of an arbitrary person in a different language community?

Here is an argument of a kind that convinces many people (such arguments are quite common in present-day linguistic theorizing): Suppose Mary Jones is an English speaker, and suppose we wish to ascertain that her word 'cat' is synonymous with the Thai word 'meew' (or with the word 'meew' as used on a particular occasion by a particular Thai speaker). We have to know that the extension of the two terms is (at least vaguely) the same to even consider accepting the *synonymy* of the two terms, and this requires some knowledge of the actual nature of the animals in Mary's environment that she (or experts upon whom she relies in doubtful cases) calls 'cats' and some knowledge of the actual nature of the animals that the Thai speaker (or experts upon whom she relies) call 'meew'. Granted that this decision can involve enormously many factors, not only Mary's speech dispositions and those of her Thai counterpart but also the speech dispositions of other members of the linguistic communities to which they belong, and information about the microstructure and evolutionary history of paradigm "cats" and paradigm "meew"; still, *if* we can make this decision and *we* are Turing machines, *then* the predicate 'word W_1 as used in situation X_1 is synonymous with word W_2 as used in situation X_2' must be a predicate that a Turing machine can employ—a recursive predicate or at worst a "trial and error predicate."[12]

This argument makes the basic empirical assumption on which functionalism depends, namely that there is some class of computers (e.g., Turing machines or finite automata) in terms of which human beings can be "modeled." If we are willing to make this assumption, then the attractive feature of the argument is that it does not presuppose that the two situations being compared involve identical "machines." All that is necessary is that the entire situation—the speaker-cum-environment—be describable in some standardized language. In short, the problem we faced in the preceding section, that it makes no sense to speak of the "same computational state" when the speakers (or the speakers-cum-environments) are not machines of the same type, does not arise if what we are asking is, "Does a certain definable *equivalence relation* R (the relation of coreferentiality) hold between an element of the one situation and an element of the other?" States of different "machines" can lie in the same *equivalence class* under an arithmetical relation, and so can situations defined in terms of such states. In short, moving from the requirement that the "states" of speakers with the same reference (or believers with the same belief) be identical to the requirement that they be *equivalent under same equivalence relation that is itself computable, or at least definable in the language of computational theory plus physical science*, gives us enormous additional leeway. What we have to see is whether this leeway will help.

Suppose (returning to the example of Mary Jones and her Thai counterpart) that our biology assures us that the animals that Mary takes to be paradigm "cats" are indeed various sorts of domestic felines (*Felis catus*) and that the same thing is true of the animals her Thai counterpart takes to be paradigm "meew." This does not show that the extension of 'cat' is the same as the extension of 'meew', for several reasons. First—to be somewhat fanciful—it might be that Thai has an ontology of temporal slices rather than things. 'Meew' might mean 'cat slice'. Second, even if we assume that English and Thai both cut the world up into 'things', 'animals', and so on, the classification used by scientific biologists might not be one either Mary or her Thai counterpart employs. 'Meew' might mean 'Siamese cat', for example. We have to know a good deal about the Thai speaker's speech dispositions (or those of others to whom she defers linguistically) to know that she would count non-Siamese cats as "meew." What is at stake, as Quine and Davidson have emphasized (not to mention European hermeneuticists such as Gadamer) is the interpretation of the two discourses as wholes.

To interpret a language one must, in general, have some idea of the theories and inference patterns common in the community that speaks that language. No one could determine what 'spin' refers to in quantum mechanics, for example, without learning quantum mechanics, or what 'negative charge' refers to without learning a certain amount of electrical theory or what 'inner product' refers to without learning a certain amount of mathematics. This creates a serious problem for the idea that coreferentiality and "synonymy" are theoretically identical with computable (or at least computationally definable) relations over properly parametrized situations.

The problem is that any theory that "defines" coreferentiality and synonymy must, in some way, survey all possible theories. A theory that figures out what people (or physically possible extraterrestials, robots, or whatever) are referring to when they speak of "spin" and that decides whether the notion of "spin" in Terrestial quantum mechanics is or is not the same notion as the notion of "grophth" in Sirian Mootrux mechanics, or an algorithm that would enable a Turing machine to make such a decision (or to reach it "in the limit") given a description of the "situations" on Earth and on Sirius, must, in some way, anticipate the processes of belief fixation on which the understanding of quantum mechanics (including the mathematics presupposed by quantum mechanics) and "Mootrux mechanics" (including the "mathematics" presupposed by Mootrux mechanics) depends. Certainly such an algorithm would have to do more than "simulate" an ability that human beings actually have. For no human being can follow all possible mathematics, all possible empirical science, and so on. This point deserves further discussion, however.

SURVEYING RATIONALITY

The fact that one cannot interpret a discourse unless one can follow it suggests that an algorithm that could interpret an arbitrary discourse would have to be "smart" enough to survey all the possible rational and semirational and not-too-far-from-rational-to-still-be-somehow-intelligible discourses that physically possible creatures could physically possibly construct. How likely is it that there is such an algorithm?

First of all, the restriction to physical possibility is not really helpful. As far as we know, physics does not rule out the possibility of an intelligent being that survives for N years for any finite N whatsoever. For example, some astronomers have suggested that a physically possible intelligent being might have a body that was a gas cloud of galactic size—the being would move with an incredible slowness, so that its time scale would be almost inconceivably slowed down by our standards, but such systems might have arbitrary complexity. The fact that such a being survives N years, for some large N, does not mean that it is "long-lived" by *its* (slowed-down) standards, of course, but it could also be incredibly long-lived by *its* standards. The point I mean this example to illustrate is that we do not *know* of any laws of physics that exclude any finite automation whatsoever from being physically realized and from surviving for any finite number N of machine stages.

Let us begin by considering a somewhat less mind-boggling question. Can we hope to survey (and write down rules for interpreting, perhaps by "successive approximation") the reasoning and belief of all possible *human* beings and societies?

Let us recall that there is no one form in which all human beliefs are cast. The predicate calculus is often treated by philosophers as if *it* were the universal language, but to put beliefs expressed in a natural language into the predicate-calculus format, one must first *interpret* them—that is, one must deal with the very problem we wish to solve. A theory of interpretation which works only after the beliefs to be interpreted have been translated into some "regimented notation" begs the question.

Moreover, the predicate-calculus format itself has problems. What should the variables range over? Analytic philosophers have a preference for material objects and sense data; but there is no guarantee that every human language and sublanguage, including the specialized sublanguages of various professions (psychoanalysis, theology, sociology, cognitive science, mathematics ...) will employ one of these standard ontologies; in fact, we know that the sublanguages just mentioned, at least, do not. Space-time points are another choice popular with philosophers; but to tell whether someone is quantifying over points in Newtonian space, or in space-time, or in Hilbert space, or in the space of supergravitation theory ..., one again has to *interpret* his or her discourse. And it is not at all clear how to represent quantum-mechanical discourse in the format of standard predicate calculus. I am not thinking of the possibility that quantum mechanics may best be understood in terms of a nonstandard logic (although that illustrates the point in a different way) but of the problem of interpreting quantum mechanics in its standard ("Copenhagen") presentation. Copenhagen theorists claim that quantum mechanics does not treat the world as consisting of objects and observer-independent properties but rather as consisting of two realms: a realm of "measuring apparatus," described by one ontology and one theory (classical physics), and a realm of "statistical states," described by vectors in Hilbert space and projection operators on Hilbert space. The "cut" between these two realms is not fixed but is itself observer-dependent—something the predicate-calculus format has no way of representing. Even if it turns out that quantum mechanics is being presented in the wrong way by its own practitioners, as many philosophers have thought (though without coming up with an agreed-upon better way), to interpret a discourse in existing quantum mechanics one must first realize that the language of those practitioners is of this "nonclassical" kind. What other languages that science (or history, or literary criticism, or ...) might use of a "nonclassical kind" are waiting to be invented?

Experience tells us that no human society is unsurpassable. For any human society, there is a possible other society that is more sophisticated, that has modes of conceptualizing and describing things which members of the first society cannot understand without years of specialized study. What is often said is true, that all human languages are intertranslatable: but that does not mean that one can translate a current book in philosophy or a paper in clinical psychology or a lecture on quantum mechanics into the language of a primitive tribe without *first* coining a host of new technical terms in that language. It does not mean that we could tell any "smart" native what the book in philosophy, or the paper in clinical psychology, or the lecture on quantum mechanics "says" and have him understand (without years of study). Often enough we cannot even tell members of *our* linguistic community what these discourses "say" so that they will understand them well enough to explain them to others.

It would seem, then, that if there is a *theory* of all human discourse (and what else could a *definition* of synonymy be based upon?), only a god—or, at any rate, a being so much smarter than all human beings in all possible human societies that he could survey the totality of possible human modes of reasoning and conceptualization as we can survey the "modes of behavioral arousal and sensitization" in a lower organism—could possibly write it down. To ask a human being in a time-bound human culture to survey all modes of human linguistic existence—including those that will transcend his own—is to ask for an impossible "Archimedean point."

The conclusion that I take from these reflections is that we do not know what we *mean* when we speak of such a theory. A theory which we could not possibly recognize as doing what the Master Theory of Discourse (or Master Definition of Reference and Synonymy in Computational Terms) is supposed to do is a "we know not what." The notion of "correctness" for such a theory is less clear than the notion of reference itself, and certainly much less clear than the propositional attitudes in their everyday use.

NOTES

1. Cambridge, Mass.: MIT Press, 1988.

2. The present paper covers the same ground as, and includes some sentences from, the fifth chapter of *Representation and Reality*.

3. See Block's "An Advertisement for a Semantics for Psychology," *Midwest Studies in Philosophy*, 1986.

4. Cf. his "Individualism and the Mental," *Midwest Studies in Philosophy* 4 (1979), and "Intellectural Norms and Foundations of Mind," *The Journal of Philosophy* 73, no. 12 (December 1986).

5. 'Meew' is the Thai word for 'cat'.

6. The idea that the problem of reducing intentional notions to nonintentional ones is analogous to the problem of reducing physicalist notions to phenomenalistic ones was advanced by Roderick Chisholm in a famous correspondence with Wilfrid Sellars in the 1950s. See "The Chisholm-Sellars Correspondence on Intentionality," in *Concepts, Theories and the Mind-Body Problem*, ed. Herbert Feigl, Michael Scriven, and Grover Maxwell, Minnesota Studies in the Philosophy of Science, 2 (Minneapolis: University of Minnesota Press, 1958).

7. For a more detailed discussion of this point, see *Representation and Reality*, 77–78.

8. To my knowledge, Frank Jackson is the only one!

9. See Lewis's *Philosophical Papers*, vol. 1 (Oxford: Oxford University Press, 1983). Lewis's views are discussed in detail in chap. 6 of *Representation and Reality*.

10. "Computational Psychology and Interpretation Theory," in *Realism and Reason*, vol. 3 of my *Philosophical Papers* (Cambridge: Cambridge University Press, 1983).

11. Cf. Carnap's *The Continuum of Inductive Methods* (Chicago: University of Chicago Press, 1956).

12. The notion of a "trial and error predicate" was introduced in my "Trial and Error Predicates and the Solution to a Problem of Mostowski," *The Journal of Symbolic Logic* 30, no. 1 (March 1965). Such predicates are limits of recursive predicates; their use is possible if one does not ask that one be able to know for sure when the value of the predicate has converged, but only that it will sooner or later converge.

TWELVE

Physicalism

Hartry Field

I take it as beyond serious doubt that there is an important sense in which all facts depend on physical facts and all good causal explanations depend on good physical explanations. Some such doctrine has played an important methodological role in guiding the development of science. It would be nice, however, if we could formulate the doctrine more precisely, and in this paper I will provide a rough sketch of what I think the more precise formulation should be like, and also indicate the lines along which I would defend the proposed characterization of physicalism against other characterizations. I take it to be a condition of adequacy on any proposal for a more precise version of the doctrine of physicalism that the proposal be such as to make physicalism weak enough to be believable but strong enough to explain how it can guide the development of science.

The methodological role of the doctrine of physicalism is double-edged. On the positive side, the doctrine tells us that when we have a putative body of facts and causal explanations that we are quite convinced are basically correct, we need to find a physical foundation for them. (If the facts and explanations are sufficiently "high-level," we will not look directly for a *physical* foundation: we will simply look for a foundation in terms of "lower-level" facts and explanations that we think are clearly unproblematic in that *their* having a physical foundation is relatively uncontroversial.) For instance, the implicit acceptance of the doctrine of physicalism on the part of most scientists has led to the successful search for the molecular foundations of genetics and the quantum-mechanical foundations of chemical bonding. The other, negative, aspect of the doctrine of physicalism is that when faced with a body of doctrine (or a body of purported causal explanations) that we are convinced can have no physical foundation, we tend to reject that body of doctrine (or of purported causal explanations). I think this is the attitude that most of us take toward astrology or telepathy: even if there were positive evidence for telepathy that we did not know how to refute, most of us would tend to disbelieve the telepathic claims (and presumably suspect the evidence) simply because it seems so difficult to conceive how such claims could fit in with a physicalistic worldview. Of course, give *sufficient* evidence for telepathy, we would look harder for its physical foundations; or we would contemplate giving up the doctrine of physicalism and replacing it by a broader "unity of science" type doctrine (much as we gave up the doctrine of mechanism late in the nineteenth century). But this last move is not one we take at all lightly, and that is what gives the doctrine of physicalism its methodological bite.

I think that most attempts to formulate the doctrine of physicalism either make the doctrine seem totally unbelievable or make it so weak that it is hard to see how it could ever have the sort of double-edged methodological importance just described. One of the goals of the project on which this paper is based is to do better. Once we have formulated the doctrine more clearly, the other main goal of the project is to say something about why the methodology of adhering to physicalism (so formulated) as a working hypothesis is a *reasonable* methodology. Of course, there are limits on what can be said in justification of any methodology: one cannot take a person that is unwilling to enumeratively induce or to reason by any form of inference to the best explanation and argue that person into acceptance of those forms of inductive inference. Still, I think that *something* can be said in favor of physicalist methodology beyond the fact that it has worked well in guiding science, even if not enough can be said to quell all possible skepticism.

The version of physicalism I want to defend is not *so* very different from classical reductionism; but it involves several differences designed to make it more believable. Before mentioning the main differences, I want to say a few things about what I understand classical reductionism to be.

Classical reductionism as I understand it consists of two interrelated parts. The first part is designed to capture the idea that all facts ultimately depend entirely on physical facts. The classical reductionist proposes that this idea be put by saying that for each sentence in the language of a successful special science like chemistry or genetics or psychology, there is a sentence in the language of a lower-level science—and ultimately, in the language of physics[1]—that in some intuitive sense "expresses the same facts." (It is this aspect of classical reductionism which seems to me too stringent, and which I shall discuss weakening shortly.)

The second part of classical reductionism is designed to capture the idea that all good explanations ultimately depend entirely on physical explanations. A minimal version of this idea already can be argued to follow from the first part of the reductionist thesis. For take any explanation in the language of a special science. By the first part of reductionism, there will be associated with each sentence S_i of that explanation a physical transcription $f(S_i)$. Now, it is plausible to suppose that if the mapping f is to associate with each special-science sentence a sentence in the language of physics that "expresses the same facts," then f must preserve deductive relationships; also, that it must preserve truth and falsity. So if the special-science explanans logically implies the special-science explanandum, then the physical transcription of the explanans will imply the physical transcription of the explanandum; and if the special-science explanation is true, so must be its physical transcription. So if an explanation of something is just any old body of truths from which the thing to be explained follows, then the physical transcription of the special-science explanation is bound to be a physical explanation. (For simplicity I have expressed the argument so as to apply only to *deductive* special-science explanations, but it generalizes without much loss of plausibility to probabilistic explanations.)[2]

The main trouble with this is that what counts as a special-science law may have as its physical transcription a physical-language sentence with no motivation independent of its role in special-science explanations. It would not seem like much of a physical explanation of the bonding of sodium and chlorine to say that the initial conditions in physics happen to be such that the physical transcription of the chemical-bonding laws come out true. Some sort of explanation of those laws is needed. So the second part of the reductionist position is simply that the higher-level laws and generalizations should themselves, when physically transcribed, admit physical explanation. This requirement is intended to be somewhat vague. I would not want to make it precise by demanding that the transcribed special-science law (even if suitably qualified and/or probabilified) be derivable from laws of physics alone, without background conditions: such a demand would rarely if ever be met in practice. (One does occasionally hear this demand, but I suspect that that is because of an unthinking extrapolation from the reduction of mathematics to set theory.) But it would be equally bad (though in the opposite direction) to put the demand as a demand that the physically transcribed special-science law be deduced from physical laws together with background conditions: that would be vacuous, since we could simply use as the background conditions the physically transcribed law we wanted to deduce, and avoid any appeal to physical law altogether. I doubt very much that an attempt at more precision here would be useful. The explanatory component of reductionism *is* vague, but despite the vagueness I think we often know when it has been satisfied and when it has not.

As I have said, I think that the reductionist thesis—especially the first part of it—needs weakening. But it is important to begin by making sure that we understand it sympathetically and that we appreciate some of its virtues. On the matter of understanding it sympathetically, I have two points to make. The first is that the requirement that a physicalist transcription of a sentence "in some intuitive sense express the same facts as" the original sentence should be taken to allow that the physical transcription has a precision that the higher-level sentence lacks: we do not want the reductionist committed to supposing that the vagueness or other semantic indeterminacy in the higher-level sentences can be exactly matched at the physical level. A reductionist will likely hold, in fact, that the vagueness or indeterminacy of terms and sentences from secondary sciences is less a matter of their having vague or indeterminate reductions than a matter of their being reducible to (more or less determinate) physical terms in different and incompatible ways.

The second point is that a classical reductionist can distinguish between *providing* a classical reduction in full detail and *sketching* one, and can hold that although full reductions are possible in principle, they would generally be so complex (even in thermodynamics and chemistry, and certainly in biology and psychology) that sketches are all we can reasonably expect to find. Physicalism gets its main methodological bite in cases where it is initially unobvious even in broad sketch how a reduction would go, and indeed where there seem to be obstacles to providing such a reduction. A classical reductionist is likely to hold that the reasons for believing in reductionism, and the reasons for believing in the explanatory importance of certain terms, are strong enough that if we can provide sketches that overcome the obstacles apparently standing in the way of reductions for those terms, then it is reasonable to believe that the reductions could in principle be filled in. In my view this is over-sanguine; but I also think that if the ideal of reduction is weakened in the ways soon to be discussed, then it becomes reasonable.

Before turning to the ways in which classical reductionism must be revised, I would like to turn to one apparent defect in it that is not genuine. Doing so will in fact reveal one of the virtues of reductionism: a virtue that is conspicuously lacking in certain alternatives to reductionism, most notably supervenience theses.

The apparent defect in reductionism emerges when we try to fill out the requirement I have vaguely expressed by saying that the physical transcription of a higher-level claim must "in some intuitive sense express the same facts." In the case where the higher-level sentences are built up using only predicates and first-order logical operators,[3] part of what this presumably involves is that the physical transcriptions are determined in the obvious way by a mapping *g* that takes predicates in the higher-level language into formulas of the physical language. This mapping *g* should correlate with each predicate of the higher-level language a formula in the language of physics with the same extension (or more accurately, a formula that does not definitely disagree in extension with the higher-level predicate—its extension may be more definite, as previously noted). But, one is inclined to say, extensional adequacy is not enough: the physical formula must be *lawfully* coextensive with the higher-level predicate.

It is here that the apparent defect in reductionism emerges. It would I think be most unfortunate if we had to appeal to an unexplicated notion of "lawfulness" in this context. The idea of a law of physics is (for many purposes anyway) tolerably clear; similarly for the idea of a law of one of the special sciences like chemistry or genetics or psychology. But it is not one of those relatively clear applications of the notion of lawfulness that we are concerned with here: rather, we are contemplating as a requirement for reduction that a statement of the form "$\forall x[Px \equiv Ax]$" be lawful, where 'P' is a predicate of a special science like chemistry or genetics and '*A*' is some candidate for a reduction into physicalist language. In this context, appeal to a notion of lawfulness seems to me of no help at all: it simply labels the problem to be solved, namely the problem of saying which true statements of the form above count as real reductions and which do not.

Fortunately, the classical reductionist does not actually need to rely on an unexplicated concept of lawfulness. Rather, the full version of the classical reductionist thesis *explicates* the sense in which classical reductions must be "lawful." The explication of the sense in which they must be lawful turns on the fact I emphasized before, that classical reductionism consists in a doctrine about explanations being ultimately physical as well as a doctrine about facts being ultimately physical. Indeed, the doctrine about explanations and the doctrine about facts are not really separable doctrines: the reductionist view is that a large part of what *makes* an assignment of physical formulas to higher-level formulas be one that preserves facthood is that it preserves explanations. In the case of the reduction of predicates, this means that in a sense no lawfulness requirement is needed: a function g that assigns extensionally correct formulas of physics to higher-level predicates will be adequate if it leads to physical transcriptions of higher-level laws that admit of physical explanation. Talk of lawfulness is needed only when we try to formulate the requirement that the facts be reduced independently of the requirement that the explanations be reduced.[4]

So classical reductionism does not, despite initial appearances, need to rely on an unexplicated notion of cross-discipline claims holding lawfully: and that is good since, as remarked before, such a use of the notion of lawfulness would simply label a problem, not solve it. This virtue of classical reductionism will be preserved on the weakening of it that I will next suggest. However, it is *not* preserved on supervenience theses: there, there is an essential use made of notions of necessity or lawfulness, *applied to cross-discipline sentences* (e.g., it is necessary or lawful that there be no mental difference without a physical difference). And it is essential to the use of supervenience by antireductionists that there is no attempt to explain this cross-discipline lawfulness—since *the only obvious way to explain it would be in terms of a reduction.* Advocates of supervenience do not rely on that explanation but do not want to put anything else in its place. (I do not think that this is the *only* problem with supervenience theses—I also think that they are far too weak to be interesting, even if one forgets the unilluminatingness of their appeal to necessity or lawfulness.)

Now for a rather quick discussion of some ways in which we need to weaken the classical-reductionist claim that for each sentence in the language of a successful special science there must be a claim in the language of physics that in some intuitive sense "expresses the same facts." It is rather easy to argue that this is implausible: indeed, one can argue that even some claims about shape that clearly ought to count as physicalistically kosher will be ruled out by this requirement. Basically, the argument is that since physical language is countable, only countably many facts about shape will be representable in it, but there are uncountably many facts about shape that ought to be represented. It turns out, though, that a very simple modification of classical reductionism will handle this cardinality problem: instead of insisting on straight-out expressibility in the language of physics, we insist on definability in the language of physics *from physical parameters.* The physical parameters can include arbitrary regions of space; this multiplies the number of physical facts we have to work with enormously and avoids the sort of worry just raised.

A second worry about classical reductionism is that it seems to be incompatible with functionalism, that is, with the fact that the same special-science predicate can be physically realized in a wide variety of very different ways. It has seemed to many (i) that if the aims of reductionism are to be achieved, then we need a single formula in physical language applicable to all occurrences of the special-science predicate; but (ii) that the possibility of extremely different physical realizations precludes this. Let us assume (i) for the moment, and focus on (ii). I think it can be made highly plausible that if one takes "the physical language" to be a purely first-order language—no predicate quantifiers, even substitutional—then it is indeed impossible to find formulas in that language that can capture the fairly abstract similarities between different possible realizations of the same special-science predicates ('pain', 'monetary transaction', or whatever). And there is some reason to construe classical reductionism as implicitly making this restriction to first-order language. But if so, then the main moral of functionalism is just that we should relax this: we should allow the physical language to contain the logical resources required for functional definition. A typical functional definition proceeds by defining something to be ψ just in case it has some property or other P that meets such and such a condition. ("Being ψ" is called the "higher-level" or "functional" property, whereas P is the "lower-level" property that realizes ψ.) So to allow for functional definition, we need to allow quantification over properties of individuals (or at any rate, predicate quantification, perhaps construed substitutionally). However, the second-order language in question is to be a predicative (or ramified) one: the only properties we quantify over are those that are predicatively construable (perhaps in multiple steps) from basic physical predicates.[5] The point of this restriction is to guarantee that the properties quantified over are independently certified to be physically kosher. (A slightly less severe restriction would also guarantee this,[6] but there is no need to go into this here.) If we liberalize classical reductionism so as to allow functional or second-order "reductions," as I think we should, then we must also demand an account, in each instance where the functional property holds, of what lower-level physical properties realize it and why they realize it. Indeed, it is in the demand for such an account of the realizations that much of the spirit of reductionism is focused.

There is a possible alternative to admitting higher-order physical language in one's "reductions": one can restrict the application of the reductions one gives, thereby denying (i); indeed, one can argue that such a restriction is not a liberalization of classical reductionism, it is what classical reductionists intended. My own view is that it is indeed fairly plausible that a classical reductionist could be satisfied with a physical account of pain in humans and a separate physical account of pain in octopuses and a third for pain in Martians: here the need for a common physical account is not all that compelling. However, the best arguments for functionalism show the possibility that the physical realization of a property like pain can vary not only from species to species but between different members of a species and even within the same member at different times.[7] This means that if one is to avoid the recourse to higher-order physical language, one must restrict the application of one's reductions not just to a given species but to a given interval of time in the life of a given individual organism. I doubt that such a way of avoiding the appeal to higher-order physical language would be satisfactory.[8] But there is no need to argue this here: the differences between this nonfunctionalist physicalism and the functionalist physicalism I prefer are not really terribly important. I see functionalist physicalism as only a slight generalization of nonfunctionalist physicalism; the differences between these two doctrines have been greatly overemphasized.

(One occasionally hears the view that psychology is fundamentally different from other sciences because its terms can only be functionally explicated. But I think in fact that to the extent that functional explication is required for psychological terms it is also required for terms much closer to fundamental physics: consider 'acidic' or 'harmonic oscillator' or 'is hotter than'.[9]

A connected view that likewise seems incorrect is that the fact that psychological theory is appropriately construed in a functionalist vein shows that a "top-down" methodology that ignores neurophysiological underpinnings is appropriate in psychology and that a "bottom-up" methodology is inappropriate. This is doubly wrong: first, a functionalist needs to be concerned with getting a theory of human psychology that can be physically realized, so that attention to neurophysiological underpinnings is quite appropriate; second, even when one has nonfunctional reductions, the complexity of the system often makes it practically indispensable to ignore the physical underpinnings in certain contexts and proceed in a relatively autonomous or top-down fashion. The fact is that in any special science, a complex interaction of "top-down" and "bottom-up" research is essential to progress: this is true whether or not the science in question is construed in a functionalist fashion.)

A third worry about classical reductionism—probably the most important worry—is that it does not seem to accommodate the fact that theories in the special sciences are not exceptionless.[10] Here I do not have in mind simply the fact that in reducing a special science we typically discover various ways in which the laws hitherto accepted in that science need to be corrected: that fact has been emphasized in the reductionist literature and is no threat to classical reductionism. Rather, what I have in mind is that there need not be any way to provide corrected laws while remaining in the special science in question: one can only correct the laws by shifting to a more fundamental discipline such as physics.[11] Laws in the special sciences typically work only in highly idealized circumstances, and even there, they work only approximately; and there may simply be no way to remove the idealization and/or the approximation while remaining in the vocabulary of the special science. These "defects" in "higher-level" laws and "higher-level" types of explanation are simply the price one has to pay for the manageability and added generality that one gets by shifting from the level of physics to the level of the special science. Now, given that laws in the special science work only in idealized circumstances and only approximately, there is little point in looking for a reduction that works outside the idealized circumstances of applicability and that is required to be more than approximately correct. I think it is clear that even the classic cases of "reduction" (e.g., of genes in terms of DNA, or valence in terms of atomic structure) provide reductions only subject to this limitation.[12] And I think that it would be silly to expect or demand any more than this in other special sciences such as psychology. In general, then, one must adjust the precision and range of applicability required of a reduction of a given term to the precision and range of applicability of the laws and explanations in which that term functions.

That's all I can say here on how classical reductionism must be weakened; I hope it is clear, though, that the weakenings I have suggested do not undercut anything very central to the spirit of classical reductionist demands. *In particular, they do not undercut what I think is the central feature of classical reductionism*: loosely formulated, it is that if we are to accept a special-science explanation of something, we are committed to the possibility in principle of finding a physical explanation of that thing *in which the structure of the special-science explanation of it is preserved.*

There are several currently popular surrogates for physicalism that do not preserve this central feature of classical reductionism. Among these weak surrogates for physicalism are:

1. "Weak sentential physicalism" or "token physicalism": the view that each true *singular* statement in the language of the special sciences is in some sense equivalent to ("reports the same event as") some true singular statement in the language of physics.
2. Purely ontological physicalism (the thesis that all entities are physical, with no requirement that all explanatorily useful ideology be reducible to physical ideology—indeed, with no requirements whatever about explanatorily useful ideology).[13]
3. Various supervenience theses.

It seems quite clear, though, that none of these weaker "physicalist" doctrines, either singly or in combination, is of any help in accounting for the important methodological role that physicalism has played in the development of science. Indeed, I think that each of (1)–(3) is very nearly vacuous.

The near-vacuity of "token physicalism" can be seen by contrasting it with functionalist physicalism. The latter requires that for the events *Jones is now in pain* and *Jones's C-fibers are now firing* to be identical, then Jones's C-fibers firing must now be part of a realization of pain theory in Jones. This places a strong constraint on what physical events can count as identical with the pain event. One of the problems with replacing functionalism by token physicalism is that it would then be unclear what if any constraints there are on what physical events are taken as identical with mental events (or other events reported in special-science language). For instance, it appears to be possible to maintain token physicalism by simply finding, on any given occasion when Jones is in pain, some arbitrary event taking place in Jones (say, an electron shifting energy levels in her toenail) and claiming that that is identical with Jones's current pain. What seems intuitively wrong with such an identification is that the event picked does not have the causal role in producing behavior, beliefs, desires, and so on that pain theory requires. The moral seems to be that unless an event realizes a certain pain theory, it cannot be a pain event. Functionalism has just this desired consequence.

The near-vacuity of purely ontological physicalism can be argued by arguing that explanations in terms of entities that are not obviously physical can usually be reformulated in a way that dispenses with the as-yet-unreduced ontology and replaces it with as-yet-unreduced ideology. Intuitively, the reformulated explanations are just verbal variants of the original, but the thesis of ontological reductionism has no application to the reformulations. I will give two examples of this. The first example is the search for the physical basis of genetics. An ontological physicalist might say that here is an example where ontological reductionism had bite: we had an entity, the gene, whose physicalistic status was unobvious; but because the scientific community accepted ontological physicalism, they were led to establish that genes were physical things after all. The problem is that it is possible to reformulate genetics trivially so that it does not quantify over genes but simply uses special predicates: for instance, 'has a haemophilic gene' (predicated of people, or ova); or failing that, 'serves as a haemophilic gene', predicated of hunks of matter. With genetics so reformulated, it is trivial in advance of scientific research that the only postulated entities are physical: ontological physicalism could play no role in motivating the search for the chemical foundations of genetics.

The second example concerns the mind-body problem. Consider a modified Cartesianism, which insists that even disembodied minds have spatial location—not that they *occupy* space, perhaps, but that their perceptions and thoughts are always from the perspective of some point or small region of space. (Suppose also that the modified Cartesianism has it that no two minds can in this sense be located at the same place at the same time.) This surely should count as an antiphysicalist doctrine. It becomes no less antiphysicalist if we redescribe it so that instead of claiming the existence of special nonphysical entities, minds, it says that the only *entities* are regions of space-time, but that such regions, in addition to satisfying predicates like 'is fully occupied by a body', also satisfy predicates like 'is the point of view of a mind'. If *this* counts as physicalism, physicalism is trivial to attain: given the natural one-to-one correspondence between regions and minds on the entity version of modified Cartesianism, the elimination of entities in favor of regions is a logical triviality.

So much for purely ontological physicalism. Turning finally to supervenience, I will argue first that nonmodal supervenience theses are incredibly weak. Then I will argue that there is a natural way to strengthen them, one that may conceivably lead to an interesting further weakening of classical reductionism than the one I have proposed, but that the usual attempts to strengthen nonmodal supervenience, in terms of modality, have little or no more real content than the nonmodal theses that underlie them.

Let's look at nonmodal supervenience theses first. If such a supervenience thesis is put as

> Any two objects that differ in any respect differ in a physical respect

it is *completely* vacuous: on even the most radically unphysicalistic views, any two entities in the same possible world differ in *some* physical respect or other. We can do a bit better by restricting to "qualitative" differences—very roughtly, differences statable without use of names or demonstratives or indexicals:

> Any two objects that differ in any qualitative respect differ in a qualitative physical respect. (S1)

This is *not quite* vacuous: it says that if there is a perfect physical symmetry in the universe, as in one of Max Black's duplicating universes,[14] then the physical doppelgängers are doppelgängers in all nonphysical respects too. But in application to any nonduplicating universe it is contentless: again, there will always be qualitative respects in which two entities differ (e.g., barring such perfect symmetry, any two entities will differ in their spatial relations to other entities, qualitatively described). We could eliminate this problem by restricting to physical differences that are "intrinsic" in addition to qualitative, where intrinsic physical properties of an object are those the object has "independent of anything external to it." But if the proposal is

> Any two objects that differ in any qualitative respect differ in an intrinsic qualitative physical respect,

then it is obviously false: objects that were identical in all intrinsic physical properties could differ in nonintrinsic properties like being a planet, being legally married, being near a light source, and so forth. Presumably then the proposal has to be

> Any two objects that differ in any intrinsic qualitative respect differ in an intrinsic qualitative physical respect. (S2)

This is undeniably better. However, it is still *very* weak: quite independent of physicalism, it is obvious that virtually any two objects differ in *some* intrinsic qualitative physical respect. Moreover, even given a science-fiction situation in which there were two women who were atom for atom duplicates, but where one had the biological property of having-a-gene-for-haemophilia whereas the other had the property of having-no-gene-for-haemophilia, one could still save the supervenience of the biological on the physical simply by declaring the property of having a haemophilic gene to be nonintrinsic.[15]

There is a natural idea for how to improve these supervenience theses without introducting modality:

> For any two objects that differ in any not-obviously-physical respect ψ, there is a physical difference between them that *explains* their difference with respect to ψ. (WEP)

("WEP" stands for "weak explanational physicalism.") The relevant sense of explanation requires some specification: obviously *causal* explanation is not what is in question here; rather, the idea is that the objects differ in respect ψ "by virtue of" a certain physical difference. (It is not enough to explain *the evidence that leads us to assert that* one object satisfies ψ and the other does not.) The strength of (WEP) depends on one's view of the sort of explanation involved. The most obvious ways to elucidate (WEP) require that one provide for each not-obviously-physical condition ψ a collection of conditions, each sufficient for ψ or its negation, with each actual object satisfying at least one of the conditions. The gap between this and the localized necessary and sufficient condition required by functionalist versions of reductive physicalism is not all that great, especially when it is remembered that reductive physicalism allows (p. 273 above) that there be indeterminacy as to which necessary and sufficient condition is the right one. Where there appears to be a bigger gap between (WEP) and reductive physicalism is in what must be explained: the goal of explaining the individual differences looks weaker than the goal of explaining the physical transcription of the laws. I suspect that the added strength of a reductive physicalism of the sort I have advocated over the "weak explanational physicalism" (WEP) is a virtue—I suspect that (WEP) is too weak to capture the methodological doctrine that actually guides the development of science—but I will not directly pursue that here. For (WEP) is not what people mean when they speak of a supervenience thesis (though it may well be that the failure to distinguish it from supervenience is what has led to the popularity of the idea that supervenience is the key component of a reasonable physicalism). Supervenience theses are supposed to strengthen S1 and S2 not by appealing to explanation but instead by appealing to modality. And the point I want to make is that supervenience theses are far too weak because they fall way short even of (WEP).

There are two obvious ways to add modality to S1 and S2. The weak way is to simply add a modal operator to the outside, as in

> Necessarily any two objects that differ in an intrinsic qualitative respect differ in an intrinsic qualitative physical respect; (S2*)

the strong way is to quantify over possibilia, as in

> Any two possible objects that differ in an intrinsic qualitative respect differ in an intrinsic qualitative physical respect. (S2**)

(S1* and S1** would be analogous.) But the excessive weakness of even the double-starred versions should be clear: one could in full accordance with S2** apply a predicate like 'has cast spells' quite freely, as long as one never applied it differently to two actual or possible entities that were alike in all intrinsic physical qualitites. (Indeed, even this restriction would not be needed if one declares 'has cast spells' to be itself nonintrinsic. In that case the only restriction would be the one imposed by S1**, which precludes only the differential application of the term to actual or possible people alike in all qualitative respects including spatial relations to other qualitatively described things.) One could apply the term freely subject only to this very weak restriction, even if one had strong reason to believe that there is no physical difference that could *explain* the difference between people that have cast spells and people who have not or cannot. Once this is appreciated, it is hard to see how supervenience theses can be given much respect: the advantage of modal supervenience over nonmodal is minimal.

(Of course, one could also add modality to (WEP), thereby slightly strengthening it: for instance, one could alter the beginning of (WEP) to "for any two possible objects.") I do not mean to argue that this would be no improvement: my point is not to oppose the invocation of modality but to insist that physicalism have an explanatory component that the invocation of modality itself does not provide.)

This completes my discussion of (1)–(3). In general, the inability of (1)–(3) to account for the important methodological role that physicalism has played in the development of science seems due to the fact that (1)–(3) say nothing whatever about the physical *explanation* of the facts stated in special-science vocabulary.

I do not want to assert dogmatically that no physicalism weaker than the more or less reductive physicalism I have advocated here could possibly capture the doctrine that has guided the development of science: such a conclusion seems to me premature, for the focus on such nonstarters as token physicalism and supervenience has tended to prevent the investigation of whether there are serious candidates for weakenings of the reductivist position. Presumably a reasonable physicalism would have to entail token physicalism and probably ontological physicalism. It would also have to entail the "weak explanational physicalism" (WEP) discussed above (which in turn entails supervenience). Finally, it would have to entail the self-containedness of physics: roughly,

> if A is any singular statement ("event statement") of fundamental physics, and F consists of all true laws of fundamental physics plus all true singular statements involving only times earlier than those mentioned in A, and S is any collection of true laws, and true singular statements about earlier times, that are not part of F, then the probability of A given F & S is identical with the probability of A given F alone. (SC)

I think that these things *are* all entailed by the slightly weakened form of classical reductionism I have advocated—or more accurately, that a rigorous formulation of them would be a consequence of a rigorous formulation of the weakened reductionism.[16] But perhaps something weaker—maybe even substantially weaker—would be enough to entail all of these things and be otherwise satisfactory.

However, there is a serious challenge that must be overcome by anyone who thinks that the kind of quasi-reductionism I have advocated is substantially too strong. The problem is that it is not clear that anything short of such quasi-reductionism will be capable of explaining why the special sciences work as well as they do.

Actually this formulation does not clearly distinguish between at least two closely related explanatory tasks. Consider any special-science theory that is approximately true. (If it is not approximately true, then not even the most staunch reductionist would expect anything like a reduction of it to physics: it would be a candidate for elimination, not reduction.) Then the first explanatory task is simply to explain in terms of an underlying science like physics why the generalizations of this theory should hold. It is hard to see how any such explanation is possible short of a quasi-reductionistic one—that is, short of specifying in the vocabulary of a lower-level science certain properties, and showing that if the concepts in the generalizations are viewed either as standing for those lower-level properties directly, or as standing for functional properties that are physically realized by those lower-level properties, then the generalizations approximately hold.

But presumably anyone wanting a substantial weakening of the kind of quasi-reductionism I have advocated is going to say that the goal of explaining higher-level laws in lower-level terms is an unreasonable goal: the inability to achieve it should not be counted against the nonreductionist. So let us shift to the second explanatory task. Here the goal is not to explain the laws of the special sciences themselves but simply to explain why the application of the special-science laws never comes into conflict with the application of the underlying laws.

Suppose that we have a psychological theory of some sort designed to explain a variety of phenomena, such as the reluctance of babies to crawl across a visual cliff. Let us say that it follows from this theory (together with suitable auxiliary hypotheses) that the probability of an infant crossing the visual cliff in the appropriate experimental conditions is extremely small. Now, if this consequence of the theory is in fact true, then were we given a complete neurophysiological description of a randomly chosen class of infants and were we able to apply the correct laws of neurophysiology to predict their movements, we would in nearly every case get a very low probability that they would cross the cliff. (This assumes that neurophysiology is sufficiently "complete" that no supplementation at the lower level of physics is required. If you like, you can substitute physics for neurophysiology; in this case the completeness assumption is given (SC).)[17] Presumably there has to be something about the general neurophysiological (or physical) structure of infants that explains why a neurophysiological (or physical) prediction, were it feasible, would nearly always yield a low probability of crossing the cliff. I do not say that this is *logically* required; one *could* say that the statistical fact about the behavior of infants has no general neurophysiological or physical basis: any neurophysiological or physical explanation of why one infant failed to cross the cliff would have nothing in common, at any level of abstraction, with a neurophysiological or physical description of why another infant failed to cross the cliff. But such a position would be very hard to take seriously; and given the assumption (SC), it would be tantamount to saying that the psychological laws governing the infants' behavior are completely fortuitous accidents.

So the demand is that we neurophysiologically explain, if not the psychological laws themselves (the laws in the theory that we are imagining explains the infants' behavior), then at least the statistical regularities that are describable nonpsychologically and which the psychological theory implies (of which the regularity in the infants' cliff-avoiding behavior is just one). This is in effect a demand that we explain why our neurophysiological laws and our psychological laws never come into conflict. Or, to introduce a convenient phrase, it is a demand that we show that our neurophysiology and our psychology "mesh." It seems to me that whenever we employ laws at different levels, there is a prima facie possibility of their coming into conflict, and it is eminently reasonable to want an explanation of why such conflict does not arise. Of course, we need not *know* the explanation to employ both levels of laws; but we ought to expect that a philosophical account of the relations between the different sciences would give us some idea as to the general outlines that such an explanation might be expected to take. This demand is weaker than the demand that we explain the laws of one science from the laws of another, and should be acceptable even to someone who rejects the latter demand.

I take it that a main advantage of reducing psychology to lower-level science, or of giving the kind of quasi-reduction I have been advocating, is that in doing so one would be able to explain the mesh between psychology and the lower-level sciences. For instance, given a reduction to neurophysiology of a psychological theory that explains the avoidance of visual cliffs, one would be able to explain neurophysiologically what it is about infants that generally leads them to avoid visual cliffs: the neurophysiology and the psychology would yield the same results. The reason one could neurophysiologically explain this is that according to reductionist and quasi-reductionist views, the structure of special-science explanations is preserved. So to get a neurophysiological explanation of why infants avoid the cliff, you basically just take the psychological explanation and "transcribe it" to the neurophysiological level, in the manner specified in the quasi-reduction. (According to the quasi-reductionist, the physical transcription may involve higher-order physical properties that can be multiply realized; it may require correcting the idealizations that are made in the special science; and so forth. But the special-science law gives at least rough directions for finding the detailed lower-level explanation.) I pointed out early in the paper that a physical transcription of a special-science explanation does not automatically count as a physical explanation; but when the laws and generalizations of the special science themselves admit physical explanation, it does, and it is part of the supposition of there being a quasi-reduction that this requirement is met.

I should remark that a quasi-reductionist explanation of the mesh between a psychological theory and neurophysiology does not actually require a quasi-reduction of psychology to neurophysiology: it would suffice to quasi-reduce both to physics. For doing this would give us an explanation of why psychology meshes with physics and of why neurophysiology meshes with physics; and two theories that mesh with physics mesh with each other.[18]

So much for the quasi-reductionist explanation of the mesh. The next question is, what should someone hostile to anything like reductionism say about how to explain the mesh between psychology and neurophysiology? I think it is very hard to come up with an answer to this question. And this, I think, is a large part of what underlies the hold that quasi-reductionism has on many of us.

My point then is that unless our theories at different levels mesh in the statistical regularities they imply, they conflict and should not be simultaneously accepted. When theories at different levels do mesh in the regularities they imply, we need an explanation of their interrelations that explains how they do this; and a quasi-reductive explanation is the only obvious form for such an explanation to take. Without a quasi-reductive explanation of the mesh in explanations between sciences, it looks as if this mesh is a total mystery. To a large extent, it is because we ought to avoid believing in total mysteries that we ought to assume that if a special scientific theory is to be accepted, then a quasi-reduction to lower-level sciences is possible.

It might perhaps be argued that we know on the basis of examples that a fundamentally nonreductive account of the mesh between two theories of different levels can be given. Consider, for instance, phlogiston theory. Within a limited domain anyway, the statistical laws about combustion based on phlogiston theory proved correct and consequently meshed with those statistical laws about combustion events that would have been forthcoming from the correct physics, even though phlogiston theory was not reducible to physics (nor were both reducible to some true theory at a deeper level). So no directly reductive account of the (partial) mesh between phlogiston theory and physics is possible. The example works, though, only because the statistical laws about combustion given by phlogiston theory are somewhat similar to those given by a competing theory at the same level—oxygen theory—*which we know to be a better theory.* I grant that it is not quite true that the only known kind of explanation of the mesh between a nonfundamental theory S and physics is a reduction (or quasi-reduction) of that theory to physics; sometimes the reduction of an *improved* theory to physics will explain the mesh. But this fact is of little help to the antireductionist: if we explain the mesh between some controversial theory in psychology and physics by means of the reduction of an improved psychology to physics, then we are granting the reductionist about psychology everything he or she ever wanted.

Actually I do not want to rule out dogmatically the possibility that there might be an explanation of a close mesh between a special science and physics which is not fundamentally reductive. What I do want to say is that the antireductionist, if he or she is to be taken seriously, owes an account of how such an alternative style of explanation of the mesh is to proceed. We need an explanation of the close mesh between special sciences and physics; without even a sketch of what a nonreductionist explanation is like, it is hard to take views that are simultaneously antireductionist and antieliminativist seriously. Certainly alternatives to broadly reductionist explanations of the mesh between on the one hand higher-level sciences like psychology and on the other hand physics are not at all easy to come by: if they were, such alternative explanations of mesh would doubtless have been proposed for special sciences like chemistry and genetics, so that broadly reductionist strategies would not have seemed so inevitable there. In any case, no such alternative explanation of the mesh is forthcoming simply from a supervenience thesis, or a token-token identity thesis, or the like: any physicalist who opposes a broadly reductionist thesis ought to go beyond espousing supervenience and/or token-token identity or whatever, and do the hard work of explaining how the mesh between psychology and physics is to be explained in a way that is not broadly reductionist.[19]

NOTES

1. This sentence should not only be in the language of physics, it should have all quantifiers restricted to physical entities, that is, to entities of a sort recognized by physics.

The physics involved need not be present-day physics; so reductionism (like other versions of physicalism) inherits whatever vagueness there is in classifying future sciences into those which are "parts of physics" and those which are not. But I doubt that this degree of vagueness in the notion is unacceptable.

2. Here is the generalization: if the special-science explanation says that condition C obtained, and also logically implies that the probability for the explanandum is high in conditions C (or higher in conditions C than it is generally; or whatever), then the physical transcription of the special-science explanation will say that the physical transcription P(C) of C obtains, and will also imply that the probability of the physical transcription of the explanandum is high in P(C) (or higher than in absence of P(C), or whatever). So as in the text, if an explanation of something were just any old body of truths that stands in the right logical/probabilistic relations to it, then the physical transcription of a special-science explanation would itself count as an explanation of it.

3. This is a very special case. In general, the higher-level sentences may contain syntactic constructions not present in the physical language. For this and other reasons, the job of making the intuitive requirement of "expressing the same facts" more precise is complicated.

4. One might indeed argue that even the requirement of extensional adequacy is needed only when we try to formulate the "fact" part of reductionism independently of the "explanation" part, but I will not pursue this.

5. In other words, either they are "level 0 properties," i.e., first-order definable from basic physical predicates; or they are "level 1 properties," i.e., definable with property quantifiers ranging only over level 0 properties; or they are "level 2 properties," i.e., definable with property quantifiers ranging only over level 0 and 1 properties; or . . .

6. See my *Realism, Mathematics, and Modality* (Oxford: Basil Blackwell, 1989), 212n and 214.

7. Note that I do not say: within the same member at the same time. It is possible, to be sure, for a *theory* of pain to be realized in more than one way in an agent at a time, but

this is better viewed as a semantic indeterminacy in the word 'pain' (there is no fact of the matter as to whether it refers to a functional property with one of these realizations or to a functional property with the other) than as the word standing determinately for a functional property with both of these realizations. The clearest argument for this comes when the functional theory involves two functional terms that are bound up together, as belief and desire are bound up together in commonsense psychology. Probably any decent theory of pain will take 'pain' to be bound up with other terms, but rather than argue this, let me just use belief and desire to illustrate my point. What would it be for a theory postulating belief states and desire states to be realized in two different ways in a given organism at a given time? It would presumably involve two sorts of belief states, $beliefs_1$ and $beliefs_2$, and two sorts of desire states, $desires_1$ and $desires_2$; corresponding to any given proposition there can be both a $belief_1$ and a $belief_2$, and similarly for desire. $Beliefs_1$ and $desires_1$ would interact in the characteristic way to result in behavior, and similarly $beliefs_2$ and $desires_2$. We should not suppose, though, that $beliefs_1$ and $desires_2$ interact in the characteristic way so as to produce behavior, or that $beliefs_2$ and $desires_1$ do. (Similarly, we should not suppose that $beliefs_1$ and $beliefs_2$ interact with each other in the characteristic manner to form further beliefs.) For if we suppose that $beliefs_1$ interact in the standard ways with $beliefs_2$ and $desires_2$, then we do not have a case naturally described as a case of multiple realization: rather, it is simply disjunctive realization, that is, 'belief' is realized by '$belief_1$ or $belief_2$', and similarly for desire.

Now, suppose a person $believes_1$ something but does not $believe_2$ that same thing. Are we to say that he believes it? The functionalist who holds that $belief_1$ and $belief_2$ are simply two realizations of the functional property of belief (i.e., of being a belief state) requires that we answer this question with an unqualified 'yes'; analogously, such a functionalist will give an unqualified 'yes' to the question, Does someone desire something when she $desires_1$ it but doesn't $desire_2$ it? But these answers lead to anomalies: unqualifiedly true belief statements and unqualifiedly true desire statements will not have the desired consequences, because of the failure of $beliefs_1$ and $desires_2$ (or $beliefs_2$ and $desires_1$) to interact in the desired ways. An unqualified 'no' answer would be similarly bizarre: it would mean that belief talk and desire talk was deemed wholly inappropriate in describing a situation that could be explained by a large body of $beliefs_1$ and $desires_1$ when there were no corresponding $beliefs_2$ and $desires_2$. I think we should instead adopt the view that in such cases the words 'belief' and 'desire' are semantically indeterminate (in a correlative way—see my "Quine and the Correspondence Theory," *Philosophical Review* 83 [1974]: 200–228). This way of looking at such cases makes them not special to functionalism: they are just analogues in a functionalist setting of the cases of semantic indeterminacy that arise in a nonfunctional context.

8. Still, I think that there is something right about the denial of (i). Even if one grants that what "reduces" a property like 'pain' is a functional property that is itself physically realized, there is good reason to allow the "reductions" to vary from species to species. For there seems little point to looking for a functional specification of pain that works for all possible organisms; all we need, presumably, is separate functional specifications of pain-in-humans, pain-in-octopuses, pain-in-Martians, etc. (The functional properties of pain-in-octopuses and pain-in-Martians are presumably quite similar to the functional property of pain-in-humans. This is one reason why invoking the species-relativity is more attractive for functional properties than for lower-level properties, where there need be no similarity.)

9. In connection with the latter two examples, see Mark Wilson, "What Is This Thing Called Pain?—The Philosophy of Science behind the Contemporary Debate," *Pacific Philosophical Quarterly* 66 (1985): 227–267. But while Wilson uses these examples in part for the same purposes as I am using them here—to show that the distinction between giving a functional explication of a term and giving a nonfunctional explication is not of great importance—he also has a more radical purpose: he is trying to argue that no explication at all, whether functional or nonfunctional, is required. On this last point I disagree; I will return to this later.

10. I assume that the laws are formulated without *ceteris paribus* clauses. To say that the correct "laws" always involve *ceteris paribus* clauses is just another way of saying that definitely formulated laws not involving such clauses are not strictly true.

11. The laws can usually be substantially improved by retaining the special-science terminology but adding conditions stated in the language of a more fundamental science to rule out some of the exceptions. But I doubt that even this is enough for fully exceptionless laws: for that, one needs to go outside the special science entirely.

12. The claim that these classical examples should be taken only as reduction sketches is reasonable, but I am claiming that they need only be (and can only be plausibly taken to be) sketches of *approximate* reductions.

13. It is sometimes said that purely ontological physicalism entails reductive physicalism, given a sufficiently full-blooded ontology of properties; or that it entails token physicalism, given a full-blooded ontology of events. More fully, the idea (in the property case) is that one could argue for reductionist physicalism from ontological physicalism as follows:

(i) There are no nonphysical entities;
(ii) Therefore in particular there are no nonphysical properties;
(iii) But (a) explanatorily useful predicates stand for properties, and (b) if a predicate cannot be reduced to physical terms, then any property it stands for must be nonphysical; so
(iv) Any explanatorily useful predicate must be reducible to physical terms.

But I think that any such argument is highly dubious, even putting aside all doubts about the realism about properties on which it depends. Consider the following apparently analogous argument:

(i) There are no nonphysical entities;
(ii*) Therefore in particular there are no nonphysical predicates;
(iii*) But a predicate which cannot be reduced to physical terms must be viewed as nonphysical; so
(iv*) Any predicate must be reducible to physical terms.

(Note the strength of the conclusion: it applies not only to explanatorily useful predicates but to predicates from scientifically disreputable disciplines, for instance, 'is telepathically communicating with'.) It seems clear that this argument turns on a pun on the reading of the phrase 'nonphysical predicate'. *All* predicates are physical entities, even predicates like 'is telepathically communicating with'. So if for a predicate to be physical is for it to be a physical entity, (ii*) follows from (i); but then (iii*) is simply false. There is though a natural reading of 'physical predicate' on which (iii*) is plausible: we take "reducible to physical terms" as the criterion for a predicate's being physical. But then the physical/nonphysical distinction for predicates is not an ontological classification of the predicates but an *ideological* classification, so that the inference from (i) to (ii*) fails. It seems to me that a similar diagnosis is plausible for the original argument (i)–(iv). If to call a property nonphysical is to comment on its *ideological* status, then part (b) of (iii) is nonproblematic; but on that reading of what it is for a property to be nonphysical, there is no reason to think that a property's being nonphysical coincides with its being a nonphysical entity, and so no reason to accept the inference from (i) to (ii). (Indeed, there are natural readings of 'physical entity' according to which no property could count as a physical entity, no matter how "physical" that property was, ideologically speaking: even the property of having mass would not be a physical entity, simply because it was a property. But there are more flexible readings of 'physical entity' that would count properties generally as physical entities, no matter how "ideologically nonphysical" they are, as long as they applied only to physical things. See for instance Geoff Hellman and Frank Thompson, "Physicalist Materialism," *Nous* 11 [1977]: 309–345.)

I conclude that the above argument for reductive physicalism should not be taken seriously. The right way of viewing things is not that the case for reductive physicalism (or for some other form of physicalism that focuses on further aspects of the sentences used in explanations than just their ontology) derives from the case for an "ontological" physicalism, via the acceptance of properties (or events or whatever) into one's ontology. Rather, the most obvious way to appreciate the virtues of physicalism is to focus on the important role it has played in guiding the development of science. But the principle that appears to have guided the development of science is not just that we should avoid the appeal to "irreducibly nonphysical" *entities* in our explanations. Rather, the principle guiding science rules out the use in explanations of *predicates* whose instantiation or noninstantiation cannot be physically explained, as even a superficial examination of the sort of examples mentioned in the second paragraph of the paper will reveal. One cannot in any way undermine the case for reductive physicalism by undermining realism about properties (as attempted in chap. 6 of Stephen Schiffer, *Remnants of Meaning* [Cambridge, Mass.: Bradford Books, 1987]): the issue of the ontological status of properties is a red herring.

14. Max Black, "The Identity of Indiscernibles," *Mind* 61 (1952): 153–164.

15. For a specific property like pain it might be proposed that we formulate our nonmodal supervenience thesis more restrictively: say, as the claim that when any two people differ as to their pains at a given time, the intrinsic physical properties of such-and-such regions of their brains also differ at that time. But of course this is not enough to solve the problem of excessive weakness: the intrinsic physical properties of corresponding regions of any two people's brains will always differ. (Moreover, in other ways the "physicalist" thesis is now too strong: it involves the specific assumption that only that region of the brain is relevant to pain, which is certainly no part of the content of physicalism.) The only obvious way to avoid the excessive-weakness problem in a nonmodal supervenience thesis is to build in the effects of a specific reduction.

16. In the case of (SC) the idea—sliding over some complexities—is that reductionism makes each fact in S in some sense "equivalent" to some collection of facts in F, so that probabilities conditional on F and S amount to the same thing as probabilities conditional on F alone.

17. Of course, 'infant' and 'cliff' and 'crosses' are not terms from either neurophysiology or fundamental physics, so the application of neurophysiology or fundamen-

tal physics to a particular infant would not yield any probability at all for the *sentence* 'The child will cross the cliff'. But it would yield a conclusion that, were it not for its complexity, we could interpret in terms of the child crossing the cliff: for instance, in the case of fundamental physics, a conclusion that the center of mass of a certain system of particles (those that make up the infant at the start of the experiment) shifted to a certain location (above the glass) would be tantamount to a prediction that the infant crossed the cliff. The claim that we could so interpret claims in physics and neurophysiology rests on some modest physicalist assumptions (which are hard to state precisely; included among them would be the assumption that infants' bodies are made up of particles and that the position of the infant depends in a systematic way on the positions of those particles); but I do not think many would question these assumptions, and they do not include assumptions about the physical basis of psychology.

18. (1) A proper elaboration of these claims would require a bit more delicate statement than I have given above of what it is for two higher-level theories to "mesh." (2) The claim that two theories that mesh with physics mesh with each other depends on some natural assumptions about physics, such as (SC).

19. My research was supported by the National Science Foundation (grant SES-8721859). I am grateful to discussion with Stephen Schiffer and comments on earlier drafts by Janet Levin and Russell Trenholme.

CONTRIBUTORS

Diderik Batens—Seminary for Logic and Philosophy of the Sciences, Universiteit Gent.

Richard Boyd—Department of Philosophy, Cornell University.

Nancy Cartwright—Department of Philosophy, London School of Economics.

Noam Chomsky—Department of Linguistics and Philosophy, MIT.

Hartry Field—Philosophy Program, Graduate School, City College of New York.

Michael Friedman—Department of Philosophy, University of Illinois at Chicago.

Clark Glymour—Department of Philosophy, Carnegie Mellon University, and Department of History and Philosophy of Science, University of Pittsburgh.

Richard E. Grandy—Department of Philosophy, Rice University.

Jaakko Hintikka—Department of Philosophy, Boston University, and Department of Philosophy, University of Helsinki.

Kevin Kelly—Department of Philosophy, Carnegie Mellon University.

Barbara D. Massey—Department of Philosophy, Chatham College.

Gerald J. Massey—Department of Philosophy, University of Pittsburgh.

Hilary Putnam—Department of Philosophy, Harvard University.

Joseph D. Sneed—Department of Human and Social Science, Colorado School of Mines.

INDEX

Designer:	U.C. Press Staff
Compositor:	Asco Trade Typesetting, Ltd.
Text:	10/12 Baskerville
Display:	Baskerville
Printer:	Maple-Vail Book Mfg. Group
Binder:	Maple-Vail Book Mfg. Group